# MASSACHUSETTS

# MASSACHUSETTS
## A Concise History

Richard D. Brown
and Jack Tager

*Picture research by*
RUTH OWEN JONES

UNIVERSITY OF MASSACHUSETTS PRESS
*Amherst*

Copyright © 2000 by
University of Massachusetts Press
ALL RIGHTS RESERVED

ISBN 1-55849-248-8 (cloth); 249-6 (pbk.)
LC 00-028629
Designed by Steve Dyer
Set in Sabon by Graphic Composition, Inc.


Library of Congress Cataloging-in-Publication Data
Brown, Richard D.
Massachusetts : a consise history / Richard D. Brown and Jack Tager ; picture
research by Ruth Owen Jones.—rev. and expanded ed.
p. cm.
Includes bibliographical references and index.
ISBN 1-55849-248-8 (alk. paper)—ISBN 1-55849-249-6 (pbk. : alk. paper)
1. Massachusetts—History.   I. Tager, Jack.   II. Title.
F64.B86 2000
974.4—dc21
00-028629


This book is a revised and expanded edition of
*Massachusetts: A Bicentennial History* by Richard D. Brown.
Copyright © 1978 by American Association for State and Local History
Published by W. W. Norton & Company, Inc.,
in The States and the Nation series

*British Library Cataloguing in Publication data are available.*

# CONTENTS

*Illustrations follow pages 45, 59, 184, 199, 240, and 274*

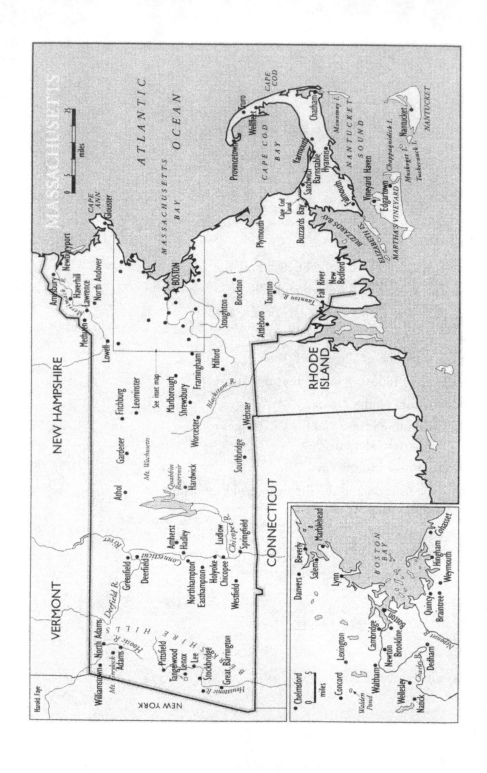

# PREFACE

M ASSACHUSETTS CASTS A LONG SHADOW. SETTLED BY THE
English almost four hundred years ago, Massachusetts and the
experiences of its people have been emblematic of larger themes in
American history in every subsequent era. The story of the Pilgrims at
Plymouth is part of the national legend, and the first Pilgrim thanksgiving is remembered as a national and family holiday. Indian warfare,
with conquest and the development of frontier boundaries, has been
part of both the Massachusetts and the American experience. During
the Revolutionary era, the Boston Tea Party, Paul Revere's ride, and the
battles of Lexington and Concord were actual events that have since
passed into national mythology.

Moreover, Massachusetts has been in the vanguard of American experience in the industrial and postindustrial periods. Its early textile
mills helped shape the industrial revolution, while its involvement with
immigration, urbanization, and ethnic conflict have also been central
to the American past. Massachusetts reformers—in temperance, public
education, women's rights, and the abolition of slavery—grew out of
the region's culture and shaped the nation decisively. In the twentieth
century, Massachusetts led the nation through a series of wrenching
industrial transformations as its economy moved from the production
of goods to the production of services—going from textiles to defense
manufacturing and then into the information era.

In public office, too, Massachusetts leaders have been central to national history. Samuel and John Adams played crucial roles in the Revolution; John Quincy Adams and Daniel Webster helped shape the early
republic and antebellum eras; and in the generations from the First
World War through the Cold War, Henry Cabot Lodge and three Kennedy brothers—John, Robert, and Edward—have influenced American

policy in substantial ways. One of the large states when the United States began, Massachusetts became a small state in the twentieth century as the result of national growth. Yet owing to its people and cultural and educational resources, it remains influential beyond its size.

At the beginning of the twenty-first century Massachusetts is very much a part of American society, yet its people also possess a sense of place and an appreciation of their state's distinctive history. This work, which revises and substantially expands Richard D. Brown's *Massachusetts: A Bicentennial History* (1978), aims to capture much of Massachusetts's unique experience as well as its relationship to the larger national history. The book is based chiefly on the scholarship of many other authors, some of whose works are cited in our Suggestions for Further Reading at the end of the text.

RICHARD D. BROWN
JACK TAGER

# MASSACHUSETTS

# CHAPTER 1

~⁂~

# The Country That the English Found

EVERY DAY THE TIDE RUSHES IN, WAVE UPON WAVE, rippling and foaming as it reaches land. Softly sloping beaches of sand and pebble, tumbles of rocks, gray and brown, meet the onrushing waters as they have for millions of years. Here, at the shifting boundary between land and sea, Massachusetts begins. The lands that lie to the west for two hundred miles—coastal plains and hillocks, uplands furrowed by a thousand streams, the great river basin, and the high, steep forests beyond—are what survive after hundreds of millions of years of punishment by wind, water, and four great glaciers. Ten thousand years ago, when people first settled what is now Massachusetts, they came to a country that had already been transformed many times.

One hundred centuries ago, the first settlers, hunters using fluted-blade stone weapons, made little impact on the land. These earliest inhabitants accommodated themselves within an environment that they could not dominate. Yet during the millennia that Stone Age peoples occupied the land, they did come to manipulate the country in significant ways. Over the years they added farming to their hunting and gathering, tilling the soil and cultivating crops brought from distant parts of America. To enhance hunting and gathering as well as tillage, they skillfully used fire to burn off the young growth on vast tracts of forest. Thus the seemingly new and underpopulated world that Englishmen explored and settled early in the seventeenth century was new only to them and underpopulated only according to their standards. The landscape they discovered had been remade a hundred times by natural forces, and remade again by its Stone Age inhabitants. The newcomers and their progeny would transform Massachusetts once more and at a speed that was unprecedented.

From the perspective of the land itself, Massachusetts is an artificial creation. Except for the ocean that washes its eastern shore, its boundaries are entirely manmade, straight lines negotiated during the seventeenth, eighteenth, and nineteenth centuries without much concern for topography. Laid out from east to west, across a landscape that includes four distinct regions running from north to south, Massachusetts possesses no natural unity. No great basin or valley unites its eight thousand square miles of territory.

In the east there is a coastal plain thirty to fifty miles wide (much wider if one includes the Cape Cod peninsula); from there a central upland region of similar breadth rises to about five hundred feet above sea level. Farther west the broad valley (often a dozen miles wide) of the Connecticut River bisects Massachusetts. This valley is the remnant of a vast glacial lake, which stretched across Massachusetts fifteen thousand years ago. The fourth region, the Berkshire hills that lie to the west, is much like the central upland although its elevation is higher, one thousand to two thousand feet. Here Mount Greylock, the highest point in Massachusetts, rises to a height of thirty-five hundred feet. This upland Berkshire region is itself divided by the narrow valley of the Housatonic River, which runs south into Connecticut before emptying into Long Island Sound.

The bedrocks that have provided the foundation for the land lie just beneath the surface of these four regions and sometimes crop up into view. Heaving up, sliding, and sinking as this particular fragment of the earth's surface cooled and shifted, the rocks were formed as long ago as one billion and as recently as twelve million years. These seemingly indestructible metamorphic rocks, among them gneisses and granite, have crumbled during the centuries, giving the land its present character.

More than once Massachusetts has been high mountains, comparable to the Rockies today. Such great peaks, some of them volcanoes, were pushed up by the working of the earth's crust hundreds of millions of years ago. Several times they rose, only to vanish as water, wind, and frost wore them down. They became plains, slightly tilted to the south and east so that water ran off in those directions. Their powdered remnants together with the lava from volcanic eruptions provided Massachusetts with a deep, rich soil that supported an abundance of plant life. Two hundred million years ago the Connecticut Valley was a lush, tropical region that teemed with dinosaurs and a hundred other species of prehistoric reptiles. As recently as one million years ago Massachusetts was a relatively flat if uneven land, its bedrock mostly covered with a thick layer of powdered-rock soil.

Then, for some mysterious reason, the climate of eastern Canada changed. Summers turned cooler by a few degrees so that the winter snowfall no longer melted entirely. Each year a little more snow accumulated until, after several hundred centuries, great glaciers formed that spread out in every direction. Those that rolled south overspread Massachusetts entirely. The dinosaurs and their cousins were frozen out. The green landscape turned white, as an ocean of ice as deep as ten thousand feet covered the land. The weight of the glaciers was so enormous that the earth's crust yielded beneath it, sinking for hundreds of feet.

The Ice Age lasted about one million years, a relatively brief period compared to the geologic eras that preceded it. Moreover, it was interrupted by three warmer periods, thousands of years long, when the glaciers melted away, the land turned green again and once more supported animal life. But though the glaciers were temporary, they gave the surface of Massachusetts its present character. Indeed, by the scale of earth history, they lasted until yesterday, about fifteen thousand years ago.

When the last glaciers melted, their impact on the land became visible. The soil that had been accumulating for millions of years from the eroding rocks had been scoured off and washed into the Atlantic. In its place rough glacial debris—till—had been deposited, an infertile mixture of clay, gravel, and rocks. In some places bedrock had been scraped off and strewn around in boulders. The rocky surface of Massachusetts and the stony subsoil beneath it are legacies of the glaciers.

The gentle hills (drumlins) one or two hundred feet high that surround Massachusetts Bay were also formed by the glaciers. These hills have no core of bedrock; they are piles of glacial till. Other ridges (moraines), including the high ground on Cape Cod, that rise above the coastal plain were formed by the runoff carrying sand and gravel to the edges of stagnant glaciers. In the same region, and farther west, the retreating glaciers stranded great freestanding chunks of ice, which melted, creating numerous ponds and upland swamps. Some of these filled up with silt, turning ponds into bogs and swamps into fertile land with a deep covering of soil.

At the end of the Ice Age the Connecticut Valley had a natural dam in central Connecticut, which created one vast lake. For thousands of years this lake trapped the silt that rain and meltwater carried off the surrounding hills. Later, when the dam gave way and the lake drained, a deep, rich soil was left covering the valley, making it the most fertile stretch of land in New England. Farther west, in the Berkshires, the glaciers scraped the narrow valleys making them a little broader but leaving the characteristic rocky soil, boulders, ponds, and swamps. The Ice Age had sharply reduced the ability of the land in Massachusetts to sustain life.

Yet the land rebounded rapidly. Even the earth's crust, freed of its burden of ice, sprang upward again, in some places by as much as two hundred feet. Within a few thousand years flora and fauna from farther south had migrated to the land and were flourishing. The country that the fluted-blade hunters inhabited provided plenty of game on land, in the air, and under water. The Massachusetts that the English were to "discover" thousands of years later was coming into being.

The renewal of life in Massachusetts depended chiefly on the climate. The global warming trend that destroyed the glaciers gave Massachusetts the moderate climate it still possesses. In January, the coldest month, the mean temperature is twenty-nine degrees Fahrenheit, although it is about three degrees cooler in the Berkshires and about three degrees warmer on Cape Cod. The mean temperature during the warmest month, July, is seventy-two degrees, about two degrees warmer in the western hills and two degrees cooler on the Cape. The difference in growing season at the two extremes is substantial. In the southeast growth occurs for a full six months, whereas in the west it lasts barely four months. Rainfall is everywhere abundant, averaging thirty-nine to forty-three inches each year.

The climate made Massachusetts a heavily forested land, but because of varying temperatures and soil conditions, the forests would be of several distinct types. In the southeast where the sandy soil retained few organic nutrients from decaying plants, a forest of pitch pine and scrub oak developed. Along riverbanks and in coastal marshes, grasses and shrubs such as bayberries, beach plums, and blueberries predominated.

In such settings, chipmunks and squirrels, rabbits and raccoons found food and cover. Shellfish flourished along the shore, feeding themselves on the organic matter in tidal flats and at the mouths of rivers. According to the seasons, alewives, salmon, and shad raced up the rivers and streams to spawn. Offshore, bass, bluefish, cod, and mackerel were common.

The coastline farther north was much the same, but inland of the immediate shore a more substantial forest grew up, with hickory and red and white oak predominating. In these varied woodlands, larger animals roamed. Deer found shrubs and young trees for browsing. Foxes fed on rodents, grouse, partridge, and pheasant. Trout swam in the streams, and bass and pickerel were the masters of the ponds. All along the coastal plains migratory birds were seasonal residents. Beaver, mink, muskrats, and otters lived in and around the streams.

To the west, in the central upland region, the higher elevations and cooler temperatures produced a somewhat different forest. Here the same varieties of trees were present, but in different proportions. Birch, beech, and maple, the northern hardwoods, were more numerous, as were hemlock and pine. In these woods the wildlife, too, was similar to the coastal plain, but there were bobcats, wolves, and black bears. Fewer migratory birds flew inland, but turkeys were more common in the woods. This same pattern of forest life flourished to the western edges of the Connecticut Valley.

In the higher, cooler Berkshires, a forest of beech, birch, and maple prevailed, with a substantial complement of conifers. Oaks and hickories became scarce, and the acorns, butternuts, chestnuts, and hickory nuts that fed the chipmunks and squirrels of central and eastern Massachusetts were much less common. This thickly forested region of steeply sloping hills, with few meadows and brushlands, sheltered large animals —wolves, bear, deer, and moose. With a shorter growing season and less fertile land, the western hills fed a smaller population of wildlife.

It is not surprising then that when the fluted-blade hunters edged their way northward into this land ten thousand years ago, they came to the coastal plains where fish and game were readily available and the climate was more like the southern land of their origin. These paleo-Indian settlers used chipped stone weapons for hunting, as well as various snares and traps. In addition to hunting they gathered the food that was accessible—nuts, berries, and shellfish. In the spring and fall they constructed dams of wooden stakes to trap the alewives and salmon that spawned upstream. These hunters were a small population, and though they may have dwelt there for several thousand years, ultimately they vanished, leaving scarcely a mark on the land.

Their successors, who may have destroyed or engulfed these earliest settlers, arrived nearly seven thousand years ago. They were more advanced, aggressive, and durable, although they, too, lived by hunting, fishing, and gathering. The size and character of their settlements remain uncertain, but their surviving cord-marked pottery (from about 2500 B.C.E. or about forty-five hundred years ago), links them to Indians of the south and central portions of North America.

Between two and three thousand years ago, Algonkin people arrived. These were people who hunted and gathered, but who also farmed. They were the first inhabitants to remake, in a limited way, the patterns of life in and of the Massachusetts forests. These Indians, whose descendants encountered the Norsemen and the English, cultivated the land. They settled on the most fertile locations along the streams and rivers of the eastern and central regions, and they added to the few natural meadows by clearing flat, low-lying tracts. Their techniques of girdling the trees to kill them and burning the underbrush enabled Algonkin men to clear sufficient farmland for a growing population. The women planted hills of corn and squashes among the stumps, fertilizing the soil with fish. The forest remained dominant, but the crops grown from imported seeds enabled them to supplement their diet of meat, nuts, berries, and fish.

Algonkin forest management included setting periodic, sometimes biannual, forest fires to clear away the underbrush, which made an open, parklike forest under a canopy of tall hardwood trees. Such forests provided a maximum of food for game and the Algonkins. Oaks and hickories as well as shrubs flourished in these conditions, enabling the small animals and deer to increase. Moreover, the open woods made Indian hunters far more effective in tracking, stalking, and killing game.

Algonkin tribes moved about seasonally in the woods and meadows and along the rivers, but they were attached to the land and possessive of the farming and hunting territory they worked. Over the centuries distinct peoples emerged as masters of a given region: on Cape Cod, the Nausets, a fishing tribe; along the south coastal plain, the Wampanoags farmed, fished, and hunted; to the north, the Massachuset tribe. The central uplands were Nipmuc country, and the Connecticut Valley and the Berkshires belonged to the Pocumtucs. All these groups had common Algonkin origins and characteristics in their languages and social customs, but each was independent and at least latently hostile to the others.

Several families occupied wood-framed lodges or wigwams covered with bark and hides, clustered together in villages. Such villages existed as long as the farming and hunting of the locale sustained them. Newly cleared land might be cultivated for a decade before it would be allowed to revert to forest.

Boys were reared to be hunters and warriors, possessing nothing but their deerskin garments and the weapons of their trade. When one married he entered the family of his wife, who retained all property rights. Inheritance, whether of goods or political status, was through the women, who cultivated the land and held it in common. These relationships were believed to be divinely ordained, and inseparably entwined with the world of natural and supernatural beings. Each person, each family, each clan within a tribe, and the tribe itself carried a mystical relationship with a living creature. The divinities, which expressed themselves in forms such as sun, fire, wind, water, and thunder, were abstract though not entirely impersonal natural forces. They demanded submission, but they might also be placated by appropriate offerings and by worship. Each year the clans of a tribe gathered in religious ceremonies where, amid rituals of chanting and dancing, the political leaders of the tribe, the sachems of the clans, met in council.

Although family practices were matrilineal and power came to men through their female kin, political authority was patriarchal. The sachems were middle-aged and elderly men who together made decisions for the tribe, adjudicating disputes, punishing misbehavior, and negotiating with other tribes. The sachems declared war and planned military operations. Warfare itself was an activity of young men, although in the event of a major defeat old people, women, and children might be captured and incorporated within the families of the victors. The chief cause of warfare seems to have been territorial incursions.

Over the centuries tribes rose and fell, and with them the extent of their lands. Tribes that survived, survived because of their strength. The availibility of food, the prevalence of disease, and conjugal practices played a much greater role than warfare in maintaining stable populations. When the English arrived at the beginning of the seventeenth century, they found a comparatively old and stable system of rivalries among the tribes and their neighbors. Only the Pequots, to the south in Connecticut, were newcomers to the politics of the New England region.

This region was not a "virgin land," nor a particularly rich or fertile one. Yet the country that the English explorers saw seemed fresh and unspoiled. One exclaimed that "the Land to me seeme[d] paradice: / for in mine eie t'was Nature's Masterpeece; / Her chiefest Magazine of all where lives her store: / if this land be not rich, then is the whole world poore."[1] Even though Algonkin peoples had been living on it since 500 B.C.E., this land seemed pristine to the newly arrived English, who came from a country that had cleared its forest and who preserved deer in a few enclaves to give sport to aristocrats. They were so impressed by what they saw that they were inspired to describe it to their countrymen in detail. The land abounded in plant and animal life; it was Nature's storehouse, and they were free to feast on it.

The climate was more extreme than England's, yet the "Sharpe Ayre" of winter did not distress the newcomers, since they found "wood in good store, and better cheape to build warm houses and make good fires." Compared with England's, this climate was healthful, and as one early settler reported, "in publicke assemblies it is strange to heare a man sneeze or cough." Fresh water was conveniently found; indeed there could be "no better water in the world"[2] than in the "sweet Cristall fountaines, and cleare running streames"[3] that watered this seemingly new land.

As did the Indians, the English considered wildlife food. The coastal marine life, which had regularly brought English fishermen to the shores of New England during the sixteenth century, was bountiful. Even the winter catch was good, and the variety of fish impressive. Sea bass was the favorite, "a delicate, fine, fat, fast fish." The technique of catching sea bass was copied from the Wampanoags: "the Fisherman taking a great Codline, to which he fastneth a peece of Lobster, and throwes it into the Sea, the fish biting at it he pulls her to him, and knockes her on the head with a sticke." Shellfish were so common that the Indians and the English seldom ate them. The first English settlers used clams to feed their swine. Lobsters, weighing up to twenty pounds, were similarly abundant and were collected among the rocks at low tide, but they were "little esteemed and seldom eaten."[4] Indians used them for bait and only ate them when bass were scarce.

In the woods, deer was the favorite game, supplying both the venison and hides that were staples of Indian life. Rabbits, like other small animals, were hardly worth hunting, and so the English gave them little notice. Birds, however, were a different matter since they could supply the table with choice dinners. The variety of doves, partridges, and pheasants compared favorably with England, but the ducks, geese, and turkeys were most remarkable. Of the geese Thomas Morton avowed "I have had often 1,000 before the mouth of my gunne." They were fatter than English geese and their feathers made "a bedd softer than any down."[5] Turkeys, the equally common year-round residents, came in great flocks, the largest fowls weighing from forty to sixty pounds. The first English observers were dazzled by such riches.

Nature inspired wonder. The very ground on which one trod offered delectable treats. There were "strawberries in abundance, very large ones, some being two inches about," in addition to blueberries, currants, gooseberries, grapes, huckleberries, and raspberries. Exotic creatures like the hummingbird delighted the eye: "no bigger than a Hornet, yet hath all the dimensions of a Bird, as bill, and wings, with quills, spiderlike legges, small clawes: for colour she is glorious as a Rainebow; as she flies she makes a little humming noise."[6] Yet though the first English observers marveled at nature, they did not share the Algonkins sense of mystery, awe, or intimacy.

To these Europeans the measure of all things was themselves. They saw lumber in the trees and dinners in the wildlife. When they studied the habitats of trees or the behavior of animals, it was for practical purposes. Beavers were fascinating because they could do what men did, felling trees "as thicke as a mans thigh, afterwards dividing them into lengths according to the use they are appointed for. If one Bever be to weake to carry the logge, then another helpes him; if they two be too weake, . . . foure more adding their helpe, being placed three to three, which set their teeth in one anothers tough tayles, and laying the load on the two hindermost, they draw the logge to the desired place." Their three-story wooden lodges were constructed to cope with flooding and frost, and were "so strong that no creature saving an industrious man with his penetrating tools can prejudice them." Beaver dams aroused "admiration from wise understanding men,"[7] while the beavers' social patterns, which included the enslavement of strangers, seemed so human that the English found it tempting to regard them as reasonable creatures.

In time the newcomers would make beavers the forest's first cash crop, purchasing them until they were virtually extinct. The Europeans did not possess the temperament required to hunt the beaver, whose "wisedome secures them from the *English* who seldome, or never kills any of them, being not patient to lay a long siege, or to be so often deceived by their cunning evasions, so that all the Beaver which the *English* have, comes first from the *Indians,* whose time and experience fits them for that employment."[8] No matter how much the English admired the landscape of the country they explored, they were not at one with it, as were the Algonkins, who had hunted over the land for two thousand years. The English were not inclined to adapt themselves to the ways of the beaver or the pace of the forest. When one boasted that "I have fed my doggs with as fatt Geese there as I have ever fed upon my selfe in England," he expressed a profligacy toward nature and its bounties that had hitherto been alien in this land.[9]

English settlers would come with the express purpose of transforming what they found. They came as conquerors to a landscape and a way of life that had gradually emerged after the glaciers. Immediately they would make themselves competitors with its Stone Age inhabitants for possession of the land itself. The coming of the English would open an epoch in the history of the land as important as the Ice Age. The coastal plain, the inland hills, and the rivers were about to be subdivided and settled in a wholly new way. The creation of a place that came to be known as Massachusetts was at hand.

# CHAPTER 2

✦❧❦✦

# The Worlds of Bradford and Winthrop

O N JULY 29, 1588, SIR FRANCIS DRAKE, ADVENTURER, seaman, and favorite of Queen Elizabeth, finished his game of bowls in the city of Plymouth and set out to battle the Spanish Armada. Two months later the job was done. Queen Elizabeth's England proudly gloried in this greatest triumph in memory. For almost two centuries England had been a weak and divided nation, torn by dynastic uncertainty and religious conflict. Now, thirty years after Elizabeth's coronation, domestic peace and prosperity had brought England to the front rank of European powers. To the English, this Protestant victory over Spanish Catholics symbolized not only the prowess of the English nation, but divine favor as well. Some were ready to proclaim: "God is English."

Queen Elizabeth's wise and judicious rule was a major reason why England flourished. Gradually Elizabeth and her advisers had created an English Church that combined Calvinism and Catholicism so effectively that it attracted broad support. There was no need or, in Elizabeth's case, any desire to persecute the Christian minorities who remained outside its generous boundaries. Religious tolerance calmed English public life and opened the way for flexibility and compromise in secular affairs. Working through shrewd and sensible councilors, Elizabeth developed a cooperative relationship with Parliament that enhanced the Commons and the Lords while strengthening the monarchy.

Elizabeth herself was the center of a glittering court life that, in London and in palaces dotting the countryside, brought England into a golden age of Renaissance culture. The arts flourished as never before, and in the poetry of William Shakespeare and the philosophy of Francis Bacon, the creativity of English high culture reached a climax. The ambition to excel bred daring and innovation.

This spirit inspired the earliest English attempts to settle in North America. For at the same time that the English were doing battle against the Spanish in Europe, they were also competing with them for North America. In 1585 and again in 1587 Sir Walter Raleigh, another of Queen Elizabeth's heroes in the war with Spain, had sent settlers to found a colony at Roanoke Island in Carolina. They were cut off from supplies from England when the Spanish Armada sailed into the English Channel and although Raleigh could not have anticipated this interruption, he had underestimated the hazards of settlement and the resources necessary to sustain it. The Roanoke colony collapsed and vanished.

Yet Raleigh's plan itself was reasonable. Where others dreamed of building forts and trafficking in precious goods as the Spanish were doing, Raleigh, who was familiar with English plantations in Ireland, conceived of transplanting English rural society to America. He was the first to send whole families to found a settlement that could be self-sufficient through farming. As it turned out, Raleigh's ideas were ahead of their time. Most of the courtiers and merchants who became interested in America thought in narrower, get-rich-quick terms.

The desire for immediate profits inspired the Jamestown settlement, which was launched almost twenty years after the Roanoke Island colony disappeared. The first settlers were mostly soldiers and gentlemen-adventurers; among the handful of tradesmen were a goldsmith and a perfumer. The purpose of overseas expansion was trade and the extraction of gold, silver, spice, and perfumes. Initially, American ventures were manifestations of the exuberant hopes of Renaissance courtiers and merchants eager to enrich themselves with glory and gold.

Yet there was another England, which was the foundation of Elizabeth's realm. This was a land of yeoman farmers, husbandmen, artisans, laborers, and fishermen who lived in villages. These people, making up 90 percent of England's 4.5 million people, struggled for survival or, if they were fortunate, savored the amenities of comfortable shelter, plentiful food, and sturdy clothing. For them the thirst for glory and the taste for novelty were alien and they viewed such goals with mistrust.

Generally speaking, they subscribed to the idea that old ways are the best ways, and in earning their livelihoods they generally shunned innovation. The common adage among farmers was, "'Tis not the husbandman, but the good weather that makes the corn grow." [1] In this world the self-assertive individualism of Renaissance culture was overmatched by conformity to age-old community values. The general good was based on people's fulfilling the roles prescribed for them by the community. Individual self-fulfillment at the expense of the orderly, everyday routine of social life was intolerable.

The people of this England were roused by the threat of Spanish Catholicism and celebrated the victory of 1588 with feasting and bonfires. But except for the Devon and Cornwall fishermen who regularly crossed the Atlantic to harvest the waters from Newfoundland south to Cape Cod, none of the common people in England knew or thought much about America. It would be more than a generation before people who lived outside the circle of the Renaissance elite became fully aware that America existed and that it might even have some bearing on their lives. It was in this country setting that the two principal founders of Massachusetts, William Bradford and John Winthrop, were born and reared.

Winthrop, a native of Edwardston in the East Anglian county of Suffolk, was born a few months after the victory over the Spanish. When he was a child, his father, Adam Winthrop, inherited the family manor house at Groton, and it was here, watching his father, that Winthrop learned the role of a country gentleman. At the age of fifteen he was sent off to Cambridge for some college education, and when he returned three years later, his father had arranged a marriage for him to Mary Forth of Essex County. Winthrop's bride brought land as a dowry and within a year gave birth to a son, John Jr. When Winthrop was twenty-one and the father of two sons, his father allowed him to share in the squire's duty of holding court for the people of Groton Manor. Several years later, Adam Winthrop, himself a lawyer as well as country gentleman, sent John for a stint at the Inns of Court at London so that he, too, might be formally trained in the law. By this time he had turned to Puritanism, but living under his father and his grandfather's roof, with a wife selected by his parents, and following his father's career, John Winthrop absorbed old family and community ideals continuously. By the time he was an adult, Winthrop was accustomed by his heritage and upbringing to a favored place in the communal social order of rural England.

Winthrop's contemporary William Bradford was born just two years later, in 1590, in the Yorkshire parish of Austerfield. Bradford's father, a yeoman farmer, died the following year, and his mother soon remarried, so the boy's upbringing was supervised by his grandfather and uncles, who were resolved that young William should follow his father's calling. Bradford was trained as a farmer, but unlike John Winthrop, he did not follow readily in the path his elders laid out for him. For both Bradford and Winthrop, the Bible was a regular part of their upbringing, but for Bradford the sacred text became supremely important. At the age of twelve or thirteen he began to follow an independent path in religion, joining the Puritan group that met at William Brewster's house in nearby Scrooby. Brewster, twenty-four years older than Bradford, treated him as a son and brother in Christ. Bradford became part of this special community of Puritans who separated themselves from the Church of England in 1606. Forever after, William Bradford was part of this tiny band of Separatists, going with Brewster and the others to Amsterdam and Leyden in the Netherlands, and ultimately to Plymouth Colony.

While John Winthrop was taking up life as a husband, father, and squire, Bradford was suffering in the wave of religious persecution inaugurated by James I, who had vowed that Puritans would "conform themselves" or he would "harry them out of the land."[2] Bradford was briefly imprisoned in 1607, and in the following year he joined his brethren in fleeing across a stormy North Sea to Amsterdam. In 1609 the group moved to Leyden and in that year, the same in which Winthrop first held court at Groton Manor, the nineteen-year-old William Bradford was chosen with Brewster, to be a ruling elder of the Pilgrim church.

For a decade Bradford and the other Pilgrims lived comfortably at Leyden, "a fair and beautiful city"[3] adorned by a university and a center of theological discussion. Bradford himself prospered; a family inheritance enabled him to purchase a house, in which he earned his living as a weaver. In 1613 he married Dorothy May and began a family. Bradford learned Dutch and some Latin and Hebrew so that he could read religious texts. While John Winthrop was being trained as an attorney, Bradford profited from the Leyden university milieu, schooling himself in Protestant history and classical literature and collecting a substantial personal library in several languages. Bradford and Winthrop were traveling in different circles. One was already a radical nonconformist in religion, a refugee; the other, a rather conventional Puritan gentleman treading the favored path of his fathers. By 1630 they would both be pioneers, dwelling in the forests at the edge of a vast wilderness. Separate routes, ultimately grounded in religion, would bring them both to Massachusetts.

Bradford's decision to join in leading a group of thirty-five Pilgrims from Leyden to America represented an assertion of a particular identity. The Leyden Separatists were, in the eyes of the orthodox, incorrigible individualists who set their own views above the wisdom and authority of the entire English political and ecclesiastical establishments. But among themselves the Separatists were devoted to an encompassing communal ideal, modeled on the early Christians. Bradford became convinced that to realize this ideal of a select holy community it was necessary to leave Leyden. The danger in Leyden was not persecution, as in England; it was hospitality, a spirit that threatened assimilation within a broadly tolerant society that made merry on the sabbath. After only a decade, the community had begun to dissolve and scatter. Some saw their children "drawn away by evil examples into extravagant and dangerous courses." Bradford and those who went with him believed "their posterity would be in danger to degenerate and be corrupted," if they remained where they were.[4]

The elders turned their thoughts to refuge in America, which Bradford described as a vast and fruitful land, "unpeopled . . . [excepting] only savage and brutish men which range up and down, little otherwise than wild beasts."[5] In 1617 the elders began negotiations for land there. By 1619 the Virginia Company of London, having given up hopes of finding gold in America, was vigorously promoting agricultural settlement, eagerly selling land to companies that would send colonists. In that year William Brewster, who had been secretly printing banned religious tracts for sale in England, was seized by Leyden authorities acting on behalf of the English ambassador. It was ironic that Brewster escaped to London, but it was there that he arranged the formation of a company of merchants who obtained land for Pilgrim settlement near the Hudson River. In this backdoor manner the settlement of Massachusetts became linked to the most conspicuous English example of Renaissance imperialism, the Virginia Company.

The actual decision to go to America seriously divided the Leyden community. The Reverend John Robinson and the majority of the church decided to stay put, preferring the known dangers of life where they were to the innumerable unknown hazards of a transatlantic settlement. When the time came to leave in the spring of 1620, only 35 of the 240 Leyden church members embarked from Holland. In England about 40 more London Separatists joined the group, as well as a handful of other Englishmen. When the *Mayflower* finally slipped away from Plymouth on September 16, its parting aroused no attention. England prospered, and most English, whatever their persuasion, were not willing to leave it forever.

Yet in the next decade a combination of events would make many people uneasy and lead a substantial number to consider permanent settlement in America. John Winthrop, the obscure Puritan layman whose chief concern was making a secure and pious life for himself and his family, was one of thousands who saw gloomy portents in the public life of his country. In the past, England had experienced much worse periods than the 1620s, but now, among Puritans particularly, there was a new restlessness. Access to America created new possibilities.

The sense of malaise in England seemed to be general. Some of its roots were economic. Over the long term a population expanding more rapidly than employment was a major source of distress. People who had once been bound to an occupation and a community were now roaming the countryside or gravitating to London, in either case facing repeated hardships and threatening the order and the property of more fortunate people. The situation was aggravated in the 1620s by a general economic depression that sharply affected the textile business of East Anglia. Troubles in the economy seemed to be manifestations of less concrete but equally disturbing changes in common attitudes.

Exactly what disturbing changes one recognized depended on one's location in the social structure. The majority of people who possessed no land believed that the world at least owed them a place, however meager, and that it was the fault of grasping landlords and merchants, not God's will, that they were groaning in poverty. The wealthy and privileged, expecting docility and deference from their inferiors, were troubled by the rising expectations and the actual mobility they saw challenging their own positions. "Observe degree, priority, and place"[6] ran the old dictum, but in a competitive, increasingly crowded commercial society, people were jostling each other for advantage. Moreover the tolerance of different opinions within the church of Elizabeth had permitted such a degree of religious individualism that the fundamental common denominators of Christian belief were in doubt. Everything from skepticism to pietism could be found in England. The familiar expectation of uniformity, so conducive to harmony and security, was repeatedly being frustrated by experience.

Uneasiness in English public life bred noisy controversies. The privilege and favoritism of monopolies and royal patronage were sharply criticized in Parliament during the 1620s, and a struggle between the advocates of royal prerogative courts and the supporters of common law courts attested to a far-reaching division among prominent people over the principles of maintaining order. At the end of the 1620s, when Charles I dissolved Parliament and determined to rule without it, the political conflict reached a climax. When the king succeeded in raising revenue by means of a forced loan, he effectively trampled the principle of taxation by parliamentary consent. Charles's objective was to establish uniformity and order within the realm by means of royal absolutism.

The English Church, which had once been pliant and tolerant, was now headed by William Laud. His drive for ecclesiastical absolutism was part of Charles I's program for the realm. As a result, Puritanism was now treated as a subversive movement to be actively rooted out of the church, the sooner the better. In the past Puritans had been under a cloud. Now the storm burst on them. Laud believed that he must achieve a total victory over the Puritans or they would, as they had started to do, take over the church. Henceforth Puritans would be ousted from the universities and church appointments, and, where they deviated from Laud's ecclesiastical policies, they would be fined and harassed. Until the end of the 1620s Puritans had clung to the hope that they could redeem an England that was sliding toward Hell. Now, when their own survival was in doubt, gloomy premonitions about the consequences of God's wrath came readily to mind. These anxieties inspired Puritans to create the Massachusetts Bay Company in 1629.

They established the Bay Company from the ruins of the Dorchester Company. During the early 1620s the Dorchester group led by the Reverend John White had attempted to found a farming and fishing colony on the shores of Massachusetts Bay. Although Puritans were conspicuous in this effort, the chief object of the enterprise was commercial. After several preliminary voyages, the Dorchester Company mounted its greatest effort in 1625 when it sent three ships and nearly one hundred men to settle Cape Ann. But as with the earlier voyages, there were no profits. The settlers' chief accomplishment was survival, although they did begin a town at Naumkeag (later named Salem), before most of them returned to England. This was not enough to save the company.

Yet John White, who had come to believe in the necessity of a purified settlement away from England, would not give up. Gaining new sponsors in 1628, White helped found the New England Company, and it was this fragile corporation that became the Massachusetts Bay Company by royal charter in March 1629. When the Massachusetts Bay Company sent its first five ships to Cape Ann in 1629, it made John Endecott, who had been the head of the Dorchester settlement, governor of the colony.

John Winthrop was not among the original 110 investors in the new company, but within the year he was drawn into the enterprise by Matthew Cradock, John Humphry, Isaac Johnson, Sir Richard Saltonstall, and the tireless John White. White's vision of a holy settlement, a fragment of England that could redeem it, appealed strongly to Winthrop. Winthrop's willingness to leave Groton Manor, the estate that had brought his grandfather into the gentry class, grew out of a careful assessment of his family's possibilities at home and their prospects in New England.

As of 1629, when Winthrop and his third wife, Margaret Tyndal, decided to migrate, they were the parents of eight children. The three eldest, sons of John's first wife, were all grown men, but none had found a secure place in the world. John Jr. and Henry had each spent some time at university, they had traveled, and Henry had married against his parents' wishes. The third son, Forth Winthrop, was training to be a minister. John Winthrop's landholdings were not sufficient to establish his three eldest sons at his own level, not to mention the younger children. His official position as a magistrate in the London Court of Wards and Liveries, which initially had seemed to be a lucrative rung on the patronage ladder, now appeared no more than a tiresome, break-even post, so Winthrop resigned it. In light of Winthrop's ambition for himself and his offspring, he was ripe for a new proposition.

Moreover, Winthrop was part of a network of Puritan gentry northeast of London. When prominent members of this group, including John Humphry and Isaac Johnson, brothers-in-law of the greatest Puritan peer, the earl of Lincoln, discussed their plans for Massachusetts with Winthrop, he listened and was persuaded to become involved. For Winthrop nothing could be more satisfying than escaping the corruption and competition of a decadent England to build a colony where Puritans would rule and land was abundant. The Massachusetts Bay Company was led by powerful men that Winthrop respected, and it nourished his visionary hopes while reassuring his practical judgment.

In the summer of 1629 Winthrop became part of a conspiracy within the newly formed company to transfer its government and its charter to the new colony. Initially Matthew Cradock, an important London merchant who was the governor of the company, proposed to the company's stockholders' meeting that they transfer actual government of the settlement "to those that shall inhabite there."[7] The company in England would thereby allow its colony substantial political independence. But Cradock's idea ran into opposition from those who believed the charter did not allow such a step and that to take it would lead to the charter's revocation. This discussion led a dozen men, including Thomas Dudley (the earl of Lincoln's steward), Humphry, Johnson, Saltonstall, and Winthrop, to meet again privately at Cambridge in late August. There they jointly pledged themselves to be ready, "with such of our severall familyes as are to go with us and such provision as we are able conveniently to furnish ourselves withall to embark . . . by the first of march next [1630] . . . to inhabite and continue in new England." But this agreement was made contingent on a crucial point, that "the whole government together with the Patent . . . bee first by an order of Court legally transferred and established to remayne with us and others which shall inhabite."[8] Two days later, on August 28, 1629, this Cambridge agreement was presented at a special meeting of the company's stockholders. On the following day, after a systematic airing of the pros and cons, the stockholders voted by a show of hands in favor of the Cambridge plan. Only 27 of the company's 125 members were present. The active minority had succeeded in imposing its will on the company.

The revolution in the company was underscored in October 1629 when the shareholders elected John Winthrop as governor. During the summer the forty-one-year-old Winthrop had emerged as a vigorous, shrewd, and conciliatory leader among a group of pious and prudent merchants and gentlemen. The Cambridge agreement now assured all of them that others of similar resources and personal commitment would share in the trials ahead. They were also assured, unlike members of virtually every other colonial settlement, that they and others who risked their lives and their fortunes would never be placed at the mercy of a company whose interests or objectives differed from their own. The special corporate vision of a purified community of God's chosen people, born in the trying circumstances of England in 1629, would be preserved and developed by those who shared the dream.

That fall and winter of 1629–30 the members of the company led the way in persuading emigrants to go to their colony. Puritan and family connections were the most effective recruiting mechanisms, as groups of farmers from Suffolk and Norfolk, Essex and Lincolnshire decided to follow the lead of Puritan gentlemen and clergy who lived nearby. No one of great wealth was tempted to go, but the sons of minor gentry like Winthrop's own sons, yeomen and their families, and a few artisans were ready to gather their resources together and invest in passage to America. Most of England was unaware of the migration that was building, and indeed only a tiny fraction of the population was responsive to the lure of overseas settlement. But when the "Winthrop fleet" of eleven vessels assembled at Southampton and Plymouth in the spring of 1630, there were more than one thousand passengers on board, with hundreds of cows, horses, goats, swine, and chickens.

Just before his ship sailed, Winthrop wrote a last letter to Margaret, "mine owne, mine onely, my best beloved." She was expecting the birth of another child, and so with John Jr. to look after her, she remained behind at Groton. The younger John, now twenty-three, was to sell the family land and then, once his father was established in the new country, shepherd his stepmother, brothers, and sisters to Massachusetts. Aboard the *Arbella,* John himself was accompanied by his nine- and ten-year-old sons, Adam and Stephen. Winthrop's spirits were high, and his words gave Margaret encouragement: "Our boyes are well and cheerful, and have no mind of home, they lye both with me, and sleepe as soundly in a rugge (for we use no sheets heer) as ever they did at Groton, and so I doe my selfe." In a midnight reverie he joyously mused: "Oh how it refresheth my heart to thinke that I shall yet againe see thy sweet countenance, that I have so much delighted in, and beheld with so great contente!" And he promised faithfully to hold to their agreement that on Mondays and Fridays at five in the evening "we shall meet in spiritt till we meet in person. yet if all these hopes should faile, blessed be our God, that we are assured, we shall meet one day, if not as husband and wife, yet in a better condition." [9] The separation from his wife and the hardships and uncertainties of what he had begun could not shake Winthrop's faith. He was confident God would protect and prosper their enterprise, and if it was his will that Winthrop and others should die in the attempt, then Winthrop felt certain of his reward. This was the faith that had sustained Bradford and the Pilgrims for twenty years. Now it launched a larger enterprise.

Under way, the Winthrop fleet was far more fortunate than the *Mayflower* had been. Although it ran into some stormy weather, it made a seasonable crossing of eight to ten weeks. On board the *Arbella* Governor Winthrop delivered a sermon to his fellow passengers that embodied the corporate vision of the colony. In England the Puritans had been individualists. Unwilling to submit to the orthodoxy of Laud's church, they had elevated their own judgments above church and state authority. Now, in Massachusetts, they sought to establish their own orthodoxy to which individual judgments must yield.

The foundation of the new community, Winthrop avowed, was a special contract with the Lord: "Thus stands the cause betweene God and us, we are entered into Covenant with him for this worke." If "the Lord shall please to . . . bring us in peace to the place wee desire, then hath hee ratified this Covenant and . . . will expect a strickt performance of the Articles contained in it." [10] Strict performance meant that the colony must be an exemplary Christian community. Speaking as the elected governor of the company, Winthrop proclaimed a utopian mission:

> wee must entertaine each other in brotherly Affeccion, wee must
> be willing to abridge our selves of our superfluities, for the supply
> of other necessities, wee must uphold a familiar Commerce to-

gether in all meekenes, gentlenes patience and liberallity, wee must delight in eache other, make others Condicions our owne[,] rejoyce together, mourne together, labour, and suffer together, allwayes haveing before our eyes our Commission and Community in the worke, our Community as members of the same body, soe shall wee keepe the unitie of the spirit in the bond of peace, the Lord will be our God and delight to dwell among us, as his owne people and will command a blessing upon us in all our wayes.[11]

Whether the people of Massachusetts Bay Colony would keep the covenant and join together in building a community of love, justice, and piety was a supreme test, not only for them, but for reformed Christianity. Certain of the covenant in his own heart, Winthrop presented his fellow settlers with a heroic view of the significance of what they were about. For if they lived up to the covenant:

wee shall find that the God of Israel is among us, when tenn of us shall be able to resist a thousand of our enemies, when hee shall make us a prayse and glory, that men shall say of succeeding plantacions: the lord make it like that of New England: for wee must Consider that wee shall be as a Citty upon a Hill, the eies of all people are uppon us; so that if wee shall deale falsely with our god in this worke . . . wee shall be made a story and a byword through the world, wee shall open the mouthes of enemies to speake evill of the wayes of god . . . wee shall shame the faces of many of gods worthy servants, and cause theire prayers to be turned into Cursses upon us till wee be consumed out of the good land.[12]

The cause of Massachusetts Bay Colony was not a temporal one aimed at profit. It was not just an effort to secure a place to live and worship as the settlers willed. Its founders believed it was a holy adventure in which the future of all humanity was at stake.

The self-consciousness of Winthrop and the Bay Company and the generous scale of its enterprise stood in sharp contrast to the Pilgrim effort that had preceded it. The *Mayflower* had sailed alone because its companion vessel leaked too badly to risk an Atlantic crossing. Because they were delayed, Bradford and the other *Mayflower* passengers crossed the sea during the stormy autumn months. At one point in midocean one of the ship's main timbers buckled; but using "a great iron screw" the ship's carpenter raised "the beam into his place" and braced it "with a post put under it, set firm in the lower deck."[13] So the *Mayflower* survived its nine-week voyage and came into harbor on November 11, 1620, at the eastern end of Cape Cod, more than two hundred miles northeast of its Hudson River destination.

The sailors, the Separatists, and the non-Separatist passengers suffered a quarrelsome journey, and when the ship landed outside the jurisdiction of the Pilgrims' patent, there was a question of who represented civil authority. To provide order, the Separatists drafted a simple agreement to join in creating a regular government, "to enact, constitute and frame such just and equal Laws, Ordinances, Acts, Constitutions and Offices, from time to time, as shall be thought most meet and convenient for the general good."[14] Before going ashore, all the healthy men signed this Mayflower Compact, establishing from necessity a government by the consent of the governed. Its first act was to confirm John Carver, an intimate of Brewster and Bradford, as governor of the colony.

Since the Pilgrims had not arrived at their intended destination, the most immediate question was where they should spend the winter. For three weeks they explored the cape on foot and in an open boat, discovering fresh water and a hoard of Indian seed corn and beans. Then on the night of December 8 the exploring party sailed into Plymouth Bay in a snowstorm. After passing two days on an island, they went ashore at Plymouth Rock on December 11. Here, Bradford reported, they "marched into the land and found divers cornfields and little running brooks, a place (as they supposed) fit for situation. At least it was the best they could find, and the season and their present necessity made them glad to accept of it." The explorers returned with the good news to their ship, but when Bradford arrived, he was greeted by the news that his wife, his "dearest consort, accidentally falling overboard, was drowned."[15] Dorothy Bradford had been traveling for nine months; now she found herself staring at the bleak, sandy wastes of America, separated from her young son who had stayed in Leyden and from her husband who was off exploring. It appears that she was a suicide, succumbing to the depression that struck some of the English when they came face to face with the new land they must call home.

The winter that lay ahead in new Plymouth presented the most devastating test of the Pilgrims' faith. Living in lean-tos and shelters they dug in the ground, not equipped to fish for food, the people fell sick. Bradford, one of the dozen heads of families who survived, related that "in two or three months' time half their company died, especially in January and February, being the depth of winter." During the worst period:

> there died sometimes two or three of a day. . . . there was but six or seven sound persons who to their great commendations, be it spoken, spared no pains night nor day, but with abundance of toil and hazard of their own health, fetched them wood, made them fires, dressed them meat, made their beds, washed their loathsome clothes, clothed and uncloathed them. In a word, did all the homely and necessary offices for them which dainty and queasy stomachs cannot endure to hear named; and all this willingly and cheerfully, without any grudging in the least, showing herein their true love unto their friends and brethren.[16]

It was a cruel sifting, and their bodies yielded to it, but not their humanity or their trust in God.

When the winter broke in March, the Pilgrims' health and their fortunes improved. After several minor brushes between the Pilgrims and Indians, an Algonkin called Samoset, who had learned to speak English among fishermen in Maine, came to Plymouth, and Pilgrim diplomacy began with several gifts. In a few days Samoset returned with the sachem of the Wampanoags, Massasoit. On his arrival Massasoit was greeted by Governor Carver, accompanied by several musketeers with drum and trumpet: "after salutations, our Governor kissing his hand, the King [Massasoit] kissed him." [17] The friendly spirit of the meeting quickly led to a durable treaty of peace and mutual defense based on the principle that neither the Pilgrims nor the Wampanoags would injure the other and that in the event of any injury or theft the offending person(s) would be returned to their own kind for punishment. Each pledged to support the other in the event of war. The newcomers were fortunate that their Plymouth settlement did not trespass on the Wampanoag territory but was instead on the land of the Patuxets, a small tribe that had been wiped out by disease (perhaps measles) in 1617. Only one Patuxet, who had been kidnapped by English fishermen and was thus absent in the fatal year, survived. His name was Squanto.

For the Pilgrim outcasts struggling to survive, the orphaned Squanto appeared a godsend. It was Squanto who showed them how to plant corn, "and after how to dress and tend it." He taught them how to catch the alewives coming up the streams and how to use them to fertilize their corn and beans. His help proved inestimable because the "English seed they sowed, as wheat and pease"[18] failed entirely that first year.

While the Pilgrims were getting their first crop planted, the *Mayflower* departed. Soon after, Governor Carver, hard at work in the fields, suffered a sunstroke and died. Now the small remnant of the men elected Bradford their governor, a post he would retain through repeated elections for over thirty years. Bradford was energetic yet stolid, reliable, and self-effacing; his sound judgment and devotion to the common good made him the lasting choice of Plymouth colony. Under his leadership the community bore their afflictions and in time prospered.

When the first anniversary of their arrival came round, it was apparent they had passed through the fire. "Being all well recovered in health and strength," their harvest gathered, the settlers "had all things in good plenty."[19] Each family was provided with a generous store of codfish and bass, ducks, geese, turkeys, venison, and cornmeal. Then Bradford organized a great feast of thanksgiving. He sent four men hunting who, in a day, returned with enough wild fowl to feed the settlement for a week:

> At which time, amongst other recreations, we exercised our arms, many of the Indians coming amongst us, and amongst the rest their greatest king, Massasoit with some 90 men, whom for three days we entertained and feasted. And they went out and killed five deer which they brought to the plantation and bestowed on our Governor and upon the Captain [Miles Standish] and others.[20]

The colonists still mourned the loss of their brethren, but they rejoiced that God had made them a community. They looked to the future with optimism.

There were, however, a number of strictly temporal problems that needed solutions. The colonists possessed no English title to the land they had settled, and the merchant company that had sponsored their crossing wanted a return on its investment. The first issue was resolved soon after the *Mayflower* returned to England. Using as a model the patent the colonists had held from the Virginia Company, they obtained a new grant from the Council for New England in June 1621. The colony was required, under the grant, to pay a quitrent of two shillings per hundred acres. In addition the merchants would have to be paid.

At first, under Bradford's leadership, property was held in common with an annual drawing for garden plots, but by 1624 the planters persuaded Bradford to make permanent allotments, so that those who improved the land would enjoy the benefits. Eight years later, when new arrivals swelled the colony to three hundred people, the move to private ownership was extended by permanent divisions of meadow and pasture lands outside the village. Farming sustained the colony during the 1620s, but it could not yield profits for the company, so the stockholders would provide no further assistance. The value of their stock plunged. As a result the Pilgrims concluded in 1626 that they must attempt to buy out the company and liberate themselves from its control. They did so, but at a fearfully high cost considering their resources: they would pay for the shares at the rate of £200 annually for nine years, and in addition pay off the company's £600 debts. By this agreement the colony itself became, de facto, a joint-stock corporation. Fifty-three men in the colony owned its assets as well as its debts, and the land and livestock were allotted among them.

It was clear that in order to accumulate the capital necessary to pay the new obligations, the colony would need to develop trade aggressively. Accordingly Bradford and seven others secured permission from the settlers to form a partnership to manage the colony's trading activities until the debts were retired. This partnership and the need to pay the debts rapidly altered the orientation of the colony toward trade. The friendly relations with the Wampanoags were a great asset as the Pilgrims exchanged steel hatchets and knives for furs, fish, and corn. In addition Pilgrim trade extended all along the northern coast, from New Amsterdam to Maine, where the colonists established important posts along the Kennebec and Penobscot Rivers. In the 1630s sales of cattle, corn, and wheat to the newcomers in Massachusetts Bay increased the profit. Yet it was not until 1639 that the five remaining trading partners completed paying their London creditors, and in order to raise the final £400, they all had to sell portions of their real estate.

The growth of Plymouth during the 1620s, while large in percentage terms, was actually quite modest. The survivors of the *Mayflower* voyage, less than sixty in all, were later joined by two hundred more Separatists and others, arriving at various times on four different ships. One of these, in 1623, carried the widow Alice Southworth of the Leyden church and her two young sons. Soon after she arrived, Southworth and Bradford were married. The three children born of this marriage, like the other children born in Plymouth, represented an important milestone in the settlement, the emergence of a new generation—people who were not refugees and who knew only the landscape of the frontier. As yet they were only youths, subject to family discipline, but one day the colony would be theirs.

Now, however, in 1630 the Separatist settlement at Plymouth, so painstakingly built up over a decade, was suddenly dwarfed by the new Puritan colony to the north. When Winthrop and the thousand other settlers landed in June and July 1630, they came to a region that their own agents had carefully reconnoitered, and they were greeted by John Endecott, former governor and leader of the handful of "old planters" of Cape Ann. In contrast to the Pilgrims, the Puritans, well financed, supplied, and numerous, were off to a running start. Indeed from the outset there was a keenly competitive element in this new colony.

Prime land was the first source of rivalry. Since Massachusetts was mostly heavily wooded, years would pass before it could be put to the plow. The Dorchester Company's people had already taken up some of the best-cleared meadowland on Cape Ann, so there was an immediate scramble for tillage elsewhere. Within two or three months the new settlers—three or four hundred families—scattered themselves around the bay, principally along the Charles River at Charlestown and Watertown, along the Mystic River, on the Shawmut peninsula, which they named Boston, and farther south at places called Roxbury and Dorchester. Their first tasks were building shelters before winter, preparing defenses against Indian attack, and, wherever possible, getting in a crop.

Governor Winthrop and the other rulers of the colony, the Assistants, were anxious about this rapid dispersion. It drastically weakened their possibilities for control, and undermined the colony's ability to defend itself. But in the turmoil of establishing government and settlement simultaneously, they could do little but accept this dispersion. At the same time they made a vigorous effort to govern, holding court at Charlestown in August and September and at Boston in October 1630. Here they appointed constables, assessed taxes, and began imposing justice on Puritans and everyone else within their jurisdiction. Their laws were the charter, the customs they knew, and their collective judgment as to what was best. Winthrop and the Assistants were struggling to establish order and their authority according to their own lights. Elsewhere local government was beyond their reach, and so it fell to the settlers themselves to establish as best they could the various borough, manor, and open-field customs they had known in England.

The Puritans' winter of 1630–31 was hard, though not as deadly as that of the Pilgrims a decade earlier. Two hundred settlers, including Assistant Isaac Johnson and his wife, died of malnutrition and disease, and within the year one hundred more returned to England. The non-Puritan settlers, a few of whom had been there for years, chafed under the imposition of Winthrop's version of a purified community. What had seemed so fresh and promising in June 1630 was already in doubt by October.

Winthrop's flexibility and shrewd judgment were largely responsible for setting things right. At the October 19 meeting of the company stockholders, General Court, Winthrop and the Assistants disregarded the charter and allowed all men present, not just the stockholders, to vote on the issues before it. This bold step broadened the government's base of consent. Soon after, Winthrop and his colleagues invited all those who wished the privilege of voting to become "freemen," thus returning the suffrage to the rules of the charter. By the following spring the Bay Colony government was far more secure, and in the towns Puritan churches had been established. The laxity and disorder of the first months had been surmounted, and Winthrop turned his efforts toward fulfilling the corporate dream.

A first step was to assure that the rule of the godly would never again be jeopardized. Accordingly Winthrop, after being elected governor once more on May 18, 1631, urged the adoption of an oath of fidelity to the Massachusetts Bay Company and its officers in New England. The freemen accepted the oath, and the majority then went on to accept Winthrop's proposal that from that day forward "noe man shalbe admitted to the freedom of this body polliticke [the General Court and its electors], but such as are members of some of the churches within the limitts"[21] of the colony. Frankly elitist in their views of society and government, the rulers of Massachusetts Bay believed that only those men who were actual converted members of the churches, not those who merely attended church, were fit vessels for authority in running the colony. In contrast to Bradford and the leaders of Plymouth who, once survival was assured, had turned their eyes to trade in order to secure independence from outside control, Winthrop, Dudley, and their colleagues now set about building the "Citty upon a Hill."

In retrospect their self-confidence is awesome. By 1635 it was apparent that Winthrop was prepared to affirm the total independence of Massachusetts Bay Colony from the authority of any English institution whatever, including the monarchy. This self-confidence was founded on religious faith, but after the first year it was also strengthened because, the colony was growing and prospering at a rate that strongly reinforced its leaders' sense of divine support. By the mid-1630s immigrants, chiefly Puritans, were coming to Massachusetts at the rate of two thousand annually. They were bringing resources in the form of people, tools, and livestock that were required to develop the colony at a rapid pace. By 1640 there were some three hundred university-trained Puritan clergymen among the settlers, who vigorously promoted the religious objectives of the colony. Under these circumstances it is no wonder that Winthrop and the assistants developed a heady sense of power. In a few short years they had gone from being semioutcasts of modest rank in England to being the exclusive leaders of a great Christian experiment.

The sense of certainty of the Bay Colony leadership is illustrated in its responses to crucial policy issues it faced during the mid-1630s. In light of the rapidly expanding population, territorial questions were most pressing. Massachusetts's response was unequivocally expansionist. With the blessing of the governor and General Court, its people settled all along the seaboard, northward along the Maine coast and southward to open land on both shores of Long Island Sound. They encouraged interior settlement as well. Ignoring Dutch claims on the Connecticut River, colonies of migrants from Massachusetts Bay began farming and trading in the rich valley, where they founded the towns of Hartford, Saybrook, Springfield, Wethersfield, and Windsor. Winthrop would have preferred a more compact, readily controlled pattern of settlement because in some cases settlers were moving beyond the Bay Colony's jurisdiction, but he and his colleagues supported expansion all the same.

They pursued this policy even though, as they anticipated, it led to a major war with the Pequot Indians of the Connecticut region in 1637.

While the immediate causes of the war were conflicts between English traders and Indians, the war was prosecuted on a scale and with a finality that was intended to eliminate the Pequot tribe and extinguish its territorial claims. In light of the surprise attack on the main Pequot fortified village, where the English set the encampment on fire, encircled it, and then shot those who fled from the flames, it is obvious that the war was not aimed at the restoration of amicable trading relations. The English captain who led the battle estimated that in half an hour six or seven hundred Pequot men, women, and children died. Surviving Pequots were sold to neighboring tribes. Pequot land was immediately occupied by Englishmen under the leadership of John Winthrop Jr., who in 1635 had become the colonial agent for the English owners of Connecticut lands. English expansion and the victory over the Pequot, set examples of English power to the other tribes of southern New England; they must accommodate the newcomers.

Within Massachusetts Bay itself, in Boston and the neighboring towns, the influx of people put intense pressure on the concept of orthodoxy. Puritans all rejected the ceremonial rituals of Anglican worship in favor of preaching, but they were not an entirely uniform or coherent body. Some tended toward Presbyterianism, others toward Separatism, and many still favored controlling and reforming the hierarchy of the Anglican Church. Dissenting religion possessed a powerful affinity with individualism. The concept of Puritan orthodoxy was itself new, and putting it into practice generated a major crisis in the Bay Colony.

The conflict that emerged with the Reverend Roger Williams in 1635 was symptomatic. Williams had come over with the Winthrop fleet in 1630 and was highly regarded, being named minister by the Salem church in 1635. But Williams's religious views were in flux, and from the Salem pulpit and in religious meetings at his home he denied the authority of the Bay Colony and its General Court to act in religious matters. Contradicting directly the fundamental position of the leadership, he called for an absolute separation of church and state. In addition Williams became a Separatist, denying any legitimacy for the Anglican Church. At a time when Massachusetts Bay governors were seeking to consolidate their power, Williams's loudly proclaimed views were intolerable. The General Court moved quickly and decisively to end his subversive challenge by banishing him from the colony. To have tolerated his insubordination would have opened the door to a wide variety of civil and religious views that were simmering in Boston and in the scattered settlements of the colony.

The following year, 1636, similar issues erupted around Anne Hutchinson. These were far less easy to contain because Hutchinson had the backing of a prominent young Puritan, Sir Henry Vane, who had just arrived in the colony. Vane, the eldest son of one of the king's privy councilors, was elected governor in 1636 because of his high rank, excellent English connections, and apparent zeal for the Puritan cause. Vane was impressed with Anne Hutchinson's extraordinary gifts for theological discourse and her intense piety. As a result he was reluctant to take action against her when she began holding prayer meetings in her home, where she pronounced sharp criticisms of conventional piety and of the clergy who encouraged it. She claimed direct, personal revelation from God on matters of doctrine, which both Anglicans and Puritans saw as heresy. Together with the Reverend John Wheelwright of the Boston church, Anne Hutchinson directly challenged the emerging religious establishment. Wheelwright threw down the gauntlet at the beginning of 1637 when he preached to his followers: "When enymies to the truth oppose the way of God . . . we must kille them with the worde of the Lorde." If this meant "a combustean in Church and Commonwealth," so be it.[22] Vane, who would distinguish himself a decade later as a champion of religious liberty in the English Revolution, became, in effect, the patron of this insurgent movement in the Boston church.

The conflict came to a head in 1637 when the General Court tried Wheelwright and, not withstanding Vane's defense of his actions, convicted him of the civil crimes of sedition and contempt of authority. Sentencing was delayed, and when the General Court met again, Vane attempted to have the decision reversed. But the deputies, led by Winthrop, stood firm against reopening the case and then went on to elect Winthrop as governor. Three months later the twenty-four-year-old Vane returned to England, depriving Wheelwright, Hutchinson, and their followers of their most effective secular spokesman.

Winthrop and the deputies, backed by the clergy, pressed their advantage. In the fall they banished Wheelwright from the colony, and disfranchised his two supporters (Boston deputies) in the General Court, as well as others who had actively supported his subversive activity.

Taking the threat of sedition seriously, the General Court ordered fifty-eight Bostonians to give up their muskets until they were ready to recant their sins. Those who would not—a substantial number—ultimately left, going to New Hampshire with Wheelwright or to Rhode Island.

Hutchinson was now virtually defenseless. She faced the choice of quiet submission or punishment when the authorities whom she had attacked brought her to trial before the General Court in March 1638. Here, after a virtuoso defense in which for hours she recanted nothing while cleverly avoiding any self-incrimination, she finally revealed the views that had brought on the conflict: loftily, she exclaimed, that her testimony was direct from God, "by an immediate revelation,"[23] and that her accusers and their posterity would be accursed, for "the mouth of the Lord hath spoken it."[24] Although the trial was anything but fair—even by seventeenth-century standards—she had finally convicted herself out of her own mouth. The ministers present voted to excommunicate her, and the magistrates voted her banishment.

These struggles with Williams, Wheelwright, and Hutchinson were crucial for the definition of orthodoxy in the Bay Colony. The disputations among clergymen that had surrounded the judgments against the three dissidents established the outer boundaries of consensus among the orthodox. Moreover the close, mutually supportive though distinct roles of church and state authority were delineated in the conflicts. In the process something that was not Anglican, or Presbyterian, or separatist, was coming into being—the New England Way—through which conventions of clergymen, meeting periodically, established their own discipline and criteria for uniformity. This arrangement allowed for a substantial degree of congregational independence, which, considering the volatile religious spirits the Bay Colony had attracted, was vital to the establishment of a peaceful, relatively harmonious Christianity. Here a durable balance was struck between individualism and corporate orthodoxy. Its future would be assured in a few years when Harvard College, which had been founded in 1636, began supplying Massachusetts with clergymen trained in the New England Way of orthodoxy.

The triumph of orthodoxy between 1635 and 1638 encouraged Winthrop to believe that Massachusetts Bay Colony might indeed build a virtuous city upon a hill. But the establishment of orthodoxy in religion, while absolutely necessary, was not sufficient. Maintaining the colony's integrity was a continuous battle, both against English interference, repeatedly invited by malcontents within the colony, and against indigenous tendencies toward backsliding. In the latter case economic individualism was the chief danger. Acquisitiveness in real estate and in trade flourished during the booming conditions of the 1630s as every year more land was settled and more furs brought to market. When the migration to Massachusetts abruptly ended in 1640 because Puritanism was blossoming in England, the land boom stopped. Prices of land, livestock, and crops declined, but the desire for individual gain continued.

Winthrop's response, analogous to the enforcement of communal religious standards, was to seek central control of business activities as well. A major portion of Winthrop's Model of Christian Charity sermon had been devoted to an explication of the proper terms of money lending for Christians. With their governor, the representatives in the General Court believed in the idea of the "just price," rather than a floating "anything-the-market-will-bear" law of supply and demand. Coming from a land where rents commonly remained fixed for fifty or one hundred years and government authorities often fixed the prices of basic commodities, these authorities were disturbed by the inflation and rapid fluctuations in prices during the 1630s. Setting prices on commodities and on wages, the General Court used the depression as a time to retrench. From the end of the 1630s onward, both secular and religious sanctions were imposed on those who violated the general sense of fair dealing.

In order to preserve the stable social hierarchy that was crucial to the corporate ideal, the General Court resorted to sumptuary laws. Hoping to keep people in their proper places, it prescribed codes of dress so that artisans and their wives would dress with the simplicity that suited their stations. Winthrop, the other magistrates, and the clergy made every effort to establish a society in which an inbred sense of mutual obligations between masters and servants, parents and children, rulers and subjects would produce a harmonious and stable community. But the pressures they faced, among themselves as well as from below, mounted. One observer remarked in the 1650s: "An over-eager desire after the world hath seized on the spirits of many . . . as if the Lord had no farther work for his people to do, but every bird to feather his own nest."[25] Religious dissenters could be banished, but not acquisitive self-seeking. At best it could be restrained.

Ultimately the question was whether the new generation of leaders would share the founders' commitment to the utopian vision of Massachusetts Bay Colony. The experience of Plymouth Colony was not promising. The Pilgrims had never possessed the powerful commitment to central institutions that Massachusetts Bay had, but Plymouth Colony was so much smaller and more intimate that during its first two decades the personal influence of Bradford and the other elders had sustained its unity far more effectively than all the courts and ministerial associations of Massachusetts Bay. Yet the same pressures were everywhere.

In Plymouth many settlers had left the old village to take up lands across Plymouth Bay at Duxbury and Green's Harbor (Marshfield), and even farther away at Barnstable, Sandwich, and Yarmouth along the Cape. Those who remained became dissatisfied with the "barrenness" of their lands, and so Bradford reported:

> the church began seriously to think whether it were not better jointly to remove to some other place than to be thus weakened and as it were insensibly dissolved. . . . Some were still for staying together in this place, alleging men might here live if they would be content with their condition, and that it was not for want or necessity so much that they removed as for the enriching of themselves. Others were resolute upon removal and so signified that here they could not stay; but if the church did not remove, they must. . . . And thus was this poor church left, like an ancient mother grown old and forsaken of her children, though not in their affections yet in regard of their bodily presence and personal helpfulness; her ancient members being most of them worn away by death, and these of later time being like children translated into other families, and she like a widow left only to trust in God.[26]

Already in the 1640s Bradford was lamenting the passing of his world. His community, initially formed at Scrooby in 1606, had survived persecution in England, exile in Holland, and the most severe physical and emotional tests of settlement only to be undermined by the lure of material success.

Bradford's counterpart in Massachusetts Bay was not yet so gloomy, though Winthrop too regretted how much "self-love" had gained a foothold and "how little of a public spirit appeared in the country."[27] Both men and hundreds of families who had come to America sharing their visions of Christian communalism within the framework of the English social hierarchy still held fast to this vision. But as settlements became widely dispersed in the region and conditions of farming and settlement no longer required intense cooperation, the original vision of New England was in doubt. Though Bradford and Winthrop still ruled as governors, their world was fading, and a dynamic provincial era was beginning.

# CHAPTER 3

꧁ꕥ꧂

# Piety and Plenty in the American Canaan

I N 1649 JOHN WINTHROP DIED AT THE AGE OF SIXTY-ONE.
Eight years later the death of William Bradford in his sixty-eighth
year marked the end of an era. A few children of Queen Elizabeth's
England still lingered on, but in both Plymouth Colony and Massachusetts Bay, leadership had passed to younger men. The founders had met
their most basic challenge masterfully, creating settlements that could
endure. Large, healthy families were making the settlements grow rapidly. Year in and year out, farmers were converting great oaks, pines,
chestnuts, and hickories into lumber and firewood, as they cleared
thousands of acres for planting. In Boston, chiefly, merchants were establishing long-distance trade, selling fish, furs, lumber, cattle, and foodstuffs to Virginia, the West Indies, and England. By the 1650s the colonies had recovered from the slump of the early 1600s and were building
the foundations for prosperity.

But Pilgrims and Puritans had not come to America for the sake of
mere survival or material success—the Pilgrims had prospered in
Leyden, and the great majority of Puritans, and their property, survived
very well in England. Among the founders of Massachusetts Bay a sense
of community had been established during a period of special adversity
when a "corrupt" society had treated them as outcasts and when they
struggled to survive in the wilderness. Now that their children were the
majority, in control of public and ecclesiastical power, what could weld
them together? The test that lay ahead was whether the society they
and their children were creating would be truly pious, or whether it
would become merely a distant colony of provincials living the ways of

the English countryside. The tension inherent in this situation proved a dynamic force during the next century as people struggled over their identity. Beneath the tension lay the question of whether the colony's corporate ideals should override individual goals or promote their fulfillment.

If the survival of the missionary vision of Massachusetts Bay Colony had rested on a handful of leaders such as Winthrop and the Assistants, or even on the broader group of leaders, the clergy, it would have had only a short and contentious life after the restoration of the Stuart monarchy in 1660. The leadership would have buckled under outside pressure from England, combined with the ambitions of farmers, fishermen, and merchants in an expanding economy. But, in fact, the original impulse had been broad as well as intense and never limited to a few lay or clerical leaders. Most Massachusetts Bay households were headed by yeomen farmers, and it was the attachment of these families to the ideal, reinforced by the policies of the General Court and the clergy, that enabled the ideal to persist.

The community of Dedham, founded in 1636, demonstrates the widespread commitment to Puritan corporatism and the way that local institutions and central authority were used to sustain it. The thirty men who founded Dedham were all part of the great Puritan migration, arriving in Massachusetts between 1630 and 1635. They were strangers from several different counties in England, but their common bond was a desire to live and own land in a Christian community. The General Court yoked these objectives in its requirements for granting townships, because it alloted them only to groups of settlers, not to individuals or absentee owners. This approach to the distribution of land was a powerful incentive for community formation.

From the beginning, the Dedham settlers planned on creating their own "Citty upon a Hill"; indeed, they proposed to the General Court that, if their petition should be granted, the town be named Contentment.[1] The court granted the group an extensive tract (some two hundred square miles) southwest of Boston, but rather than innovate, the court named it after a village in the shire of Essex. The founders cleared their title with the Wampanoags of the region and rapidly began their settlement in 1636.

The first action of the founders in Dedham was to draw and sign a community covenant. Its first article was a mutual pledge to "practice one truth according to that most perfect rule, the foundation whereof is everlasting love."[2] In addition they agreed to obey the common rules made by the group. The covenant included a procedure whereby any disputes between Dedham people would be submitted to an arbitration committee selected from among their neighbors. The Dedham settlers wished theirs to be a harmonious community of like-minded people, but they were not totally exclusive. The covenant provided that others might settle if it appeared that the newcomers would be "of one heart with us" and were prepared to sign the covenant.

The willingness to practice what they preached is evident in the way the settlers treated their land. Instead of dividing it all among themselves to satisfy individual speculative ambitions, they parceled it out to create a compact village within their extensive township. Since they believed in a social hierarchy, the land was not divided equally, but the range between largest and smallest grants was narrow and depended for the most part on a family's ability to work the land and the number of people in a household. The grants were so sparing, so oriented to present ability to improve the land, that twenty years after Dedham was settled, when the number of admitted families had grown from thirty to seventy-five, the town still retained 97 percent of its original grant.

After the selectmen had laid out the village, the townspeople began work on forming a church. Their first task was to know each other's minds so they could work out common fundamentals for inclusion in a church covenant. Since they had not come from any single parish and were not the followers of a particular clergyman, it was a lengthy undertaking. Meeting weekly from late 1637 into the following year, the people spoke their minds and gradually came to agree on principles. Though only God could know who was truly saved, theirs would be a church of "visible saints," of people whose outward and inward piety were so well known that it seemed probable that they were God's elect. Several of the most pious men, including the Reverend John Allin, were chosen to act as an admissions committee to interview every prospective member. One year after the townspeople had begun discussing a covenant, they were ready to form a church, so, in the presence of clergymen from other churches and magistrates from the General Court, they signed their covenant and inaugurated their church. It had no meetinghouse; it was a body of visible saints. Within a decade four-fifths of the men and women in Dedham became admitted members of the church.

Dedham's first twenty years fulfilled the villagers' ideal of a Christian community. Working and praying together, they accommodated their wishes to one another. The arbitration system was so effective that Dedham people had no need for courts. The town meeting, where heads of households elected local officials and voted on town policy, operated through consensus, and the decisions of the annually elected executives, the selectmen, were never challenged. Common interests—material and spiritual—furnished a setting in which a harmony based on orthodoxy flourished.

Then in 1657, the year of Bradford's death, the people of Dedham laid down a policy that, while aimed at preserving their community just as it was, signaled the legitimation of self-seeking at the community's expense. The immediate decision was to stop admitting new settlers into Dedham so the town's growth would be limited to their own descendants. They feared that if this were not done, the town would become too large and diverse to remain a unified community. However, the way in which the policy was spelled out suggests that selfishness was also at work. The public land of Dedham, which had been thought of as belonging to the community, was made the common property of the specific individuals who were presently members of the town. They made themselves the proprietors of the town land, and only they, their heirs, and people to whom they sold proprietary shares would partake in future divisions of the town's remaining 125,000 acres. Until now Dedham had been a corporation open to like-minded Christians. Now it became a hereditary corporation, although membership could also be purchased. While the immediate consequences of the new policy were minimal, its implications were profoundly significant for the Puritan ideal of community. In time the people of Dedham would be divided into two classes: the first comprised the descendants of proprietors, who had hereditary access to land within the township; the second, made up of newcomers and their progeny, was much less securely rooted and had to purchase land whenever and wherever they could.

In the church, too, there were signs of decline: by the early 1660s the percentage of young people experiencing conversion had fallen so sharply that the day was approaching when only a minority of Dedham people would be church members. For a time the church rejected the "halfway covenant," a widely used innovation whereby the children of admitted members could be admitted into the practices of the church (except for communion) provided they committed themselves to living by the Bible. Dedham had made access to communal land a hereditary privilege in 1657, but it was not until the 1670s that people were prepared to accept a similar principle in the church, and even then there were misgivings. If incoming clergymen had not demanded the adoption of this provision in order to expand membership and their own base of support, it seems unlikely that the Dedham church would have accepted the halfway covenant. The circle of people devoted to the original faith was contracting, but it did not disappear.

When Dedham and communities like it were challenged by the dispersion of a growing population away from the old villages in the late seventeenth century, their responses were ambivalent. Usually the process began, as it had in Bradford's Plymouth, with the requests of people living distant from the center to be permitted to form a separate church society in their own locality. Often this proposal met heated opposition, because it meant the original church would be left with fewer people and smaller revenues. After separate religious societies were formed, it was often only a matter of time until the same people sought full political separation from the parent town. That, too, meant a loss in revenues. But, generally, the old towns and their deputies in the General Court accepted this process of division because it preserved and renewed the communal ideal, which was tied to settlements of no more than several hundred families. The easiest way to recapture a sense of community in a town where rancorous, geographically based divisions had erupted was to create new towns through legislative surgery. As the population of Massachusetts Bay grew to more than 100,000 by 1700, the average size of towns was stabilizing in the range of two to three hundred families.

By this time, however, a community covenant such as that of Dedham was becoming rare. Even in the 1630s all towns had not begun with Christian covenants. The fishermen of Gloucester and Marblehead, many of whom were not Puritans, scorned to give up the least iota of their individual rights. Even Puritan farmers such as those who settled the town of Sudbury, ten miles northwest of Dedham, did not enter a town covenant. For them, as for others, town founding had been a secular matter, and material questions had made their town meeting a forum of conflict even though the townspeople organized a church and worshiped as a group.

The fact that all towns were not harmonious Dedhams and that from time to time bickering and even serious divisions occurred does not mean that the corporate impulse and the sense that individual judgments and actions should be subordinate to the common good had died. Everywhere an ideal of community remained a powerful force shaping people's expectations and behavior.

As at Dedham, the initial strength of the ideal had been drawn from religious commitment. But from the beginning it also depended on secular attitudes and institutions that were common to agricultural settlements in much of Britain and the Continent in the seventeenth century. Here the crucial decision had been made by the General Court when, both for religious and practical reasons, it had determined that settlement would be by groups of people clustered in towns, in contrast to the scattered, isolated grant system that was used in colonies to the south. Granting land to groups of people and requiring them to establish communal institutions—town government, churches—meant the creation of a highly localized pattern of face-to-face relationships, frequently renewed. Since the land grants were large enough to provide for several generations of inhabitants, the basis for continuity was established at the outset. Loyalties to familiar people and places were bound to grow, reinforcing the vitality of the community.

Pulling together for the common good in frontier settlements was also highly functional in the most mundane, practical terms. Road construction was literally a public-work project, demanding the collective efforts of townsmen; erecting the frame for every house and barn in a settlement required the labor of several families, at least. In the absence of specialized workers and a cash economy, subsistence required cooperation and common labor from settlers. The physical creation of a village and its amenities, such as roads and bridges, contributed substantially to the formation of a psychological community even in towns where a covenant like Dedharn's was never considered.

Over time, the political and ecclesiastical structure of the colony reinforced the corporate identity. Towns and congregations were not mere administrative subdivisions of Massachusetts Bay. Collectively, they were the colony. Within wide and generally flexible boundaries fixed by all the towns and churches, each town and each congregation displayed autonomy. Towns conducted their elections, tax collection and disbursement, other internal business, and relations with neighboring towns without supervision from outside. Their conformity with colony laws was voluntary for the most part, and coercion from the General Court, which came in the form of fines, was infrequent and subject to negotiation. The colony's military force was composed of town militia units that were largely self-trained and self-governing. Formal secular institutions provided a structure to sustain the vitality of community.

The New England Way of church polity allowed an even greater degree of liberty. Churches hired their own clergy and managed their own affairs. Outsiders were called in only rarely, and then to confirm local decisions or to adjudicate disputes. After a church was founded, total autonomy was common for a generation or two. Under these circumstances, where local institutions were controlled by local people, the town belonged to its people in the fullest sense and group possessiveness toward the community flourished. Informally as well as officially, townspeople effectively squelched selfishness when it interfered with common goals.

Consequently the survival of a vigorous corporate ideal was never in doubt. But was it Winthrop's ideal community? Did people "uphold a familiar Commerce together in all meekenes, gentlenes, patience and liberallity"; did they "delight in eache other, . . . rejoyce together, mourne together, labour, and suffer together . . . in the bond of peace?"[3] To some degree they did. The life of Anne Bradstreet of Ipswich and North Andover in Essex County offers a rich example. Bradstreet, a daughter of the magistrate and sometime governor Thomas Dudley, had come to Massachusetts in 1630 as the eighteen-year old wife of Simon Bradstreet. Throughout her life, her primary occupation was maintaining an orderly Christian home for her husband and children. (Her husband, the son of a clergyman, was a Cambridge graduate. In later years, he served twice as governor.) Like countless other men and women, she would have remained obscure to all but her immediate family if she had not taken time away from her chores and devotions to write poetry. Her literary endeavors were private until 1650 when her brother-in-law took copies of her poems to London and had them published without her knowledge or consent. The title he gave to her book, *The Tenth Muse Lately Sprung up in America. Or Severall Poems, compiled with great variety of Wit and Learning, full of delight,* suggests that he saw Bradstreet's learned poetry as one of the glories of New England culture, one that would be all the more remarkable in the eyes of English Puritans because it was written by a woman.

Anne Bradstreet was, indeed, early America's first notable poet though, as befitted her station as a woman, she was a private and domestic author. Six years after her death, a second edition of her book appeared in 1678, and then she was identified as "A Gentlewoman of New England." This second edition contained additional pieces, and these later poems were more straightforward and original than her earlier verse. Though they resembled some of the English Metaphysical poetry of the preceding generation, much of their content and imagery could have come only from a woman living in New England and observing the passage of its seasons. Most of all, however, Anne Bradstreet's poetry reflected her faith, as when she wrote in anticipation of her own life-and-death struggle with childbirth:

> All things within this fading world hath end,
> Adversity still our joys attend;
> No ties so strong, no friends so dear and sweet,
> But with death's parting blow is sure to meet.

Her piety, Puritan piety, was closely tied to the divine gift of human love, as when she wrote "To My Dear Loving Husband":

> If ever two were one, then surely we.
> If ever man were loved by wife, then thee.
> If ever wife was happy in a man,
> Compare with me, ye women, if you can.
> I prize thy love more than whole mines of gold,
> Or all the riches that the East doth hold.
> My love is such that rivers cannot quench
> Nor ought but love from thee give recompense
> Thy love is such I can no way repay;
> The heavens reward thee manifold I pray.
> Then, while we live, in love let's so persever,
> That when we live no more we may live ever.[4]

This was a love poem, to be sure, but it speaks not of the youthful, romantic love of Shakespeare's sonnets. It expresses the mature, committed love of a godly woman to her faithful companion in life's journey. Anne and Simon Bradstreet cherished the tenderness of their relationship as one of God's blessings. For, as she noted, "Sore laborers have hard hands, and old sinners have brawny consciences." Bradstreet exemplified both the otherworldly piety and the earthly vitality of seventeenth-century Puritan experience.

As the decades passed, especially following the restoration of the monarchy in England in 1660, the intensity of Puritanism faded on both sides of the Atlantic and worldly ambitions became more prominent. In Massachusetts the communal ideal now showed evidence of a good deal of earthy secularism. Economic interests often came before Christian generosity. Poor people who were not born in a township were quickly sent away to become charges of their native locality. Even Dedham, with its abundant supply of land, was insistent about maintaining control of every acre within its boundaries when, in the 1670s, the Indian missionary John Eliot needed some land for Christian Indian farmers. Piety flourished, but it was a *social* piety more than a *spiritual* piety. People still favored the common good over the individual, but in defining the good, the balance had shifted from salvation toward material security and well-being.

It was this trend that made the halfway covenant so generally desirable in the late seventeenth century. In the second and third generations of settlement new church memberships were no longer common, especially among young men. Whereas the majority of heads of families in each town had been church members, the situation now was reversed and nonmembers were in the majority. The political consequences of this shift were serious. Enthusiasm for supporting churches waned, and pulpits sometimes remained empty for several years. Moreover, the circle of voters eligible to choose representatives to the General Court contracted. Since the pillars of the social order—the church and the state—were both founded on regenerate Christians, the colony faced the choice of letting these institutions become separate from the body of the people, governing them substantially without their consent, or of letting every man participate, church member or not. In light of the colonial leaders' ruling principles, neither of these courses was acceptable. To clergymen especially, the idea that the population would become generally outsiders to the church was a dismal reproach. The clergy's influence would decline and infidelity would flourish.

Taking the lead in solving this problem, a synod of ministers agreed in 1662 to allow the children of members into church membership without requiring conversion. The church would become theirs, and, it was hoped, they would later come into full membership. The halfway covenant was a recruiting device for the churches and a means of promoting a broader colonial political franchise. Yet because of the congregational church structure, the synod's decision was in no way binding. Each church had to become convinced that it should open its membership in this way. Gradually in the forty years following the synod the new arrangement gained acceptance. When members saw their children and grandchildren straying from their own path, they came to adopt this practical, if doctrinally doubtful measure. Together with hereditary access to town lands, the halfway covenant promoted an almost tribal sense of family identity that became intertwined with communal bonds.

In the late seventeenth century there were two major external threats to the colony—one from Indians and the other from the king—that tested community vigor and unity. The first began in June 1675 when Wampanoag braves attacked the village of Swansea in Plymouth Colony, burning part of it. Several days later, as Plymouth prepared its defenses and called on God's assistance through fasting and prayer, eleven Swansea men were killed and King Philip's War began in earnest. Now the Bay Colony joined with Plymouth in seeking to isolate the Wampanoags and Massasoit's son and successor, Metacom, whom the English called Philip. The colonists' first measures were diplomatic, sending messages to their Indian allies the Narragansetts in Rhode Island and the Pocumtucs in the Connecticut River valley. Then, together with Plymouth forces, they moved to capture Metacom. Throughout the summer of 1675 the Wampanoag chief eluded them and gained Indian allies of his own in what was becoming a drive to curtail English settlement and reassert Indian supremacy. By autumn both the Narragansetts and the Pocumtucs joined the Wampanoags.

When the Nipmucs in the central upland region also joined, the settlers faced the worst military threat in their entire history. Communications between east and west were disrupted, and the valley towns, including Springfield, Hadley, and Northampton were burned. By the beginning of the winter of 1675–76 most of the frontier had to be abandoned. In this first phase of King Philip's War, the Indians clearly won.

But the tide turned. In late December, Governor Josiah Winslow of Plymouth led militiamen from both colonies in an attack on Chief Can-

*A pilgrim meetinghouse, late 17th century.*
From Z. A. Mudge, *Views from Plymouth Rock,* 1869.

*Attack on Hadley during King Philip's War, 1675–1676.*
Engraving by E. H. Corbould and J. Stephenson, 1880.
Courtesy Ruth Owen Jones.

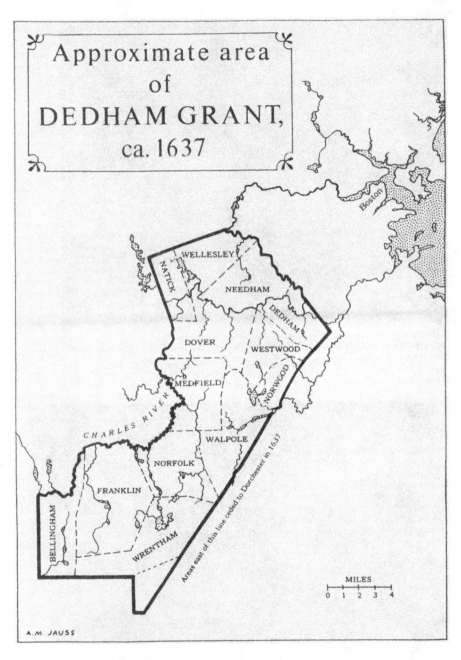

*Map of original Dedham grant, c. 1637.*

Drawn by A. M. Jauss. From Kenneth A. Lockridge, *A New England Town: The First Hundred Years*. Enlarged ed. Copyright © 1985, 1970 by W. W. Norton & Company, Inc. Used by permission of W. W. Norton, Inc.

*Puritan meetinghouse, Hingham, built 1681–1682.* From Justin
Winsor, ed. *Narrative and Critical History of America*, vol. 3, 1884.

*Interior of Hingham meetinghouse, constructed like an upside-
down ship.* Photo Dorothy Abbe. Courtesy The Old Ship Meetinghouse.

*Cotton Mather (1663–1728).*
After a painting by Peter Pelham.
From Samuel Adams Drake, *Nooks
and Corners of the New England
Coast*, 1875.

*Jonathan Edwards
(1703–1758), Northampton
Congregational minister
who led a return to stricter
Calvinist practices.*
Engraving by S. S. Jocelyn and
S. B. Munson, after c. 1750 oil.
Photo Edgar Sabogal.

onchet and the Narragansetts, the most powerful of King Philip's allies. The Indians were encamped (as the Pequots had been forty years earlier) on a rise in the middle of a great swamp located along the Chippuxet River, ten miles west of Narragansett Bay. Ordinarily this would have been a secure defensive position. But cold weather froze the swamp, and the militia mounted a fierce attack. By the day's end the colonists had suffered 240 casualties; their enemies lost over 900 killed and wounded. The Narragansetts were not destroyed, but they were neutralized, allowing Plymouth and Massachusetts Bay to concentrate their efforts on defense.

Yet the crisis was not over. Through the months of February, March, April, and May, increasingly desperate Indian attacks continued. The Indians needed to capture vital food supplies, so they raided settlements. Dozens of towns were attacked; one, Medfield, originally part of Dedham, was only eighteen miles west of Boston. As people fled to the safety of garrison houses and to relatives in towns surrounding Boston, their hard-won homes, their tools, and their scanty furnishings were destroyed. Scores of settlers were killed, and others taken prisoner.

As terror mounted, atrocity stories bred vengeance, which fell on friendly Christian Indians as well as allied tribes. The authorities at Boston, unable to protect the praying Indians in their villages from irate frontiersmen, put many of them in protective custody on an island in Boston Harbor, where large numbers died from illness and lack of adequate provisions. Later in the summer of 1676 Christian Indians were in the vanguard of the settlers' counterattack, making a major contribution to the ultimate victory of the white settlers because Metacom and his followers lacked the resources for sustained warfare. Their aggressive tactics brought them through the winter, but when spring came, they needed to return to fishing and farming if their tribes were to survive another year. So King Philip's warriors gradually slipped away, and Metacom himself returned to his home camp. There on August 12, 1676, an English musket shot ended his life and the war.

For Plymouth and Massachusetts Bay the war had been a severe test. Nearly five hundred of their militiamen died of battle wounds, exposure, and disease; many civilians died as well. The loss of capital goods—buildings, tools, and livestock—set the economy back substantially, impoverishing the colonies for years. But the colonial governments functioned adequately, and loyalties were strengthened. In contrast to the hard times of the Pequot War and the early 1640s, when there had been a significant remigration of settlers back to England, almost no one abandoned Massachusetts in 1676. Most of the settlers who had fought Metacom and his braves were American natives too.

The threat posed by England ten years later was more complicated and less immediate than Indian warfare. The colonies in New England, since their founding, had been free of English control. Indeed, in the 1650s, during the period of Cromwell's commonwealth, Massachusetts Bay had begun minting currency and operating very much as an independent state. With the Restoration of the Stuarts in 1660, however, the dissenters in Massachusetts began to be subjected to English control. King Charles II and King James II did not forget that New England had given sanctuary to the men who had killed their father. There were others eager to garner the profits of empire now that the region was flourishing; they wanted to exploit New England trade and real estate. Consequently, in 1685 the crown founded the Dominion of New England to rule over colonies in what are now New York, Massachusetts, Maine and New Hampshire, as well as Rhode Island and Connecticut. The plan was to create a central administration that would operate out of Boston and would control trade, land, and defense against the French and their Indian allies. The first president of the council of the dominion, appointed by the crown, was Joseph Dudley, a native of Roxbury, Massachusetts, the son of Winthrop's colleague Thomas Dudley and Anne Bradstreet's half-brother.

The extent to which some of Massachusetts Bay Colony's sons had departed from the ideals of their fathers is illustrated by their complicity in overturning the colony's charter. Joseph Dudley, who possessed "as many virtues as can consist with so great a thirst for honor and power,"[5] had been sent by the General Court to London in 1682 to head off the threatened revocation of the charter. Betraying this trust, Dudley secretly encouraged the king to dispense with the charter and to give him a major post in the new regime. Dudley and other Boston entrepreneurs recognized tremendous possibilities for insiders to profit from the new dominion. The scope of Boston trade as well as administrative fees would expand, and the insiders would dispense the favors of the government, its patronage, supply contracts, and land patents. Massachusetts Bay leaders had long sought to expand the jurisdiction of the colony and had recently purchased the patent to a vast part of

Maine. In the minds of those supporting the dominion, and they included one of John Winthrop's grandsons, opportunity lay at hand.

But after Sir Edmund Andros displaced the eighty-three-year-old Simon Bradstreet by assuming the governorship of the Dominion of New England in December 1686, the distressing consequences of losing the autonomy of the charter became apparent. Andros, setting aside the General Court, imposed taxes as an executive act. Townspeople bristled, and at Ipswich the Reverend John Wise led a determined effort to nullify Andros's taxes as being contrary to the Magna Carta and the rights of Englishmen. Andros jailed Wise and then fined him, and so succeeded temporarily in gaining the upper hand. Settlers complained, but they submitted.

This opposition, however, led Andros to take another crucial step. He forbade town meetings except for the purpose of the annual selection of town officials. With this action the dominion struck at the heart of civil communities everywhere in Massachusetts Bay. Andros went on to deny towns the right to collect church tithes used to support the clergy. At the same time he commandeered a Congregational meetinghouse and used it ostentatiously to promote Anglican worship in Boston. Puritan church members and the clergy were enraged; even Joseph Dudley, the young Winthrop, and the merchants who had supported the dominion began to be uneasy.

Andros completed the alienation of the people by threatening them with quitrents. In the past land had been granted in fee simple—full ownership. Now future grants would be subjected to a quitrent of one pound per eight hundred acres. For Dedham this would have come to over two hundred pounds. Existing land titles, on which there was no such rent, were to be reviewed by Governor Andros, who would personally establish what sum should be paid retroactively to reestablish titles. Within one short year the dominion was undermining the foundations of political, religious, and economic security.

Had the dominion become entrenched and its policies enforced, Massachusetts Bay Colony would have been extinguished as an entity. A pattern of exploitation of New England paralleling English rule in Ireland would have emerged. But the dominion's potential success rested on English support, so when news arrived in Boston in April 1689 that Andros's sponsor, King James II, was being overthrown by

Protestants behind William of Orange, the people of Boston, led by their old magistrates, staged a coup, capturing Andros and his associates. The insurgents, acting as a "Council for the Safety of the People," put forward the eighty-six-year-old Simon Bradstreet to resume his term as governor, which had been interrupted by the dominion. Bradstreet, Anne Dudley Bradstreet's beloved husband was one of the few survivors of the original migration of 1630, the father of eighteen children, and the epitome of a Puritan patriarch. Immediately he called for a meeting of town representatives, and when they learned that William III had indeed succeeded in the Glorious Revolution, they restored the old charter government. Acting on their own, the people vindicated the political principles of the Puritan commonwealth.

But the leaders of Massachusetts Bay, both lay and clerical, could not turn the clock back to the 1630s or 1640s. Imperialism was gaining strength in England, and the autonomy that Plymouth and the Bay Colony had enjoyed was no longer acceptable to royal administration, Protestant or Catholic. A mercantilist trading system was being developed, and political control over the colonies was necessary to promote a coherent system that would serve the needs of British trading and real estate interests. A new charter, consolidating Plymouth and the Bay Colony and setting a royal governor over the new province of Massachusetts Bay, was written.

Yet the Boston leaders did have some voice in shaping the new charter. The Reverend Increase Mather, son of the great preacher Richard Mather and a Boston native, had been sent to England even before the Glorious Revolution to see if Governor Andros could be replaced. In 1690 and 1691, he helped negotiate a charter that restored the General Court as the legislative assembly, the legal system, and allowed the deputies in the lower house of the General Court to nominate the members of the Governor's Council, the upper house. The new charter also permitted the Congregational establishment and its supplier of clergymen, Harvard College, to remain intact, although a policy of religious tolerance for other sectarians—chiefly Baptists, Anglicans, and Catholics—was now required.

Increase Mather was particularly successful in lobbying for a compatible governor. The appointee was Sir William Phips, a newly knighted sea captain from Kennebec in the Maine district and a Puritan follower of Mather in the Boston congregation. In contrast to Andros, the new governor was friendly to the religious as well as the secular objectives of the tradition-oriented Massachusetts Bay elite.

It was partly for this reason that he fell prey to the witchcraft anxiety that captured Massachusetts Bay in 1692. When Governor Phips arrived in 1692 bringing the new charter, he was greeted by news of a satanic epidemic at Salem, twenty miles northeast of Boston. Here, in the sharply divided second parish the daughter of the Reverend Samuel Parris and several of her friends were claiming to be attacked by witches. Their tormentors, they said, were middle-aged women outcasts and the Reverend Mr. Parris's opponents in the congregation. Phips took all of this very seriously, and not being one to appear soft on Satan, he quickly created a special court to deal with the suspects.

The court, which met during the spring and summer of 1692, condemned to death by hanging nineteen villagers, both men and women, including the congregation's former minister, the Reverend George Burroughs, who had taken a pulpit in Maine. One more victim of the proceedings was Giles Corey, an elderly farmer who wished to assure his heirs possession of his property, and therefore refused to plead. In the circumstances Corey figured that if he pled not guilty, he would be convicted, executed, and his property confiscated. If, however, he refused to plead, he could not be convicted. His death came when, in accordance with English custom, he was pressed (by placing stones upon his chest) until he was willing to plead. But determined not to plead, Corey's final words were "more weight";[6] then his chest caved in.

The prosecutions were postponed at the end of 1692, and later stopped as the General Court, seeing that hundreds now stood accused in Salem and neighboring towns, reasoned that something was amiss and that innocent people were being victimized outrageously. Salem itself had become the epitome of the perversion of Christian community, where half-forgotten grievances were resurrected to settle old scores. The Reverend Mr. Parris, apparently a stranger to the religious idea of charity, secured his tenure in the congregation by venting his hostility. The well of community spirit remained poisoned for years thereafter.

Massachusetts Bay recovered slowly. The majority of towns had not been touched by witchcraft accusations, but concern for the preservation of the old Puritan values and anxiety about the devil and sin-ful conduct were general. The turmoil connected to the Dominion of New England had been profoundly unsettling, especially because it had revealed a major divergence in the aims of the Bay Colony's leaders. Some, it seemed, were ready to jettison the heritage of pious, frugal independence in favor of imperial political and commercial integration. England, after all, was no longer the realm of James I or William Laud. Parliament controlled the monarchy, and dissenters were now officially tolerated. Massachusetts Bay natives, who had never known religious persecution but who had suffered the economic hardships of King Philip's War firsthand, were eager for the prosperity that British commercial development promised.

Many felt ambivalent. In Boston a competitive, ostentatious "codfish aristocracy," which delighted in the latest English fashions, was emerging. Perhaps the most visible symbol of the mixture of attitudes was the new pretentiousness of meetinghouse architecture. The ambition to match London was evident in soaring spires, richly carved interiors, and the brilliance of cut-glass and brass chandeliers. Pulpits rose to new heights, complete with paneled sounding boards. The men who stood in the pulpits and preached to the prospering merchants, tradesmen, and their families were themselves ambivalent in their aspirations. They yearned to recapture the holiness of the early settlers and preached nostalgically of the golden age of the great migration. Scolding their congregations for backsliding, they coaxed them to return to the simplicity and humility of their grandparents. Yet at the same time the clergy longed to cut figures of distinction in this world.

Cotton Mather, son of Increase Mather and grandson of Richard Mather and John Cotton, was born in Boston in 1662, the year that the halfway covenant was approved. He illustrates the conflicting impulses that were generally at work. As the son and grandson of notable divines, and as his father's assistant, he was eager to restore and revitalize the religiosity of the founders. Indeed, filial piety was an ever-present theme in Mather's sermons. Of the hundreds of titles he published in a forty-year career, Mather's history of the Puritan churches in America, *Magnalia Christi Americana*, was his greatest work. It stood as a monument to the founders of Massachusetts and as both an exemplar and a reproach to their heirs.

Yet Cotton Mather did not himself live the life of his grandfathers. He was terribly aware of his provincial situation within the British empire, and he labored tirelessly to distinguish himself on the larger stage. His mania for writing was not introspective; he wished to exhibit his brilliance and erudition to the world. As a dissenter he could never gain the plaudits of the English establishment so he did not confine himself to theology but turned to natural science as well. Ultimately his efforts in astronomy, botany, and physics were rewarded with an international correspondence among natural philosophers and with election to the Royal Society in 1713. Considering the resources of turn-of-the-century Boston, a town of twelve thousand people, Mather's achievements were truly extraordinary. What is most significant, however, is the way Mather combined the desire to maintain the old Puritanism with the thirst for cosmopolitan experience and fame. Other clergymen, Harvard professors, merchants, and magistrates shared these ambitions, if not always with the same intensity.

In time, however, as the eighteenth century progressed, the intense devotion to the Puritan past waned among ordinary farmers as well as wealthier, more cosmopolitan people. In the port towns, Boston, Salem, Newbury, and in a handful of others, commercial prosperity encouraged more and more involvement with the Atlantic trading world. Sailors speaking foreign tongues and worshipping alien gods became part of the landscape, and in Boston prostitution became a fact of life. In the country towns no such exotic influences were visible, but secularism was rife among farmers, whether they were frontiersmen clearing their land or yeomen who marketed their surplus crops, gradually improving their living standard with imported luxuries.

In Boston, religious tolerance, forced upon Massachusetts Bay by the new charter of 1692, gained general acceptance. By the 1720s Cotton Mather was proud to announce that he personally had admitted Baptists and Lutherans to communion in addition to Anglicans and Presbyterians. This broad-minded cordiality would have been unheard of when Mather was first ordained in the 1680s. In most Massachusetts congregations such tolerance remained alien. Cosmopolitanism, secular and religious, did not penetrate far into the province socially or geographically. Insularity and communal intolerance were widespread in towns that, by the 1720s and 1730s, were often genealogically extended cousinages. Old ways, in social and religious life, were the best ways, and the forms of old Puritanism, if not always the substance, survived notwithstanding cupidity and profane ambitions.

But in the 1730s a reaction set in against empty piety and covetous secularism. By this time church membership had so diminished that in most congregations only a minority of townspeople, including just a handful of men, were members. The halfway covenant had slowed the decline in the late seventeenth century, but now even it was too stringent to attract most people. Sexual morality, one indicator of piety in practice, had become so relaxed that the parents of children born within seven months of marriage were frequently treated as if they had not engaged in fornication, even though its fruits were publicly acknowledged. Since one-third to one-half of all first children being born in the 1730s were conceived out of wedlock, it is apparent that among betrothed couples chastity was a dying virtue. Communal values were following individual behavior, not prescribing it.

A reaction in favor of total submission to the will of God began in the town of Northampton, a major farming and trading community in the northern part of the Connecticut River valley. For over sixty years the Northampton congregation had been the home of the Reverend Solomon Stoddard, a vigorous evangelist who had been instrumental in promoting the halfway covenant. In 1729 his successor in the Northampton pulpit was his grandson Jonathan Edwards, a native of Connecticut who had been graduated from Yale in 1720. Edwards was a brilliant scholar who would become the most original thinker in eighteenth-century New England. At the beginning of the 1730s Edwards, like many other clergymen, was preaching against depending on merely pious behavior for salvation. Instead, he called on people to rely as of old on God's power to bring forth a redeeming experience, for conversion and salvation. Then, at the end of 1734 and in the early months of the new year, Northampton was mysteriously transformed by a remarkable spiritual awakening. Suddenly scores of people were converted. By springtime the church boasted over three hundred new members, and the whole community became thoroughly absorbed in religion. Never before, Edwards reported, was the town "so full of Love, nor of Joy, and yet so full of distress."[7]

Originally the revival was a purely local affair. But while Edwards's gifts were unique, his message was not, and the spiritual needs of his congregation were very much like those of people elsewhere in Massachusetts. In a few years, partly as a result of Edwards's writing about the Northampton revival, it began to sweep over the entire province.

By 1740, when the English evangelist George Whitefield visited Massachusetts, a general revival was at hand. Whitefield preached for a month at Boston, converting hundreds of people, sailors, slaves, and apprentices as well as merchants and manufacturers. He went on to cross the colony, preaching at Concord, Sudbury, Marlborough, Leicester, and Edwards's own Northampton before heading south to Connecticut and New York.

Whitefield's tour more than Edwards's effort set off a wave of revivalism in Massachusetts and Connecticut. Loose women, impudent boys, and hardened sinners suddenly felt themselves filled by the workings of the Lord's spirit. The message of God's unique power to redeem sinners spoke directly to people who were guilty about the ways in which they had abandoned the spiritual piety of the early Puritans. The preaching techniques that emerged in the revival, flamboyantly exploited by George Whitefield, moved people emotionally as conventional preaching had never done before. Revival sermons were dominated by bold metaphors and similes drawn from common experience instead of logic and appeals to reason, and they awakened heartfelt identification among audiences. Whitefield himself pulled out all the stops in a lush, sentimental approach—pointing the finger of accusation, throwing his hands up to heaven, shouting, weeping, crying aloud. Often his listeners responded in kind, writhing in torment, crying in exaltation. At their most extreme, revival preachers were chiefly concerned with immediate effects, and they tried to capture souls with emotion rather than reason.

This assault on the time-honored plain style of Puritan preaching aroused defensive reactions from clergymen who neither knew nor wanted any other way, as well as laymen who had long been pious without such "artificial" stimulation. When Whitefield began to draw distinctions among clergymen, pointing out those associated with him as being especially close to God, he encouraged a divisive censoriousness. One minister was more Christian than another; one church more regenerate; one congregation saved and another damned. This Great Awakening, inaugurated in Massachusetts by Edwards and dramatically extended by Whitefield, would not unite townspeople in the Christian harmony of early Dedham. In the end it divided the people into two camps, those who saw the new light, and those who, unmoved, continued to worship under the guidance of the old light.

The Great Awakening recalled seventeenth-century Puritan experience in the intensity of religious involvement and in the way it turned people away from material concerns. In its focus on individual emotional spirituality, it approached the Puritanism of Anne Hutchinson more nearly than that of John Winthrop and orthodox Puritans because it set great store on individual judgment, rather than on the reasoned wisdom of expert, ordained clergy. Consequently, it provided the impulse—and the rationale—for numerous church divisions as "New Lights" struggled with "Old Lights" for control of parishes. By the mid-1740s the Great Awakening left Massachusetts society more divided than ever before. Corporatism lost much of its meaning for towns where congregations had divided, and two different strains of the Puritan faith were now competing with each other. Originally town and congregation had been overlapping communities—now as a result of dispersed settlement and religious differences, they were distinct. Both lost a crucial dimension.

Though people were reluctant to accept the fact, Massachusetts had become pluralistic. The ideal of uniformity remained alive, but actually economic development had laid the foundation for a complex social order, and religious controversy had shattered the illusion of one orthodoxy. Piety remained a powerful force, and the zeal for harmony through uniformity lived on in country towns; they had to compete, however, with other values in a province that was economically integrated into the world of imperial commerce.

By the middle decades of the eighteenth century, that imperial world of affairs impinged more and more on Massachusetts. Indeed, in the 1740s its people participated actively in an imperial war that did not directly affect their borders or their safety. England and France, enmeshed in a series of dynastic rivalries, went to war in 1740 for reasons that had nothing to do with Massachusetts. In America the conflict generated frontier hostilities and was called King George's War. Massachusetts, like some other colonies, could have followed the war at a distance, in dispatches from London. It could have limited its participation to trading with the active parties to the dispute, as indeed it did for several years. Yet in 1745, supporting the leadership of the royal governor, William Shirley, Massachusetts enthusiastically mounted a four-thousand-man attack on the French stronghold of Louisburg on Cape Breton Island, which guarded the Gulf of St. Lawrence. An armada of nearly one hundred ships, mostly merchant and fishing vessels, carried the militiamen to their destination. Here, after a fifty-day cannonade that dropped nine thousand cannonballs on the fort, the French surrendered the gateway to Canada. Although its soldiers were not rewarded with much booty, Massachusetts Bay had won a great victory for the British empire.

The victory at Louisburg was the fruit of a new spirit in the province, British patriotism. Fifty years before, even twenty-five years earlier, the General Court would not have committed its constituents to overseas warfare, and if the idea had been presented by the royal government, it would have encountered vigorous opposition from Massachusetts farmers as well as their leaders. But during the years when the province was declining as an insular Puritan stronghold, identification with Britain had grown. There had been new emigrants from the old country, there had been the official encouragement of the royal governor and his entourage; and, together with the rising standard of living, there had been a broad importation of British culture. English secular books and newspapers had become the common fare among influential people. Most important, the Hanoverian monarchy ruling in conjunction with Parliament had become the fortress of Protestant power and the emblem of constitutional liberty in the world. From a Puritan standpoint the Glorious Revolution had substantially redeemed the mother country; it had not, as once feared, become the home of papist tyranny. So the descendants of Bradford and Winthrop chose to view its recent history as compatible with their own forefathers' hope for England.

The peace treaty that temporarily ended the war in 1748 dealt a significant, disillusioning blow to Massachusetts's nascent British patriotism. The crown decided that Louisburg could be returned to the French, effectively repudiating the great Massachusetts victory. Parliament passed an act reimbursing the province for most (not all) of its expenses, but pounds sterling were small recompense for patriotism scorned. The colonists could not return to the mentality of the founders, where the secular pride of nationality had no place. Massachusetts needed patriotism to create the sense of unity that people craved in a diverse and competitive society. The willingness to sacrifice for the common good was still esteemed as a civic virtue—among Old Lights and New Lights, Anglicans and Baptists, among frontiersmen and Atlantic merchants.

In the century that had passed, Massachusetts had changed so dramatically that Bradford and Winthrop would have been aliens in the prosperous British province that their struggling settlements had become. They would have mourned the distance that had grown between church and state, the diversity, the self-interested competition, the enthusiasm for things of this world that gripped their progeny. That the first magistrate, the governor, was now an Anglican chosen in the king's court would have grieved them deeply. Massachusetts was no longer theirs. But in the concern for the common good, in the seriousness with which laymen viewed questions of religion and morality, and in the sense of separateness that still ruled Massachusetts, the world of Bradford and Winthrop endured.

# CHAPTER 4

# Revolutionary Vanguard

I N 1750 THE FUTURE DIRECTION OF MASSACHUSETTS AND its people was uncertain. The dissenting spirit of spartan moralism and earnest self-improvement flourished together with a righteous Yankee independence.[1] Town meetings, a distinctive New England institution, symbolized the emergence of indigenous culture. At the same time, the influences of eighteenth-century British society proliferated. Royal government brought contemporary English ways to the capital at Boston and into the county seats, the "shire towns" from Falmouth in Maine to Barnstable on the Cape and Springfield in the Connecticut Valley. Commerce, a far more pervasive day-to-day force, brought London tastes in fabric and pottery and, more important, in polite letters and social customs to every village in the Bay Colony. At midcentury, Yankee culture and British culture—the one ascetic and oriented toward fulfilling the aspirations of common farmers and tradesmen, the other, frankly elitist and cosmopolitan, aimed at refinement, excellence, and order—were rivals for the future dominion of Massachusetts.

In the 1760s British policy brought these two hitherto indistinct, parallel, and overlapping streams of social development into direct conflict. Enforcement of the new commercial legislation following the French and Indian War, culminating in the Stamp and Tea acts, polarized not only Massachusetts politics but social visions as well. Promoting obedience to British government came to signify an attachment to the orderly, hierarchical world of patronage and privilege. To counsel resistance became emblematic of the Yankee heritage of Puritan ancestry, political autonomy, and the lean, thrifty ways of life practiced by independent freeholders. Consequently the Revolution, which was fundamentally a political conflict, carried broad social implications that would become explicit in the republicanism it spawned. By the 1780s the people of Massachusetts had become self-conscious republicans who, building on their new state constitution, were eager to establish a republic of virtue as a successor to the Puritans' city upon a hill.

The very earliest stirrings of the Revolutionary impulse can be traced far back into the eighteenth century and even back to the overthrow of Governor Andros. Certainly the idea of provincial autonomy based on a constitutionlike charter was a Puritan legacy. Yet in the sense of a continuously connected set of events, the first sparks of Revolutionary opposition to British government began in the early 1760s. In the following decade both the royal governor Thomas Hutchinson and the future president of the United States John Adams, two very different but very Massachusetts people traced their "genealogies" of the Revolution back to the events of the first year or so of Governor Francis Bernard's administration. Hutchinson and Adams, sharing an inflated, provincial sense of the importance of what happened in Massachusetts, began their stories of the American Revolution with the same individual, James Otis. But the differences in the way they viewed people and events, even each other, reveal the conflicting visions of what Massachusetts was and what it should be, that gave the Revolution there its character.

Thomas Hutchinson, born in Boston in 1711, was the great-great grandson of Anne Hutchinson, but his own heritage was one of mercantile materialism rather than religious intensity. His father, also named Thomas and also a native Boston Congregationalist, was the scion of a line of merchants and tradesmen stretching back to sixteenth-century London. His mother, Sarah Foster, came from a similar Boston background. Thomas himself aspired to succeed as a merchant, in the manner of his ancestors. At Harvard in the 1720s, while other students kept spiritual accounts in nervously written diaries, Hutchinson "kept a little paper journal and ledger, and entered in it every dinner, supper, breakfast, and every article of expense, even of a shilling, which practice," he later recalled, "soon became pleasant."[2] Where his classmates spent their undergraduate leisure dreaming of excellence in poetry and rhetoric, Hutchinson concentrated on investments. While at Harvard, by "adventuring at sea," he multiplied many times the small capital

*Thomas Hutchinson (1711–1780) was governor of Massachusetts from 1771 to 1774.*

Painting by Walter Gilman Page, 1900, after 1741 oil. Courtesy Commonwealth of Massachusetts.

*John Adams (1735–1826), second United States president, helped write the Massachusetts Constitution, which was used as a model for the Federal Constitution.*

From George Bancroft, *History of the United States*, vol. 4, 1866.

*Boston Massacre, 1770.*

After an engraving by Paul Revere. From
Justin Winsor, ed., *The Memorial History
of Boston, 1630–1880*, vol. 3, 1883.

*"View of the Attack on Bunker's Hill with the
Burning of Charles Town, June 17, 1775."*

From James H. Stark, *Antique Views
of Ye Towne of Boston,* 1882.

*Mercy Otis Warren (1728–1814) published an account of the Revolution.*

From Elizabeth F. Ellet, *The Women of the Revolution*, vol. 1, 1888.

*John Hancock (1737–1793), first to sign the Declaration of Independence, served as Massachusetts governor from 1780 to 1785 and again from 1787 to his death in 1793.*

1883 print, after 1775 oil by John Singleton Copley. From Justin Winsor, ed., *The Memorial History of Boston, 1630–1880*, vol. 4, 1883.

(several hundred pounds of fish) his father had given him for the purpose of investing.[3] When he married, advantageously, several years after
graduation, he had already become a successful Boston merchant.

Shrewd, prudent, rational, and wellborn, Hutchinson built a public
career on the same advantages and talents that established his commercial prosperity. At the age of twenty-six, the young merchant was
elected by the Boston town meeting to its two highest offices, selectman
and representative to the General Court. To begin a political career at
such an elevated level was extraordinary. It marked Hutchinson's outstanding reputation among Bostonians and his distinguished lineage as
grandson of a governor's councillor and son of a current councillor who
had been holding office for nearly twenty years. For most provincial
officeholders election as selectman or representative would have been
the pinnacle of their careers, attained only after a generation's service
in lesser offices. But Thomas Hutchinson was someone special.

In the General Court he quickly became an active member of the
inner circle of legislative committeemen who led the delegates. A decade later, after almost continuous reelection to the court, he became
its speaker. By then Hutchinson had become a leading spokesman for
the hard-money Boston merchants, but at the same time his base of
support was narrowing, and in 1749 the Boston town meeting turned
him out of the General Court. Following the family tradition, however,
he was chosen to serve in the Governor's Council, where he remained
for the next seventeen years. In 1752 Governor William Shirley appointed Hutchinson a judge of probate and of common pleas in Suffolk
County (which included Boston and eighteen other towns). Within the
Massachusetts elite, he had become a key figure who could always be
relied on for carefully calculated, reasonable advice on delicate provincial or imperial questions, whether details of patronage or large issues
of transatlantic significance. As Massachusetts's delegate to the Albany
Congress in 1754, convened to promote intercolonial military cooperation, Hutchinson, with the Pennsylvania delegate Benjamin Franklin
(a Boston native five years his senior), became a major proponent of
intercolonial union. Provincial in his background, Hutchinson had been
led by his political and mercantile experience to embrace a British imperial vision of the colonies. No one was better qualified by training, prior
service, or political acumen than Hutchinson when he was appointed
lieutenant governor in 1760.

Hutchinson was an ambitious, self-serving man. He cultivated opportunities for political preferment and financial gain, but he was not consumed by ambition or avarice and he was content with his achievements. His personal pleasures were refined and retiring. In Boston he lived in a mansion inherited from his maternal grandfather and redecorated in the "modern" taste. At Milton, several miles southeast of Boston, in 1743 he constructed an unpretentious country residence for weekends and summers with his family. He had no desire to overawe his neighbors in Milton or in Massachusetts at large. Indeed his highest ambition was to become the preeminent, most exemplary Massachusetts subject. With a zeal surpassing even Cotton Mather's, an awesome figure during his Boston youth, Hutchinson made himself the archivist and historian of his native colony. For decades he collected documents and privately labored over them, drafting a systematic political narrative of Massachusetts that was a model of factually correct, balanced, eighteenth-century scholarship. In it he made Massachusetts's rough edges smooth, vindicating it, and himself, for posterity. He pictured his own role as that of steward, the champion and conservator of the Massachusetts traditions with which he identified.

Coming to the politics of the 1760s from this position of moral certainty, it is hardly surprising that Hutchinson viewed his opponents' motives as wrong-headed at best and vicious at worst. Personally acquainted with all the major figures in provincial politics and fully cognizant of their families' reputations, Hutchinson naturally, and characteristically for his age, understood events in highly personal terms. He believed the opposition of Samuel Adams was rooted in Adams's father's reversals in the land-bank conflicts of 1739–42 when Hutchinson had emerged on the winning, anti–land-bank side. He attributed John Adams's attachment to the antiadministration cause to Adams's frustrated ambition to become a great man instantly. Indeed, looking back later on the origins of the Revolution from his vantage point as an exile in England, Hutchinson was inclined to focus on the implacable enmity of the Otis family. James Otis, angry over Hutchinson's appointment to the judgeship that Otis's father coveted, had declared war on Hutchinson, and so the Revolution had begun. "From so small a spark," Hutchinson concluded, "a great fire seems to have been kindled."[4]

When Hutchinson interpreted John Adams's conduct in terms of towering ambition, he grasped an essential truth about Adams's personality. Born to a family of yeoman farmers who had worked the stony fields of Braintree for a century, John Adams developed the most intense, romantic ambitions for greatness. His father, a respectable farmer, shoemaker, and deacon of the First Church, was himself ambitious and compelled John to prepare for Harvard. Thereafter his son's aspirations needed no further encouragement. All his life Adams thirsted for fame based on the intellectual and moral excellence he ceaselessly sought to cultivate. Adams, an outsider to Boston in the 1760s, relatively poor, yet eager to establish a reputation among Massachusetts lawyers and men of affairs, envied Hutchinson keenly. This was one reason why, in his first year in Boston, Adams fixed on Hutchinson as villain and identified with another outsider, James Otis, as hero in the drama he saw unfolding.

Over fifty years later John Adams vividly sketched the scene in the council chamber of the Town House (Old State House, today) where the Writs of Assistance case, testing officials' powers of entry and search, was tried in February 1761. Here "round a great fire, were seated five Judges, with Lieutenant-Governor Hutchinson at their head, as Chief Justice, all arrayed in their new, fresh, rich robes of scarlet English broadcloth; in their large cambric bands, and immense judicial wigs." All the barristers of Boston and of neighboring Middlesex County were seated as spectators at a long table in their "gowns, bands, and tie wigs." On the walls hung "two portraits, at more than full length, of King Charles the Second and of King James the Second, in splendid gold frames . . . these were as fine pictures as I ever saw; the colors of the royal ermines and long flowing robes were the most glowing, the figures the most noble and graceful, the features the most distinct and characteristic." As the case proceeded, "Otis was a flame of fire!" With "a profusion of legal authorities" and "a torrent of impetuous eloquence, . . . [he] hurried away every thing before him. . . . Then and there the child Independence was born."[5] In retrospect, both Adams, seated at the long table with the other barristers, and Hutchinson, sitting impassively in a great chair by the fire, saw the emergence of the Revolution in this modest room, removed from the people of Massachusetts and distant from the seat of empire.

That participants personalized these events and invested such a heightened sense of their importance in them illustrates the character of provincial politics in the 1760s. At the time Massachusetts possessed a compact political community, including crown officials, the judiciary, the members of the General Court, and a handful of others dwelling in and around Boston. The chief actors in the Revolutionary crisis were already prominent—the Adamses, James Bowdoin, John Hancock, Hutchinson, the Olivers, the Otises, the Quincys, the Sewalls, the Warrens. In the next decade scarcely a stranger would intrude as Boston and the General Court became arenas for repeated imperial confrontations. Here events large with significance for Massachusetts and all the colonies had a local, personal character for eyewitnesses. But forces much greater than one person's pride or another's thirst for power were operating. Gradually the protagonists came to take on symbolic importance as representatives of constituencies in England and in Massachusetts that diverged more and more. They became heroes to their friends (King George III would hold a reception in Hutchinson's honor, and Hancock would commission a portrait of Samuel Adams to adorn his drawing-room) and villains in the eyes of their enemies (Hutchinson was seen as a traitorous serpent, and Adams, so vicious that if one "wished to draw a picture of the Devil, . . . he would get Sam Adams to sit for him").[6] Between 1765 and 1775 the people of Massachusetts mobilized around these leading figures and the outlooks and ideologies they personified.

From the time popular Revolutionary activity began in opposition to the Stamp Act in 1765 until the battles at Lexington and Concord a decade later, the conflict in Massachusetts, as elsewhere, centered explicitly on the question of taxation and representation. The Stamp Act, designed to raise a revenue to help support imperial administration, set taxes on legal and commercial documents, newspapers, and playing cards. It was a form of excise long used in England and later employed by the United States government. The taxes were a nuisance from the colonial standpoint, but though they did threaten to drain off some hard money, they did not have major economic importance. Their actual economic impact probably would have been exceeded by the commercial regulations successfully imposed the previous year by the Revenue Act (also called the Sugar Act). But the Revenue Act affected only merchants immediately, and though the Boston town meeting protested it on constitutional grounds, Massachusetts, like the other colonies, accepted it within the established framework of imperial regulation of commerce. People outside Boston and the port towns paid little attention to it. In contrast, the Stamp Act, which touched the general population directly and concerned not only merchants, but also newspaper readers, printers, and attorneys on a daily basis, broadly crystallized opinion. The issue of taxation became the focus for a powerful assertion of political autonomy founded on eighteenth-century Yankee culture.

In Boston, as in other colonial ports where the stamps would be landed and the act first implemented, there were peaceful as well as violent demonstrations in July and August that forced the resignation of the officials who were commissioned to administer the law. Here self-proclaimed "Bodies of the People" declared opposition to taxes and, indeed, to any law made without the consent of the people or their delegates. Outside Boston for the first time there were widespread assertions of political rights. The specter of direct taxation by outsiders was so fearsome that selectmen and other local leaders brought the issue directly to the attention of their neighbors in town meetings.

Here, in gatherings where for over a century nearly all men had been eligible to vote on town policy as well as election of officials, the culture represented by the Adamses spoke its mind. In Braintree, it was John Adams, still an obscure young provincial lawyer, who drafted the town's sentiments in the form of instructions to their representative. The substance of the statement as well as its form bespoke the intensity of the popular commitment to individual liberty within the context of corporate self-government.

The Braintree Instructions concentrated on the three major evils of the Stamp Act which together made it so alarming. In the first place, the townspeople asserted, it "would dreign the Country of Cash, strip multitudes of the poorer people of all their property and Reduce them to absolute beggary." Even if the law had been constitutional, which Braintree denied, it would destroy the economic subsistence that Yankees believed was crucial for personal independence and political liberty. The act was unconstitutional because it contradicted the principles of the Magna Carta, "that no Freeman should be subjected to any Tax to which he has not given his own consent in person or by proxy." Even worse, the enforcement of the law was under the jurisdiction of vice-admiralty courts where "no Juries have any concern," and "one Judge presides alone." The Braintree town meeting warned that stripped of

perty without their consent and denied the right of trial by jury,
ople would soon become "the most sordid and forlorn of Slaves."[7]

To John Adams's surprise, the declaration of principles he prepared
for his neighbors in Braintree spoke also for Massachusetts townspeople generally. Within a few months forty towns adopted the same or
similar instructions as their own manifestoes. Adams himself discovered that "the People, even to the lowest Ranks, have become more
attentive to their Liberties, more inquisitive about them, and more determined to defend them, than they were ever before."[8] This spirit, manifested in varying degrees among the colonies, was ultimately influential
in bringing Parliament to repeal the Stamp Act in 1766.

When word of the repeal arrived in Boston, there were bonfires and
celebrations. In the West Church the pastor, Jonathan Mayhew, took
as his text "the snare is broken, and we are escaped," a sermon thanking
God for delivering Massachusetts "from a slavish, inglorious bond-
age."[9] Some months later, the Sons of Liberty, a loose association of
defenders of the province, mounted a major parade and procession that
culminated in a vast open-air feast to commemorate their demonstra-
tion that had led to the stamp master's ouster the previous year. Many
believed that the imperial threat to their way of life had been ended.

Yet what had actually occurred was not so simple or clearcut. Parliament had accompanied repeal with a Declaratory Act asserting its total
competence to legislate, "in all cases whatsoever," so the threat of imperial control remained alive.[10] Moreover the resistance of 1765 had begun to shake the foundations of Massachusetts society.

No one was more aware of this than Lieutenant Governor Hutchinson who, in spite of his record and reputation for public service, had
become the local target of enmity. In August his ancestral mansion in
Boston had been all but destroyed by a nighttime mob from which he
himself had only barely escaped. The furnishings, the silver, and the
contents of the wine cellar were destroyed or stolen, and the building
was left open to the sky, in ruin. Hutchinson, the native son who advocated submission to Parliament while himself enjoying the privileges
and emoluments of imperial favor, had become the symbol of the political and cultural forces that Massachusetts Yankees found most alarming.
His gorgeous mansion, his luxurious furnishings, his multiple offices
(three judgeships, a council seat, and his lieutenant governor's position)

and Oliver family connections, and his intimacy w~~~~
English functionaries combined to indict him as a turn~
make Massachusetts over in the corrupt English style. V~
havior suspiciously, outsiders of Hutchinson's exclusive circle~
take his professions of concern for Massachusetts seriously; th~
them as a subterfuge for self-aggrandizement.

The attack on Hutchinson's house expressed these hostilities, but it
was also unsettling to Bostonians in general. Hutchinson himself feared
that Boston had become prey to a leveling mobocracy, and local property holders, whether friendly to the lieutenant-governor or not, were
worried by the implications of the attack for the security of their own
homes and stores. Except for crown officials, no one was eager to identify publicly and prosecute the men and boys who had participated in
the affair, but Bostonians did not want the scene repeated. Even Jonathan Mayhew, who had preached on the right of revolution as long ago
as 1750 and who was the most outspoken clerical opponent of British
policy, drew back from the vision of chaos he had glimpsed in Boston.
In the same sermon in which he celebrated repeal, Mayhew reminded
his listeners of how close they had come "to anarchy" when "some
profligate people . . . took an opportunity to gratify their private resent-
ments [by] . . . committing abominable outrages and excesses on the
persons or property of others." Resistance to Britain had exposed the
long-standing tension in Massachusetts between liberty and license, a
tension that John Winthrop had elaborated in a speech in the 1640s
and that Mayhew now recalled in a quotation from the Apostle Paul:
"Brethren, ye have been called unto LIBERTY; only use not LIBERTY
for an occasion to the flesh, but by love serve one another." [11] Liberty
meant the right to do that which was just, good, and lawful in the eyes
of the community, not the untrammeled expression of personal will.
The perennial problem for Revolutionary Massachusetts was to assert
and maintain liberty without degenerating into licentiousness. It was
the old question of reconciling individual and corporate rights in a
new form.

From this time onward, resistance to British measures was more controlled than it had been in 1765; no more houses were destroyed, in
Boston or in any other towns. But a year later, when news arrived of
the passage of Prime Minister Charles Townshend's Revenue Act of
1767, laying duties on a variety of imports, Bostonians again took the

lead in organizing opposition. Drawing a lesson from the Stamp Act resistance, merchants began by joining in a nonimportation movement that embraced all the major colonial ports from Portsmouth, New Hampshire, to Savannah, Georgia. Peaceful economic pressure, they hoped, would lead English shippers to join the colonists in pressing for repeal as they had two years earlier. The newspapers of Massachusetts blazed with the rhetoric of approaching slavery, corruption, and tyranny, but people in Boston and in country towns remained quiet. In the Connecticut River valley, where even the Stamp Act had not aroused much notice, the established leaders who were tied to Lieutenant Governor Hutchinson by bonds of friendship and patronage remained serene. Conversing with them at court sessions and reading their letters, Hutchinson was reassured that Massachusetts was returning to normal and that the frightening events of 1765 had been an aberration fomented by Samuel Adams and the handful of malcontents surrounding him.

To one who had gradually become distant from the day-to-day existence of ordinary farmers and tradesmen, to one who had not attended town meetings around the province, such a view was as persuasive as it was wishful. Certainly the idea that Massachusetts people were on the verge of denouncing British government and society and of asserting their own independence was unthinkable. In reality, however, it was people like Samuel Adams and his cousin John who had an accurate understanding of public opinion. Yankees had no taste for a closer relationship with England and were apprehensive about imperial innovations. When word arrived in 1768 that royal troops would be stationed in Boston, ostensibly to defend the city against French invasion but actually to strengthen British administration, especially customs enforcement, Massachusetts recoiled. Still, there was no violent opposition to the landing of the troops.

The governor, Francis Bernard, blocked efforts to bring the General Court back into session since he was reluctant to give his opponents a forum for recriminations. To his surprise, the Boston town meeting issued a call for a convention of towns as a surrogate for a legislative session, and about one hundred towns sent delegates. This convention of towns, whose members came chiefly from eastern and central Massachusetts and southern Maine, was ridiculed as ineffectual by Bernard and Hutchinson. Certainly it did not head off the peaceful landing of the troops. But had crown officials been more perceptive, they would have been alarmed that so many towns, where the majority of the population lived, chose to join Boston in an extralegal body to protest administration measures. Selectmen and other townspeople believed that they had the right to meet, speak their minds, and join with other towns, freely—whether the governor liked it or not. The belief in political autonomy was widespread in Massachusetts, and deference to the prestige, pomp, and dignity of royal government was waning.

Still, for nearly a year and a half after the landing of troops, Massachusetts was peaceful. By 1770, when all of the Townshend duties were repealed (except for the duty on tea), the nonimportation movement in Massachusetts and other colonies was flagging. Ironically, it was at this moment that the British blunder of stationing troops in Boston brought on the bloody fray known as the Boston Massacre. After months of abrasion between Bostonians and the troops, where name-calling and fist fights had been common, there was finally an explosion. On the night of March 5, 1770, groups of soldiers seeking to settle a score over a previous fight broke the curfew that required them to be in their barracks after eight o'clock, and instead went out in the streets with clubs looking for victims. Townspeople quickly turned out and a vast crowd collected, ultimately concentrating on the lone redcoat guarding the Custom House. When a handful of soldiers were sent to assist him, they were pelted. In self-defense they leveled their muskets to threaten the crowd. Then they fired pointblank, killing five civilians. Now Boston was on the threshold of warfare. Troops and more civilians poured out. Fearing the worst, Lieutenant Governor Hutchinson hurried from his home to address the crowd. Stepping out onto the balcony of the Town House, from the chamber where nearly a decade earlier he had listened with John Adams to James Otis's flamboyant rhetoric, Hutchinson appealed for order under the law. Murder would not go unpunished; he would order an inquiry immediately and, he promised, "The law shall have its course!" [12]

Although some Bostonians jeered Hutchinson's words, many more decided to heed his entreaty and return to their homes. The Boston selectmen were circulating in the crowd giving the same message—go home. For the moment at least, most people seemed chastened by the gunfire and carnage. But the following morning, after people had reflected on what they now called a "massacre," Bostonians resolved that the troops must leave the town. A hastily arranged town meeting sent the selectmen to Hutchinson and the Governor's Council to urge the troops' removal, and a committee led by Samuel Adams reported to Hutchinson that only the departure of the soldiers would pacify Boston. The lieutenant governor, who believed that yielding to public pressure would be disastrous, refused to give such an order, arguing that he lacked authority over the troops. By the afternoon, however, after the councillors unanimously advised him to comply with the popular demand, Hutchinson yielded and requested (not ordered) the commanding officer to move the troops to Castle William in the harbor. Within the week they were gone, and if Boston was not quiet, at least the danger of a general battle had been forestalled.

Now the clamor was to prosecute the eight soldiers who had committed the "murders." Few attorneys wished to defend them, and for their own safety the soldiers wanted lawyers who were popular in Boston as defenders of colonial rights, so they appealed to John Adams and Josiah Quincy Jr. to take their cases. The two agreed, after consulting with Samuel Adams, who was eager for the trials to demonstrate that mobbish anarchy did not prevail in Boston as Tories claimed. He hoped the trials would prove that Boston was a town where the people were committed to constitutional principles of justice.

In the end perhaps the trials lent support to that view. After weeks of investigation and deposition taking, and following several months of delay at the hands of the newly appointed Governor Hutchinson, the soldiers were tried. The jury, packed in favor of the defendants as far as Hutchinson was able, and presided over by Peter Oliver, a close friend of the governor's and related by marriage, was lenient. Six were acquitted of all charges, and two were convicted of manslaughter for firing prematurely. By using the legal loophole "benefit of clergy" (whereby anyone who could read or pretend to read a verse in the Bible might be exempted from hanging) they escaped serious punishment and were sentenced to branding upon the hand. From Hutchinson's perspective the outcome was satisfactory. Boston and Massachusetts seemed pacified, and though the troops had not been entirely exonerated, they had not become scapegoats to popular rage either.

But the massacre was not forgotten. Bostonians opposed to the royal government, Whigs, used it as the occasion for an annual memorial oration in which they repeatedly warned against the tyrannical tendencies of standing armies in a free state. From the perspective of royal officials and those attuned to the social outlook of contemporary English gentlemen, the episode was merely a popular tumult that furnished additional evidence of the turbulence in Massachusetts society. But to Yankees the massacre represented the logical outcome of needlessly stationing a corrupt military among subjects who were loyal to both the crown and the constitution. Massachusetts did become calmer than it had been at any time since the Stamp Act, but while the occasions for direct conflict between colonial and English expectations had diminished, the divergence between them continued to increase.

On the surface, however, Massachusetts seemed to have returned to the halcyon days of Governor Shirley's rule in the 1750s. Trade prospered, agricultural prices were favorable to farmers, and popular involvement in provincial affairs declined to a level that Governor Hutchinson believed proper. Many hoped that time would heal the political wounds of the past decade so that, if the clock could not be turned back to Shirley's time, at least Massachusetts could remain as it was, a prosperous British colony enjoying a close commercial relationship with the empire together with substantial political autonomy.

But in little more than a year, Massachusetts politics became heated once more, and a spiral of conflict developed which led to independence. It began in the spring of 1772 with what seemed to many a minor issue—the salaries of the governor and judges. In the past the General Court had always paid these salaries out of provincial revenues, but now the administration announced plans to pay the judges and actually began to pay the governor. The object was to integrate these offices into the British civil list and thus eliminate any dependence they might have on the colonists. If their pocketbooks and taxation were all the people of Massachusetts cared about, the crown's taking over of these salaries would have been welcome. Indeed, had it been done a generation or two earlier, it is unlikely that such a move would have caused any protest. By 1772, however, Massachusetts Whigs had embraced a view of politics that explained virtually every action of the cabinet and Parliament as part of a scheme to subvert English and American liberty. They believed that power-hungry conspirators close to the king wished to pay Massachusetts officials so they would always do their bidding and loyally serve the cause of tyranny. People like the Adamses, who believed that officials should be responsible to the constituents they served rather than to their patrons in the royal administration, saw the salaries issue as fundamental to the liberty of Massachusetts. If the governor and judges were perpetually bribed against the subjects, what hope could people have? In the Boston town meeting, in the General Court, in the *Boston Gazette,* Samuel and John Adams raised the hue and cry.

On half of the issue, the payment of the governor's salary, they lost. After all, if it was constitutional for the crown to appoint a governor, as provided in the Massachusetts charter, then surely it was proper for the crown to pay that appointee. True, it had always been customary for the General Court to appropriate the governor's salary, but it had often been done with ill will, and this custom had no constitutional standing in the eyes of most observers. The General Court protested the innovation, but the protest died there. Most people took little notice, and they were not eager to pay for Hutchinson's luxuries out of their own pockets. By the summer of 1772 the clamor died, and Hutchinson pocketed his stipend without incident.

In the autumn, news arrived of the implementation of the other part of the scheme, to pay the judges as well. Once again Whigs protested. In Boston Samuel Adams, who had for some time been weighing a plan to create committees of correspondence to keep alive Whig views of constitutional liberty, chose this issue as an occasion to act. After fruitlessly trying to persuade the governor to assemble the legislature and consider the issue, Adams persuaded the Boston town meeting to adopt his motion and create a committee of correspondence to state the town's views and to solicit the opinions of all the communities in Massachusetts. At the time the governor and his friends believed this was the desperate tactic of a dying opposition faction. They fully expected that the issue of the judges' salaries would be even less controversial than that of the governor. Such questions were not matters of local concern, they believed, so townspeople would go about their business and ignore the antics of Samuel Adams and the Boston town meeting.

Hutchinson was wrong. Viewing the countryside from atop his hill in Milton, he saw in it an image resembling rural England where, had such a question ever been raised, it would have been quietly snuffed out by the local gentry. Yeoman farmers, busy with their fields, their orchards, and their herds, would not have blinked. But, as he learned to his distress, Massachusetts was not an English county. Towns with English place names were radically different from their home-country counterparts. The local response to the Braintree Instructions in 1765 and to the convention of 1768, it turned out, had been merely preludes to the political excitement that now rippled across eastern and central Massachusetts.

The Boston Committee of Correspondence had asked townspeople to consider current affairs and to communicate their sentiments to Boston so that the views of the inhabitants generally would no longer be liable to misrepresentation by the governor. To ease the way, the committee provided each town with a highly partisan expression of Boston's views in pamphlet form. The "Boston Pamphlet," as it became known, contained a statement of the colonists' rights "as men, as Christians, and as Subjects,"[13] in addition to a lengthy list of grievances. In the pamphlet the issue of the judges' salaries was emphasized within a larger pattern of repeated violations of the Massachusetts charter and the British constitution. People were exhorted to inform themselves of their rights and to assert them vigorously if they meant to remain free men rather than allowing themselves and their posterity to slide into slavery. While Hutchinson's politics, and that of imperial officials generally, was grounded on a calculating pragmatism, Whigs like Samuel Adams turned the issues into a moral drama and called on the people of Massachusetts to defend the virtuous legacy of their forefathers in terms that Yankees, both Old Lights and New Lights, often found irresistible.

By December 1772 the local response to the issue of judges' salaries and the larger drift of British policy began to emerge. Although their specific language and emphasis varied, a consensus of political views was made explicit. People reasoned that their forefathers had spent their blood and treasure on settling in the "howling wilderness" of Massachusetts because they wanted to enjoy "civil and religious" liberty.[14] Their ancestors had not risked their lives in order to diminish their own rights. It was self-evident then that the inhabitants of Massachusetts should of right possess the same liberty as Englishmen. Central to that liberty was the right to hold property without being subjected to arbitrary taxation and the right to impartial justice. Without the secure possession of these rights everything they had or would ever have would be insecure, and they would effectively become dependents on the will of officials. This meant slavery. Faced by such a threat, townspeople were eager to put themselves on record as defenders of their heritage and stewards for their posterity.

As Governor Hutchinson learned of the response that the Boston Pamphlet was eliciting, he grew alarmed. His assumptions about the broad support the administration possessed and the merely factional character of opposition were cast in doubt. Now he called the General Court into session so as to lead a swift counterattack that would cut through the demagogy and bring the light of informed reason to the well-meaning but oft-deceived majority. In the first days of the new year Hutchinson put the finishing touches on his clear, carefully argued speech. On January 6, 1773, he appeared before nearly two hundred councillors and representatives pressed into the same chamber where he had heard the Writs of Assistance case.

Standing not a hundred yards from the site of the Boston Massacre, Hutchinson approached his listeners in his recognized role as the pre-eminent authority on Massachusetts history, lecturing the assembly on the colony's long-standing recognition of Parliamentary supremacy. Until recently, he reported, no one had doubted that acts of parliament were binding in the Bay province. But now people were making novel claims that the General Court, a subordinate legislature, possessed exclusive powers to legislate wholly beyond the competence of the supreme Parliament. They were even asserting that English subjects residing in a colony must enjoy all the liberties of Englishmen in England. These claims, he said, had no basis in the Massachusetts charter; they were wholly fallacious. If someone left England, that person voluntarily relinquished the right to representation in Parliament. No one could claim that because he had left, Parliament no longer possessed supremacy in the empire. Migrants could not dictate the authority of Parliament or compromise its powers by the fact of their migration. Starkly exposing the central constitutional issue, Hutchinson carried his argument to a climax that he hoped would shock his listeners to their senses: "I know of no line that can be drawn between the supreme authority of Parliament and the total independence of the colonies." [15] By raising the bogeyman of independence as the only alternative to submission to Parliament, Hutchinson dared the members of the General Court to oppose him at their peril.

The delegates were stunned. Doubtless, many of them had long been aware of the ultimate implications of the constitutional debate, but to have their seasoned governor and colleague, the Thomas Hutchinson who was famous for prudence and circumspection, speak so boldly was breathtaking. Their immediate response was silence, and Hutchinson believed that he had successfully opened people's eyes to the necessity of submission. It was more than two weeks before the Council and the House of Representatives formally answered his address, and by then he was so convinced of his success that their rejoinders only stimulated him to press his points home in further debate. If they meant treason by pressing for independence, he wanted the issues brought out into the open where he was certain loyalty to Britain would triumph.

But Hutchinson had blundered grievously. The members of the House of Representatives and the Council, whose two houses formed the General Court, and the people generally, rallied around Whig arguments rooted in the legacy of the Puritan commonwealth, that the General Court did enjoy the exclusive right to tax. If a line must be drawn between submission to Parliament and independence, they were not afraid to choose the latter; although they had no wish to draw any such line, nor would they propose one unilaterally, without the consent of "all the other Colonies . . . in Congress." The House of Representatives reproved Hutchinson by grieving that "the ill policy of a late injudicious Administration" had raised the question, and that the governor had "reduced us to the unhappy Alternative, either of appearing by our Silence to acquiesce in your Excellency's Sentiments, or of thus freely discussing the point."[16] Hutchinson, they made clear, must bear the onus for whatever consequences flowed from the challenge he had thrown down. John Adams's reactions crystallized Massachusetts's response to the debate over "the greatest Question ever yet agitated." Like others, Adams was "amazed at the Governor, for forcing on this Controversy." In contrast to Hutchinson's wishful assessments, Adams's own postmortem on the affair proved accurate: "He will not be thanked for this. His Ruin and Destruction must spring out of it, either from the Ministry and Parliament on one Hand, or from his Countrymen, on the other."[17] Hutchinson's superiors in England saw his polemicizing as self-defeating, the worst possible tactic to regain the tranquility they sought, and his adversaries in Massachusetts were delighted that he was now on record explicitly as an opponent to constitutional liberty. Several months later, Benjamin Franklin furnished the legislature with a collection of Hutchinson's private letters from the 1760s, which were published to underscore Hutchinson's view that a colonist could not possess the full measure of "English liberties."[18]

By that time the governor's isolation from the people of the province was almost complete. Scores of towns, a majority, had now responded to the Boston Pamphlet in kind, and even in western Massachusetts Hutchinson's allies in Hampshire and Berkshire counties reported that the countryside was growing restless. In June the House of Representatives, stung by the contempt for colonial assertions of right revealed in the letters, had condemned Hutchinson and his brother-in-law, Lieutenant governor Andrew Oliver, by the overwhelming vote of 101 to 5, calling upon the king to remove them from office. Hutchinson, repudiated in his attempts at the art of persuasion, at last realized that he no longer possessed a substantial base of support in Massachusetts. Thereafter, believing that any lenity on the part of the administration was self defeating, he became inflexible. Personally he was deeply hurt, not only because his speech had failed to block the tide of opposition and his private letters had been published, but also because, as John Adams had predicted, the ministry in London frowned on his judgment. Governor Hutchinson longed for an opportunity to vindicate himself and to bring the force he believed was necessary to bear on his enemies, the opposition in Massachusetts.

Several months later, in the autumn of 1773, controversy over the recently passed Tea Act provided the occasion he had been seeking. The Tea Act, which was specially designed to relieve the East India Company of its surplus inventory, promised to interrupt if not destroy the existing system of tea trading by giving the company the opportunity to sell its tea directly in the colonies through its own agents (consignees), with duties payable on arrival of the goods in America. If it succeeded, tea smuggling would end, enforcement of the customs revenue would increase, and tea traders who were not fortunate enough to be consignees would be cut out of most of their business. Up and down the seaboard, colonial merchants and their allies in elective offices protested the political and economic consequences of this new parliamentary statute. In Massachusetts trade and politics centered in Boston, and that was where protests began.

They started in an extralegal, or in the governor's eyes an illegal, way when Boston's North End Caucus called for a public meeting at the

Liberty Tree, where the consignees would be called upon to renounce their commissions and so block the implementation of the new law. If public demonstrations could stop the Stamp Act, they could also nullify the Tea Act. But the consignees, two of whom were Hutchinson's sons and strongly backed by the governor, himself a substantial investor in the East India Company, refused. Several days later, after the Boston town meeting had formally adopted resolves opposing the Tea Act and calling for the consignees' resignation, those men continued to stand firm. Now the involvement of the colony as a whole broadened as the Boston Committee of Correspondence invited committees from neighboring towns to join in the resistance effort. Later, after the tea ships arrived, the Boston committee called a great Meeting of the People where men from the surrounding towns joined Bostonians in resolutions forbidding the consumption of the tea, and again pressed the consignees to resign. But Governor Hutchinson, confident that he was upholding the law and that the navy would support him, held the consignees loyal to the East India Company and their commissions, while refusing to allow the tea ships to leave unless the duties were first paid according to law.

Finally, on December 16, 1773, time ran out. Either the tea would be shipped back or the duty paid. The Meeting of the People, under the guidance of Samuel Adams and the Whig leadership of Boston, made one final effort to have the tea sent back, obtaining the consent of all the interested parties except the governor. Hutchinson, reached by express rider at his home in Milton, again refused to bend or break the law and allow the vessels to leave. He would vindicate himself in the eyes of the ministry by his staunch devotion to the enforcement of law; if the opposition did anything radical or violent, then the need for repression would be evident in London. Whatever the event, Hutchinson believed, the soundness of his own behavior, past and present, would be demonstrated.

But the Tea Party that evening still shocked him. He had expected the Whigs to back down. He was not aware that the North End caucus and other Whig groups had anticipated his refusal to let the ships pass and had made their plans accordingly. The governor had not the least inkling of the plan to send dozens of men (perhaps as many as sixty), disguised as Mohawks, aboard the ships to dump the tea, ninety thousand pounds of it worth £9,000, into the harbor. So he was distraught when he learned the next morning that in two hours the tea, all of it, had been destroyed. Immediately he had private second thoughts about his own conduct, but officially he set out to defend his policy and argue the necessity of strong measures against Boston and Massachusetts.

His adversaries were jubilant. "The Sublimity of it, charms me!" John Adams exclaimed, gloating over the near-surgical precision of the Mohawks. "The Town of Boston was never more Still and calm," he said; "all Things were conducted with great order, Decency, and perfect Submission to Government." The only private property that had been destroyed, other than the tea, was a single brass padlock, and that was carefully replaced. Considering the entire period "since the Controversy, with Britain, opened" in his first year at the bar, Adams concluded that now "the Dye is cast: The People have passed the River and cutt away the Bridge: . . . This is the grandest Event, which has ever yet happened."[19]

Once again John Adams's political judgment after the event was more acute than Hutchinson's judgment beforehand. Hutchinson, who believed fundamentally that, if left to themselves, the people of Massachusetts were sound, docile, and capable of following wise leaders as they had in the 1740s and 1750s, could never accept the idea that his enemies, Whig leaders like the Adamses, truly represented the people. He was convinced that they were merely demagogues who held power through deceitful machinations, and so he repeatedly returned to the hope that ultimately their extremist follies would expose them for what they were, once and for all separating them from the yeomanry of the province. In the aftermath of the Tea Party he briefly clung to this hope.

Samuel Adams knew otherwise. Letters arrived almost every day assuring Whigs "that our Friends in the Country approve of the Conduct"of the opposition. Adams was confident "we have put our Enemies in the wrong,"[20] and in the early months of 1774 the consolidation of provincewide support behind Whig leadership confirmed his judgment. For the moment, the Tea Act had been nullified, not only in Massachusetts, but in all the colonies. The next move was up to the British government.

In England news of the Tea Party had caused a furor. The attention of the political nation turned to the American colonies as never before. Parliament and the ministry had been insulted, and for those who believed in stern measures the moment had come to rally support. The ministry, led by Lord North, proposed that the port of Boston be closed to all trade as of June 1, 1774, if the town refused to make restitution to the East India Company and to pay the duty on the tea. Members of Parliament who argued that, according to this logic, the port of London should also be closed owing to recent political riots there, were derided by the majority who passed the bill in March. The Port Act, intended to punish Boston and teach the colonies submission, was quickly succeeded by a series of administrative reform bills, which would be known in America as the Coercive Acts. Their chief focus was Massachusetts.

These Coercive Acts were drawn up and passed in the heat of anger over the Tea Party, but their substance reflected long-standing complaints of colonial officials like Governor Hutchinson. He and others had frequently argued that Massachusetts suffered from too much popular participation in government—democracy—and that crown officials were hindered in doing their work because of public pressure. The Administration of Justice Act, sealed by King George on May 20, 1774, spoke directly to this point by providing for the transfer of royal officials charged with capital crimes to England for trial. Since customs officials had sometimes been intimidated with countersuits and criminal-trespass charges which were tried in local courts, the act strengthened officials considerably.

The Massachusetts Government Act, passed the same day, spoke to the larger question of the province's political structure. At a stroke it nullified the Charter of 1692 and strengthened royal power. It prescribed the royal appointment of the Governor's Council in place of its election by the lower house; it authorized the governor to appoint and remove all judges; it empowered the governor's appointees, the sheriffs, to appoint jurors instead of towns' selecting them; and it limited town meetings to a single annual one for the purpose of managing strictly local affairs, as authorized by the governor. In a single statute the ministry, following the lines of criticism it had long been hearing from its appointees in Massachusetts, attempted to terminate the system of responsive government by consent that the inhabitants had developed over generations. Deliberately, although unwittingly, the ministry was fulfilling the prophecies of the Braintree Instructions of 1765 and the more recently expressed fears of scores of towns and thousands of people all over Massachusetts.

Three days later the last of the Coercive Acts, the Quartering Act, became law. Feeding ancient horrors of quartering a standing army among civilians and recalling the Boston Massacre, the bill paved the way for stationing troops in any American colonial settlement. It empowered governors to open uninhabited buildings for the use of soldiers whenever they saw fit. Violating the sanctity of private property, it seemed to foreshadow military rule by the English over the colonists. In conjunction with the other acts that remade Massachusetts government along authoritarian lines, the Quartering Act gave notice to all the colonies that their own governments and liberties existed at the sufferance of Parliament. Although the ministry had hoped to isolate Massachusetts to suffer alone, the colonial response to the Coercive Acts was to see the case of the Bay Colony as their own at one remove and to call for a Continental Congress to plan concerted opposition.

For Massachusetts the test of public commitment to government by consent, according to ancestral ways, came during the summer of 1774. Boston town meeting would not reimburse the East India Company for the damages of the Mohawks, nor would the people of Boston yield to duress and pay the tea duty that they continued to oppose on principle. Consequently the blockade of Boston began in June, entirely cutting off its economic lifeblood, water-borne commerce. Within weeks, Boston was threatened by large-scale unemployment and the specter of impoverishment, and a wartime mentality began to emerge.

The province as a whole was outraged. Frontier communities along the Kennebec River in Maine and towns in the Berkshires one hundred miles west of Boston joined in an opposition that was far broader and deeper than ever before. Judging from public reactions, the Coercive Acts were tantamount to a declaration of war on Massachusetts, and in meeting after meeting called in disregard of the new law, townspeople considered what must now be done. For the most part they were led by the same selectmen and representatives who had earned their trust in years past, although in a few places, such as Worcester and Springfield where local officials were loyal to their friend and patron Governor Hutchinson, it was necessary to raise up new leaders. In nearly every town the determination to resist approached unanimity.

The hard question was how to resist. The lesson of past conflicts was that economic pressure through nonimportation, nonconsumption, or a total boycott of English goods was effective. However, the choice among these alternatives was not clearcut. If it was not made carefully, the decision, and its timing, could damage colonial merchants as well as people in particular trades and divide the colonial cause. When the Boston Committee of Correspondence pressed for an immediate boycott of all English goods, to be backed up by a secondary boycott against those who declined to join in the primary boycott, people in Massachusetts were unwilling to take up this initiative. Some of their neighbors and commercial associates would suffer, while local and provincial unity would be sacrificed. Surely, they believed, they could find more satisfactory ways of resisting if they took the time to consult each other.

As towns met to determine their course of action a solution emerged —county conventions. If delegates from all towns within a county deliberated together, they could be sure that decisions, whatever they were, would enjoy broad support and that no town would be isolated by its intemperate or idiosyncratic action. Between July and September 1774, the towns in eight of the nine Massachusetts counties and in two of the three Maine counties, excepting only Barnstable on Cape Cod (where Hutchinson's allies retained control) and Cumberland in Maine, held conventions to determine the next steps. As Hutchinson departed for England in June 1774 and turned over the royal government to his successor General Thomas Gage, an insurgent government was already beginning to appear. That summer it was the county conventions that functioned as a loose interim government until the autumn when a transformed General Court, calling itself a Provincial Congress, became the effective central government of Massachusetts.

During the summer the conventions agreed on the basic pattern of Massachusetts conduct. Asserting their general support for a boycott, they would take no immediate action with respect to trade. To be effective the boycott would have to be a joint, intercolonial effort, so the matter of designing it and establishing its effective date would be left to the Continental Congress, which was scheduled to meet in Philadelphia at the beginning of September. In the meantime it was necessary to assert fundamental political principles—that the people of Massachusetts enjoyed the same natural and constitutional rights as Englishmen, and that submission to the Coercive Acts would mean the surrender of those rights. From the outset, the conventions made it clear that they were not going to acquiesce in the destruction of their liberty, and they took immediate steps to nullify the Massachusetts Government Act. Appointees under the act were pressed to resign their positions, and meetings of the people—great crowds (Tories called them "mobs")—were called to prevent any courts from sitting under the new law. Quickly the county conventions made the Massachusetts Government Act a dead letter. They went on to recommend that town militia companies be activated and that military supplies be laid by, ready for immediate use. Massachusetts assumed a defensive posture.

All the while popular enthusiasm blossomed. The patriotic fervor was expressed in dozens of large public acts and thousands of private ones. Bostonians found to their great relief that their countrymen really believed the town was "suffering in the common cause," as donations of food, clothing, and cash flooded into Boston. From all over Massachusetts, and from colonies near and far, pork and mutton came in on the hoof, as did bushels of flour and barrels of wheat. Merchants in Salem, setting past rivalries aside, volunteered the use of their facilities to blockaded Boston merchants. Bostonians could only be elated when contributions from persons and places unknown—like £50 from the Fairfax County, Virginia, planter George Washington—came in. For Massachusetts a year of almost ecstatic patriotism and self-sacrifice, which were both self-righteous and intolerant of contradiction, had begun.

The ardor was so explosive that on September 1, 1774, a rumor, the Powder Alarm, nearly touched off a war. That night British troops, who had occupied Boston as part of the blockade, marched to Mystic and destroyed the gunpowder that had already been collected there. Rapidly, the false rumor spread through the countryside that Boston was being attacked, that cannonballs from British ships were destroying the town, and that the streets ran with the blood of the inhabitants. Immediately militiamen armed themselves and began marching to the relief of Boston. By morning some three thousand men had collected on Cambridge common, and ten thousand more were within twenty miles, converging on the capital. As far west as the Connecticut Valley the Minutemen had been alarmed, and reports came in of forty or fifty thousand surrounding Boston by nightfall. A few days later Samuel and John Adams, who had joined the Continental Congress at Philadelphia, learned that "the people from Hampshire County crowded the county of Worcester with armed men; and both counties received the accounts of the quiet dispersion of the people of Middlesex with apparent regret, grudging them the glory of having done something important for their country."[21] Psychologically, Massachusetts was ready to fight, and its people were perhaps even ready for independence.

Yet no one wanted Massachusetts to stand and fight alone. Even the most eager and impulsive patriots recognized the need for intercolonial cooperation in order for resistance to succeed. The Continental Congress rather than unilateral action represented their best hope. So Massachusetts rejoiced when Congress, barely two weeks after the Powder Alarm, publicly endorsed the resolutions of the Suffolk County Convention, denying the authority of the Coercive Acts, calling for a stoppage of trade with Britain, and directing the people to prepare for war. For John Adams, "this was one of the happiest Days of my Life. . . . This Day convinced me that America will support the Massachusetts or perish with her."[22] For the present, the task of patriots was to remain peaceful while readying their defenses.

Through the autumn and winter of 1774–75 Massachusetts stood firm. After the Continental Congress voted a trade boycott in October and resolved to meet again the following May, people could be confident that other colonials would join them in defense of "the common cause." In the blockaded town of Boston there was a war of nerves that repeatedly threatened to ignite a conflagration. If Boston could not trade, then neighboring towns decided they would not supply General Gage's troops with provisions, lumber, or skilled workers. Finally, with his men facing a winter in tents on the Boston Common, Gage imported workers and materials from Nova Scotia and New York to construct barracks. Meanwhile many patriots departed the occupied capital, taking their families to reside in outlying towns among family and friends.

On the surface Massachusetts remained quiet during this winter of waiting. But public attitudes that had become polarized during 1774, rather than moderating, became more and more fixed. One tiny incident, related by a Boston merchant, reveals that even schoolboys were politically conscious. When General Haldimand's servant destroyed their sledding path by strewing ashes on it, "the lads made a muster, and chose a committee to wait upon the General, who admitted them, and heard their complaint . . . that their fathers before 'em had improved it as a coast for time immemorial." Haldimand redressed their grievance by ordering their path repaired. When General Gage learned of it, he reflected that "'twas impossible to beat the notion of Liberty out of the people, as it was rooted in *'em from their Childhood.*"[23]

Gage's comment revealed his own ambivalence about his mission in Massachusetts. Deep down, he did not really believe that coercion would bring about the loyal submission Britain craved. But his duty to reassert imperial authority, at gunpoint if need be, was clear. Faced with this dilemma, he stalled, hoping that the ministry would send him the thousands of additional troops he believed necessary to make an effective show of force. But British officials were skeptical. Gage was the governor, after all, and he already possessed a force of four thousand regulars. Surely, they reasoned, he should be able to overawe the troublemakers and restore the supremacy of the multitudes who, they supposed, were loyal to Britain. Gage, who had a long record of experience in the colonies and whose wife was American, had witnessed the Powder Alarm, and he knew better. He delayed. If he did not receive reinforcements, there was always the chance that a political solution might be found. War, he recognized, could be had any time.

And time would not stand still. His own officers were restless, and in mid-April 1775 the ministry informed him that he would have no more troops and that he must act. Accordingly, as governor and general, Gage set into motion a secret plan to seize the Provincial Congress's military supplies stored twenty miles west of Boston at Concord. Because Concord was four times farther away than Mystic, the operation would be difficult. But Gage had good intelligence about the objective and the route to it, and so he believed the job might be quickly done with a minimum of disturbance to the inhabitants. He wished to avoid touching off another Powder Alarm.

The commander of the expedition, Lt. Col. Francis Smith, did not learn the objective of his sortie until he opened his sealed orders on the night of April 18. But patriots had already guessed where the troops who had been bustling around Boston were headed. Concord was an obvious target; the only question was whether the troops would take the longer land route through Roxbury and Brookline, or save a few miles by crossing the mouth of the Charles River to Charlestown and proceed from there. When Paul Revere, the Whigs' courier, learned that the troops were assembling around the rowboats on the banks of the Charles, he sent the sexton of the Old North Church up the church tower with two lanterns to signal the Provincial Congress's executive body, the Committee of Safety, which was waiting in Charlestown. Immediately the committee sent a rider to warn Concord. A little while later Revere and William Dawes set out. Even though there were British scouting parties out patrolling the roads to intercept messengers, several riders would succeed in raising the alarm all the way to Concord and beyond. This time it was no rumor of destruction. The British were marching against the stores of the Provincial Congress and might even be aiming to seize its leaders, Samuel Adams and John Hancock, and its treasury.

Meanwhile the British raiding party got off to a late start and then delayed its march from Charlestown. Though the raiders passed through Menotomy (Arlington) in the dark, it was already light by the time they reached Lexington, six miles east of Concord. Here they met a militia company of nearly seventy men—fathers and sons, uncles and nephews, cousins, in-laws—standing assembled on the common to "observe" the British. When the redcoats drew within musket range, the British command was not to fire, but to surround and disarm the militia. Simultaneously Captain John Parker ordered his militiamen to disperse. As they turned and scattered, overanxious redcoats pulled their triggers, and a brief, pointless massacre ensued. Eight militiamen were killed, more were wounded; only a handful returned the British fire. But in those chaotic moments the war began. The British would skirmish again around the North Bridge at Concord and later, after destroying a small quantity of supplies, head back to Boston. But that afternoon as they retraced their steps, the blood they had so impulsively shed that morning would haunt them. The corpses in Lexington were real, not imagined, and among militiamen the urge for revenge and vindication overflowed. As the redcoats marched east, the woods and pastures, the fieldstone walls, the barns and sheds and villages were no longer peaceful. Snipers were everywhere. Through the shrewd intervention of a relief column, the troops finally made it back to Boston, but for each militiamen hit by the infantry at Lexington, twenty-five redcoats would bleed. By nightfall on April 19, nearly three hundred of the king's soldiers and almost one hundred colonists lay dead or wounded. Massachusetts was at war with Great Britain.

The long months of waiting were over. Within a few days tens of thousands of militiamen from Massachusetts and the neighboring colonies poured into the Boston area, surrounding the capital so thoroughly that General Gage and his troops were helpless to act. Within three weeks the Continental Congress reconvened at Philadelphia, and by mid-June it was organizing a Continental army to defend Massachusetts and the other colonies. On June 15 John Adams, to the chagrin of his Braintree boyhood friend John Hancock, nominated George Washington as commanding general. A Massachusetts–Virginia alliance had been forged in Congress that would form the cornerstone of the national union.

Before Washington had time to set out to organize the army, there was more news from Boston. On June 17 General Gage, now reinforced by Generals Howe, Clinton, and Burgoyne and one thousand troops, decided to attack the colonial emplacement that had been set up on Breed's Hill, just to the south of Bunker Hill in Charlestown, overlooking Boston. General Howe directed the frontal assault by the redcoats up the hill. Twice they fell back under the murderous fire of the outnumbered but well-fortified defenders. On the third attempt Howe's troops succeeded, though only because the provincial militiamen had run out of powder. As the Yankees retreated, they left behind over one thousand injured British, which represented more than twice their own casualties. Howe had gained his objective, the high ground at Breed's and Bunker hills, but at a dreadful cost. More British officers died that day than in the remainder of the war. Gage's reinforcements were entirely spent, and British military morale plummeted. Even before Washington's arrival, the New England militia had shown that it could meet Britain's best in a pitched battle. The ardor of April 19 was confirmed by the battle of Bunker Hill.

Now a new period of waiting began in Massachusetts as imperial politics gradually caught up with events. The practical demands of creating a durable army, trained and equipped, still remained to be filled; meanwhile Congress attempted a final round of petition and negotiation with the king. In Pennsylvania and New York especially, influential men were eager for a reconciliation with Britain and fearful of the conflict and the chaos that independence might generate. Until these major colonies became reconciled to independence, political strategy dictated a pause, although by this time people in Massachusetts were generally ready, even eager, to cut loose from Britain.

As Boston entered its second winter of British occupation, it became a Loyalist refuge. In the countryside outspoken friends of Britain were treated with suspicion and hostility. They feared for their lives, even though relatively few were molested. What frightened them particularly was the recognition that power was now entirely in popular hands. As friends and kinsmen of Governor Hutchinson's circle and as admirers of English standards of society and government, they had always put their trust in elite, hierarchical rule. Consequently the county conventions and the expansion of popular rule manifested in town meetings and Whig committees of correspondence, safety, and inspection, that investigated and punished suspected Tories, often led them to panic. Anarchy and mob rule seemed to flourish. Fearing the worst, they fled to the safety of British troops.

These fears, while exaggerated, were certainly not groundless. Loyalists were being purged from all positions of trust and became easy targets of private and public animosity. Some were publicly humiliated, occasionally with pine tar and feathers, and their property was often vandalized. Popular authorities did not go out of their way to protect Tory rights, and in some localities local officials actually led the charge against them. Britain and its sympathizers had become "the enemy" as Massachusetts mobilized for full-scale war.

The occupation of Boston, and Massachusetts, ended finally in March 1776. Cooped up in a garrison town, surrounded by far more numerous American troops, the army had been immobilized since the Bunker Hill battle. Still the British refused to leave, until Washington's troops, supplied with cannon captured ten months earlier at Fort Ticonderoga, threatened Boston by mounting the artillery on Dorchester Heights. Once again the British were forced to act. General Howe prepared to attack the Heights, but bad weather intervened, and Howe, thinking back on the losses he had sustained assaulting Breed's Hill, changed his mind. To preserve his army he would leave Boston for the friendly port of Halifax. Within two weeks Boston was "liberated," and what remained was a disheveled town where looting and vandalism by the troops and an outbreak of smallpox cast a pall that even the jubilation of Continental soldiers could not dispel. Except for some coastal marauding a few years later, no more front-line warfare occurred in Massachusetts.

In July the Congress caught up with Massachusetts and declared independence. The news of it "diffused a general Joy" in the province. Massachusetts's opposition to British measures now achieved sublime vindication. One patriot, a descendant of a Pilgrim who had sailed into Plymouth harbor with Bradford that snowy night in 1620, proclaimed that "every one of us feels more important than ever; we now congratulate each other as Free men."[24] Independence was heady news.

Thomas Hutchinson, who learned of the declaration a month later, read it with a sense of exasperation and personal bitterness. The calumnies and distortions he had tried to eradicate now reigned triumphant in America. Defeated and angry, he composed a polemical reply to the Declaration of Independence that he humbly laid at His "Majesty's feet."[25] Writing from his own sense of Massachusetts, he denied that Americans ever "were a distinct people from the kingdom." Politically, he maintained, the relationship of the colonists to England was "just the same before the first Colonists emigrated as it has been ever since." Bradford, Winthrop, and all their successors had always been subject to "the Supreme Legislative Authority," Parliament.[26] The problem, he reiterated, was that bands of unprincipled, demagogic agitators had conspired to poison the minds of the people against England in order to achieve separation. In Hutchinson's mind the reality of a loyal, monarchy-loving English population overseas had been transformed into a nightmare of democracy, anarchy, and treason. He would never grasp the fact that the Massachusetts of his youth, for all its provincial imitation of England, had always possessed a profound attachment to individual autonomy and toward authority that was grounded on consent.

John Adams, the provincial lawyer of yeoman stock, knew better. Yet Adams also knew that independence was only a beginning. At the moment of jubilation in Philadelphia after Congress had voted the Declaration of Independence, he invoked the central concerns of the Massachusetts Yankee culture, even as he celebrated: "It may be the Will of Heaven that America shall suffer Calamities. . . . If this is to be the Case, it will have this good Effect, at least: it will inspire Us with many Virtues, which We have not, and correct many Errors, Follies and Vices, which threaten to disturb, dishonour, and destroy Us." Hutchinson saw Massachusetts as having been overrun with viciousness. Adams saw vice and virtue locked in a struggle and immediately raised his voice for reform:

the new Governments . . . will require a Purification from our Vices, and an Augmentation of our Virtues or they will be no

Blessings. The People will have unbounded Power. And the People are extremely addicted to Corruption and Venality, as well as the Great. . . . I must submit all my Hopes and Fears, to an overruling Providence, . . . unfashionable as the Faith may be.[27]

Now that the British were gone and independence belonged to American citizens, exhortations to moral reform would ring throughout the new state. The time had come to try to create a government true to the Revolution and to the past, one that liberated individuals and simultaneously upheld communal ideals.

# CHAPTER 5

❦

# A Republic of Virtue or Liberty?

I N MASSACHUSETTS ON A SUMMER'S DAY IN 1776 IT WAS
easy to support independence. One's own life, liberty, and property
were immediately at stake. Nearly everyone agreed that ancestral birth-
rights, bequeathed by heroic Puritan forefathers, must be transmitted
intact to the next generation and to all posterity. Defense against British
oppression provided people with an appealing basis for consensus. But
creating a new government and a new society was a far more complicated and controversial undertaking than asserting independence.
Though people were eager to denounce British tyranny, many still clung
to British conceptions of political and social order. Others, more rooted
in Yankee ways, hoped to create an austere *American* republic in which
simple manners and individual political liberty were preeminent. All
agreed that the state of Massachusetts must be a republic, but whether
it should be ruled by the best people for the interests of all or governed
by ordinary men responsive to popular wishes remained a central issue
for two generations. Rhetorically, the contest between the few and the
many became a debate between virtue and liberty, the two most broadly
appealing ideals in Massachusetts public life.

These were recurrent themes from the late 1770s, when Berkshire
constitutionalists pressed for more responsive government, through the
1780s, when Shays's Rebellion erupted in Hampshire County (which
then included Hampden and Franklin counties as well), and on into
early decades of the nineteenth century, when the conflict became routinized and finally diluted in the electoral contests of Federalists and
Jeffersonian Democratic-Republicans. Moreover the operations of the

independent Commonwealth of Massachusetts awakened regional and religious conflicts that the royal government had effectively contained. Its new majoritarian political structure encouraged—even required—debate. Its tradition of an active, widely patronized press and its heritage of voluminous, articulate public debate made Massachusetts a key American forum for the issues of the day.

When the war began in Massachusetts, economic activity had already been gravely disturbed by the blockade of Boston and the patriotic boycott of English trade prescribed by the Continental Congress. During the summer of 1775 militia service and enlistments in the Continental army added to the burden as thousands of able-bodied men worked with rifles instead of plows, hoes, and harvest tools. Although the year following the battles at Lexington and Concord was the peak year of military activity for Massachusetts people, the financial drain continued throughout the war, ruining thousands of families and driving thousands more into serious debt. For farmers and tradesmen who had always lived frugally, close to the margin, the combination of high taxes and time lost for military service produced extensive hardships. In thousands of homes where fathers and sons were killed or disabled, the stress of war was even more intense. In April 1775 doing battle with redcoats was a glorious adventure, but as the years dragged on, the war became a malignant, demoralizing force. The social and economic side effects of a long war were profound on an agricultural and commercial society that lacked the insulation of great surpluses.

One crucial source of discontent was the fact that the war conspicuously enriched some people while it was impoverishing others. Armies, after all, have to be supplied, and the heavy taxes raised out of the pockets of all found their way finally to the pockets of those who were advantageously involved in supplying the troops. The most numerous beneficiaries of wartime economic conditions were prosperous market farmers who were scattered all over Massachusetts, though concentrated in the east and the Connecticut Valley. Crop prices rose more rapidly than production costs, so farms large enough to produce substantial surpluses yielded unusual profits. From 1777 onward there were repeated public complaints about exorbitant farm prices and the readiness of farmers to withhold their crops from market until they could get the best price. The majority of farmers lacked sufficient land and labor to benefit from the high prices, since other costs were also rising. But the number who did prosper was significant, and in the 1780s enlarged and sometimes newly constructed Georgian houses would become durable monuments to the selective agricultural prosperity generated by the war.

Even more conspicuous were the mercantile fortunes that the war created. Opportunities abounded for merchants whose connections in the countryside enabled them to become conduits in the supply network, as well as for those who were associated with the patriot leaders. Moreover the departure of Tory merchants from Boston and the North Shore ports created a vacuum that their competitors rushed to fill. In addition, from 1776 onward New York trade was interrupted by British occupation, so Massachusetts merchants enjoyed renewed profits from transatlantic and coastal commerce. When the French arrived in 1778, they brought with them naval supply contracts that made a handful of merchants rich. Thereafter privateering became a spectacular, if hazardous, source of wealth. The Cabots and Lees of Beverly, the Derbys of Salem, and the Bostonians John Codman, Stephen Higginson, and Thomas Russell were among more than a score of merchants whose fortunes were founded on capturing British merchant vessels.

Because their assets were always in motion, these fortunate merchants were far less damaged by taxation and inflation than were farmers and tradesmen. Watching the changes, Robert Treat Paine, a delegate to the Continental Congress, observed that "the course of the war has thrown property into channels, where before, it never was, and has increased little streams to overflowing rivers: and what is worse, in some respects by a method that has drained the sources of some as much as it has replenished others."[1] Because the arbitrary economic consequences of the war impoverished some, strained many, and enriched a few, the divisiveness of wartime political questions was intensified. Policies respecting taxation, currency, and price controls were bound to have unequal effects. In a time of heightened anxieties, when people worried not only about their immediate economic well-being but also about the survival of the United States and the establishment of an equitable republican government, Massachusetts's political structure and the men who controlled it faced their severest challenge.

Contrary to the expectations of Thomas Hutchinson and other Loyalists, Massachusetts did not collapse into anarchy when it became an independent state. One major test came in the summer of 1776 when the Provincial Congress successfully reopened the courts that had been closed for two years since the enactment of the coercive Administration of Justice Act. The authorities acted gingerly, recognizing that debtors and their kinsmen might be happier to see the courts remain closed.

A second major test of Massachusetts's political equilibrium came when the General Court sought permission from the electorate to draft a new constitution, since the legitimacy of all government was doubtful now that the Massachusetts charter was void. During the autumn of 1776 people all over the state weighed the issue, and a majority finally rejected the proposal. While the reasons varied, the consensus was that the General Court contained so many inexperienced members and was so burdened with day-to-day affairs that it should not be entrusted with the awesome responsibility of drawing a constitution. In any case, many people believed a constitution would require popular ratification, not merely legislative enactment. The decision to delay the creation of a constitution did not unleash an orgy of disorder, nor did it incapacitate the provisional government.

The presence or absence of anarchy was contingent on local government during the war as it had been during the colonial era. In the towns, the cooperation of citizens was based on tradition, shared ideas about the rules of politics, and personal trust. The fact that town meetings, like the state government, could not control prices did not produce alienation. Towns were highly responsive if not always effective, and local administration was normally flexible. People who really needed tax abatements generally got them. Families whose survival was threatened because husbands or sons were off in the army received town aid. Draft quotas were filled by paying bonuses to volunteers, which were financed by taxing those who had cash to create bounties that attracted landless young men. Except for the raising of troops and supplies, state government was remote. Every town seemed to have its own constitution, written in the minds of its inhabitants and preserved in the multitude of precedents contained in the town records. Maintaining order was the routine achievement of the people in nearly three hundred communities around the state.

Yet the statewide issues of taxes, inflation, and the administration of justice were lively and divisive. The interests of merchants and prosperous market farmers, who were chiefly located in the eastern counties, were not the same as those of the semisubsistence farmers who were most numerous and influential in Worcester, Berkshire, and upland Hampshire towns. As time went on, the framing of a state constitution became entwined with these economic inequities since their resolution was contingent on the makeup of the General Court. Ultimately the most controversial question for constitution writers would be who would be represented. More than any other, this issue generated highly self-interested maneuvering for competitive advantage.

One consequence was delay. In most states, constitutions were rapidly drafted and approved during the first years of the war. But in Massachusetts the call for a constitution was rejected in 1776 and even when the House of Representatives did draw up and approve a constitution in early 1778, the voters turned it down. The explicit reasons for opposing the 1778 constitution varied widely. The weakness of the governor and the failure to create a strong, independent upper house were criticized in eastern Massachusetts. In the west the fact that property qualifications for senators and the governor were proposed was as objectionable as the fact that poor men would be disfranchised from voting for these offices. Moreover, the compromise on representation that had been negotiated aroused widespread criticism. Eastern towns complained that by allowing a representative for every town, regardless of population, sparsely settled communities would enjoy undue influence and the whole legislature would be so large as to be unwieldy. Western communities, for whom the cost of sending a representative had often seemed prohibitive, complained at the provision that each town must be responsible for the travel and per diem costs of its delegates. Divisions of interest, partly economic and partly regional, were so acutely felt that it is unlikely that any constitution would have achieved broad support in 1778.

Independence from Britain had not dissolved the social bonds of civil order in Massachusetts towns, but it had destroyed the network of royal patronage that had furnished a major source of intercounty political integration for provincial government. Until the 1780s, when a new gubernatorial patronage network slowly emerged, there were few concrete, particular loyalties that bound the leaders of all the counties together. Instead, certain legislative issues, a few family linkages, and a generalized patriotism for Massachusetts and the United States furnished the means of cohesion. Single-minded patriotic ardor quickly receded after independence, but it remained a potent source of corporate unity, within communities and in the state at large.

Consequently, even though there was considerable dissatisfaction with the provisional government and widespread war-weariness, Massachusetts was not restive. By 1779 there was so much self-confidence in the American cause that Loyalists who had fled in 1774 and 1775 were beginning to drift back to their homes. Although they were widely excluded from public office, only the most prominent remained targets of acute hostility. Most of the Loyalists were able to retain their property and regain a measure of acceptance. Confiscation laws only affected major crown appointees and others who had left behind substantial debts. In the latter case property was seized and sold—not for vengeance but to satisfy creditors. Old standards of equity in government endured.

It was in the spring of 1779 that the townspeople voted to hold a special convention to draft a constitution. It would be more expensive than having the legislature do it, but many believed it would also be more productive. In September the convention opened at Boston. Its members, drawn from almost every part of the state, included the major Revolutionary leaders. John and Samuel Adams and John Hancock, as well as rising figures such as Benjamin Lincoln, Caleb Strong, and James Sullivan, played active roles in the convention. Ultimately it was John Adams, the key political and legal theorist among the old patriot group, who drafted the new constitution. Drawing on the most enlightened political science of the day and on Whig ideals, Adams designed a modern governing structure that enshrined the traditional ideals of the Bay Colony.

A firm believer in the guiding powers of correct rhetoric, Adams opened the constitution with a preamble recalling that of the Declaration of Independence, which he had worked on three years earlier. The purpose of government was "to secure the existence of the body-politic; and to furnish the individuals who compose it, with . . . their natural rights and the blessings of life." Explaining precisely what was meant, Adams defined the body politic in terms reminiscent of the Mayflower Compact and Puritan political thought. "Formed by a voluntary association of individuals," he said, the body politic was "a social compact, by which the whole people covenants with each citizen, and each citizen with the whole people, that all shall be governed by certain laws for the common good."[2] In theory, corporate and individual good merged, although it was clear that common interests superseded those of individuals.

The first section of the constitution consisted of a declaration of rights in which the basic elements of free republican government were spelled out. Procedural rights protecting citizens from government oppression were enumerated, together with Whig safeguards including a free press, free assembly, and the right of the people "to keep and bear arms for the common defence."[3] In several instances particular British offenses of recent years, such as the Quartering Act, were forevermore prohibited. Corporate, communal power would be supreme, but not absolute. Individuals were the source of government, and their rights would be guaranteed.

At the same time the people, through their government, were empowered to create a religious establishment "for the support and maintenance of public protestant teachers of piety," and to direct inhabitants to attend services, provided they could "conscienciously [sic] and conveniently" do so.[4] Taxes raised for religious support would be paid to whichever local denomination each taxpayer preferred, provided he attended a local church; otherwise the sums raised would go to the majority church in the town. Protestant religion was so generally regarded as a public good that individual rights of conscience were recognized only within the framework of regular church attendance. For Baptists, Methodists, and Quakers, whose numbers had grown since the Great Awakening, the multiple religious options that were established by this constitution represented a long step toward disestablishment and full religious liberty in a state where Winthrop's commonwealth was still widely revered, and where the Congregational clergy and the Congregational-led, Harvard College, enjoyed public financial support.

The main body of Adams's draft was the Frame of Government, laying out the powers of the legislature, the executive, and the judiciary, and the boundaries between the branches.[5] The form of government, which anticipated the federal Constitution of 1787, had to compromise on the most divisive political issues, especially the matter of representation. Here the solution was to give something to nearly everyone. The upper house of the legislature, the Senate, would be chosen annually, as were all elective officers, and apportioned according to equal tax districts. The rich and populous counties of Suffolk and Essex would each have six senators, while others would have from one to five senators. Nantucket and Martha's Vineyard would share a senator. Senators themselves must own land of at least £300 value or personal property and real estate worth a minimum of £600. Their electors, too, must meet a property test. The Senate was explicitly meant to represent the principle that one's stake in government was partially proportional to wealth.

The lower house carried the same relatively low property test for electors, but its actual composition was clearly intended to represent all regions and the common mass of people. Every incorporated town would have one delegate, regardless of its size, although future towns would have to possess at least 150 taxable men (about 700 people) to be represented. Larger towns could have more delegates according to a formula that, while discriminating against the people of large towns, still provided Boston with six representatives. One key complaint of small towns distant from Boston, that the expense of representation hit them unfairly because of transportation costs, was met by the stipulation that in each session one round-trip journey for every delegate to the legislature would be paid out of the state treasury. Although in its property tests for voters as well as delegates the House of Representatives retained some of the elitism of the colonial past, this lower house was designed to be broadly based and close to the people.

In contrast, John Adams and the convention chose to elevate the governor's office. Unique among all officials, the governor was given the title "His Excellency." He must also be a rich man, owning a Massachusetts freehold worth at least £1,000, and he must "declare himself to be of the christian religion."[6] His powers, largely modeled on those of his colonial predecessors, included calling and dismissing the legislature, commanding the state's military forces, and vetoing legislation. Notwithstanding their unfortunate experiences with Governors Bernard and Hutchinson, the Revolutionaries in Massachusetts, unlike those in most states, did not create a weak governor. Experience since 1775, as well as John Adams's application of political theory, demonstrated the necessity for a vigorous executive. Since each term of office was limited to a year, the possibilities of executive abuse appeared to be curtailed.

The constitution of 1780, which was as deliberately and rationally devised as political circumstances would permit, was conceived within a vigorous tradition of representative government. Moreover the corporate values of the Massachusetts Bay Colony were adapted to the new era. The presumption of a close link between high social status and public office endured in the governor and the Senate. The public commitment to a society of sober morals was underwritten by retaining a modified Congregational religious establishment. Revolutionary republicanism, as it was understood in Massachusetts, was consistent with the Puritan heritage.

Public support for education, a major feature of the General Court's program under Winthrop in the 1630s, was recognized as critical for the new commonwealth and written into its constitution. Where the objectives had once been public piety and clerical training, the new constitution asserted that "the encouragement of arts and sciences, and all good literature, tends to the honour of God, the advantage of the christian religion, and the great benefit of this and the other United States of America."[7] Harvard College and the public schools must be maintained. There was no need for, and little sense of, a break with tradition. Yet underlying these formal, institutional continuities with the past, a new vision was evident. The secular utopianism of the Revolution was explicit in the injunction that

> it shall be the duty of legislatures and magistrates, in all future periods . . . , to cherish the interests of literature and the sciences, and all seminaries of them; . . . to encourage private societies and public institutions, rewards and immunities, for the promotion of agriculture, arts, sciences, commerce, trades, manufactures, and a natural history of the country.[8]

The constitution pointed toward a Massachusetts that would be increasingly enlightened, advanced, and productive.

In March 1780 the convention completed work on the constitution and sent it out to the towns, urging them to ratify it. In an address to their constituents the delegates admitted that this was not "a perfect System of Government: This is not the Lot of Mankind." Yet they urged that the proposal be viewed carefully and sympathetically since, they asserted, it was the product of conscientious deliberation and repeated compromise. Recognizing that some provisions might be controversial, they explained the reasoning behind the new Protestant religious establishment, the property requirements for suffrage, and the system of legislative apportionment. The tone of the entire address from "Your Delegates" to their "Friends and Countrymen" was mild and ingratiating.[9] Nearly all those who had spent months laboring over the document were eager to see it accepted. Their commitment to the constitution of 1780 was chiefly responsible for its ultimate success.

Townspeople did not blindly defer to their leaders and shower their handiwork with accolades. In town after town a querulous individualism marked the evaluation of the document. As the convention had anticipated, the complaints clustered around the religious establishment, voting qualifications, and apportionment. Why not complete liberty of conscience? some asked, while others fretted over the fact that the Congregational monopoly was broken. In the poorer towns of Worcester County and farther west, there were many who found outrageous the disfranchisement of citizens, including Revolutionary soldiers, because of their poverty. In populous eastern towns some complained that they were underrepresented in an overlarge assembly because of the inclusion of delegates from every single town. But there were also more idiosyncratic criticisms against the creation of certain offices like that of lieutenant governor and Governor's Council, against the wording of particular oaths, against the distribution of specific powers among officials. Collectively the towns' review of the constitution illustrated not only the penetration of Revolutionary ideology among the people, but also the individualistic, uneven ways they combined it with older ideas and local political expectations. The ratification process revealed the absence of a coherent, integrated outlook toward state government. Individualism had not degenerated into the chaos of every man for himself, but there were hints of the spirit of every town and every interest group for itself. At the state level, independence had destroyed an effective traditional system of political integration —the patronage and deference once commanded by the provincial government of colonial days.

While the ratification of the constitution revealed the absence of statewide political integration, it successfully marked the beginning of a new era. For the convention evaluated the returns on the constitution of 1780 as approval, however narrow, and they moved to establish the new government without further delay. An election was quickly called, and in October 1780 John Hancock, the overwhelmingly popular choice, was inaugurated as the first governor of the Commonwealth of

Massachusetts. Out of all the turmoil of resistance to Britain it was he, not one of the Adamses, who emerged as the central figure in Massachusetts public life during the crucial decade of the 1780s.

John Hancock had been born in the North Precinct of Braintree in 1737, just two years after his father, the Reverend John Hancock Jr., had baptized Deacon Adams's son John. But unlike his schoolmate John Adams, young Hancock was plucked out of Braintree and brought to Boston soon after his father died when he was adopted by his wealthy uncle Thomas. By this time Thomas Hancock, the second son of "Pope" Hancock, the Lexington pastor, had made a fortune in trade and, childless, was eager to make John his apprentice and heir. Later on the now wealthy youth would be educated at Harvard as his forebears had been.

When he was graduated at the age of seventeen, he immediately went to work for his uncle. After nine years he became a partner, and at Thomas Hancock's death in 1764 he became the sole proprietor of the business. Within the next several years Samuel Adams would draw him into Boston and provincial politics. By late 1774 when he was elected president of the Provincial Congress and chairman of its Committee of Safety, Hancock had become the most prominent Whig in Massachusetts. His national stature was similarly elevated; indeed it was as president of the Continental Congress that Hancock seized the opportunity to display his bold signature on the Declaration of Independence. But in spite of long service in Congress, Hancock never achieved the national role he coveted as commander of the Continental army. Still, he was pleased to return to Massachusetts as His Excellency, the governor of the commonwealth.

At home Hancock had created a broad following among people from all regions and walks of life. From the 1760s onward he had displayed his wealth in a generous, public-spirited way, providing employment and a variety of charitable donations including the gift of Bibles to struggling congregations. As a member of the inner circle of Massachusetts Whigs, he kept his purse always open to the patriot cause. During the war Hancock made himself conspicuous among Boston merchants by donating firewood to the poor and willingly accepting Massachusetts and Continental notes in payment for debts. Hancock was unique among his peers in that he actively cultivated popularity as a means of enhancing his political stature. By breaking the political code of republican gentlemen and courting the people, he became the target of the gentry's private scorn. But Hancock's use of his wealth, together with his sensitivity to tides of opinion, ultimately elevated his career in Massachusetts beyond that of his early mentor Samuel Adams and his rivals John Adams, James Bowdoin, and James Warren. Hancock was the all but unanimous popular choice for governor in 1780. Thereafter he was reelected with 70 to 90 percent majorities whenever he ran, until his death in 1793.

As his colonial predecessor Thomas Hutchinson had done, John Hancock managed personally to exercise an integrating influence on state politics. He was better known personally throughout the state than any other leader; his private and public patronage, together with his reputation as a sterling patriot—one who had been singled out for punishment by the British in 1775—enabled him to blunt the edges of regional and interest-group conflict during the early 1780s. Yet Hancock, for all his patriotic glitter and political maneuvering, did not lead in solving the problems of taxation and finance, and in time these came to a head. Hancock's response was to retire from office in 1785, claiming reasons of health. His successor was his erstwhile electoral challenger James Bowdoin, now allied with Samuel Adams and James Warren.

Bowdoin, in contrast to Hancock, wanted to resolve Massachusetts's financial crisis, whatever the cost in popularity. His approach, which appealed to creditors and mercantile interests broadly, was to raise taxes to pay off the war debt over a fifteen-year period. For farmers who were already having trouble meeting their taxes because of the slump in farm prices, the prospect of additional direct taxation was alarming. Since Bowdoin was also deaf to cries for the relief of debtors, tension mounted until 1786, when a rebellion broke out in Hampshire County.

Hampshire and Berkshire had never been thoroughly integrated into provincial or state politics due largely to geography. Patterns of trade and settlement in the west ran north and south along the river valleys, connecting the area almost as closely to Connecticut as to Massachusetts. During the colonial era government patronage had tied county notables to the royal government; within the western towns people had typically deferred to the leadership of this regional elite. But the Revolution disrupted both of these sources of cohesion, so social and economic tensions came to focus on the shortcomings of state fiscal policy, a policy that more nearly met the needs of eastern merchants and tradesmen than of semi-subsistence farmers.

Indeed, the Bowdoin administration's policies combined with the depressed economy to make thousands of farmers all over the state—in Worcester County and even in the eastern counties of Middlesex and Bristol—restive. But in central and eastern Massachusetts the breadth and depth of alienation were less acute, and allegiance to the state government was stronger. When Daniel Shays, Luke Day, and a handful of other Revolutionary veterans organized armed resistance to the courts of Massachusetts, they would have sympathizers throughout the commonwealth, but not supporters.

The insurgents of 1786, like those of 1774, began with a county convention to formulate common grievances and call for their redress. Meeting in late August at Hatfield in the central part of Hampshire County, delegates from fifty of the fifty-seven towns met to identify the "many grievances and unnecessary burdens now lying upon the people" that were sources of "great uneasiness" and "discontent."[10] When they finished, they had specified no less than seventeen complaints. Several aimed at the constitution of 1780. The Senate and the Courts of Common Pleas and General Sessions, which had thwarted debtor relief, should be abolished. The system of representation was no good, and all officers of the government, they argued, should be annually elected and made dependent on the House of Representatives, instead of a fee system, for their support. These were the constitutional issues.

Most of the grievances, however, were wholly questions of policy. The table of fees for using the courts was unfair. The system of taxation and appropriation was no good because it operated "unequally between the polls and estates, and between landed and mercantile interests."[11] The refusal to issue paper money and other fiscal matters were distressing. Government policy was wrongheaded and, these farm representatives believed, discriminatory. Why, after all, must the General Court meet in Boston instead of a site farther west? A populist tone ran through all the Hampshire complaints. The people were fed up with officials and especially lawyers.

The delegates from Hampshire wanted to have a special legislative session to deal with their grievances and to have the wheels set in motion for constitutional revision. In the meantime, just as conventions had done a decade before, they called on the people to "abstain from all mobs and unlawful assemblies."[12] But having delivered a frontal assault on the legitimacy of the Massachusetts Senate and the courts, the convention had not encouraged a mood of restraint. Within a week a crowd of over a thousand armed men seized the courthouse at Northampton and so, for the time being, abolished the objectionable Courts Common Pleas and of General Sessions.

Governor Bowdoin proclaimed these actions treason, but official threats did not curb popular discontent. In early September a crowd of several hundred men occupied the courthouse in Worcester and blocked proceedings there. When it began to appear that farmers in Middlesex and Bristol in the east as well as those of Hampshire, Berkshire, and Worcester might resort to arms to close the courts, Governor Bowdoin began to take military action to assure the maintenance of the state government. To protect the Supreme Judicial Court, which was scheduled to meet at Springfield in late September, Bowdoin ordered six hundred loyal Massachusetts militia troops to occupy the courthouse there. When more than a thousand insurgents arrived, led by Daniel Shays, it proved impossible to transact business, and though Shays may have been chagrined that government troops occupied the courthouse first, there was no question but that his show of force had intimidated the supreme court into retreat. The judges retired east from Springfield, wholly abandoning their original plan to go on to Berkshire County.

By early October the General Court, meeting in emergency session, had begun to consider both the insurrection and the grievances that lay behind it. Some members favored immediate suppression of the rebellion, but the majority, sympathetic to at least some of the complaints and wanting to hear and consider the numerous petitions that had poured in from scores of towns, blocked swift or vigorous repression. The House of Representatives wished to end the uprising by conciliating the insurgents with reform legislation. At the end of October, however, the Shaysites issued a call for a second county convention in Hampshire and also invited towns to prepare for war, requesting that provisions be laid in and that, as in 1774, men should "stand ready to march at a moment's warning."[13]

When news of these measures arrived in Boston, the governor's hand was strengthened. The assembly passed a riot act and temporarily suspended the right of habeas corpus. At the same time the General Court provided exemption from prosecution under the act to all insurgents who would swear allegiance to the state and behave accordingly by the first of January 1787. The determination to suppress the rebels was joined with the desire to conciliate them, and so, in addition to relief acts dealing with taxation, lawsuits, and court fees, the General Court took steps to reassert its authority with a forty-five-page address to the people of Massachusetts, explaining and justifying the operations and expenses of government. The court took the position that "misinformation" was chiefly responsible for the wide popularity of the rebel movement. Using clear, step-by-step terms, the court presented a financial accounting of its stewardship to the public, hoping to silence rumors of government extravagance. The address also lectured the people on the vices of paper money, likening demands for it to the Israelites' call to Aaron "to make them a calf." Ultimately, the General Court maintained, the legislators were being made scapegoats "as if they had devoured them [the people],"[14] whereas the fundamental sources of unhappiness lay within the people themselves.

The climax of the address was an appeal by the official leadership of Massachusetts society for a reformation of morals that would create a rebirth of republican virtue. Since American independence corruption had made alarming headway:

> habits of luxury have exceedingly increased, the usual manufactures of the country have been little attended to. That we can buy goods cheaper than we can make them, is often repeated, and is even become a maxim in economy, altho' a most absurd and destructive one. While these habits continue, the wisest Legislature will not be able to remove our complaints . . . we have indulged ourselves in fantastical and expensive fashions and intemperate living. . . . Without a reformation of manners, we can have little hope to prosper in our public or private concerns. . . . That virtue which is necessary to support a Republic, has declined; and as a people, we are now in the precise channel, in which the liberty of States has generally been swallowed up. But still our case is not desperate; by recurring to the principles of integrity and public spirit, and the practice of industry, sobriety, economy, and fidelity in contracts, and by acquiescing in laws necessary for the public good, the impending ruin may be averted, and we become respectable and happy. . . . In such a cause we may hope, that the God of our fathers, who has defended us hitherto, will prosper

the work of his own hands, and save the fair structure of American liberty from falling into ruin.[15]

Massachusetts's leaders hoped that ultimately, if the people were exhorted to follow the banner of virtue and to support *their* government, the rebels could be effectively isolated and would quickly seek the promised indemnity. To assure thorough circulation of the message, the Senate ordered that the address be read to town meetings by town clerks and to congregations by the ministers on Thanksgiving Day. Hereafter insurgents would be on notice that in attacking the government they were attacking the rights of individuals as part of the corporate rights of the body politic of Massachusetts.

The effects of this remarkable republican homily from the representatives to their constituents are uncertain. In rebel towns it never had a hearing, nor did it abate the willingness of Daniel Shays to pressure the courts with armed men. Finally Governor Bowdoin decided it was best to delay further court sessions until January. Postponement would give insurgents time to reconsider their resistance, while allowing government troops time to assemble and prepare their attack. Bowdoin recognized that as the cold winter set in, the rebels would be undermined by the scarcity of food and shelter. By the beginning of the new year, 1787, he was confident that the courts, supported by troops, could reopen.

In mid-January Governor Bowdoin gave orders to General Benjamin Lincoln, a Worcester native, to move west in command of the entire militia. After a three-day march from the outskirts of Boston, Lincoln's troops arrived in Worcester on January 22 in time to witness the opening of the courts the following day. As Bowdoin had hoped, the firm show of force had intimidated the rebels, so no opposition of any sort was raised. Now Lincoln and his men moved west to Hampshire County.

Before they arrived, however, blood was shed at Springfield. There Shays, together with Eli Parsons and Luke Day, had collected about two thousand troops. They planned to use their superior numbers to force nine hundred government troops under General Shepard to abandon their position at the arsenal overlooking Springfield village. If the Shaysites succeeded, they would establish effective control of the county and occupy a strong position in any future negotiations with the government. On January 25, Shays made his move, although in a more symbolic than tactical manner. Not fully believing Shepard's troops would fire, he ignored all warnings from Shepard and marched a column of troops to within two hundred, then one hundred yards of Shepard's encampment. Now Shepard ordered his artillerymen to fire over the insurgents' heads, but when they still kept coming, Shepard ordered the cannon to fire at the center of the approaching column. The cannonballs succeeded where all previous political maneuvers had failed. Shays's troops broke ranks and fled, leaving three of their own Massachusetts men dead, the first victims of this civil war.

The "victory" of Shepard's government troops exposed the weakness of the insurgent movement. For while farmers and tradesmen had shouldered arms against the commonwealth, they called themselves "Regulators" and their intentions were reformist, not revolutionary. They were ambivalent about how far they should go in pressing their resistance, however they did not mean to commit treason by taking up arms; they merely intended to mount pressure on the governor and legislature. When these authorities, represented by Shepard's and Lincoln's armies, showed they were ready to fight, the rebels had second thoughts. Within the week Shays, whose troops had reassembled twenty-five miles northeast of Springfield at Pelham, pressed for a settlement based on a general pardon. In a letter to General Lincoln and in a petition to the legislature, the Shaysites admitted that "we have been in errour, in having recourse to arms, and not seeking redress in a constitutional way," and they asked the General Court "to overlook our failing," to accept the innocence of their intentions, and to grant a pardon in exchange for laying down their arms.[16] A single skirmish had brought them to the edge of surrender.

But Lincoln and the General Court rejected these terms because the Shaysites remained in arms. The rebels had missed their opportunity to surrender before January 1 in exchange for a pardon; now it was said that they sought to dictate it at gunpoint. When, early in February, Shays unexpectedly moved his men across the Worcester County line to Petersham, Lincoln acted decisively. In an overnight march through a snowstorm, he led his militiamen thirty miles from their encampment at Hadley to Petersham where the exhausted militia surprised the rebels. Shays and the other leaders escaped across the state line to the north, but the rest of the rebels, after being disarmed and swearing an oath of allegiance, went quietly home. There was no battle, no formal surrender, only collapse. Elsewhere, in Worcester, Hampshire, and

Berkshire counties, there would be a few more confrontations in the coming months—two rebels were killed and thirty wounded at Sheffield on February 27—but the rebellion or "regulation" was broken. The legitimacy of the commonwealth, which even the rebels ultimately accepted, had been vindicated.

The political and psychological wounds of this civil war were slow in healing, however, and memories of the rebellion exercised a profound influence on Massachusetts public life for a generation. Nothing could have more powerfully impressed people with a realization of the difficulty of satisfying diverse constituencies within a republic. Shays's Rebellion was the most immediate object lesson in the fragility of republican government, and it helps to account for the special excitement which controversies over the French Revolution would have in the Bay State during the 1790s. After 1800 the citizens of Massachusetts came to accept the idea of opposition as routine in party competition at the ballot box. But recognition of the legitimacy of political opposition within a competitive structure required a new perspective for people all over New England and the United States.

In 1787 Massachusetts returned to the security of reelecting John Hancock to the governor's chair. After his death in 1793, Hancock's successor would be none other than his ally Samuel Adams. Each in his own way, the two old Revolutionary heroes helped unify state politics. Neither possessed an organized following, but memories of their Revolutionary exploits attracted broad support.

At the town and county level the aftermath of the rebellion was divisive, as the victorious "friends of government" settled scores with former rebels by excluding them from office and by administering the laws of property and indebtedness harshly. In many instances young Shaysites moved on, immigrating to New Hampshire, New York, and Vermont. Indeed with each passing year the turnover in local populations caused by migration to the north and west, as well as movement from agricultural to commercial towns, generally reduced the bitter heritage of the rebellion.

Nevertheless the deeper issues of the revolt remained alive. In the autumn of 1787 townspeople elected delegates to the convention that would meet in January 1788 to ratify or reject the United States Constitution drafted the previous summer at Philadelphia. The debate over the federal Constitution was in some ways an extension of the controversies that had racked Massachusetts so recently and went to the heart of republicanism. Centralization was set against government close to the people. The interests of merchants, manufacturers (including artisans), market-oriented farmers, and creditors seemed in conflict with those of the semisubsistence upland farmers who had supported the insurrection. Everyone wanted a republic of virtue, but would national government, providing secure credit and conducted by a cosmopolitan elite, be more conducive to virtue than the confederation, where state governments were essentially autonomous? In a sense the old questions of Winthrop's day were being posed in different terms. The vision of corporatism and an elevated magistracy was embodied in the Constitution. Opposition to it traded on the same concern for individual liberty and anti-statism that Puritans had also voiced. Now the issues were framed in the secular language of political science. The covenant became a constitution and the voice of the majority assumed a quasi-divine authority.

When Massachusetts's ratifying convention met in early 1788, a narrow majority of its members opposed the new federal Constitution. Whatever the political and commercial benefits of national union, many greeted it with suspicion. The discussion surrounding the new proposal reiterated many of the arguments that had been expressed during the Revolutionary crisis. Would liberty be secure if a distant national authority was created with the power to tax? Could liberty be safe if officials were elected for two- to six-year terms of office, instead of being subject to the recall mechanism of annual elections? Would the people of Massachusetts retain the autonomy that was a legacy from their ancestors as well as from their own recent past? Many citizens were alarmed because in contrast to Massachusetts's own constitution, this new Constitution carried no religious requirements for officeholders. Infidels and freethinkers might someday gain control of the government. A decade later, when Thomas Jefferson sought election to the presidency, this anxiety would intensify opposition to his candidacy in Massachusetts. One of the leading voices raised against ratification was that of Mercy Otis Warren, the firebrand James Otis's sister, who would later be known for her three-volume *History of the Rise, Progress, and Termination of the American Revolution* (1805). Writing anonymously, she produced a powerful Anti-Federalist polemic, *Observations on the New Constitution,* (1788) a pamphlet that until the

1960s was attributed to Elbridge Gerry, one of the state's delegates to the constitutional convention and a prominent opponent of ratification. Warren, the informally educated daughter of the Barnstable County magnate whose disappointed ambitions Thomas Hutchinson claimed had planted the first seed of revolutionary opposition, was the wife of James Warren, a prominent Plymouth leader. By the time of the ratification controversy this homebody and mother of five was forty-nine, but she had already achieved a certain literary notoriety. Back in the 1770s she had penned several satirical dramas attacking Governor Hutchinson, whom she named "Rapatio," together with his circle including "Brigadier Hateall," "Judge Meagre," and "Sir Spendall." She had first circulated these dramas among friends for their amusement, but she later published them anonymously in newspapers. Using a London drawing-room style, Warren displayed a biting, partisan wit. That she concealed her identity when she went into print is evidence of the continuing power of the ruling convention that women's voices should not be heard in public, especially on political subjects.

It is no wonder then that, in order to assure that her arguments would be taken seriously, she used the pen name "A Columbian Patriot" to conceal her authorship of *Observations on the New Constitution*. This attack on the proposed Constitution was a classic expression of Anti-Federalist thinking, in which she presented eighteen reasons why the new scheme of government was dangerous. They ranged from the lack of a bill of rights guaranteeing freedom of the press and the rights of individuals, to the indirect, antidemocratic method for electing the president. Warren's direct, point-by-point commentary won a substantial hearing and, after first appearing in Boston, *Observations* was reprinted in New York.

In time, however, the Federalists succeeded in persuading some of the delegates to change their minds. Most important, Samuel Adams and Governor John Hancock, whose followings overlapped, both decided to support ratification. They became convinced that the federal Constitution did contain sufficient structural safeguards to warrant support, and they both were eager for the commercial and diplomatic advantages that a vigorous national government could provide. Both men, deeply enmeshed in the fate of Massachusetts, were also veterans of the Continental Congress. They knew and convinced others that the political and economic interests of Massachusetts and the United States were complementary. In contrast to state leaders in New York and Virginia, Adams and Hancock ultimately brought decisive support to the federal cause by backing a recommendation that a Bill of Rights be added to the national Constitution.

Within a few years their judgment seemed vindicated by a new surge of prosperity. Every part of the state flourished as agricultural prices rose and trade and manufacturing expanded. Merchants and sailors had not only regained access to their old markets in the Atlantic and Caribbean, they also had opened new ones from the Baltic to the ports of China. After 1793, when Europe entered a decade of recurrent warfare, Massachusetts became more prosperous than ever before. Everything people produced found a profitable market, and with cash in their pockets farmers and tradesmen as well as merchants and lawyers became consumers of store-bought goods on an unprecedented scale. In a republican society the urge for luxury and display was somewhat chastened, finding expression in the elegant understatement of classic architecture and the English decorative styles of Adam and Hepplewhite. For the first time classical columns and pilasters gleamed white among the clusters of weathered clapboard houses in country villages. In the port towns, from Newburyport and Salem south to Hingham and Plymouth, elegant town streets displayed the new, self-conscious urbanity bred by the cosmopolitan experience of successful interstate and international trade.

The few who were wealthy, like Harrison Gray Otis, the Boston merchant and real estate developer who built not one but three city mansions over a period of years, seemed to revel in their sterling and silk. The many, who were fortunate if they had some pewter and a few coin-silver spoons, now tasted amenities they had seldom known. Cane sugar was preferable to a steady diet of the homemade maple variety. Imported cotton and woolen textiles supplemented homespun. Newspapers and pamphlets found broader markets than ever before. Voluntarily, if not always eagerly, the people of Massachusetts ceded the economic independence of the old semisubsistence life in favor of the interdependence of a more specialized, commercial society.

This shift, reminiscent of the change that had occurred in the 1730s and 1740s, also generated anxiety and conflict, both religious and secular. The sense that a revered past was being supplanted awakened a keen desire to preserve old virtues. In both religion and politics, a rhetoric emerged that shared some of the concerns of the Great Awakening. A social mobilization, raising the consciousness of inhabitants in religious and civic affairs and engaging their active participation, was sustained by the prosperity of the federal era.

The religious mobilization had two major thrusts. The most profound and wide-ranging was the collection of activities included in the movement called the Revival, or Second Great Awakening. Congregationalists turned in the direction of heartfelt piety, emphasizing conversion with renewed vigor. As in the 1740s, some churches split, with scores assuming the name of "evangelical Congregationalists." Baptists, whose evangelical views put them in a permanent state of revival, enjoyed a wave of growth in numbers and prosperity.

At the same time there was also an "awakening" of sorts in the orthodox clergy. As a result of the constitutional provisions of the new government in the commonwealth, clergymen found themselves thrust into an uncongenial, competitive, religious environment. On one hand they were beset by lay preachers and Baptists in their parishes, while on the other, a new rationalistic deism was spreading. Some of the clergy tried to bend with prevailing circumstances, either becoming revivalists themselves or else moving in the direction of Unitarianism, a religion that was peculiar to eastern Massachusetts. More often, however, the orthodox clergy dug in, mounting rhetorical counterattacks. By the 1790s, when traces of the deism promulgated by English freethinkers and the French republic cropped up in Massachusetts, the ministers' tone was shrill, apocalyptic, almost hysterical. Irreligion and vice, evident in public indifference to established clergymen, led them increasingly to form associations among themselves and to seek political allies.

They found their allies within their own congregations. Deacons as well as other parishioners worried about the erosion of their churches' financial base of support, in addition to larger questions of social morality. The secular establishment of selectmen, justices of the peace, lawyers, and merchants were often among their parishioners, and men in these positions were also fearful of the violent disorders of Revolutionary France and, more immediately, distressed by the decline in customary respect due to social leaders like themselves. Here, too, the republican structure of government was partly to blame since it had created a fertile climate for electoral competition. At the same time, dynamic economic growth was shuffling local hierarchies of wealth. For the majority of Massachusetts people the political outlook known as Federalism seemed to provide the most reassuring answers.

The presidential election of 1800, which pitted Massachusetts's own John Adams against the Francophile Virginia Deist, Thomas Jefferson, mobilized Federalism on a broad scale. The now ancient Samuel Adams, who remained the staunch Congregationalist he had always been, vainly tried to defend Jefferson against malicious attacks in the press and from the pulpit. But Adams no longer possessed the health and strength to make a difference, and his old "Puritan republicanism" was becoming anachronistic. The new Republicans in Massachusetts were friendly to Deists and Baptists—they were champions of complete freedom of religion—and they were tinged with anticlerical sentiments. Republicans were a vocal and competitive minority during the early years of the nineteenth century.

Federalism became the new source of integration in Massachusetts public affairs. Pledged to sustain the orthodox religious establishment and to defend the interests of commerce and manufacturing tradesmen, it commanded great support in eastern Massachusetts and in the more prosperous, commercially developed towns to the west, particularly in the Connecticut Valley. The Republican minority, which stood for more open opportunities in religion and economic life, enjoyed its strongest appeal among the poorer farming towns where Shaysites had once been numerous, and in Maine. Yet the Republicans also commanded support among some artisans and merchants in eastern towns. Massachusetts was becoming decidedly more heterogeneous in a variety of ways.

The willingness to accept diversity, however, came slowly. Federalist hegemony meant that full religious equality for Baptists and other minority denominations awaited the 1830s. Minorities, whether religious or political, were much quicker to recognize the necessity of pluralism than were the majorities who still cherished the ideal of uniformity. Congregationalists understood that they would never regain the dominant position they had held, yet they fought a rearguard action to retain the advantages they still possessed. Federalists, permanently defeated at the national level, still believed they might preserve the commonwealth as a right-thinking enclave. Organizing both inside and outside the legislature, they developed a party structure that reached down to the towns and to precincts within them. By means of their Washington Benevolent Societies they created popular membership associations that included thousands of citizens. Although nominally nonpartisan, these societies were instruments of Federalist views. Since most people saw themselves as patriots rather than partisans, membership in a society explicitly devoted to the principles of George Washington was satisfying.

In time the competitive nature of public life became accepted, even ritualized in party politics. Though the rhetoric of religious and secular party conflict remained intense as the issues were refought year after year, the effect of the words diminished. Customs developed which recognized that the purpose of invective was no longer to destroy the opponent, but rather to arouse one's friends to action. The contestants learned to speak to their own constituencies instead of wasting their effort preaching to opponents who were deaf to their arguments. Within a decade of Jefferson's first election this general acceptance of inflated public rhetoric signaled the emergence of a new era in which diversity and competition would supplant uniformity and unity as reigning public ideals.

The Massachusetts Federalists, self-proclaimed champions of virtue, were a reluctant vehicle of this transition from the colonial past stretching back to Winthrop and Bradford. They won most of their electoral battles with the Republicans, but they lost the war. Like the Puritan magistrates, the Federalists were devoted to the moral and material leadership of men of learning, piety, wealth, and leisure, in the interests, they claimed, of all. The Puritan ideal of a stable, orderly, uniform society, in which people knew their places and behaved accordingly, was also a Federalist ideal, but by the early nineteenth century it was only a dream. Reality required the few to court the many if they hoped to gain their favor. Reality required that competition, within the majoritarian provisions of republican government determine which persons and policies would rule. Ultimately Massachusetts would be a republic of liberty because liberty was public business, and virtue had become a religious, and therefore private, matter. The commitment to virtue remained powerful, but it was no longer a central objective of the state. For the present, the perennial tension between corporate and individual good was being resolved in favor of individuals. The corporate good, the job of the new republican state, was to promote liberty for individuals. The preservation of virtue would be their responsibility.

# CHAPTER 6

# Hive of Industry and Elite Paternalism

B Y 1860, LITTLE MORE THAN A QUARTER CENTURY AFTER
the death of John Adams, Massachusetts had been transformed. The raw young minutemen who had marched off to battle on April 19, 1775, now lay in graveyards all over the Bay State and scattered throughout the United States. By the time Abraham Lincoln led the new Republican party to its landslide victory in Massachusetts, romantic legends of the colonial past were springing up, replacing living memory. Agriculture and waterborne commerce maintained their economic hegemony into the first decades of the nineteenth century, but the situation was beginning to change. Political continuity with the colonial past had been broken in the 1770s. After 1800 the economy of Massachusetts took on a new character. The population of the state doubled by 1820, then tripled by 1880, even though the eastern district—Maine—had become a separate state in 1820. Urban life became predominant. In 1875, after two centuries, farming was surpassed decisively by manufacturing as the chief occupation and leading source of income in Massachusetts.

The religious and ethnic homogeneity that had prevailed during the eighteenth century, preserving a link between the Revolutionary generation and Winthrop's Bay Colony, yielded to diversity. Innovation and variety became characteristic of religious and social life as well as of economic activity. The ideals of uniformity and orthodoxy in religion and politics were overshadowed as competition became the ruling principle in the marketplace of Massachusetts. The vision of the Puritan commonwealth, in which the corporate good defined individual liberty, was reversed. Now it was the thirst for individual liberty that was paramount, defining the public good. Just as the immigrant newcomers to Massachusetts had done, the grandchildren of the minutemen departed from the paths of their ancestors. They were creating new monuments in the Massachusetts landscape—factories, railroads, cities—while they learned to live in unfamiliar surroundings with people who held different views.

Massachusetts's maritime importance in the first decade of the nineteenth century owed itself to the activities of the people of its three largest towns and the island of Nantucket: Boston (33,250, the fourth largest town in the country), Salem (12,613), Newburyport (7,634), and Nantucket (6,807). Boston shipping in 1807 alone totaled 310,309 tons, more than one-third of the United States' entire merchant fleet. With imports valued at $10 million annually, and almost one thousand ships entering the port each year, the hub bustled with commercial activity. The U.S. Census of 1810 counted 412,040 inhabitants of the state, with 79 percent of them dispersed in rural areas or in villages of under 2,500 people. Although most farmers lived in the eastern half of Massachusetts, the four western counties (Berkshire, Franklin, Hampshire, and Hampden) were home to a quarter of the population (112,182), the greatest proportion that region ever achieved. Rum, the most important product, was Boston's principal export. There were thirty distilleries in the port towns, and in addition, the region boasted eight sugar refineries. Shipbuilding, a longtime staple, was a prominent industry in both Boston and its neighbor Charlestown. Other prime Boston exports were cordage, hats, plate glass, tobacco, sail cloth, and paper. Salem's imports were valued at some $3 million a year, with shipping of forty thousand tons and some 150 vessels involved in foreign and domestic trade and fishing. The third port, Newburyport, concentrated on fishing, shipbuilding, and rum, with some 160 vessels sailing to Europe and the West Indies, and at least 50 more fishing the Grand Banks. After Newburyport, the next largest towns—Gloucester (5,990), Marblehead (5,900), and New Bedford (5,600)—were all active in fishing, whaling, shipbuilding, and the carrying trade. Also significant in wealth and population was the whaling island of Nantucket, with some 120 ships and several communities where whale "works" produced spermaceti candles.

The thriving markets of the commercial towns were more advanced than the towns of the inland regions, but from the 1790s to 1860 the interior also became more market oriented. There was a shift from semisubsistence farming toward dependence on outside markets, and a changeover from household production to workshops and factories. In the eighteenth century slow, expensive overland transportation meant that the agricultural population was only partially engaged in commercial intercourse with the rest of the world. There was little incentive to produce surpluses or improve growing methods, except in suburban towns like Concord and those towns along the Connecticut River that enjoyed access to ports downstream. The distance from markets discouraged investment in capital improvements, and crop yields did not create regular surpluses. However, transportation improvements after 1800, with stage roads, turnpikes, and canals, opened outside markets and provided incentives for surplus production. Rural people also turned to manufacturing on a small scale. While the household economy still dominated, an entrepreneurial spirit was on the rise.

In 1800, the typical farm township had between one and three thousand people, although many towns in central and western Massachusetts were smaller. Two-thirds of the state's population lived in these rural towns, whose villages typically included a few stores, a grist mill and a sawmill, perhaps a potash works, churches, and a few taverns. With only a sprinkling of tradesmen, professionals, or merchants, there was little specialization of labor. Almost everyone was involved in agriculture directly or indirectly, but there was an increasing drive to produce surpluses for a wider market.

Most of the goods manufactured between 1790 and 1810 resulted from the household production of textiles and handicrafts or the labor of village artisans working in small shops where they turned out consumer goods like shoes, furniture, and clocks. In eastern Massachusetts there was a small iron industry with furnaces, forges, trip hammers, and rolling and slitting mills. Ore, dredged from bogs, fed the furnaces and mills that turned out cast and bar iron. Men in Taunton, Plymouth, Middleborough, and Bridgewater made nails, spades, nail rods, scythes, axes, edge tools, and muskets on a limited scale. In addition, however, by 1810, there were some fifty-four cotton manufacturing plants in the state, all small-scale operations. The Napoleonic wars in Europe bolstered prices of agricultural goods, but Massachusetts's maritime supremacy was put in serious jeopardy by the Jeffersonian embargoes.

Yet at first war in Europe in the early years of the nineteenth century proved lucrative for Bay State shipping interests. By 1807, because of harassment of shipping and impressment of American seamen, President Jefferson recommended and Congress passed the Embargo Act, which forbade all trade with Europe. The voters of Massachusetts, who had helped elect Jefferson in 1804, reacted with anger. The economic impact of the Embargo Act on Massachusetts was calamitous. In 1808, exports dropped by three-fourths from the previous year and shipbuilding fell by two-thirds. The Federalist mood found expression in irate polemics and ironic verse:

> Our ships all in motion once whitened the ocean,
> They sailed and returned with a cargo;
> Now doomed to decay, they have fallen a prey
> To Jefferson—worms—and embargo.[1]

All sectors of the state's economy suffered, and the political reaction restored the Federalist party to power in state politics. The Embargo was repealed in 1809, but its political legacy was lingering hostility to the Democratic-Republican party of Jefferson and widespread support for the Federalists. The Republicans made a respectable show statewide, controlling the governorship in 1807–9 and 1810–12 and also winning substantial gains in the legislature. But Boston was loyal to the Federalists from 1807 through 1812. Massachusetts was a very reluctant participant in the War of 1812, refusing to supply troops and generally opposing the war. Indeed Massachusetts merchants even traded with the enemy. When peace came in 1815, the Federalist party's near "traitorous" stance destroyed its national stature, though it continued to dominate politics in Massachusetts until the early 1820s. The wartime experience as a whole was a catalyst for a turn toward manufacturing as the dynamic component of the economy.

Indeed, the sharp growth in the population of Massachusetts after 1780 demanded a transformation of the economy. Had people remained chiefly dependent on agriculture, they would have sunk ever more deeply into poverty. Before the Revolution, during the middle decades of the eighteenth century, Massachusetts witnessed a marked slowdown in population growth that was significantly related to the scarcity of productive land. But after 1780 and especially in the decades after 1820, the population grew swiftly, at rates comparable to the most dynamic periods of colonial settlement. Moreover, even though the state was not growing so rapidly as the new nation, the sheer numbers were staggering, given the size and physical character of the state. In 1780 the population had stood at 270,000 people. By 1820 the figure had grown to more than half a million, and in 1860 it reached 1.2 million. The population density had risen from 33 persons per square mile in 1780 to 153 persons in 1860. Massachusetts became the most thickly settled state in the union, save only for tiny Rhode Island.

The growth of Massachusetts's population was closely connected to a general pattern of urbanization that was not tied simply to a few cities like Boston or Worcester or Springfield. All over Massachusetts, communities with no more than two or three thousand people at the time of the Revolution grew to five, ten, even twenty thousand by 1860. Because water transportation was largely confined to the eastern counties, eastern Massachusetts enjoyed the most spectacular growth, from Fall River and New Bedford north to Gloucester, Lowell, and Newburyport. Yet inland towns also grew dramatically. Worcester, connected to Providence by means of the Blackstone River and canal, grew twelve-fold, from twenty-one hundred people in 1790 to twenty-five thousand in 1860. Along the Connecticut River, Springfield, Hadley, and Northampton became urban centers, as did Adams and Pittsfield in Berkshire County. Here the shift to industrial production arrested an exodus from the region, which between 1810 and 1820 had caused a decline in the population of that county and the smallest statewide growth rate (11 percent) of the nineteenth century, less than one-third of the national rate.

The urbanization of Massachusetts took several forms. Along the seacoast, old colonial ports had long possessed a quasi-urban character. Many of their inhabitants had always engaged in some branch of commerce with the fisheries or the building, furnishing, and maintenance of shipping. Here the diversity of occupation, wealth, and social background characteristic of a commercial city such as Boston had been visible by the time of the Revolution. Although the people of such North Shore towns as Newburyport, Gloucester, and Marblehead or the South Shore ports of Hingham and Plymouth might trade in faraway places, they were more insular than they were cosmopolitan. Their greatest passions were aroused by parochial questions, for instance, the threat of contagion from the Marblehead smallpox hospital, the operation of which in the 1770s had led to riots among neighbors who carried bitter grudges for years. Even after 1800 in Salem, at that time the most populous and urbane community after Boston, the great national division between Federalists and Jeffersonians was transformed into a village feud by the fierce rivalries of political cliques. Urbanization certainly was already more advanced in port towns than in the farm hamlets and county seats of the interior. But after 1800 the economic and social diversity in settlements, as well as awareness of the world beyond town and state, would grow to make such communities truly urban.

It was not until 1815 that commerce could resume on the global scale of the previous decade, and by then critical changes had occurred. American merchants were no longer middlemen and carriers for a Europe locked in warfare. English competition was intense and successful. Henceforward the port towns would regard the years before the embargo as a halcyon era; and it would be a decade before they returned to comparable levels of activity. Newburyport and Salem on the North Shore and Plymouth to the south would never regain their commercial importance. Only the commercial eminence of Boston would be enhanced as a centralization of overseas trade developed in the 1820s and 1830s. The urbanization of the lesser port towns might have halted entirely had they not emulated their inland neighbors and become sites for manufacturing.

The rise of industrial enterprises in the interior of Massachusetts was connected directly to the fate of agriculture. As long as farming prospered, few men looked elsewhere for their bread, but from the middle of the eighteenth century onward, more and more farm communities were suffering from a long-term, though intermittent decline. Their populations grew, but the quantity of arable land was fixed, and its productivity was diminishing. The initial response was migration to vacant lands. People went first to the northern half of Connecticut and to central and western Massachusetts. After the Revolution they went north into Vermont, New Hampshire, and Maine. By 1800 a stream of settlers was again heading west, now into the Mohawk valley in New York and beyond into Ohio. Massachusetts's role as exporter of literate, industrious Yankees was established.

Migration, however, was only one solution. The evidence suggests that many farm boys and girls were so strongly committed to their families and their communities that they preferred to sink or swim in Massachusetts. It was this attachment of ordinary people and of merchant capitalists to their native commonwealth that would transform the social and economic landscape of the state within the lifetime of the post-Revolutionary generation. Declining agriculture would stimulate the creation of new transportation facilities, new industries, and specialization in nearly every sphere of activity. These developments exploited existing concentrations of labor and created new ones.

In farming communities, whether county seats or meetinghouse villages, industries typically began on a tiny scale. Grist mills and sawmills operated by two or three men had long taken advantage of the water power available in almost every township. Now a paper mill was added, or carding and fulling mills to process homegrown wool were begun. This industrial activity usually processed local farm products such as grain, hides, and fleece, or it supplied common articles of consumption like iron, farm tools, nails, and pins. Most often the industrialization began almost imperceptibly, requiring little capital and employing only small numbers.

Simultaneously people found themselves driven by the lack of other opportunities to engage in cottage industries, not only spinning, weaving, shoemaking, basket-making, and fashioning wooden implements, but also making wheels and wagons, clapboards and shingles, barrels and pottery. In the past these jobs had been done in hours left over from farming and food processing and during the winter season. Now, with many farms dwindling in size or having excess labor, they assumed new importance, often becoming the chief source of cash. By the first decades of the nineteenth century industry was unobtrusively preserving a veneer of agricultural prosperity in the countryside. Had people been relying on the soil alone, fewer houses would have been neatly painted and fewer of their inhabitants decently clothed.

The more people turned to market production, even on this small scale, the more thoroughly they became enmeshed in the world of commerce. The costs of transportation assumed enormous importance, since every dollar spent on transportation meant a dollar lost to the producer. And if inland people wanted to buy what they did not produce, they must pay the freight. For this reason turnpike and canal building and, after 1830, railroad building enjoyed widespread interest and a measure of public support. The locations of these facilities, their crossings and termini, were magnets producing concentrations of population. Market agriculture and market industry thirsted for cheap access to customers. As urbanization developed at village crossroads and water sites, it was magnified by new and improved transportation.

The first stages of factory development were initiated usually by the investments of local merchants and gentry in the rural towns of southern New England. Typical factories were small and administered by the local owners. These factories were family organizations in which some of the operations, such as weaving, were given out to nearby farmers and artisans who worked in their own dwellings. This system of putting-out work and "cottage industry" became more widespread when the English immigrant Samuel Slater, financed by the Providence merchant Moses Brown, introduced water-powered spinning to Rhode Island in the 1790s. By 1850, more than half the textile factories in southern Massachusetts were located in rural townships, such as the Slater-dominated towns of Dudley, Oxford, and Webster, which were just up the Blackstone River valley from Pawtucket. In many instances, however, these small family or Rhode Island–style factories were undercapitalized and had difficulty surviving economic slumps. The first mill set up in the Dudley–Oxford area, the Merino Wool Company of 1812, went bankrupt in 1816; but later ventures were more successful. As historian Jonathan Prude wrote:

> The textile industry would have achieved an enduring presence in Dudley and Oxford even if Slater had not appeared on the scene; such was the momentum toward economic expansion operating both throughout the region and within these communities. But Slater's arrival made a difference. It provided a direct, personal link between the rise of local manufacturing in the United States—and so adds special luster to developments within these communities. And Slater's presence also contributed to the specific shape of post-1810 events in the two towns. With significant interests in both communities, Slater was a figure whose priorities, even whimsies, inevitably affected the face of local industrialization.[2]

Wealthy Boston entrepreneurs (and a few Springfield investors), however, led Massachusetts's transition toward large-scale industrial society. Seeking to overcome the high risks inherent in maritime overseas trade, they chose to invest in the more secure high technology activity—textile manufacturing.

This large-scale, conspicuous industrialization and urbanization required major capital expenditures, and it was not until these were forthcoming in the decades after 1810 that dramatic changes took place. The merchants of Boston and the other port towns were the chief sources of this capital. By the 1790s they already had begun to invest in turnpikes to expand their access to farm and forest products. Later, when Napoleonic warfare and Jeffersonian policy interfered with their trade, they began to consider investments in factories. Yet because industrial profits were small compared to trade, in spite of equivalent risks, there was no rush into industry. Merchant capitalists did not shift their interests until a handful of the boldest and most farsighted among them had demonstrated the immense opportunities for secure, profitable investment in textiles.

The basic technology of textile mills had already been imported from England into Rhode Island and had shown some limited success by the first years of the new century. As a result a boom in cotton-spinning mills had occurred before the onset of the War of 1812. In Massachusetts these tiny mills, each employing several people, were erected in towns that lay along the Merrimack River in Essex County, the Charles in Middlesex County, the Somerset (now Taunton River) in Bristol County, and the Blackstone in the southeast quarter of Worcester County. From an economic standpoint their impact was minimal, and in the entire state they employed scarcely one hundred people. Yet they provided a beginning in the development of a wide pool of mechanics familiar with the rudiments of mill construction and machinery, and they inspired some wealthy men with a vision of far more substantial and sophisticated industrial possibilities.

The most important of these men was a merchant, a native of Newburyport, Francis Cabot Lowell. By 1810 Lowell was well established in Boston and had accumulated substantial reserves of capital. But the uncertain climate of trade made him restless, and in 1810 the thirty-five-year-old Lowell took his wife and children to England for an extended vacation that was supposed to strengthen his health. In 1811 the trading firm of Joseph and Henry Lee failed, which almost ruined Lowell's brother-in-law, Patrick Jackson. Lowell wrote to Jackson in

1811 of his anxiety: "The hazards of business are much greater now than they ever were in my day."[3] In England, where the Lowell family lived for two years, Lowell became an industrial tourist, exploiting his mercantile connections to gain access to a wide range of Lancashire and Scottish textile operations—from the smallest one-room mill to the great, four-story brick factories where power looms wove hundreds of yards daily. When Lowell returned to Massachusetts in 1812, he had worked out a plan to create a single factory in which he would house all the varied processes required to turn raw cotton into finished cloth. He would need $100,000 in capital, one-sixth of which ($15,000) he was prepared to invest himself. He raised the remaining sum from a small circle of fellow merchants, including his brother-in-law Jackson, who was eager to manage the company. With his investment of $20,000, Jackson became the largest single stockholder in the new Boston Manufacturing Company. Lowell and Jackson, who had known each other since boyhood in Newburyport, worked closely together to provide the impetus for innovations that would transform the American textile business and act as a catalyst for the industrialization and urbanization of Massachusetts.

Jackson selected a site six miles west of Boston along the Charles River, at Waltham, for the great experiment. He bought out an existing paper mill, its land, and its water rights and it was here that Lowell, with his chief mechanic Paul Moody, created the factory and its machines. Moody was a native of Newbury who had worked as a weaver, in a nail factory, and, most recently, in Amesbury constructing carding machines for the dozens of small carding mills that were springing up. Like Jackson and Lowell, he was a person of proven abilities and in his mid-thirties.

Building and equipping the new factory occupied much of 1813 and 1814, so it was not until 1815, after the War of 1812 had ended, that the Waltham mill began to produce for the market. By then the English were flooding America with their textiles, and the small mills that had so recently flourished became idle. Postwar reconstruction compounded their problems, and many went bankrupt. The economic climate was so gloomy that from 1817 through 1820 only six new factories were incorporated in the entire state, less than two per year. In 1817 Lowell died, but under Jackson's gifted leadership and Moody's careful and inventive supervision, the Waltham mill succeeded. Sales grew tenfold from $3,000 in 1815, the first year of operations, to $34,000 in 1817. They then multiplied ten times more in the next five years, with annual sales reaching $345,000 in 1822. By this time, a second, larger mill had been erected. The capital assets of the company had swelled from the initial $100,000 to more than three-quarters of a million dollars, and annual dividends were running between 12 and 28 percent. The Waltham mills proved conclusively that even under adverse economic conditions large-scale mills, where all fiber-processing, spinning, and weaving operations were integrated, made money.

The new mills and their dormitories for one hundred, then two hundred, mill girls, had substantially altered the face of the town. Still they were augmenting an ongoing process of industrialization and urbanization, and their workers were a minority of the townspeople. The scale of the Waltham mills, while larger than any others, was not so great that it overwhelmed existing patterns of social and political life. The town had absorbed the mills rather than the reverse.

In 1812 and 1813 Lowell had solicited only a half-dozen others to join the Boston Manufacturing Company. One of them, Nathan Appleton, a prosperous Boston merchant from New Ipswich, New Hampshire, had been a reluctant participant. Lowell had asked him for $10,000, but since he had lost earlier investments in cotton manufacture, Appleton had only subscribed $5,000 in what he then believed was a risky venture. A decade later, with Waltham's profits soaring, Appleton was more than happy to open his purse when Jackson approached him with a visionary scheme for the creation of an entire city of mills. Waltham had been good for the Boston Manufacturing Company, and the water site Jackson had arranged there had fully met the original requirements. But the mills at Waltham were enclosed by the existing small-scale industrial and farming settlements and water power was limited, so there was little opportunity for expansion. By 1820 Jackson realized that what he, Lowell, and Moody had done at Waltham could be multiplied elsewhere almost indefinitely. He wanted to begin at once, and with the backing of Appleton and the Boston trading house of the Scotsmen Boott and Sons, he set about opening a new era in Massachusetts industrial and urban history. In 1820 Jackson and the newly organized Merrimack Manufacturing Company bought the Pawtucket Falls site in northeast Chelmsford, and they set out to transform a pastoral landscape.

Chelmsford, a town of fifteen hundred people in 1820, twenty-five miles northwest of Boston, was much like a hundred other farming communities. Two-thirds of its inhabitants were farmers, producing the wide range of grains, meats, fruits, and dairy goods needed to feed themselves, with enough surplus for the market. The Merrimack Canal, built in the 1790s to augment Newburyport's lumber supply for ship-building and its provisions for trade, ran through Chelmsford, so it was a more market-oriented town than most in Middlesex and Worcester counties. But its mixture of farming with small industries (employing 31 percent of its adults) made it typical in other respects. Chelmsford village, located in the central part of the town a mile south of the Merrimack and several miles from the Pawtucket Falls site, had its meeting-house, a few stores, shops, and dwellings. Jackson and the new Merrimack Manufacturing Company did not seek to disrupt it. Their mill city would rise on the open land adjoining the falls and the canal.

Moody and Jackson learned of the site in 1820 and quickly set about acquiring land and water rights. In 1821 they bought up farms and several small mills as well as the existing canal, which ran a mile and a half around the falls. In the following year Jackson's dream began to take shape. Moody and Jackson began by building a dam across the river and widening and deepening the canal. The latter task required fifty tons of gunpowder for blasting and $120,000—more than the entire capital that founded the Waltham mills. In 1823 these jobs were completed, as was the erection of two mill buildings. Machinery for them had already been constructed at the Waltham factory and was installed as soon as the buildings were finished. On September 4, 1823, production began. Moody, who had overseen its construction, called the mill wheel "the best in the world," exclaiming he had never seen "machinery start better."[4] Immediately, work began on a third mill, and two more were started the next year. In 1825 the machine shops were moved from Waltham to the new location, where they were housed in a large five-story brick building. Under Jackson's leadership merchant capital was flooding in. The following year, 1826, the four-square-mile area containing the water site and the surrounding real estate was set off from Chelmsford as a new town, which was named Lowell after the deceased founder of the Boston Manufacturing Company, Francis Cabot Lowell. This first company town, whose population reached

3,500 in 1828, would prove an important model of urbanization for Massachusetts and the United States in the nineteenth century.

In contrast to Waltham, the creation of Lowell required a full range of urban development to provide housing and amenities for a labor force that was drawn from far and wide to an essentially vacant location. At Waltham it was chiefly local men who were employed to construct buildings and their machinery. Moody, Lowell, and Jackson had supervised the carpenters, masons, and smiths already residing nearby. But the enterprise at Lowell would have exhausted the local labor supply and would have held back the pace of development. Consequently, Jackson imported workers: from the British Isles, from rock-strewn farms, and from lesser mills—including five hundred Irish laborers to work on the dam and canal and, a few years later, hundreds of mechanics to build, assemble, and maintain the machines that were used locally and sold to mills in nearby New Hampshire, southward to Rhode Island and Connecticut. In addition to dormitories for mill girls, the company built row housing for families and stores. Indirectly it built schools, churches, and other public buildings. As *the* real estate developer for Lowell, the company fulfilled Jackson's dream of a spacious, fireproof brick city on a gridiron plan, where efficiency, order, and regularity ruled.

Lowell was truly an instant city. In 1836, ten years after it was set off as a town, it was formally incorporated as a city with a mayor, aldermen, and common council. By then the population had grown to nearly eighteen thousand and the diversity and cosmopolitanism characteristic of an urban center were evident, not only in the complexity of its economic life but also in Lowell's five newspapers and five religious denominations. The city's religious composition, like its economic base, dramatically illustrated the profound departure from the colonial past. There was a Catholic church and a Universalist church, as well as two Methodist, three Baptist, and three Congregational chapels and meetinghouses. What was happening in Lowell, urbanization based on industry, was far more rapid and intense than in other towns. Yet the direction was the same almost everywhere in Massachusetts during the first half of the nineteenth century.

The pace of industrialization and urbanization depended on a variety of circumstances. In Worcester the construction of the Blackstone Canal, financed by Rhode Island merchants to expand their commercial hinterland and completed in 1828, provided a major impetus for economic development. Here, no single business was dominant, and cotton and woolen mills flourished in the 1830s together with shoemaking, machine shops, paper milling, foundries, and coach making. At Springfield the first major industry was the United States Armory, whose gun production thrived during the War of 1812. Later, in the 1820s, Jonathan Dwight Jr. and his brother Edmund, scions of a powerful dynasty of Springfield merchants, bought the water rights and real estate that lay along the south side of the Chicopee River, four miles south of Springfield Village. Copying the model of Jackson and the Merrimack Manufacturing Company, the Dwights formed the Boston and Springfield Manufacturing Company, raising its $500,000 capital from Springfield and Boston merchants, including several who were already investors in Waltham and Lowell. Although the scale never matched that of Lowell, the company created a mill village that had two thousand people by 1835, a decade after production began. These major textile enterprises, together with the armaments and paper industries, which in the 1830s each employed more than two hundred workers, gave Springfield an unusually broad base of large industries together with a wide range of smaller ones.

Men like Lowell, Jackson, Appleton, and the Dwight brothers, the successors to the maritime patriciate of eighteenth-century New England, had constructed an ethos—a set of ideas, attitudes, and institutions dominated by economic needs—that gave them control over the banking, politics, and professions of Massachusetts. These elites, who came to be known as the Boston Associates, were primarily concerned with commerce and the commercial life; they were imbued with the values of diligence, order, thrift, prudence, personal restraint, and self-improvement. Through intermarriage between families and a degree of openness to talented newcomers they forged a merchant aristocracy. In a world where security of investments required trust and reliable communication, this elite turned to family members. John Cushing, William Sturgis, John Murray Forbes, and John Bennett Forbes all worked for their uncle, Thomas H. Perkins. The interrelated Lees, Higginsons, Tracys, Jacksons, and Cabots formed partnerships, employed sons, nephews, and cousins. The result was the recruitment and training of several generations of businessmen who were devoted to commerce and shared a common outlook. The values of this upper stratum became the embodiment of one variety of the American capitalist ideal, sometimes called the Protestant ethic, the bourgeois ethic, or the gospel of wealth philosophy. These men, who moved to industrial development in the early nineteenth century, wanted to protect and enhance their families' fortunes.

Manufacturing offered the expectation of regular returns unlike other commercial transactions, each one of which had its own peculiar risks. Another factor in the Associates' decision was politics. Whereas the British empire was devoted to mercantile interests, the new United States represented a wider range of interests; and the Jeffersonian ascendancy meant second-class status for maritime commerce. Fearing for the future, Lowell's friends and colleagues welcomed his mastering of the principal features of the English power loom. A steady income from textile mills could provide these merchants with the time and energy to pursue activities outside the arena of business, particularly in philanthropy, which was considered a "gentleman's" activity. In 1826 the industrialist Amos Lawrence complained in his journal of his "*over-engagedness* in business. . . . I now find myself so engrossed with its cares, as to occupy my thoughts, waking or sleeping, to a degree entirely disproportioned to its importance."[5] He believed that commerce was too narrow an interest and "it served no larger sense of purpose." Assured of a secure return of at least 6 percent annually over five to seven years, the elite could live well and preserve the family fortunes for the generations to follow. As the historian of the Boston Associates, Robert Dalzell, wrote: "Far from the production of wealth in the usual sense, the goal was the preservation of fortunes already made, positions already won."[6] These leaders would now be able to direct their attention to the promotion of philanthropic and societal needs, thus transforming themselves from a maritime elite to a true "ruling class."

These Boston elite merchant shippers, ship owners, captains, traders, importers, and exporters redirected their surplus capital to start new industry on a large scale. They developed new techniques of manufacture, and devised a system to sell their products. The Boston Associates recruited, trained, and housed a labor force, sometimes building new communities, like Lawrence and Lowell, in the process. They contributed heavily to the construction of a transportation system vital to their own needs, which served others as well. Furthermore, the growth of their mills triggered a massive demographic movement with enormous social consequences. Because sizable numbers of farm women and children were attracted by the wages of the factory system, the family structure was significantly affected. Beginning in the late 1820s the Boston Associates also introduced substantial numbers of foreign workers to inhospitable communities, a measure that generated xenophobia, ethnic tension, and group conflict. In the years following, housing and health problems were created that gave rise to the need for new urban services. Industrialization promoted new forms of social mobility together with the exploitation of mill workers. When mill owners cut wages during the 1830s, they stimulated union organization and, later, ethnic politics. The Boston Associates were crucial agents for transforming Massachusetts into an industrial commonwealth.

By 1850, the Boston Associates, including Edmund Dwight, Kirk Boott, Patrick T. Jackson, William Sturgis, Harrison Gray Otis, T. H. Perkins, Israel Thorndike, Abbott and Amos Lawrence, Nathan Appleton, the Lowells, the Cabots, the Quincys, and the Eliots, controlled most of the entire New England region's large cotton mills. Their names could be found on the boards of directors, or as major stockholders, in virtually all the cotton factories of the day. They managed or owned one-fifth of the entire U.S. textile industry with a complex array of interlocking directorates. These men controlled production by exchanging information on costs, posting similar bids for raw cotton, and by attempting to fix the price of finished goods. They monopolized regional water power sites, had substantial interests in the subsidiary manufacture of textile machinery, and often built and rented out the houses of the workers. To gain access to new markets and to support new profitable ventures that would reduce their risks, they invested in the first railroads of the state, holding interest in one-third of the state's railroad mileage by the late 1840s. By 1848 they possessed 40 percent of Boston's bank stock and 38 percent of the state's insurance industry. The investment pursuits of Boston's capitalist elite helped make Massachusetts first in the nation in the high proportion of workers involved in manufacturing and nonagricultural activities.

A combination of local and outside investment capital was common. Thousands of small enterprises in Massachusetts were financed locally and scores of these, as they grew, attracted support from capitalists in Boston and the other cities. Large-scale enterprise was seldom totally financed by local investors. Yet the all-pervasive industrialization of the state did depend chiefly on local ingenuity, thrift, and continuous rein-vestment. In Massachusetts during these decades, even the most ag-ricultural town had more industry than the traditional gristmills, saw-mills, and tanneries. An 1837 survey shows that woven palm-leaf hats or pocketbooks, wallets, scythes, buttons, or pins were commonly pro-duced in those few towns that did not possess at least one cotton, woolen, or paper mill. Everywhere the pressure of a rising population on a declining agriculture forced people to use their wits to devise new modes of production.

By 1860 Yankee ingenuity had carved a record of thousands of small successes, dozens of which were truly spectacular. Massachusetts, in addition to leading the nation in shoemaking and textiles, contained industries representing practically the entire spectrum of American manufacturing from A (artificial limbs) to Z (zinc oxide). Indeed, of the six hundred industrial, commercial, and agricultural occupations listed in the United States census of 1860, people in Massachusetts were engaged in more than three-quarters of them. From the standpoint of employment and volume of business, however, there were six areas of activity that dominated the industrial economy: leather goods, textiles, machine-building, metalworking, the extractive industries (forest, fish-ery, and quarry products), and consumer goods.

Boot- and shoemaking, which employed more than 60,000 people in 1860, more than 28 percent of the state's entire industrial labor force, had a long history. Farmers in Lynn, a poor Essex County township just to the south of Salem and Marblehead, had built up a large cottage industry of shoemaking before the Revolution, and in succeeding de-cades Lynn shoes became a standard item in Atlantic trade. By 1860 shoemaking had grown into a vast factory industry with over twenty-five thousand workers in Essex County, twenty thousand more in Mid-dlesex and Worcester counties, and another fifteen thousand in Plym-outh and Norfolk counties. In addition, the demands created by shoe manufacture had led to the development of major leather-processing shops nearby. The boot and shoe trade had such far-reaching influence in the industrial economy that Massachusetts's prosperity rose and fell with it.

In dollar volume, textiles were even more important than shoe-making. Although cotton and woolen mills, being far more intensively capitalized and mechanized, employed fewer people overall, still, with more than fifty thousand workers, these mills accounted for nearly one-quarter of all industrial employment. Located in every region from Essex and Bristol counties west to Berkshire County, cloth and carpet manufacture was more broadly diffused across the state than shoemaking. Middlesex County, the home of Lowell, possessed the greatest concentration of textile workers (13,000), followed by Essex (9,000), Hampden in the Connecticut Valley (7,000), and Bristol (6,000). By 1860, however, the trend in both shoemaking and textiles was toward concentration in fewer companies with larger factories. Dependence on a particular industry was fast becoming the rule in many locales.

Machine building was highly important, for the mechanization not only of the shoemaking and textile industries but of other industries in Massachusetts and all over the United States. By 1860 Massachusetts was one of the leaders in the production of machinery and machine tools. Although the growth of machine building was directly tied to textiles and shoemaking, its origins lay in the colonial era.

Every colonial town had its mill and its blacksmith. The woodwork required to build a water wheel, power transmission gears and shafts, as well as spinning wheels and looms for home use, had made some carpenters into mechanics; elaborate iron crafting had done the same for blacksmiths. These men built the cotton and carding mills of the 1780s and 1790s and the machinery inside them. Using wood for the structural members and iron at points of pressure and friction, they adapted the skills and designs of the agricultural past to make machines that had been invented by the more advanced English textile industry. By the early years of the nineteenth century, demand for such machinery had grown so rapidly that two- and three-man machine shops began to appear, first in Rhode Island and then in Massachusetts. It was in such a shop in Amesbury that Francis Lowell found Paul Moody, and in constructing the machinery for the Waltham mills they intensified the pace of machine building dramatically. Later Moody created and ran the great machine shop at Lowell, which possessed a wide variety of drills, lathes, and equipment for cutting, stamping, and hammering. By the 1830s cast iron was replacing wood in machine frames, and within two decades machine building would become a chiefly metal-working craft. Because of the need for high capital investment and a concentration of highly skilled labor, machine building tended to be, as at Lowell and Newton Upper Falls, directly tied to a textile company or, as in Lynn, connected to a shoemaking firm.

Yet independent machine shops also emerged. Usually they were small, specializing in simple, widely needed devices and in the production of particular parts used in other factories. Sometimes they built machines that performed a single operation in a complex manufacturing process. In a few cases such small shops grew in size and sophistication to become major suppliers to an entire industry. The Whitin Machine Works, located twelve miles southeast of Worcester, in Northbridge on the Mumford River, was among the most important and outstanding examples of the indigenous development of machine building. Beginning in 1831 as an offshoot of the Whitin brothers' cotton mill, by the 1840s it became the Whitins' chief source of profit on the strength of John C. Whitin's patented cotton-picking machine, which was the best in the cotton industry. In the following decade Whitin was employing over five hundred men in his new factory, and his workers were producing a full line of cotton textile machinery. Business acumen, a ready supply of skilled workers, and Whitin's fortunate location near the textile mill markets both in Rhode Island and eastern Connecticut enabled his enterprise to prosper without infusions of merchant capital.

By 1860 machine shops like Whitin's employed only a fraction of the men engaged in metalworking industries. The old colonial crafts of the clockmakers and the smiths—gun, silver, and iron—were the source of the skilled men who had rendered these crafts obsolete while creating new ones. Paul Revere's odyssey from artist in silver to industrial pioneer, reveals one way in which the transformation to industrial metal work occurred.

At the time of the Revolution, Revere had already risen to the pinnacle of his craft in America. After the war, however, he turned his back on the expanding luxury market in silver table settings and tea services. Instead he and his son Joseph Warren Revere started a foundry in which he could tinker with metallurgy. Revere's first important product was church bells: by the 1790s he was casting them in abundance. Revere also produced marine hardware and developed new techniques for machine-drawing and hammering copper and bronze so that the bolts, spikes, and fittings he manufactured undersold English imports. In

1795 Revere won the contract to outfit two United States frigates being built at Boston, and he was able to supply all the necessary parts save the copper sheathing for their hulls, which was imported from England.

In 1800, at the age of sixty-five, Revere set out to remedy this missing link by establishing a rolling mill. A native of Boston who had spent his entire life there, he was now forced to leave in order to obtain water power. The site he selected in the newly incorporated town of Canton was a dozen miles south of Boston's North End shipyards. Here, on the Neponset River, he transformed an old slitting mill into the first American rolling mill. Within a year he was producing sheet copper for marine use and roofing. Revere's copper would not only sheathe American ships; it would also cover the dome on Charles Bulfinch's Massachusetts State House and the roof of Benjamin Latrobe's New York City Hall. Within a few years Revere would be making copper boilers for steam engines, including the one used on Robert Fulton's first successful steamboat. In later decades when steam engines came into wide use, the technical skills in forging and working copper and brass developed at Canton would help sustain their manufacture in Massachusetts.

Revere was one silversmith who turned from decorative to practical metal work, but most silversmiths stayed with silver, enjoying the popular demand for consumer luxuries that upward aspirations, the spread of refinement, and commercial prosperity nourished. Here, however, the craft was transformed by the desire to meet the burgeoning market for table silver, jewelry, and Victorian ornament. Initially, in the first years of the nineteenth century, craftsmen and their apprentices turned to nickel silver to satisfy their customers. But Brittannia ware, an amalgam of antimony, copper, tin, lead, and zinc, was imported from England and undersold it. In the 1820s a Taunton silversmith succeeded in making Brittannia metal in his own shop, and from this discovery grew the Reed and Barton factory, which recruited and trained local people. By 1860, when over one hundred men and women worked side-by-side with Henry Reed and Charles Barton, the silversmith's craft had been subdivided out of existence. Some people specialized in design, others in casting, rolling, pressing, spinning, or soldering. The final appearance was created in separate polishing, plating, and engraving operations. Reed's standards of craftsmanship were the highest in the industry, but while his product surpassed the work of a journeyman silversmith, it would never match the aesthetic heights of a Revere. For the decorative arts like silver and cabinetmaking the new mass production had drawbacks as well as benefits.

When it came to wholly utilitarian goods, however, mass-produced articles equaled or exceeded the standards of old-time artisans. Factories in Bristol and Worcester counties made cutlery and edged tools—scythes and axes, hoes, shovels, and plow blades—that were cheap and durable. Machine-made wire, nails, spikes, and other hardware were equally satisfactory and had the additional advantages of uniformity and, increasingly, standardization. Metalworking shops were never as large as the great textile mills, but they did concentrate labor around water power sites.

Early in the nineteenth century the nation had suffered from a scarcity of labor. Industrialization required transforming farm workers into an industrial labor force, often necessitating resettlement in urban locations. The Boston Associates took the first steps in this process by securing an adequate labor force. In order to create a reliable supply of workers, and avoid what Nathan Appleton described as "the degradation" of the English factory operatives, the Boston Associates began to recruit unmarried young women and youth from the farms of New England. To ensure control over the workforce and to avoid labor discontent, the factory owners developed a system of paternalistic labor relations called the "Waltham system."

Thousands of young Yankee farm women and children streamed to work in the mills and to live in factory-owned boardinghouses. They came for many reasons, not the least of which was to escape from the unproductive farms of New England. Fathers sent their daughters to the mills and collected their wages to pay off mortgage, or to send their sons to college. The 1821 wage book of the Waltham Cotton Mills shows one Gideon Haynes coming regularly to collect the wages of his children: Cynthia, $2.25 per week for work in the cloth room; Ann, Sabre, and Sophia, all working in the card room, $1.25, $2.00, and $2.08 per week respectively.

Many young women went to the mills to make money and to claim some independence for themselves. One such young worker, who turned out not to be very typical at all, was Harriet Hanson Robinson.

Writing many years later about her time in the mills, Robinson, who became an author, extolled the new industrial experience as liberating. Indeed, to work in a factory and earn one's own wages, no longer carrying out the unpaid drudgery of the farm family, became a major moment in the history of women's liberation. This newfound freedom was particularly important for the poorest women. She wrote:

> The cotton factory was a great opening to these lonely and dependent women. From a condition approaching pauperism they were at once placed above want; they could earn money, and spend it as they pleased; and could gratify their tastes and desires without restraint, and without rendering an account to anybody. At last they had found a place in the universe; they were no longer obliged to finish out their faded lives mere burdens to male relatives.[7]

Thus, Robinson generally praised her factory existence, especially the fact that work in the mills could mean a step up the ladder of success and also save a family from destitution.

Her own arrival in Lowell resulted from an ordinary misfortune, the death of a parent. Harriet Hanson was born in Boston in 1825 and six years later her father, a carpenter, died, leaving a widow and four young children. Robinson's mother, also Harriet Hanson, tried supporting the family by running a small general store, but the business failed. Mrs. Hanson heard about the many possibilities available in Lowell from her sister, who ran a boardinghouse owned by the mills. The family moved to Lowell and Mrs. Hanson was able to also gain a position managing a boardinghouse for the mills, taking care of the needs of more than forty workers. At first, young Harriet helped with the housework, but soon it became obvious that the family needed more income, so, at the age of ten, she entered the mills as a "doffer," changing bobbins on spinning frames, working fourteen-hour days in a six-day cycle, with only a half hour for her lunch and another half-hour for dinner. But it was not constant work, and she remembered the many games and good times she had with the other girls in between the times when she had to change bobbins. She recalled it as "a pleasant life," except for "the great hardship" of the long hours for the children.

She stayed in the mills for ten years before leaving to marry William S. Robinson, a journalist. While at the mill she had contributed to its famous literary periodical, *The Lowell Offering*. She went on to have four children, and she became a supporter of women's clubs and a leading suffragist. Besides verse, she wrote four books, her most famous being *Massachusetts in the Woman's Suffrage Movement*.

The paternalistic approach to factory life of the Waltham system caught the attention of European travelers who described the factory system. In 1834, Harriet Martineau, an English visitor wrote:

> I visited the corporate factory establishment of Waltham within a few miles of Boston. The establishment is for spinning and weaving of cotton alone and the construction of the requisite machinery. Five hundred girls were employed at the time of my visit. The girls can earn two and sometimes three dollars a week besides their board. The little children earn one dollar a week. Most of the girls live in houses provided by the corporation . . . they save enough out of their board to clothe themselves and have two or three dollars to spare. Some have thus cleared off mortgages from their father's farms; others have educated the [male] hope of the family at college; and many are rapidly accumulating independence. . . . The people work about seventy hours a week on an average. . . . All look like well-dressed young ladies. The health is good, or rather it is no worse than elsewhere.[8]

It did not take long, however, before the female workers in the factory towns began to express outrage at both the strict paternalism and the wage policies of the factory owners. Increased competition in the textile industry, especially from New York and Pennsylvania, led mill owners to cut wages as the quickest way to lower their costs. Wage cuts alarmed the working girls who depended on fixed wages. The "Daughters of Freemen," like their male counterparts in the workingmen's movement, began to organize against the long hours in poorly ventilated and dangerous factories, speed-ups, regulations, wage cuts, and attacks on their independence. Even Harriet Hanson became upset. Recalling the labor discontent, she later wrote: "One of the first strikes of cotton-factory operatives that ever took place in this country was that in Lowell, in October 1836. When it was announced that the wages were to be cut down, great indignation was felt, and it was decided to strike, en masse. . . . It is hardly necessary to say that so far as results were concerned this strike did no good."[9] For her role in the strike the company punished her by firing her mother from her job of running a boarding-house.

While the orderly Waltham system satisfied the consciences of the Boston Associates by "rescuing" the farm women from the "idleness" of rural life, it had entailed instituting a new labor system that gave employers extensive control over their workers. Strict regulations in boardinghouse and factory were intended to assure that work was done on time and costly work stoppages due to labor unrest were avoided. Supervisors and foremen were all men, who were paid a considerably higher wage than the mill women, which caused resentment among the women. Life in the boardinghouses was controlled by matrons like Harriet Hanson's mother, which limited the mill women's newfound freedom. Behavior was watched closely, codes determined dress habits, church attendance was compulsory, no male visitors were allowed, and the doors were locked at ten o'clock.

Feeling exploited, mill girls like Sarah Bagley became militant. Bagley is one of the ordinary people who appear only briefly in the historical record, make a notable place, and then disappear. There is no listing of her birth or death, but in the 1830s she became one of the first female labor leaders in the nation's history. She seems to have worked in the mills for a while, contributing to the *Lowell Offering*. In 1836, she worked at the Boston Associates' Hamilton Cotton Mills in Lowell, and she was present during the strike in which Harriet Hanson took part. Responding to the rapid decline of working conditions in the mills, Bagley organized a women's labor organization, the Lowell Female Labor Reform Association, in 1845. Starting with a few dozen members, it soon had five hundred and became an important rallying force for the ten-hour workday movement, which had been a worker demand for some years. (The nation's first strike for a ten-hour day was in 1824 by Boston mechanics). Bagley wrote exposés, led petition drives, and did all in her power to publicize the plight of factory women, generally with no immediate success. In 1845 she charged that the company publication, the *Lowell Offering,* was captive to the interests of the owners. She and a few other young women published differing views in local newspapers and in *Voices of Labor,* a male labor journal. Bagley denounced the mill owners for cutting wages that were already too low, for increasing workloads, and for imposing long hours that left little time for social or intellectual pursuits. A pioneer labor organizer, Bagley began the long hard drive for worker equity that was not to come to fruition until well into the twentieth century. By 1847 she had left the mills, become a telegrapher, and, like many other workers, vanished from history.

The high cost of a planned community developed according to the moral principles of an urban elite ran headlong into conflict with the economic imperatives of the 1830s and 1840s. It was not long before the Boston Associates abandoned the Waltham system and sought out a cheaper and more malleable labor supply, one that was not imbued with republican and middle-class expectations. Moreover, the Associates' economic concerns meant that they were required to continue their interest in the political life of Massachusetts, particularly in the center of their power, Boston.

In Boston, the hub of commerce, politics, and administration, production of consumer goods had become the leading occupation. No one regarded Boston as a factory city, nor was it dominated by large-scale industries in the manner of Lowell, Chicopee, or Fall River. Yet as early as 1820 the census had shown a majority of its workers employed in production rather than trade. At that time, in the early decades of the century, shipbuilding and rum distilleries remained the largest industries, and most of the others catered directly to the needs of trade, like barrel making, or else to the urban market. Boston itself grew rapidly after 1790, breaking out from the commercial plateau that had held the population close to 16,000 for two generations since the 1730s. By 1800 Boston grew to 25,000, and in the 1830s, when the population shot past the 60,000 mark, Boston was being transformed into an immense city. By 1860 its population exceeded 180,000, ten times its size in 1790. The political change from town into city was formalized in 1822 by the granting of a new charter. While the Federalist party was doomed as a national party, elite Bostonians maintained their control over the Massachusetts capital. Boston, like the new factory system, needed to enter the modern age. The man responsible for this urban accommodation was Brahmin Josiah Quincy.

Born into the merchant aristocracy in 1772 and the son of the patriot of the same name who died in 1775, the maverick Quincy was to turn himself in a political cult figure who modernized the city of Boston while helping to destroy his own Federalist party. Educated at Phillips Academy and Harvard, where he graduated first in the class of 1790, he practiced law for a few years before entering politics in 1804, when he was elected as a Federalist state senator. Later that year he won election as a U.S. congressman. His years in Congress were controversial and it was in these years that he and Federalist leader Harrison Gray Otis began a lifelong quarrel. The enmity resulted because Quincy sometimes took positions that were ill conceived and repudiated by his own party. To the dismay of his party, in 1811 he joined the war hawks in Congress, mistakenly believing that requiring his fellow representatives to vote on war would force them to pull back from hostilities. When his scheme misfired and they voted for war, he resigned in disgrace in 1813 and returned to Boston.

He spent the next few years dabbling in agriculture and trying to build up political support for his pet ambition, the governorship. To gain that end he mended fences and was elected to the state Senate where he served until he once again upset the Federalist party leaders. In 1820, Federalists tried to use the constitutional convention to separate Republican-dominated Maine from the commonwealth. Their strategy was narrowly political, aimed at ensuring Federalist supremacy in Massachusetts. Quincy was opposed to this tactic and joined forces with a group emerging within both parties, called the Middling Interest, whose purpose was to dislodge the aristocratic Federalist monopoly in Boston and the state as a whole. For his vote against Maine separation, the party punished Quincy by denying him nomination to the state Senate the following year.

Now openly opposed to Federalist leaders, Quincy was able to win election to the Massachusetts House, where the delegates selected him as Speaker because of his growing popularity. Recognizing that his goal of becoming governor was now impossible because of Federalist enmity, he turned his political attention to Boston and what it could offer him. In 1821, he resigned as Speaker of the House and accepted appointment as a Boston municipal court judge. As judge he took several positions that favored the working classes over the interests of the rich, which greatly increased his popularity with the middle-class Middling Interest. His nemesis, Harrison Grey Otis, had already decided that he wanted the governorship for himself and he devised a plan to achieve that end, which eventually worked in Quincy's favor.

Fearful of the increasing influence of the men of the Middling Interest, Otis and his cronies decided to whittle away their position by centralizing power in the town of Boston. Their scheme was to change the charter and make Boston a city with a mayor and legislative council, doing away with the unwieldy and more democratic town meeting. The plan called for Otis himself to become the first mayor, and then from there to move on to the governor's office. Otis and his allies succeeded in turning Boston into a city, over Quincy's and the Middling Interest's opposition. But to Otis's dismay, in the first mayoral race in 1822, Quincy ran against him as an independent, supported by a Middling Interest made up of Republicans and unhappy Federalists. Both candidates were unable to obtain the necessary majority to win and they both withdrew allowing a compromise candidate, John Phillips, to become the first mayor of Boston. Swept into office with Phillips was the Middling Interest's slate of aldermen and councillors.

The lackluster and ailing Phillips satisfied no one. Moreover, a significant portion of the city's Federalists feared their loss of control over the city. In 1823, a new election was scheduled and the prominent candidate seemed to be Quincy. To guarantee victory, by stealing a march on the Middling Interest, the Central Federalist party now offered the party's nomination for mayor to the once cast-out Josiah Quincy. Otis was enraged and publicly announced he would not vote for Quincy. Quincy narrowly won the election by getting most of the Federalist votes and about half of the Middling Interest votes. The shrewd Quincy recognized that to stay in power he would need to rid himself of any party ties and create a coalition of the disaffected of all parties and classes based on the power and strength of his personality and character.

While at the apex of his power, he began his mayoralty by marshaling popular support against the city's several standing commissions that were in the way of centralized decision making. Going way beyond the charter, Quincy strengthened his authority and began an urban renewal process that was to change the face of Boston. He reformed the volunteer fire corps, hired more police constables, took charge of public health matters, ordered that streets be swept and paved, introduced a municipal water system, created a House of Industry to separate debtors from criminals, and revamped the crowded market district by initiating a project that resulted in the Faneuil (or Quincy) Market. Quincy, afterward dubbed the "Great Mayor" by historians, led the transformation of a backwater colonial town into a modern urban center. After five one-year terms (1823–27) he had created enemies who complained about his dictatorial ways, and he was defeated in 1828. Quincy went on to an appointment as president of Harvard University in 1829, where he served until he resigned in 1849 at the age of seventy-six. He spent his declining years in literary endeavors and died at ninety-two in Boston, on July 1, 1864. His service as mayor of Boston is noted not only for impressive public accomplishments, but also for his part in finally destroying that bastion of conservatism, the Federalist party.

The Federalist party died in the 1820s, and if Josiah Quincy was the man most responsible for its decline in Boston, it was his cousin, the leading political figure of Massachusetts, John Quincy Adams, who undermined it at the state level. The eldest son of president John Adams, John Quincy Adams symbolized the shifting party structure of the times and the difficulties that arose among Massachusetts elites who fought each other over local and national issues. For example, although Quincy and Harrison Gray Otis were rivals, Otis and Adams hated each other. Otis never forgave Adams for ditching the Federalist party and its platform to become a follower of Thomas Jefferson. Adams keenly felt the stinging criticism articulated by the vengeful Otis and his Federalist cohorts. His response was to destroy the Federalists once and for all.

Adams was many things, certainly an intellectual and devoted public servant, but he was also a curmudgeon who badgered one of his sons so badly that gossips contended Adams goaded him to suicide. A stickler for duty, he was pugnacious and quarrelsome, even if he ended up a loser defending unpopular causes. Such "lost causes," however, often triumphed later on, after Adams had left the political arena. Born in Braintree in 1767, his life seemed to be an endless struggle to measure up to the high standards set by his famous father and ambitious mother, Abigail. In 1781, at the precocious age of fourteen, he started his public career by becoming secretary to the U.S. minister to Russia, and the following year he worked in that capacity for his father, who was minister to Britain. He attended Harvard, graduating in 1787. Later his father, the vice president, encouraged his appointment as minister to the Netherlands in 1794 and minister to Prussia in 1797. When President John Adams lost the presidency to Jefferson in 1800, his son had to leave Washington with him. But family connections helped Adams's election to the Massachusetts Senate in 1802. The seeming heir to a major political future, Adams was elected the next year by the Federalist Massachusetts legislature to the U.S. Senate.

Demonstrating the rash streak of independence that epitomized his life, he began taking positions that the Federalist leaders back home found intolerable. He infuriated his party by voting for Jefferson's purchase of Louisiana. But the moment of crisis came when he voted for Jefferson's Embargo Act of 1807; that was anathema to New England merchants. Furious at his maverick stance, Massachusetts's Federalist-dominated legislature ordered him to vote for the repeal of the embargo in 1808. To the horror of his friends, and the everlasting enmity of Harrison Grey Otis, he refused. Instead, he resigned and joined Jefferson's Republican party.

Spurned by the Federalists, the Republicans grudgingly took him into their fold and appointed him to various diplomatic posts where he would do the least harm. Recognizing his expertise in foreign affairs, Republican president James Monroe honored Adams by appointing him as secretary of state in 1817, a position that was widely viewed as a stepping stone to the presidency. All the while he was gathering supporters in the Republican and Federalist parties in a bid to satisfy the wishes of his father, and take back the presidency for the Adams family.

To achieve this goal meant destroying the old, now discredited Federalist party, which he did by organizing a new party, the National Republicans. Under this banner, he ran for the presidency in 1824, contending against another ex-Republican, Andrew Jackson, who also created a new party, the Democrats. In the confusion of party ebb and flow, others joined the race—two Democratic-Republicans, Henry Clay and William Crawford. Jackson won the most electoral votes, with Adams placing second. However, Jackson did not receive the necessary majority required by the Constitution, so the choice was thrown to the House of Representatives for a decision. There Clay worked an accommodation with Adams, and the second-place contender was elected president of the United States. Once again Massachusetts led the nation.

Forgetting that compromise had won the day, Adams initiated a nationalist federal program that was not well received by Clay and his Jeffersonian Republicans. Adams called for many changes, among them the creation of a national system of canals, turnpikes, and railroads, the establishment of a national university and a naval academy, federal support for exploration of the western territories, and the setting up of a uniform system of weights and measure. Parts of this farsighted and progressive program were not enacted until years later, and in office Adams's administration was divided by bitter infighting and petty quarrels.

Adams possessed few leadership abilities suitable to the give-and-take of American popular politics and his National Republican party was unable to marshal sufficient support to win his reelection in 1828. Losing to Andrew Jackson, who ran a populist, national campaign, the disappointed Adams returned to Massachusetts in virtual disgrace. But to the surprise of everyone, and to his own delight, the people of his home district south of Boston elected him to Congress in 1830. The following year, Adams quit the National Republicans to become an Anti-Mason. Subsequently he had an important congressional career, usually standing alone attacking the southern "slavemasters" and their policies. He was also an advocate before the Supreme Court for the liberty of the *Amistad* captives.

One of Adams's most famous victories was against the "gag rule." In the 1830s, abolitionist sentiment in the North led to a fierce southern reaction. The South showed its political power when southern congressmen were able to pass, in 1836, a gag rule that forbade presenting the petitions of abolitionists, or reading from them in the House of Representatives. Adams along with many northern whites was outraged that freedom of speech should be destroyed by the slavocracy, and he led a long campaign for its repudiation. Fighting virtually alone, Adams devised a series of parliamentary strategies to bring the issue up for debate. Withstanding threats against him, including expulsion from the House, Adams's persistent struggle gradually won support from a growing number of northern abolitionists, and in 1844 he succeeded in persuading the House to abolish the gag rule. "Old Man Eloquent," as he was dubbed, often opposed the Whigs as well, led by Massachusetts senator Daniel Webster and Adams's old colleague Henry Clay.

Contentious to the end, Adams died in harness when he suffered a stroke and collapsed on the House floor after delivering a vote on February 21, 1848. He died two days later. Although he found it difficult to work well with others and to make the compromises necessary for political success, John Quincy Adams of Massachusetts was a brilliant, principled advocate, a skilled diplomat, and farsighted policy maker who was instrumental in changing party structures in the Bay State and the nation. His advocacy of abolition and equal rights was instrumental in promoting equality for all.

It was the state's patricians who provided the wealth and leadership to transform the Commonwealth of Massachusetts into an urban and industrial society. Along the way, some of them, like Josiah Quincy and John Quincy Adams, brought liberty and justice to Massachusetts and the nation, as well as prosperity. Motivated by the principles of revolutionary Republicanism and by a Christian sense of moral steward-ship, they funded private charities as well as providing monetary sup-port for public institutions. The Perkins School for the Blind, the state reform school, Boston's Children's Infirmary and Hospital, the Young Men's Benevolent Association, the Boston Provident Association, the Massachusetts Charitable Congregational Society, Massachusetts Gen-eral Hospital, and the Board of Overseers of the Poor in Boston were all beneficiaries of their social philanthropy. They made cultural contri-butions by supporting Harvard, the Boston Athenaeum (a private li-brary), the Massachusetts Historical Society, the *North American Re-view* and the *Atlantic Monthly,* the Boston Academy of Music, and a host of public libraries, Bible societies, and Sunday schools. Most of these philanthropists calculated their vision of service to serve their no-tion of a stable and harmonious community in which their own inter-ests were secure. The new industrial and urban system they created, however, would generate challenges to their hegemony that would even-tually lead to their eclipse as shapers of the destiny of the Bay State. The first such assault on them came not from the new working classes, but from reform-minded Protestants bent on a mission to cleanse the "impure" conditions emerging in Massachusetts.

# CHAPTER 7

# Missions to the Nation

T HE FIRST HALF OF THE NINETEENTH CENTURY IN
America was an age of paradoxes. Physical expansion, economic
development, and material prosperity nourished boundless optimism,
while at the same time evangelical preachers proclaimed to millions of
eager listeners that depravity and corruption lurked everywhere. Perfec-
tionist optimism flourished alongside millenarian gloom. Americans
celebrated individual self-assertion and autonomy, while they urged
others to conform. Libertarian beliefs echoed from pulpits and plat-
forms, as did eloquent apologias for the virtues of both chattel slavery
and wage labor. Individualism and corporatism prospered, as did com-
mitments to egalitarianism and hierarchy. America was a society where
contradictory impulses fed repeated conflicts.

In the minds of contemporaries these were struggles between fundamental truths, commanding loyalties that erased the boundaries between states. When the future of the nation, perhaps all mankind, was
at stake, one's attachment to a single locality was overshadowed. It was
in this context that Massachusetts, like other states, began to lose its
particular identity. More than in most places, the people of the Bay
State became involved with the general issues that excited concern. Indeed Massachusetts emerged as a nursery for the missionaries of a hundred causes. The dollars-and-cents commercial and industrial energies
of Massachusetts people, which sent their products all over the United
States, found a counterpart in the religious and social activism that
spread their ideas and doctrines across the continent. Massachusetts
was the metropolis of New England during the era of that region's cul-

tural imperialism. Though Massachusetts's distinctiveness was waning, its people put their stamp on the culture of the American republic.

They were concerned with everything. Some embraced highly controversial, divisive causes like abolition, temperance, and women's rights, while others pursued objectives that were broadly appealing: improved education, moral reform, and higher standards of public health and personal hygiene. Advocacy of a cause was always clothed in benevolence, but traces of partisan, denominational competition showed through. Advocates of every ideal were propelled onward by a spirit of optimism. Even the most apocalyptic visionaries raised their voices, confident that people could act to save themselves and their fellows. The promoters of prison reform and therapeutic care of the physically and mentally handicapped represented the quintessential merger of the optimism and altruism that were widely evident. Such movements transcended Massachusetts, but they were shaped by people who had not only been born and raised there, but who also had begun their public careers confronting the failings of their native commonwealth. Their criticisms of American society began at home, in the state where rapid social and economic changes made the contradictions between individual and collective goals and between new aspirations and old values especially acute.

The sensitivity to the faults of this world as well as the belief that people must actively intervene to erase them had both secular and religious origins. The republicanism of the early national era was profoundly moralistic, and virtue—private and public—was one of its fundamental tenets. The United States, if it possessed virtue, would become a utopia of liberty, justice, and social happiness; therefore the good citizen was obliged to cultivate improvements in a public as well as a personal way. The Second Great Awakening, which emerged in the 1790s and endured for several decades, prescribed a kind of piety that was parallel to this civic virtue. Moreover the awakening generated a contagious energy and immediacy to the drive for virtue. In peacetime, as patriotic fervor waned, the ambition for salvation more than took up the slack. Gospel piety, even more than patriotism, propelled people to seek out others and exhort and persuade them to support virtuous causes.

Like the first Great Awakening, the evangelical movement of the early nineteenth century had no political boundaries. In Massachusetts the movement had no central leader nor any particular geographic source. Everywhere the second half of the eighteenth century had witnessed a decline in religious concern and a tendency toward a placid Arminianism, where ethical conduct and sober respectability were sufficient for grace. In the more cosmopolitan towns in eastern Massachusetts, this turn away from orthodox Calvinism had become a trend, and even before 1800 a liberal (in the sense of nonsectarian) Unitarianism was evident in a handful of congregations. In Massachusetts, the second Great Awakening was an effort to reverse this trend, to reestablish divine will, conversion, and faith as the essence of Christianity. Whether Congregational, Baptist, or Methodist, this was the crucial objective.

The conflict between religious liberals and conservatives lasted for generations and was fought in thousands of communities across the United States, and in hundreds in Massachusetts. But the single most important battlefield in the Bay State was Harvard College, still the training school for Congregational Massachusetts. The struggle began in 1803 when David Tappan (uncle of the abolitionists Arthur and Lewis Tappan) died, thus vacating the Hollis Professorship of Divinity. By this time the faculty of Harvard and its trustees were evenly divided into orthodox and Unitarian factions, and the Hollis professorship promised to tip the balance decisively one way or the other. For two years the professorship remained vacant as the battle raged in college halls and drawing rooms. Finally, in 1805, the Unitarians triumphed, naming one of their own, the Hingham pastor Henry Ware, to the post. Pressing their advantage, they replaced the acting president, who was orthodox, with another Unitarian. Defeated, the Calvinist trustees and faculty resigned from the college in a storm of protest, and Unitarianism became the new Harvard orthodoxy. Until the Civil War and beyond, Harvard would remain the principal beacon of the "Christian Enlightenment" in America and the school for numerous social commentators and reformers.

The orthodox retreated from Harvard, but they were not defeated. Although their resources were dispersed, their supporters were numerous and intensely devoted. Within two years they had created a rival theological college at Andover, financed chiefly by people from Newburyport, Salem, and Andover. In 1808 they admitted the first class, housed in a new four-story brick building. From the outset they flourished, and so by the 1820s the school was expanded to accommodate more than sixty students, drawn from several colleges, principally Williams, Yale, and later Amherst. Andover became a center of the awakening in Massachusetts and a focal point for a whole range of missionary endeavors.

The New England Tract Society, founded at Andover in 1814, was to serve as a starting place for numerous efforts on behalf of virtue. English evangelists had already demonstrated that distributing tracts by the millions was both practical and effective. The New England society, renamed the American Tract Society in the 1820s, was built on the premise that "god has made every man responsible for the use or abuse of his personal influence," and everyone was "sacredly bound to employ it in doing good." Cheap tracts enabled all Christians to do the work of salvation actively. For people who were personally diffident, for anyone who lacked "the talent of talking to those he meets with, especially to strangers, on subject of religion," the tracts offered *"an easy way of doing good."*[1] The movement to place uplifting homilies in the hands of the masses was led by clergymen who were often distribution agents, but the dues-paying members who enlisted in the cause were mostly laymen, merchants, shopkeepers, lawyers, teachers, and middle-class farmers and artisans. A mood of pious condescension toward those who were too ignorant or too poor to provide themselves with the gospel pervaded the movement.

The problems of lack of faith, obviously, were not unique to Massachusetts, and the objectives of the founders were national in scope. But the motivation for the society and the methods it adopted were closely related to the growing commercialization and urbanization of the state. More people were "free-floating" in society, unattached to any church. As commerce and travel expanded and village populations rose, the pious became more aware of profaneness in the behavior and beliefs of others. At the same time the expanded commercial network and the ready access to the printing press made the idea of mass distribution of tracts feasible. In a few years thousands of people in Massachusetts, both men and women, would be contributing their pennies, dimes, and dollars to a cause that relied on a Christian cosmopolitanism that had been almost unknown in eighteenth-century communities.

In one sense, however, the national and even global objectives of

Massachusetts organizations like the tract society and the later American Bible Society and the Sunday School Union were highly provincial in that Massachusetts virtue became the standard for people everywhere. Winthrop's old vision of Massachusetts as a city upon a hill was revived and extended so that not only would Massachusetts become the model to be admired and emulated from afar, but its citizens would personally sally forth to awaken those who slumbered, whether in New York, Ohio, or the Ottoman Empire. The missionary activities spawned in the Second Great Awakening would influence the character of penal reform, temperance reform, and many other secular endeavors.

The viewpoint of religious liberals was more thoroughly cosmopolitan. With their headquarters at Boston, the commercial hub of New England, the Unitarians were appropriately tolerant and urbane. Their foremost leader, William Ellery Channing, was a native of the sophisticated, pluralistic seaport, Newport, Rhode Island. Channing had come to Harvard for college in the 1790s, and after a brief period as a schoolmaster in Richmond, Virginia, returned permanently to Boston in 1803 as pastor of the Federal Street Church. From this prestigious pulpit Channing came to exert a profound influence on young reformers and intellectuals in eastern Massachusetts. Many of them—Ralph Waldo Emerson and Theodore Parker, Horace Mann and Charles Sumner, Dorothea Dix and Thomas Wentworth Higginson—regarded him as their mentor for a time, and after his death in 1842 Channing was described as "the saint of the Unitarians."[2] Channing's ideas were complex, but at their core lay a simple faith in the necessity of supporting universal truths that were, by their nature, good. Reason and morality permitted humankind to distinguish good and evil, and it was everyone's responsibility to be a moral agent. Though the inspiration was different from Cotton Mather's, the injunction was the same: to do good.

Both the Christian conservatives and the liberals placed great confidence in the individual's ability to grasp the truth and to develop self-discipline. Moreover, even though the Calvinists were pessimistic about the essential nature of humanity, they were hopeful that untold millions could be saved by God's grace. In this setting nearly everyone was taught at an early age to make personal moral judgments and was pressed to develop an active conscience, no matter what his or her denomination, social class, or community. The missionary generation of antebellum Massachusetts was nurtured in an era of strong partisan identities in politics and religion. The willingness to advocate one's beliefs, to stand up and be counted, was a normal requirement of growing up.

Missionaries and reformers were born in all parts of the commonwealth, from the eastern district of Maine to Berkshire County. Yet Boston was a major site for most of their activities. Boston, after all, was the seat of state government and possessed the greatest concentration of population and wealth. It was also the chief communication center for New England. Moreover Boston's rapid growth during the first half of the century made its problems of poverty, drunkenness, and crime especially conspicuous. Some of the causes espoused by reformers were universal and had no particular connection to urban or industrial development, but because Boston was increasingly becoming the central metropolis, it was a place to launch movements and was a magnet for them.

Dorothea Lynde Dix, born in the frontier town of Hampden, Maine, in 1802, was descended from prominent Boston and Worcester families, but her own parents were poor, and she learned to endure hardships early. Her mother suffered chronically from poor health, and her father, who had no head for business, became an itinerant Methodist preacher who was frequently away from home. Until she was twelve, Dorothea Dix often had charge of her two younger brothers, but then her grandmother Dix intervened and moved Dorothea to Boston to live with her. Two years later she was sent to live with a great aunt in Worcester, and it was there that her talents began to emerge. In her great aunt's barn, at the age of fourteen, Dorothea opened a school to teach poor children their *abc*'s. Although she was herself largely self-taught, Dix would later make a career in Boston as a schoolmistress. Her first published writings would be a children's textbook in science and a collection of poetry designed for children. Then, in the late 1820s, she became governess in the family of her new pastor, William Ellery Channing. Under Channing's influence, Dix became an author of liberal devotional writings for youth, and in the 1830s she opened a school of her own in Boston. In 1836, however, she suffered a nervous breakdown and was forced to give up the school. When her doctor prescribed travel, she visited the British Isles, staying with Channing's acquaintances. It was here that she first became seriously aware of humane methods of caring for people who were mentally disturbed. Dix returned to Boston the following year and, supported by her grandmother's legacy, spent several years visiting friends, traveling, and "resting."

Dix's "conversion" to the work of a reformer occurred in 1841 when, at the request of a Harvard divinity student, she volunteered to teach a Sunday school class to the women in the East Cambridge jail. Here she discovered disturbed women who were treated cruelly although they were guilty of no crime. Dix identified with these forlorn souls, and she was outraged. Immediately she took the matter to the Middlesex Court, and to Channing's friend Samuel Gridley Howe, who supported her cause in the press. Here Dix won her first victory, and the jail was renovated, the better to accommodate the mentally ill.

For Dorothea Dix this was all new and exciting, but actually others had been working for a generation to provide not merely humane conditions, but genuinely therapeutic care for people who suffered with mental sickness. In 1818 a private hospital, McLean, had been opened at Charlestown, and in the same period Louis Dwight's Boston Prison Discipline Society had been working to improve conditions in jails and in the treatment of inmates and to separate the poor, the sick, and the juveniles from criminal convicts. During the years when Dix was running her school, Horace Mann was leading the movement in the General Court to create a state mental hospital, and in 1833 it was opened at Worcester. Six years later it was already overcrowded, so Boston established its own lunatic asylum. Thus Dorothea Dix, who became involved with the cause of the mentally ill in 1841, was a latecomer to a movement that had scored major advances in Massachusetts and several other states. Yet it was she who transformed the cause into a national campaign by her contagious zeal, her audacity, and her masterful appeals to public opinion. Encouraged by Howe and Channing, Dix began by making a thorough personal inspection of every jail and almshouse in the entire commonwealth. For eighteen months she traveled from town to town making herself the unrivaled expert on the actual conditions that prevailed. Then, in 1843, she presented the legislature with a devastating written report on the cruelty, degradation, and disease that she had found. Weeks later the General Court voted the funds to expand Worcester State Hospital, in spite of arguments that such a policy represented a further unwarranted expansion of the state government and its budget at the expense of the towns.

With this victory, Dorothea Dix became something of a celebrity among reformers, and she was soon in demand in other states. In 1844 and 1845 she extended her investigations to Rhode Island, New York, and New Jersey, in each case preparing a muckraking report that called on the legislatures of those states to follow Massachusetts's example and create (or expand) a state mental hospital. Her *Remarks on Prison and Prison Discipline in the United States* (1845) was widely read, and during the next several years Dix was active in southern states— Kentucky, Maryland, Mississippi, Alabama, Tennessee, and North Carolina—as well as northern ones—Pennsylvania, Ohio, and Illinois. Though singlehandedly she could never arouse a legislature to action, her influence was formidable, and in 1848 she set her sights on the creation of a national trust to finance a program to care for disturbed people throughout the country. The public lands were being used to finance schools and railroads, Dix argued, so why not mental hospitals? In time the scheme won support, passing both the House and the Senate in 1854. But President Franklin Pierce, echoing the arguments that had been heard in Massachusetts and elsewhere, asserted this would be an improper extension of national powers. The problem, he said, belonged to the states, and he vetoed the bill.

Dix was sadly defeated, and as she had twenty years before, she turned to Europe. Now, however, she needed no introductions. Soon she became involved in promoting the cause in Scotland and all over the Continent, from France to Russia and even into the Ottoman Empire. Before she returned to America, Dix had pressed her views on a wide array of dignitaries, including Pope Pius IX. No one from Massachusetts, and no American woman had ever possessed such a far-reaching influence in the United States and abroad.

Yet by the late 1850s the American effort on behalf of treatment for the mentally ill was largely spent. Even in Massachusetts the public hospitals had become custodial welfare institutions for the indigent, rather than centers of medical treatment. Dix and her colleagues had eliminated the worst physical abuses, and they had succeeded in liberating their charges from jails, but they could not fulfill the promise of therapeutic care. It was beyond the reach of taxpayer support and also largely beyond the capability of psychiatric medicine. The state mental hospitals that were Dix's legacy—she was directly involved in the creation of over thirty around the country—were a distinct improvement over local cellars and outbuildings, but lacking the capacity for treatment, they gradually became prisons of a sort, where society hid its least fortunate people from view. Dix's crusade had been founded on the optimism of her generation, a faith that flourished in the early decades of the century.

Samuel Gridley Howe was just a year older than Dorothea Dix, but his upbringing and gender gave him a very different start. In contrast to Dix, Howe began with opportunities. He was born into a well-to-do Boston family and educated at Boston Latin School. He would have attended Harvard; however, his father, who was fed up with stuffy Federalists, broke with convention and sent Samuel to Brown, where he was a contemporary of Horace Mann. Upon graduation in 1821, Howe returned to Boston to enroll in the Harvard Medical School. But he did not pursue a medical career in the usual way. Indeed Howe quickly distinguished himself as the archetypal romantic, albeit a Massachusetts Yankee. When his studies were complete, he did not open an office, but enlisted instead on behalf of the Greek war of independence from Turkey. He sailed to the Mediterranean where he became a soldier and surgeon who for six years fought with and cared for the Greek and Polish revolutionaries. He also led a fund-raising drive in Massachusetts and throughout the United States so that the cause of independent republicanism could triumph in distant lands.

When Howe returned to Boston at the age of thirty, he had had his fill of swashbuckling heroics and the destructiveness of warfare. Possessing independent means, he turned to philanthropy at the most intimate level by creating a school for six blind children in his own home. Before departing from Europe he had studied treatments for the blind that were being used in England, France, and Germany, and so had begun to prepare himself. During the next forty-five years Howe would continue his work with blind children, developing techniques that would be employed all over the country.

Initially he created a system of raised lettering that allowed his students to learn the alphabet and then to read. In these early years Howe was eager to demonstrate that blind children actually could be taught to read, and so he exhibited the children's achievements to gatherings around the state. Thomas Handasyd Perkins, a wealthy merchant-capitalist who witnessed one such exhibition, was so impressed by Howe's work that he offered to donate his mansion for use as a school, provided Bostonians would raise fifty thousand dollars to sustain the institution. The appeal of Howe and the children was so moving among the Boston bourgeoisie that Perkins's terms were quickly met, and the school expanded, becoming the Perkins Institute.

It was here in 1837 that Howe scored the most remarkable success, teaching Laura Bridgman, an eight-year-old who was not only blind but also deaf and dumb, to communicate. When she was brought to Howe, she knew only a primitive, homemade sign language that conveyed her most basic needs and responses like "yes" and "no." But Howe, defying the prevailing view that anything more was impossible, set out to teach her the alphabet, and then to label common household objects with raised lettering so that Laura could connect words that she could not hear with objects she could not see. For months they worked on it, and Laura came to master the system, but only in a mechanical way. At last, however, "the truth began to flash upon her: her intellect began to work: she perceived that here was a way by which she could herself make up a sign of anything that was in her own mind, and show it to another mind." Howe and Laura were ecstatic: "At once her countenance lighted up with a human expression: it was no longer a dog or a parrot: it was an immortal spirit, eagerly seizing upon a new link of union with other spirits!"[3] Laura Bridgman had rewarded the physician whose therapy rested more on humanitarian faith than on scientific knowledge.

In contrast to Dorothea Dix, whose achievements in Massachusetts launched a national career, Howe stayed rooted in the commonwealth although his influence and example were widely recognized. In the mid-1840s he actively worked on legislation to improve systems of training for the deaf, collaborating with Horace Mann. At the same time Howe took up the cause of mentally retarded children—idiots, as they were then called.

As an investigator for a state commission Howe visited sixty towns and personally examined hundreds of afflicted children. His final report appealed to the legislature to provide for the children with kindness and decency. In 1848 Howe's efforts led to the creation of a state program for retarded children at the Perkins Institute. He also worked to provide foster homes for juvenile delinquents. For Samuel Gridley Howe no human being was beyond redemption.

The final decade in Howe's odyssey of good works was spent as president of the Massachusetts Board of State Charities as well as head of the Perkins Institute. As board president Howe was to lead in establishing rational, systematic policy and administration for the congeries of public welfare institutions that had been created in the state during his lifetime to care for people who were sick, disabled, poor, and criminal. By now Howe's enduring optimism had become old-fashioned, and a snobbish, pessimistic determinism that linked mental illness, poverty, crime, and breeding was coming into vogue. Incarceration, "to protect society," was the new policy, which Howe could never really accept. For Howe the good of each individual, even blind, dumb Laura Bridgman, defined the corporate good. Howe hated large, bureaucratic, custodial institutions. He believed that "the care and treatment of the dependent and vicious classes" should be diffused throughout society, in homes and workshops, churches and schools. "We should enlist," Howe argued, "the greatest number of individuals and families in the care and treatment of the dependent"; public institutions should be kept small and used "only in the last resort."[4] Penny-pinching legislators all around the United States would pervert Howe's intentions and use his words to justify skimpy budgets. After the Civil War, Howe's romantic optimism, grounded on personal commitment and faith in humanity, had become anachronistic in social-welfare programs. When Samuel Gridley Howe died in the centennial year of 1876, some of the utopian hopes of the Revolutionary era died with him.

Both Howe and Dix fought uphill struggles for decades against the inertia of old habits and institutions and against people who believed they were impractical and naive. In political forums they had been met with resistance from those who begrudged the cost of reform and those who believed that government had no business assuming responsibilities that could be left to private individuals and agencies. Yet however controversial their proposals, their objectives—the care of mentally ill and physically disabled people—did not assault popular sensibilities or prevailing values. Their reforms operated within a broad consensus of charitable attitudes, and so they never excited harsh antagonisms. Other Massachusetts missionaries were less fortunate. When they came to espouse the rights of women and the liberation of slaves as part of the fulfillment of individual rights promised by the Revolution, they were treading on the personal values and interests of millions of their fellow citizens, so they aroused bitter, even violent hostilities. What was needed to maintain their advocacy was a powerful inner sense of the truth and the reinforcement, psychological and material, of some like-minded people. In the Bay State they found what they needed, and as the Pilgrims and Puritans who first settled Massachusetts had done, they proceeded according to their own unpopular convictions.

One of the most vigorous, effective pioneers of the women's movement was Lucy Stone, who was born in 1818 at West Brookfield in the western part of Worcester County. Her family was comfortably well off by local standards; her father, the son of an officer in the Revolution and in Shays's Rebellion, ran a farm and a tannery with his wife and eight children. Lucy was raised as an orthodox Congregationalist, and she was a pious child. However, in her early teens she began to question, particularly the doctrine that men should rule over women. She suspected the Bible was being misinterpreted, so she resolved to learn Greek and Hebrew to enable her to judge the question for herself. But because her father believed such subjects were not fit for a girl, she had to content herself with English, and at the age of sixteen she took a job as teacher in a local district. Lucy Stone used her earnings to further her own education at academies in the neighboring town of Warren and in Wilbraham, about twenty miles west. When she was twenty-one, she was ready to enter Mount Holyoke Female Seminary at South Hadley. Stone studied there for several years and then, seemingly the perpetual student, she moved to Ohio to enter Oberlin College in 1843. The journey was justified because at Oberlin, the first coeducational college, Lucy Stone could pursue her biblical studies. Oberlin itself was a western outpost of a whole range of Yankee causes, especially evangelical piety and abolitionism. Since Stone had been a reader of abolitionist writings for the past decade, Oberlin's climate of opinion was congenial.

At Oberlin, Stone learned Greek and Hebrew and realized her ambition to reexamine scriptural statements on the relations of the sexes. Her conclusion, that absolute sovereignty over women distorted the true gospel, fed her feminism and fostered her challenge to the limitations that even Oberlin placed on women. At the time of her commencement in 1849, when she became the first Massachusetts woman to graduate from a classical college, Stone refused to prepare a public address because the school officials insisted that one of her male colleagues would have to deliver it, as it would be inappropriate for a woman to speak to a public meeting.

A few months later Lucy Stone's career in public speaking began when her brother, a minister at Gardner in the northern tier of Worcester County, took the radical step of inviting her to speak from his pulpit. Now William Lloyd Garrison, who had met Stone at the Oberlin commencement, took her on as a lecturer from the American Anti-Slavery Society. Because of her gender, she drew crowds as a curiosity; but her earnest rhetoric was persuasive. Stone's emphasis, however, quickly moved from the cause of slaves to the ideologically related question of women's rights. As she put it: "I was a woman before I was an abolitionist. I must speak for the women."[5] Within a year she was an active feminist, taking a leading role in calling the first National Women's Rights convention, which met at Worcester in 1850. It was here that Stone met her contemporary Susan B. Anthony, a native of Adams in Berkshire County. Anthony was not yet a committed feminist, and Stone's oratory had a powerful effect on her.

A few years later, in the 1850s, Lucy Stone was dismissed from her orthodox church because of her controversial speaking career on behalf of women and abolition. Soon after, she became a Unitarian. When she married in 1855, it was the Unitarian abolitionist Thomas Wentworth Higginson who performed the radical ceremony in which Stone and her husband, Henry Blackwell, protested the marriage laws of Massachusetts, which subjected a wife and her property to the control of the husband. As a symbol of her independent identity, Lucy Stone did not take Blackwell's name, although their daughter Alice, born two years later, did.

During the Civil War, Stone curtailed her public career to devote herself to the nurture of little Alice. As the child grew older, Stone returned to promoting women's rights, which, now that blacks were enfranchised, centered on the suffrage. In 1869 she settled in the Dorchester section of Boston, and she spent the rest of her life there, serving as an executive of the American Woman Suffrage Association and, with her husband and daughter, publishing the *Woman's Journal*. Between them, Lucy Stone and, after her graduation from Boston University in 1881, Alice Stone Blackwell made their journal into the oracle of the women's movement for half a century.

The feminist cause that Stone proclaimed was not a distinctly Massachusetts movement. Yet a roll call of its major figures includes a disproportionate share of Massachusetts people: the author Lydia Maria Child; the lecturer Abby Kelley Foster; the essayist and critic Margaret Fuller; and the physician Harriot K. Hunt. Although the majority of women in Massachusetts, as elsewhere, accepted their subordination to men in varying degrees, many refused to, believing that their individual, independent identities must be realized. As long ago as 1776 a member of their grandmothers' generation, Abigail Adams, had issued a warning. "Remember the Ladies," she said, for "if particular care and attention is not paid to the Laidies we are determined to foment a Rebellion, and will not hold ourselves bound by any Laws in which we have no voice, or Representation."[6] In Massachusetts, where the Revolution was recalled with reverence, women found encouragement for proclaiming the libertarian message of those heroic times. The united front of men and women who had always in the past asserted traditional female subordination, cracked. Men joined women in advocating civil rights for their mothers, their sisters, and their daughters.

The question of women's rights, after all, was not considered in isolation from the whole range of reform objectives. The drive for women's suffrage and property rights gained momentum in the wake of the movement to eliminate property requirements for voters, to end the religious establishment in Massachusetts (which was done in 1833), and to abolish imprisonment for debt. The reformers, Channing, Dix, Howe, and Stone, as well as others, tried to press the whole range of humanitarian and libertarian reforms to fulfillment.

They were met, however, by powerful opposition and widespread indifference. An ideology of "Christian Capitalism," which was wedded to individual and corporate profit seeking, as well as pragmatic popular desires to "get ahead," combined to elevate the selfish pursuit of gain. Concern for others was shouldered aside in favor of economic interests throughout the United States. In Massachusetts these attitudes had been growing for more than a generation. They were rooted in the Yankee commercial tradition and in the justifications that had surrounded the economic development which transformed the state between 1800 and 1860. At the same time Massachusetts was the breeding ground of reform missionaries, it was also a center for capitalist ideology. In 1837, the year when Wendell Phillips rose to prominence in abolition, his old mentor, Justice Joseph Story, was sitting in judgment in the United States Supreme Court on the Charles River Bridge case, a keystone for corporate devolpment. If the bridge at Concord was a shrine in the crusade for liberty, then this bridge from Boston to Cambridge became a landmark on the road toward democratic, laissez-faire capitalism. During the antebellum era, in addition to altruistic causes, people from Massachusetts were becoming missionaries for a capitalism clad in Christian robes.

Harvard became the college of capitalism. From the 1820s onward, Boston businessmen established their supremacy over the administration and even the faculty. Josiah Quincy, the ex-mayor of Boston, was appointed president, ending the long line of clergymen who had led the college in the past. Faculty members who worked strenuously on behalf of reform causes became unwelcome in the eyes of the trustees, and in 1835, the year of the anti-abolition "Garrison mob," one professor was fired after publishing a pamphlet endorsing abolition. Financially, Harvard became dependent on the munificence of great capitalists like the Appletons, Cabots, Lawrences, and Lowells, who valued classical and scientific learning, but resented any threat to their Whig social, political, and economic views. Being elitist in principle as well as practice, such men would never resort to the "vulgar propaganda" of the advocates of temperance, women's rights, or abolition; but they did underwrite professorships and textbooks. These men were the sponsors of Francis Bowen, the Harvard professor whose book *The Principles of Political Economy* (1856) was dedicated to "A Highly Honored Class, THE MERCHANT PRINCES OF BOSTON, Who Have Earned Success By Sagacity, Enterprise, and Uprightness In All Their Undertakings."[7] For a generation of American college students, Bowen's *Political Economy* was a standard text.

Francis Bowen, born in Charlestown in 1811, the same year as abolitionist Wendell Phillips, did not enjoy Phillips's advantages. After attending school in Boston and taking a term at the Phillips Academy in Exeter, New Hampshire, he became a publisher's clerk, then briefly taught school before entering Harvard. After graduation in 1833 he returned to Exeter to teach mathematics. In 1839 Harvard hired Bowen as a tutor. When John Gorham Palfrey resigned as editor of the *North American Review* a few years later, the Whigs who financed the *Review* brought Bowen in as editor. This was the platform from which Bowen launched his career as philosopher, littérateur, and spokesman for Christian capitalism.

Ten years later his distinguished record for wide-ranging, socially approved scholarship was rewarded by appointment to the Harvard faculty as Alvord Professor of Natural Religion, Moral Philosophy, and Civil Polity. As professor of natural religion, Bowen enjoyed wide latitude with respect to theology, and indeed his intellectual orientation was far more secular than religious. A careful and critical reader of contemporary British and French commentators on economics and politics, Bowen was nonsectarian in approaching secular questions, and as a critic of France and Britain he had an outlook that was distinctly democratic, or, as he would have put it, "republican." The huge concentrations of wealth overseas and the inheritance laws and customs that held these intact were dysfunctional in Bowen's eyes. "Capital and land," he maintained, "are not mere instruments for the production of wealth . . . ; they are also necessary means for the support and happiness of the whole nation; and in this capacity, like rain and fertilizing agents for the soil, they produce the more effect the more evenly they are distributed."[8]

Yet Bowen was not an advocate of even distribution, of leveling. In his view the divinely ordained "natural" laws of economics dictated that wealth be accumulated according to the talent of particular entrepreneurs to employ it productively. He ranked inherited wealth below earned income, which was an instrument of general prosperity. Bowen proclaimed a democratic capitalism in which small capitalists could band together to form corporations for large projects, and in which all were free to accumulate (or dissipate) wealth. His highest encomiums went to the nouveaux riches:

> the most natural and sensible way of deriving personal gratification from newly acquired wealth, and of making a show of it in the eyes of the world, is to give largely to public charities. The sums which are contributed here [in the United States] by individuals for the support of schools, colleges, churches, missions, hospitals, and institutions of science and beneficence, put to shame the official liberality of the oldest and wealthiest governments in Europe.

Bowen's apologia for new wealth was forthright. In Boston six million dollars had been given in donations from 1800 to 1850 and, Bowen asserted, everyone knew "that the most numerous and magnificent gifts and bequests are made, not by men who have inherited their fortunes, but by those who have amassed them by their own exertions."[9]

The moral philosophy sustaining Bowen's views was a bland, beneficent Christianity. It was morally right for some to acquire great property and others to suffer in misery. The law of private property was a divine absolute. When a man sought his own profit, this was not destructive self-seeking, because individual gain also benefited the community, "lending aid to thousands of human beings whom he never saw." Bowen claimed that "we are all servants of one another without wishing it, and even without knowing it; and we are all cooperating with each other as busily and effectively as the bees in a hive."[10] Economic laws, like Christian principles, were natural laws, and all operated in harmony. The economic transformation of Massachusetts, its industrial and urban development, was fundamentally good. Great capitalists were instruments of progress. Reformers who interfered with them were challenging nature as God in his wisdom had created it. People who denounced the status quo were in their ignorance retarding the fruition of Christian progress. Here Bowen laid the foundations for the "gospel of wealth" that would sustain the Republican party, and many Democrats, in the post–Civil War era.

The people who dwelled in Massachusetts had never been more divided in their attitudes, objectives, and ideals than on the eve of the Civil War. Some, both Irish and Yankee, were ethnic provincials, and some were cosmopolitan friends of mankind. Some believed the history of Massachusetts demanded that they actively pursue the selfless ideals of the Puritan and Revolutionary past, while others took their inspiration from the Yankee ingenuity that had brought prosperity to the thin, stony soil and rocky harbors of the state. As an industrial society emerged, remnants of the older commercial and agricultural order lingered, and those who earned their bread from industry and its economic byproducts did not always shed the views of their agrarian youth, whether it had passed in Worcester County or County Cork. From earliest times, the people of Massachusetts had been struggling with the tension between self-assertion and corporate goals. Now people from the "Bowen school" of capitalists argued that individual economic self-assertion led to the fulfillment of collective goals, but at the same time they denied the legitimacy of collective efforts by legislatures and unions to interfere with one minority class, the entrepreneurs, who claimed to know better. In contrast, reformers of every kind were active interventionists, seeking to impress their individual moral certainties upon the whole society through both persuasion and legislation.

To a large degree Massachusetts missionary activists were talking past their opponents rather than to them. Their proselytizing, after all, knew no bounds; and it was far more effective to try to convince people who were uncertain or indifferent than to confront people whose minds were made up. Massachusetts, like the nation at large, had become a plural society where contradictory views flourished. But the people of the commonwealth, like people in other states, were not yet pluralistic, not yet prepared to accept the legitimacy of beliefs and opinions that they did not share, so they were tense and competitive. Massachusetts continued to industrialize and urbanize, with an inevitable impact upon the lives of its citizens. Besides the missionaries' efforts to reform society came the transformed conditions generated by the new labor force of Irish immigrants. Their presence challenged the notion of industrial paternalism held by Massachusetts's elites.

# CHAPTER 8

# Irish Immigration and the Challenges to Industrial Paternalism

B ECAUSE MASSACHUSETTS BECAME INDUSTRIAL AND URBAN before the rest of the nation, and because its people were facing the challenges of competition and pluralism, the tensions in Massachusetts society anticipated those of the nation at large. In formal political terms, perhaps, Massachusetts was lagging, but in adapting to a dynamic, heterogeneous world, Massachusetts was in the vanguard. The key social and political issues of the day were being tested in the Bay State. Questions of race and ethnicity, of education and social responsibility, of economic development and individual and corporate goals emerged repeatedly as the Massachusetts of old, where farmers, fishermen, tradesmen, and merchants were bound together in a deferential, congregational society, was transformed into an urban, industrial commonwealth.

Almost at once the growing factory system had a positive impact on the state's agriculture. A "mini-boom" began by 1820 for farmers of the inland areas because they now had a home market. There was an increased demand for foodstuffs and raw materials to supply the factory towns and their rising populations. This growing demand affected the very nature of farm life. Both location and the specific advantages of natural resources required jettisoning the semisubsistence ideal of farming in order to specialize in cash crops. Market gardening and dairy farming expanded in Essex, Middlesex, Worcester, and Hampshire counties and the farmlands surrounding Lynn, Lowell, Lawrence, and Boston.

One example of this agricultural improvement was Concord. The historian Robert Gross wrote: "Thanks to the coming of the railroad in 1844, Concord farmers played milkmen to the metropolis and branched out into market gardening and fruit raising as well." He went on to note that a "revolution" in agriculture occurred. "Without it, the creation of an urban industrial society would have been impossible."[1] Beef cattle herds could be found in northern Massachusetts, tobacco was grown in the Connecticut River valley, and sheep were raised in the hilly regions of western Massachusetts.

The extractive industries—quarrying, lumber, and fishing—had a smaller impact on urbanization. Towns did not grow into cities because of local quarries, forests, or fishing grounds. Quarries, like those at Quincy, were worked by small teams of men and animals. After blasting and cutting, they hauled the stone to a railway or a barge. Because transportation costs were high, no quarry could serve an extensive area, so the common pattern was of small localized quarries producing marble, granite, and slate.

The pattern for lumber was similar, although for different reasons. Timber trees were scattered through much of central and western Massachusetts and were most often logged by farmers during the winter. Centralization of milling, except to a degree along the Connecticut River, was not feasible. Consequently the dispersion of sawmills characteristic of the colonial era continued. But the mills grew in size and in the complexity of their operations as circular saws, planers, and other milling machinery came into use. Still, few mills had as many as a dozen employees. It was pulp-paper mills, just beginning in the 1860s, far more than lumber mills, that would create large factories and urban concentrations.

Even more than forest industries, fishing was tied to its colonial origins. On the North Shore, Gloucester and Marblehead, fishing centers for two centuries, remained fishing ports as their role in sea-borne commerce declined. Fishing also remained important in the town of Plymouth. On thinly populated Cape Cod, fishing was, next to farming, the chief occupation. Cod and mackerel supported about two thousand families, almost one third of the population. Primacy in whaling, once belonging to Nantucket and Martha's Vineyard, had passed across Buzzards Bay to New Bedford. Like other forms of fishing, whaling was entering a decline, but in 1860 it still supported fifty thousand people in southeastern Massachusetts and the islands. In New Bedford, supplying the whale ships and processing and distributing their catch provided the employment to generate major urbanization, and the population of the whaling port exceeded ten thousand by the mid-1830s. By 1860, New Bedford and the adjoining textile city of Fall River formed one of the largest urban areas in the entire United States, both ranking among the top twenty-five manufacturing cities in the nation.

The production of consumer goods—items like clothing, home furnishings, musical instruments, and books—reflected the radical change in American ways of life between 1800 and 1860. These were the years when semisubsistence farming all but disappeared, and the ideals of bourgeois comfort and amenities characteristic of the Victorian age supplanted the rustic simplicity that religious beliefs and economic realities had forced on the majority of the people from Winthrop's day to John Hancock's. But Massachusetts produced consumer goods for the national market as well as for home consumption. As a result, though consumer industries were located in every corner of the state, they were concentrated in the most commercially accessible areas—Boston and its environs and along the railways that now connected Massachusetts to neighboring states.

The range of such industries was almost endless: buttons and bedsteads, cigars and spectacles, stove polish and perfume, candy and combs. Virtually anything money could buy was being produced in the state where, two centuries before, sumptuary laws had required frugality. In farming areas some of this production was still cottage industry; farm wives wove straw baskets and bonnets.

The change to a market economy exposed farmers to direct competition with western states and their cheaper farm products. By the onset of the Civil War, Massachusetts's commercial agriculture declined severely, causing the abandonment of large numbers of upland farms. Habits of self-sufficiency and traditions of independence were eroded by the new realities of cash crops and reliance on ready-made goods. Since the 1820s women, children, and young men had left farms to work in factories. Machine-made textiles ended forever the homespun household economy, and new industrial techniques were brought into the home by the putting-out system of production. Yankee farm families joined the procession of countless migrants who moved to the burgeoning towns and cities of Massachusetts to find opportunities for employment and social mobility that came with the full flowering of the industrial revolution.

One obvious significant change in rural family life was the rise in women's participation in the wage labor market. While much has been written about the mill girls of eastern Massachusetts, women in other parts of the state were also involved in the industrialization process. In rural areas of central and western Massachusetts and along the Connecticut River valley there was no clear boundary in the transition from a household economy to a factory one. Women produced shirt collars, cloth buttons, paper products, and palm-leaf hats through the putting-out system, either at home or in temporary workshops. In the western rural counties by 1860, the U.S. Census of manufacturing shows that, depending on the industry, from 28 to 53 percent of the manufacturing labor force were women. At the same time that women's roles in factories increased, so did their time devoted to cheese and butter production and maintaining boarders in their homes. The ability of women to earn money from domestic production and from wages was an important factor in loosening their dependence on men in farm households.

Between 1820 and the Civil War, Massachusetts turned toward industry and away from agriculture. From a labor force where 60 percent of workers were in agriculture, by 1865 only 13 percent were on farms. By 1875, half of the state's working women were in manufacturing occupations, while three-quarters of the laboring men held jobs in industry, trade, and transportation. Now workers were largely employees, no longer owning property or small businesses. The demand for skilled artisans declined, and self-employment became unusual. Workers had become dependent on others for employment; and the old putting-out system of the farms disappeared. The transformation from agrarian to industrial society sustained the emergence of new elites: industrialists, financiers, and railroad builders. They, along with British investors, committed large sums to the new textile and woolens mills of New England. At the same time, impoverished farmers and their families left the rural areas to be joined by poor peasants from overseas, to form a new industrial working class living in densely populated factory towns. By 1875, Massachusetts and Rhode Island were the most densely populated states in the union, with a majority of their citizens living in urban areas rather than in the countryside.

Paradoxical though it may seem, the period of intense economic concentration and the increasing wealth during the second quarter of the century also witnessed the beginning of a general economic decline for the working poor of the large cities. The lower classes faced serious reductions in their real wages while their living expenses went up dramatically. Inequality in wealth and income had risen dramatically during the age of Jacksonian Democracy, so that by 1860 over 51 percent of the nation's adult male urbanites were propertyless. The cramped housing, periodic unemployment, and growing discontent of the lower orders were stark contrasts to the opulence of the rich.

According to the historian Arthur B. Darling, the period from 1824 to 1860 in Massachusetts "was a time of seething unrest"[2] among the laboring classes. Two severe depressions leading to unemployment and suffering affected Massachusetts, the first in 1837–40 and the second in 1857–59. A short-lived workingmen's movement arose in the early 1830s, protesting long hours, poor working conditions, production speed-ups, lower wages, and periodic unemployment due to factory closings. Although exact numbers for unemployment are not available for the antebellum period, Alexander Keyssar, the historian of Massachusetts unemployment, argued that increased industrialization, urbanization, immigration, and the severing of ties with agriculture, removed an important safety net for temporarily unemployed workers. They could no longer return to farms in times of stress to wait out a panic or a downturn in the business cycle. For example, in the textile industry

> major downturns in business activity often produced swift and simultaneous layoffs for large numbers of operatives. At least once each decade between 1810 and 1870, trade became so slow that many mills either closed altogether or sharply curtailed their schedules, releasing large numbers of employees. The phenomenon was cyclical, but its impact was not: each time the mills shut down or cut back, more jobs were at stake and more jobs were lost. With every succeeding slump in trade, workers who were laid off were more prone to hardship, less able to cope easily with their loss of income.[3]

In fact, the more Massachusetts industrialized, the more commonplace was unemployment. Turning the majority of working people into dependent, propertyless wage earners accentuated the differences between the classes.

The historian Gloria Main postulated that a big jump in inequality began first in the period that lasted from the end of the Revolution to the 1830s, because of "the growth of wealth at the top rather than expansion of the propertyless."[4] Yet in Boston inequality was more pronounced than in other urban areas, as in 1834, when wages stood still. By 1845, 4 percent of Bostonians owned more than two-thirds of the city's wealth. In this decade, unskilled and menial service workers faced a marked decline in wealth while the richest citizens were improving their holdings. By 1860 the wealthiest 1 percent held 65 percent of the city's aggregate wealth, whereas over half the men of Boston "had no wealth at all." In his statistical study of the "plain people of Boston," Peter Knights concluded that between 1830 and 1860 "the proportion of propertyless taxpayers rose" and "more wealth was in fewer hands." It became clear, as Steven Herscovici reports, that "the distribution of wealth in nineteenth-century Boston was very unequal,"[5] as it was throughout the industrializing world.

The increasing proletarianization of labor and the growing divisions of wealth gave rise to class differences that became apparent to many in Massachusetts. Nationwide, as well, political differences among regions concerning policies such as the tariff and expansion of slavery generated a politics of conflict. The Boston Associates worried about instability and dissension and sought to find ways to foster harmony and avoid conflicts that would jeopardize their enterprises and their social standing. Influencing Massachusetts politics became vital for the Boston Associates. Their movement into the Whig party was intended to avert the chaos of politics dominated by individuals. They sought to blunt divisiveness and to promote a prosperity that would mollify malcontents. They worked behind the scenes, provided financial support, and promoted their own stalwart defender, Daniel Webster.

Webster, like John Quincy Adams, came to epitomize the interests of an important Massachusetts constituency, becoming the major New England political personage of the 1830s and 1840s. A legendary orator, Webster's words "had the force of a fleet of battle ships."[6] He toiled to preserve the Union and at the same time advocated the Massachusetts manufacturing and commercial interests that paid for his extravagant life style.

Webster's career illustrates the tangled web of Massachusetts politics from the demise of the national Federalists after the War of 1812,

through the creation of the Whigs in 1834, to their disintegration by 1854, with the birth of the Republican party.[7] Webster was born January 18, 1782, on a farm in Salisbury, New Hampshire. He went to Dartmouth College where he began building his reputation as an orator. After graduation in 1801, he taught school and prepared for a career in law by reading in the office of a Boston law firm. Then he opened his own office in Portsmouth, New Hampshire in 1807. He wrote an anonymous pamphlet against the Embargo, and his antiwar stance in 1812 helped him win election to Congress as a Federalist. As a good Federalist believing in states' rights, he did everything he could to stymie and harass the administration of President James Madison. Although he was reelected by his New Hampshire constituents in 1814, the bad times brought by the war's deleterious effect on trade caused him to leave Portsmouth and move to Boston in 1816. It was there that he became the legal adviser of the Boston Associates, earning large fees and building his reputation by transfixing juries with his spellbinding oratory.

He gained a national reputation as a defender of conservatism in several cases that he won before the Supreme Court in 1819, including the Dartmouth College case and *McCulloch v. Maryland*. In the Dartmouth College case the Republican state legislature of New Hampshire revised the charter of Dartmouth College, changing it from a private to a public institution. Defending the trustees of the college, Webster argued successfully that the grant setting up the college was a "contract," and that corporation charters as contracts could only be voided by mutual agreement, not by legislative decree. *McCulloch v. Maryland* brought up the issue of state versus federal sovereignty. The state government of Maryland attempted to tax the Baltimore branch of the Federal Bank of the United States. Defending the bank, Webster convinced the court that the United States government had the right to charter banks and that because the power to tax was the power to "destroy," no state had the right to tax, and therefore destroy, a part of the federal government. Brought fame by his skill as an attorney, Webster was elected to Congress from Boston in 1823, and he served to 1827. He came out against the protective tariff, largely because the Boston Associates, the giants of the textile industry, did not need it and still had major interests in trade. Later in his career Webster would switch his position to become the main advocate of tariffs when Massachusetts

manufacturing interests changed their position on protection. In 1824, now a National Republican, he voted for John Quincy Adams for president when the election was decided by the House. Three years later the Massachusetts legislature elected Webster to the U.S. Senate. There he led the fight for the Tariff of 1828, which the South termed an "abomination." From being a states' right advocate as a Federalist, Webster, still faithfully representing the dominant entrepreneurial interests of his region, now became a defender of the national government's prerogatives. That was his stance in the famous debate with Senator Robert Y. Hayne of South Carolina.

The Webster-Hayne-Benton debates took place between January 18 and 27, 1830. The original issue was a query by a senator concerning limiting land sales on public lands. This brought a furious attack by Senator Thomas Hart Benton of Missouri, who claimed this was a typical ploy of the eastern establishment to check western settlement and keep factory workers under control. Senator Robert Hayne of South Carolina joined Benton's attack on the East, raising the issue of the misuse of federal power that was threatening the sovereignty of the states by such nefarious acts as the tariff. Hayne went on to connect Webster with this eastern aggrandizement and then brought up the issue of "interposition." This was the southern doctrine that maintained that a state could interfere against or block measures of the federal government when it deemed federal policy unlawful or unconstitutional. Webster took it upon himself to exonerate the East from the charges that it discouraged western settlement, but, more important, he attacked the notion of interposition.

Webster compared interposition with nullification, which was unconstitutional and would result in violence. He rejected the South's notion of the Union as a "compact of states"; instead he argued that the Union derived from "popular consent." The federal government was not an agent of the states but had powers given it by the people through the Constitution; and he went on to remind the Senate of *McCulloch v. Maryland.* "It is, sir, the people's Constitution, the people's government, made for the people, made by the people, and answerable to the people." Article 6 provided that the Constitution and the treaties and laws of the United States were "supreme law." Article 3, Webster went on, gave the federal judiciary the power as sole arbiter of constitutional questions. "These two provisions cover the whole ground. They are, in truth, the keystone of the arch! With these it is a government; without them it is a confederation." Webster closed with the words: "Liberty and Union, now and forever, one and inseparable." Webster's eloquence brought him fame as the "Defender of the Constitution." One biographer called Webster's concept of the Union his greatest contribution, one that would "triumph over the discredited notion of a loose compact of sovereign states."[8]

Webster's growing concern over the possible destruction of the Union led him to take positions that sometimes did not sit well with his constituents. When a rogue South Carolina declared its "nullification" of the Tariff of 1828, he sided with the Democrat Andrew Jackson. He would alternate between supporting Jackson or Henry Clay, his major competitor, depending on the issue of the moment and his own political ambitions. In 1836, he became one of the Whig party's nominees for the presidency, but lost badly to Democrat Martin Van Buren. Webster defended the national bank of the United States, favored government support for internal improvements, and continued to defend protectionism. In all this he was consistent and faithful to his business backers. When Whig William Henry Harrison won the presidency in 1840, Webster became his secretary of state. With Harrison's death, Webster retained this office under John Tyler, to the dismay of the Whigs in Massachusetts. By 1845 Webster was once more back in the Senate, though his accommodations to the interests of slavery—to preserve the Union and the cotton business at any cost—turned the "conscience Whigs" against him. Moreover, his support of the enforcement of the fugitive slave law and the Compromise of 1850 made him anathema to the growing antislavery forces in Massachusetts. When the Whig party split over this issue, Webster was left without a party and with few supporters. The death of another president, Zachary Taylor, in 1850, momentarily halted Webster's political decline, as Millard Fillmore appointed him to return to the office of secretary of state. Yet his separation from national and regional issues for international ones symbolized his growing impotence as a national political figure. When he died at the age of seventy in Marshfield, Massachusetts, in 1852, he was a leader from the past era of the supremacy of the Boston Associates. By the 1850s, these manufacturing interests were undergoing a major transformation.

The expansion of the textile industry, increased competition, and

growing labor militancy croded employer paternalism after the 1840s. The Waltham system, started by Francis Cabot Lowell and his friends at the beginning of the century, was gradually abandoned because of the large-scale growth of the textile industry. A competitive capitalism, unfettered by the paternalism, that had once dominated the mills of Rhode Island and Connecticut, now became the guiding principle for Lowell and Lawrence as well as newer factory towns, such as Fall River and New Bedford. One Fall River factory agent bluntly characterized the new situation in 1855: "I regard my work-people just as I regard my machinery. So long as they can do my work for what I choose to pay them, I keep them, getting out of them all I can. What they do or how they fare outside my walls I don't know, nor do I consider it my business to know."[9] No longer would mill owners spend money on housing their laborers. The free market quickly turned former dormitory buildings into slums.

Lowell, the proud creation of Boston's financiers, became a factory town of twenty-thousand people—congested, disease ridden, and a place of misery for its working poor. Various ministers and reformers reported on the dank, dark living conditions. The *Lowell Courier* noted in 1847 that one such investigation found a house "occupied by one store and twenty-five different families embracing 120 persons, more than half of whom were adults." In 1849, a minister wrote that in "one cellar of two rooms lived four families of twenty-two persons." In general, the period from 1840 to 1860 was one of excellent profits for business, "and a lowering of standards of the industrial population."[10] Amid capital prosperity, the industrial worker lost ground.

The other major industry of the Bay State, boots and shoes, also underwent a major transformation after 1850. Originally an industry based on Yankee craftsmen and women, the invention of new machines made it easy to mass-produce shoes. A Massachusetts native, Elias Howe, perfected sewing machine techniques, creating the lockstitcher that allowed for factory production of shoes. Howe was born in Spencer in 1819. He learned about machines as an apprentice in a Lowell cotton mill and when he worked in machine shops in Boston and Cambridge. In 1844, he invented a sewing machine that was capable of sewing 250 stitches a minute. For years Howe struggled with patent problems while others used his device. Eventually he won his cases and became a millionaire. More important, his sewing machine transformed an industry based on the putting-out system and small independent shops into one characterized by division of labor with workers as machine operatives performing single and simple tasks. Increased production of shoes resulted in periods of overproduction, forcing the closing of factories. The cyclical nature of the shoe markets, varying from year to year, resulted in bankruptcies for owners and uncertain employment for the now-unskilled shoe factory workers.

Both the introduction of sewing machines and the depression of 1857–59 sorely affected skilled shoe workers, such as binders. Household production was changing over to factory production and the result was lower wages. Years of depression and deskilling led to the nation's largest pre–Civil War strike, the Great Shoemakers' Strike of 1860. Centered in Lynn, the strike enveloped the Merrimack Valley of Massachusetts and New Hampshire, with more than twenty thousand men and women workers leaving their jobs in protest over reduced wages. At first the strikers employed parades and demonstrations to win over community support. But the manufacturers would not budge, successfully continuing production by the widespread use of strike-breaking workers. Finally, when strikers in Lynn spied cases of shoe stock being sent by railroad to outworkers, they reacted violently. Workers began destroying the shipments, and then fought police who tried to protect the cases. At first the police were overpowered, but reinforcements from other cities and the state militia soon repelled the strikers, who were forced to yield. The financial staying power of the manufacturers and the use of the institutional force of police and militia broke the strike and defeated the workers.

A key influence helping to undermine the Waltham system in the textile industry and creating the growing unemployment in the shoe industry was new and cheaper supplies of labor, the first being the Irish of the famine era, who came by the tens of thousands from overseas and Canada. Business welcomed these newcomers as important sources of cheap labor that reduced production expenses while making the costly paternalism of the Waltham system superfluous. But the arrival of immigrants intensified the fears of the Yankee working classes, who envisioned the Irish as subverting Protestant society and culture while taking away "American" jobs.

Even before the great migration of the Irish, which took place after 1846, Massachusetts citizens had expressed their dissatisfaction with newcomers. From the early 1600s to 1820, the majority of the state's settlers came from England, with smaller numbers from Scotland, Wales, and Ireland. In Massachusetts by 1790, 95 percent of the population had either come from Britain or been born of British parents. These Yankees dominated the Bay State for two hundred years without any competition apart from the Indians whom they and the British had defeated in the seventeenth and eighteenth centuries. Religious motives as well as economic drives motivated Puritans to settle on the Shawmut peninsula in 1630. Like almost all seventeenth-century people they were intolerant of other religions. In addition to expelling Roger Williams and Anne Hutchinson for religious deviations, they hanged four Quakers who persisted in evangelizing after they had been banished. They only began to tolerate Catholics when the new colonial charter required it in 1692, and even so, Catholics could not worship publicly in Massachusetts until 1780, when toleration became the enlightened policy of the state constitution's Declaration of Rights. Not until 1788 did Boston get its first Catholic church. By 1820, an amended state constitution allowed Catholics to hold office, but only Protestants could be school teachers. In the same decade, hysterical fears of Irish Catholic subversion revived dramatically when a small number of Irish immigrated to Boston.

In 1820, Boston's population was more than forty-three thousand, only two thousand or 4.6 percent of whom were Irish. By 1825, the number of Irish more than doubled to five thousand or 8.6 percent, and by 1830 there were seven thousand Irish inhabitants, 11.4 percent of a population of over sixty-one thousand. Moreover, Boston was a major port for Irish entry. Most of the new arrivals went into the hinterland to seek work in construction or in the factories of New England. But to many Bostonians, the large numbers who arrived with no intention of remaining in the city could not be distinguished from those staying, and this uncertainty was alarming. The Irish in Boston gave their support to the Jacksonian Democrats in 1828, while Yankee Bostonians overwhelmingly gave their allegiance to John Quincy Adams. The national defeat of Adams caused anguish among Yankee voters, and they blamed the Irish for Jackson's victory. Native-born workers feared their incomes would diminish and that Protestant dominance was threatened. After two hundred years of Anglo anti-Catholicism, the Catholic newcomers were targets of Yankee wrath.

Workers' fears of Catholics were supported by the growing number of Protestant religious groups who had joined in a new evangelical crusade against Catholicism and new anti-Trinitarian Protestant sects, such as the Unitarians and the Universalists. This nationwide fundamentalist movement rejected the liberalism that came out of the American Revolution. Revival leaders called for a return to the purity of Puritanism and highlighted the menace of Catholicism as a danger to American democracy and Protestantism. The first newspapers dedicated to attacking "Popery" and "Romanism" were the *Boston Recorder,* founded in 1816, and the *Boston Watchman,* established in 1819. "To maintain Protestantism and to oppose Popery," was the "cause of all mankind," editorialized the *Recorder* on November 18, 1829. Tract societies, Bible groups, missionaries, and Sunday schools—all set their sights on attacking Catholicism. Revivalist preachers who came to Boston, such as Charles G. Finney and Lyman Beecher, compared Catholicism with Satanism and anti-Republicanism. Their incendiary preaching contributed to the rising level of agitation against Irish Catholics. Lacking the political power to redress their economic grievances and made fearful by their ministers, some working-class Protestants resorted to violence.

Several attacks upon Irish Catholics occurred, the first in 1823, and then again in 1825, 1826, 1828, and 1831. The mayor of Boston, Charles Wells received a petition in 1832, "praying that some measure may be taken to suppress the dangerous riots, routs, and tumultuous assemblies in and about Broad Street." [11] Charlestown, adjoining Boston and later incorporated, witnessed a nativist riot on Thanksgiving in 1833. In December of that year five hundred Yankee workers, reinforced by volunteer firemen from Boston, marched on Charlestown's Irish Catholic neighborhood, looting and burning. Throughout New England, Irish Catholics suffered from increasingly violent encounters with "lower class people," as one newspaper put it. [12] This explosive anti-Catholic antagonism led to the burning of an Ursuline convent in Charlestown in 1834.

Many disparate threads woven together made the convent the perfect target for attack. A Protestant pornography of rumors circulated of scandalous sexual activities, murder, and kidnapping of babies and girls in nunneries and monasteries. The convent, although a finishing school for a small number of Catholic girls and for Boston's upper-class Unitarians and Episcopalians, was a convenient target. The period was one of Protestant evangelical fervor heightened by the schism that occurred when Boston's upper classes turned to Unitarianism and away from the stricter Calvinist and Trinitarian ideas of their Puritan ancestors. The orthodox ministers and their flocks connected the Unitarians with the Catholics, sensing a plot against the "true religion." One newspaper, the *Mass Yeoman*, shrilly commented: "Atheists and infidels will always be ready to sympathize with Catholics, to unite with them in crushing Protestantism preparatory to the subversion of Christianity." One eminent Boston Unitarian who sent his daughter to the school wrote afterward that he was convinced the "mob" believed "that the Nunnery at Charlestown was an immoral and corrupt place, where all sorts of vice and superstitions were practiced: and that Protestant parents who sent their children there for instruction were guilty of a heinous sin." Years later, the accused leader of the Ursuline rioters, John Buzzell, remarked: "we looked upon the nunnery with disfavor, and many stories of cruel practices within its walls were told and believed."[13] The substantial new buildings of the convent seemed to represent ostentatiously an unholy alliance between Catholics and Unitarians, while symbolizing the breach between the Yankee rich and poor.

Rumors spread of a nun, Sister Mary John, being forcibly held in the convent after attempting to leave. A large crowd of workers from Charlestown and Boston gathered outside the convent on the evening of August 11, 1834. Trying to stave off violence, the mother superior, Sister Mary Edmond St. George, further incensed the crowd when she threatened that an army of twenty thousand Irish laborers were on the march to protect the convent. The *New England Galaxy* reported that thousands watched and applauded as some fifty rioters, "disguised with masks and fantastic dresses and painted faces," entered the convent, began looting, and then set it ablaze. The nuns and the children escaped by the rear garden before the violence began. The assailants and the cheerful onlookers were the poor Protestant laborers of Boston and Charlestown—truckmen, brickmakers, sailors, firemen, apprentices, and assorted teens—men "from the poorest and most ignorant strata" of the community.[14] They returned the next night and set more fires and destroyed the convent completely.

Boston's elite leaders met at Faneuil Hall and condemned the action of the crowd as "a base and cowardly act," setting up a committee made up of such luminaries as Josiah Quincy, Harrison G. Otis, William Sturgis, Nathan Appleton, Henry Lee, and Charles Loring to bring "the villains to justice." But in an interesting sidelight to the riot story, Boston's upper strata demonstrated their own anti-Catholic and anti-Irish fears. Rumors spread that Irish workers were advancing on the area, perhaps because of the threats of the convent's mother superior, and "that the Library of Harvard College was doomed to assault and destruction by the Irish Roman Catholics." Believing the story, the elite sons at Harvard organized and armed themselves. Young Franklin Dexter and Robert Winthrop were chosen as captain and lieutenant, and "sentinels were stationed at the doors and windows, patrols were sent out on the streets and roads, and every preparation was made for defending the building and the books at all hazards."[15] For the entire evening the elite students of Harvard waited anxiously to defend their precious books from the depredations of an army of Irishmen that never appeared. This bizarre episode demonstrates the level of prevailing community hysteria and the Yankee belief that things Catholic and Irish were a threat to republican values.

While several of the rioters were arrested and eventually went to trial, all but one were acquitted by juries of their peers. Class divisions, religious enmity, and nativism were evident in the legal proceedings. Even before the arrest of thirteen men, posters and anonymous letters appeared threatening prospective witnesses. The *Bunker Hill Aurora* of August 23, 1834, reported a poster that read: "all persons giving information in any shape or testifying in a court against anyone concerned in the late affair at Charlestown may expect assassination, according to the oath which bound the party together." Another handbill evoked republican sentiments in favor of the rioters:

> Liberty or Death!
> Suppressed Evidence.
> Sons of Freedom! Can you live in a
> Free country, and bear the Yoke of
> Priesthood, veiled in the habit of a
> Profligate Court?[16]

The attack on the integrity of the court symbolized workers' suspicion of the upper strata because Judge Lemuel Shaw, a member of the upper class, presided over the Supreme Judicial Court proceedings. The first trial was against the apparent ringleader, brickmaker John Buzzell. The defense statement to the all Yankee jury was simple: all the witnesses against the defendant were Catholics, thus suspect; the jury should reject Catholic "imported testimony" in favor of "domestic testimony." Notwithstanding the wealth of evidence against him, the jury acquitted Buzzell.[17] This manifestation of anti-Irish Catholic sentiment did not abate, as another major riot took place in Boston in 1837.

The Broad Street riot reflected the continuing animosity of the Yankee workers toward the newcomers. Boston at this time had neither a professional police nor fire department. When violence erupted the mayor's only recourse was to call out the militia, which largely comprised the same Yankee workers who generally made up the riot contingent. Putting out fires was the work of volunteer fire companies, who also came from Boston's working classes. On Sunday, June 11, 1837, a volunteer fire company had returned from a fire when it discovered that a large funeral cortege of four or five hundred Irish was forming in front of the firehouse. After some shoving, fighting began, and the firemen rang their bells to summon more companies. When more firemen arrived a full-scale battle erupted. The Irish fled to their homes off Broad Street in the North End, only to be pursued by ever larger numbers of firemen, who were joined by men and women from all over the city. In vain, the Irish tried to defend their homes, but they were outnumbered by a crowd estimated to be near fifteen thousand. Several Irish homes were set on fire, furniture was vandalized and tossed into the street, and scores of the Irish were severely beaten. No record remains of the total number of deaths or injuries, because no hospital or police records existed. Property damage was in the thousands of dollars, with many Irish families left homeless. Finally, after several hours, the violence ended with the appearance of the mayor and the militia, over eight hundred strong. Using force, the militia dispersed the crowds and patrolled the neighborhood. As was generally true with mob violence, no one was punished for the attack. Boston's ruling class, which had spoken out against the Ursuline Convent rioters after the fact, made no comment on this firemen's riot, but they ended forever the unruly behavior of volunteer firemen by establishing a permanent fire department a few months later, in September 1837. After 1846, when Ireland inundated Boston with large numbers of potential voters, even the patricians awakened to the "foreign menace."

The famine Irish were, for the most part, landless peasants escaping from potato blight and English oppression. Starting in 1846, about one thousand were entering monthly into an already overcrowded Boston. The next year a record-breaking thirty-seven thousand Irish immigrants came to a hostile city that was ill prepared to provide work or shelter for these large numbers. Arriving penniless and without the job skills required for the commercial city of Boston, they congregated in Boston's North End slum, where they hoped to get jobs on the docks as stevedores or day laborers. Unskilled work, however, was limited in Boston, so unemployment, ill health, and crowded, pestilential housing plagued the new arrivals.

In 1849, during a cholera epidemic, of the 700 fatalities, 509 (73 percent) were Irish. One doctor reported that living conditions were so bad that he saw thirty-nine people living in a cellar that repeatedly flooded. The doctor observed that planks were put down as bridges between stools and beds, and he spied a dead baby sailing about the room in a coffin. Open drains and unsanitary living conditions worsened, and another cholera epidemic broke out in 1854. A police officer described collecting bloated bodies that were so swollen they could not fit into coffins.

Finding themselves among a community that feared and hated Catholics, the majority of Boston's Irish eked out a miserable existence. Largely hired as laborers when they could find employment, many Irish men had to leave their families to work outside the city on the construction of railroads and mills in order to survive. Irish women—farm raised and trained only for farm- and housework—became domestics. They filled an acute shortage felt by middle-class Yankee families who wanted help at home. By 1850, some 2,227 Irish women took up the trade as "Bridget" for well-to-do Bostonians.

Irish peasants with rural habits and no jobs to train them in industrial discipline sought escape in alcohol. Increased public displays of Irish drunkenness infuriated frightened Yankee Bostonians, who at that time were struggling to curb their own alcoholic vices through prohibition.

The Yankee response to Irish immigrants was mostly hostile and intolerant. The Irish were depicted as drunk, idle, thriftless, vicious, criminal, profligate paupers, who preyed on taxpayers because of their need for public charity. Discrimination became rampant, with the expression, "Positively no Irish need apply," frequently used when jobs were advertised. Smug jokes, often imported directly from England, about "Paddy's" drinking, fighting, and irrational, spontaneous passions helped informally to reinforce the Yankee sense of superiority. The clash between Yankee and Irish, Protestant and Catholic became particularly vitriolic in Boston, indeed "unique," according to a historian of the Boston Irish. "The generations of bitter and unyielding conflict between the natives of Boston and the newcomers from Ireland would forever mold the social and political character of the Boston Irish in ways not found elsewhere." [18]

The Irish flocked in large numbers to the rising mill towns, such as Lawrence, which itself was incorporated in 1847 shortly after the outbreak of the Great Famine. It was in Lawrence that the term "shanty Irish" emerged, a reference to the wooden huts the immigrants built for shelter along the Merrimack River and above the dam constructed by their compatriots for the Boston Associates. These were shacks of raw lumber with dirt floors, put together around a stove-pipe chimney. A large family with several relatives and boarders usually lived in the cramped one-room space. As in Boston, such dense living quarters resulted in unsanitary conditions, and Lawrence had its share of disease, with a particularly severe typhoid fever epidemic in 1850. Matters worsened because the river running through the town was filled with the sewage that came from its upstream neighbor, Lowell.

It was the Irish who were the construction workers who built the factories, the dam for water power, and the canal linking the factories with the river. By 1855 Lawrence had six cotton mills and five woolen mills. The Irish in 1850 worked for less than a dollar a day, which was not enough to support a family, and most family members were forced to work. The Irish endured long hours under sometimes hazardous conditions. One notable disaster occurred at the Pemberton Mill, on January 10, 1860. Observers watched in horror when the five-story factory, filled with 670 workers, collapsed. Although only several were instantly killed, hundreds were injured. Many were trapped in the ruins, awaiting rescue. To add to the horror, one of the rescue workers mistakenly started a fire which quickly added to the tragedy. Finally, the grim toll was 88 dead and 116 badly injured.

The historian Oscar Handlin wrote: "Thousands of poverty-stricken peasants, rudely transposed to an urban commercial center, could not readily become merchants or clerks; they had neither the training nor the capital to set up as shopkeepers or artisans. The absence of other opportunities forced the majority into ranks of an unemployed, resourceless proletariat, whose cheap labor and abundant numbers ultimately created a new industrialism in Boston."[19] Thus, the factory system came to Boston because of surplus Irish labor. The new jobs became the ladder for Irish social mobility.

The popular notion that the Irish were depressing the wage scale was obvious to an English traveler in 1849:

> Within five miles of Boston, some of the newly arrived emigrants of the lower class of Irish, may now be seen living in mud huts by the side of the railway cuttings, which they are employed to dig, who are regarded by many of the native-born laborers with no small disgust, not only as the most ignorant and superstitious of mortals, but as likely, by their own competition, to bring down the general standard of wages. The rich capitalists, on the other hand, confess to me, that they know not how they could get on with the construction of public works, and obtain good interest for their money, deprived of this constant influx of foreign labor.[20]

The job-hungry Irish spread throughout the state in the 1850s, working in railroad camps, on construction crews, and in the mills. By 1855 there were 181,000 Irish-born inhabitants in the commonwealth.

By then many of the famine migrants had been in Massachusetts for the required five years and thus could vote, usually for the Democratic candidates. The majority Whigs were nativist, temperance, and a portion of them were antislavery. The Irish and Democrats generally were against prohibition, and they feared that if southern slaves were freed, they would move north and compete for jobs. These immigrants also suspected that antislavery tampering with the Constitution to abolish slavery might lead nativists to change the document that protected Irish liberties. Thus, a weak but growing minority aligned itself with the state's minority political party, increasing their alienation from the majority Yankee Protestant Whigs. Because of their intensifying presence and their political position, Irish Catholics continued to experience hatred. This time it flared up in the form of a political party.

Suddenly, in the middle of the 1850s with the collapse of the national Whig party over the issue of slavery expansion, a populist nativist movement, dominated by Yankee working and middling classes in a coalition with a wide variety of splinter groups, took over every major political office in Massachusetts. Besides attracting fierce anti-Catholics, these reformers found support among discontented former Whigs and Democrats, Free Soilers, and temperance and antimonopoly supporters, in a revolt against established political parties. A grass-roots, secret movement of average men, this nativist party was called the American or "Know-Nothing" party, because its members pledged to tell nothing about their organization if asked. This was a reform party whose goals were to drive out the unresponsive political organization regulars, make politics more democratic, and stop the incursions of the immigrants.

The Know-Nothing party won an astounding victory in 1854. They garnered 63 percent of the vote, winning the entire congressional delegation and capturing every state office, including the governorship. Know-Nothings won all 40 state Senate seats and 376 seats out of 379 in the state House of Representatives. As a result, they ruled Massachusetts without opposition from 1855 to 1858. They passed laws that removed Irish paupers and mental patients from state institutions, deporting them to Britain. They disbanded the much feared Irish militia units, one of which had assisted in the return of the fugitive slave, Anthony Burns, in 1854. The Know-Nothings reduced the role of the state courts in naturalization matters and ordered the daily reading of the Protestant Bible in the public schools. They failed in an attempt to change the state constitution to deny Catholics and naturalized citizens the right to vote or hold office for twenty-one years. They set up a special legislative committee to inspect nunneries and convents, Catholic schools, and the College of the Holy Cross in Worcester, but when the committee members began terrorizing some Catholic religious orders, public sentiment turned against Know-Nothing extremes, and that practice ceased.

The Know-Nothing agenda, while based on a rabid nativism, also included broader populist reforms. Recent historical analysis suggests that this nativist party was successful in passing a series of reform measures beneficial to the Yankee working classes that elected them to power: a strict temperance law, tax exemption for homesteads, a law protecting mechanics from credit liens, abolition of debtors' prison, a law forbidding state officials from returning fugitive slaves, and the desegregation of the Boston school system. While it has been suggested that the desegregation of the Boston schools was somehow an attempt to defuse the growth of Irish power in the city, it cannot be denied that the African American community had long fought the Boston School Committee for equality in the schools, and that it was the Know-Nothing state legislature that ended the racial injustice of school segregation.

Paradoxically, the Know-Nothing attacks sometimes had the opposite effect than they desired, as happened in Lowell. The fierce hatred Know-Nothingism expressed was epitomized by the Yankee townspeople's way of responding to the swift creation of an ugly factory town infested by hordes of foreigners. A historian of Lowell, Brian C. Mitchell, suggested: "In Lowell, those Yankee voters who feared Irish power . . . turned to the Know-Nothing party because the traditional political parties, particularly the Whig party to whom they had always given undivided support, no longer acted upon these concerns. . . . Even more important, it was the Whigs who had betrayed Lowell's Yankees when the mill owners opened Lowell's mills to Irish."[21] Know-Nothing outbursts against the newcomer Irish were particularly venomous when it came to the public school system.

The harsh realities of an active nativism finally served to bring the divided Irish together under the protective banner of the Catholic Church. The church, through its priests and nuns, acted as a bulwark for the oppressed Irish and helped significantly in creating a new American identity for the "Irish Americans" of Lowell. "The verbal, physical, psychological, and intellectual attacks of the Know-Nothings had drawn Lowell's Irish together under the leadership of the O'Briens [two brothers who were Catholic priests]."[22] Under the banner of the church, and led by these two priests, the Irish community stopped feuding and banded together in a communal effort at self-protection. The result was a stronger immigrant community better able to withstand nativist hostility. Although the Know-Nothing party had enjoyed astounding success at first, it soon fell apart due to political ineptitude and because the issue of nativism paled in contrast to the emerging national conflict over the expansion of slavery.

# CHAPTER 9

# Abolition and the Civil War

B EFORE THE OUTBREAK OF THE CIVIL WAR, MASSACHUSETTS
had a reputation as a hotbed of abolitionism and as the leading
opponent of returning fugitive slaves. Massachusetts abolitionists and
others were soldiers in a second American revolution founded on the
principles of the first. "Life, liberty, and the pursuit of happiness"
should be the right of all Americans, not a particular class. The two
most prominent Massachusetts abolitionists were William Lloyd Garrison and Wendell Phillips. Though very different from each other, these
two men whose careers intertwined epitomized the independent, assert-
ive, self-righteous spirit of the abolitionists that emanated from the Bay
State in the antebellum era.

Garrison, the son of an immigrant sea captain, was born at Newburyport in 1805. Three years later his father deserted the family. In 1814
William was placed under the care of Ezekeil Bartlett. From the age of
nine onward the boy was apprenticed to tradesmen, first a shoemaker,
then a cabinetmaker, and finally a printer. As a "printer's devil" Garrison showed real aptitude, and at the age of thirteen he was taken on as
an apprentice by a local newspaper. Working for the *Newburyport Herald,* Garrison rose to become a full-fledged journeyman in a trade that
was rapidly expanding but that was nevertheless over crowded. At the
age of twenty-one he left the *Herald* to become the editor of the Essex
County *Free Press,* one of the thousands of short-lived American newspapers of the era. Garrison soon moved on, going in 1828 to Boston,
where he briefly edited a reform paper, the *National Philanthropist,*
and then on to Vermont. This peripatetic career, common among young

printers who wanted to run their own papers, landed Garrison in Baltimore in 1829. It was here in the slave state of Maryland that he realized his calling as an abolitionist, working with the Quaker Benjamin Lundy as editors of the *Genius of Universal Emancipation*. Together they were jailed for libel, beginning Garrison's war with conventional politics.

Garrison was not long in prison, and after he got out he went back to Boston. At Boston he found support among African Americans for a new abolitionist paper. In Massachusetts, where slavery had been outlawed by the constitution of 1780, the issue of abolition was quiescent. The cotton textile industry thrived on the product of slave labor, and few people were disposed to challenge the status quo in the slave states. Indeed urban development and rising race consciousness were proceeding in tandem in the Bay State. Increasingly, formal patterns of segregation curtailed the freedom of blacks. Their discontent and their subscriptions sustained Garrison in his new vocation as editor of the *Liberator*.

On January 1, 1831, standing "within sight of Bunker Hill and in the birthplace of liberty," Garrison demanded the immediate abolition of slavery. Rejecting the colonization movement that he had once supported and condemning all forms of gradualism, the twenty-five-year old Garrison declared:

> I *will be* as harsh as truth, and as uncompromising as justice. On this subject, I do not wish to think, or speak, or write, with moderation. No! no! Tell a man whose house is on fire to give a moderate alarm; tell him to moderately rescue his wife from the hands of the ravisher; tell the mother to gradually extricate her babe from the fire into which it has fallen; but urge me not to use moderation in a cause like the present. I am in earnest—I will not equivocate—I will not excuse—I will not retreat a single inch— AND I WILL BE HEARD. The apathy of the people is enough to make every statue leap from its pedestal, and to hasten the resurrection of the dead.[1]

For the first time, a white Massachusetts native took up the crusade that David Walker, a black second-hand clothes dealer had preached for several years. Garrison's energy, commitment, and skill would soon make him the principal leader of a movement that eventually transformed American attitudes toward slavery.

*View of Boston Common and State House, c. 1810.*
Watercolor by Andrew Ritchie, from a c. 1810 sketch by J. R. Smith.
From Justin Winsor, ed., *The Memorial History of Boston,*
*1630–1880,* vol. 4, 1883.

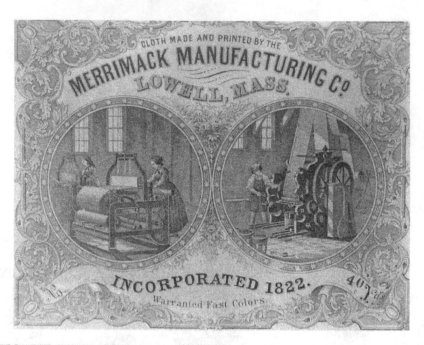

*Advertising trade card of the Merrimack Manufacturing Company, Lowell, which made and printed cloth.*

Courtesy American Antiquarian Society, Worcester.

*Cover of the December 1845 issue of the* Lowell Offering, *a magazine written by women factory workers.*

From *New England Magazine,* vol. 1, 1889.

*Lucy Stone (1818–1893),
advocate of women's rights
who helped organize and
served as president of the
American Woman Suffrage
Association.*

Photo Studio Home Portraits,
Ansonia, New York. Sophia Smith
Collection, Smith College.

*Irish emigrants embarking from County Cork
for Boston, Quebec, or New York, 1851.*

From *Illustrated London News*, May 10, 1852.
Courtesy Eugene Worman.

*William Lloyd Garrison (1805–1879), publisher of Boston's abolitionist newspaper,* The Liberator *(est. 1831).*

After an 1853 daguerreotype by Chase. From Justin Winsor, ed., *The Memorial History of Boston, 1630–1880,* vol. 3, 1883.

*Masthead of* The Liberator.

From *New England Magazine,* December 1890.

In the *Liberator* Garrison lamented public apathy, but within a year or so, that apathy was replaced by active antagonism. Garrison, not content with just a newspaper voice, led in the formation of the New England Anti-Slavery Society organized at Boston in 1832 in emulation of the flourishing American Tract Society. Speakers, agents, pamphlets, and subscriptions would spread the message throughout New England and the nation. The evangelical spirit, as well as its techniques, infused abolitionism. Grounding their appeals on Christian principles as much as on the ideals of the Revolution, the abolitionists effectively challenged the status quo with verbal assaults.

Outside Massachusetts, in the South particularly, a repressive response was almost immediate. Incendiary attacks on the established order were intolerable, and in Congress the effort began to bar abolitionist writings from United States mail and to ban abolitionist petitions to the House and Senate. The chief defender of abolitionists in Washington was John Quincy Adams, the ex-president who returned to Congress to represent a southeastern Massachusetts district. Adams was not yet an active abolitionist, but he vigorously defended the republican principle of free speech against the gag rule in the late 1830s. The abolitionist cause suffered severe setbacks before any progress was made.

The year 1835 was critical. By then the New England Anti-Slavery Society had joined with the American Anti-Slavery Society in a national propaganda campaign that included mass mailing as well as full-time paid agents. Opposition to slavery in the Bay State had a knotty history. In this period, the upper classes of businessmen, industrialists, and gentry were hostile to Garrison and his small band of abolitionists. On several occasions, according to the historian Leonard Richards, these prominent men—"doctors and lawyers, merchants and bankers, judges and congressmen"—employed violence to intimidate and crush abolitionist sentiment in their midst. These "gentlemen of property and standing" feared that abolitionism would disrupt the mutually advantageous political economy of the industrial and commercial Northeast and the agricultural South, thus challenging their economic, social, and political dominance. They needed to continue good relationships with that area that provided the raw cotton for their textile mills; and the fact that the Garrisonians openly called for the abrogation of the Constitution, since it sanctified slavery, was to them outrageous. Moreover, most northerners, regardless of class, dreaded the possibility of interracial marriage—"Amalgamation"—that might result from the freeing of the slaves. They also strongly opposed the abolitionist reliance on women's antislavery societies, which threatened the patriarchal order.[2] In an attempt to squelch anti-slavery propaganda, a large number of anti-abolitionist riots, aided and abetted by prosperous gentlemen, occurred between 1833 and 1837 in Massachusetts and the rest of the nation, with at least twelve taking place in 1835 alone.

Violent protests against abolitionist agitation were endemic across the United States, and in Massachusetts crowds at Lynn and Boston nearly killed the visiting British antislavery advocate George Thompson and Garrison. The "Garrison mob," as it was later called, began by breaking up a small meeting of the Boston Female Anti-Slavery Society that gathered on the afternoon of October 21, 1835. Garrison had been invited to address this group of thirty women at the *Liberator's* building on Washington Street, but a crowd of young men invaded the hall and finally succeeded in grabbing Garrison, notwithstanding the effort of Mayor Theodore Lyman, a Harvard-educated Jackson Democrat, to extricate him. Tied up by the mob, Garrison was dragged through the streets to the site of the Boston Massacre. Here, he was stripped to his underwear, but though he was verbally abused, two burly men protected him from being physically beaten. Ultimately Lyman returned with constables and they wrenched Garrison away, driving him by horse and carriage at breakneck speed to a local jail for safekeeping. The next morning Lyman and several other officials persuaded Garrison to leave Boston for several days "to tranquillize the public mind." No effort was made to arrest any of those who had led the crowd or attacked Garrison. Garrison himself believed that the episode was "planned and executed, not by the rabble, or the workingmen, but by 'gentlemen of property and standing,'" and "evidently winked at by the city authorities."[3] Garrison's suspicions were plausible; only two months earlier Lyman had led a meeting at Faneuil Hall at which the mercantile elite of Boston criticized the efforts of abolitionists and proclaimed support for the constitutional guarantees that protected slavery in the South.

Yet the abolition cause continued to win converts. In 1837 the abolitionist editor Elijah P. Lovejoy, a native of the frontier town of Albion in the old eastern district of Maine, was killed defending his press in Alton, Illinois; and fellow abolitionists instantly elevated him to martyrdom. In Boston William Ellery Channing, among others, petitioned Mayor Samuel A. Eliot and the aldermen for permission to use Faneuil Hall to protest Lovejoy's death. After initially rejecting the petition, the authorities yielded. When the meeting came to order, both the friends and foes of abolition were represented, and after Channing addressed the assembly on the importance of free speech, the attorney general of Massachusetts, James T. Austin, issued a rejoinder. Lovejoy's right to free speech, he said, was no more legitimate than Parliament's right to tax the colonists, and so the men who killed Lovejoy were great patriots, the equals of those Massachusetts sons of liberty who had gloriously dumped the tea in Boston Harbor. Lovejoy was merely pitiful, Austin declared: he "died as the fool dieth."[4] When the attorney general sat down he was loudly cheered.

But Austin did not have the last word. Wendell Phillips, a twenty-six year-old lawyer with some prior experience in platform oratory, rose to answer him. Phillips became indignant when Austin "asserted principles which place the murderer of Alton side by side with Otis and Hancock, with Quincy and Adams." Pointing to their portraits which hung around the hall, Phillips exclaimed, "I thought those pictured lips would have broken into voice to rebuke the recreant American, the slanderer of the dead. . . . For the sentiments [Austin] has uttered, on soil consecrated by the prayers of Puritans and the blood of patriots, the earth should have yawned and swallowed him up." Phillips went on to explain that the patriots of 1776 had battled to defend constitutional rights, whereas Lovejoy's assailants fought to destroy the constitutional right of free speech. "James Otis," he said, "thundered in this Hall when the King did but touch his *pocket*. Imagine, if you can, his indignant eloquence, had England offered to put a gag on his lips." Insisting on the abolitionists' share of the Revolutionary heritage, Phillips concluded that "when Liberty is in danger, Faneuil Hall has the right, it is her duty, to strike the keynote for these United States."[5] The people of Massachusetts possessed a historic responsibility to cleanse the nation. When Phillips sat down, he had created a new career for himself as spokesman for Garrisonian abolition and advocate for the oppressed.

Like Garrison, Phillips came to his calling indirectly. Born in 1811 as the eighth child in a prosperous Boston merchant family, young Wendell enjoyed all the advantages of wealth, talent, and health. At Boston

Latin School he won the prize for declamation and then went on to Harvard College, from which he was graduated in 1831. After three years' training at the law school with Supreme Court justice Joseph Story, he entered practice in the conventional way on Court Street. But since Phillips's family provided him with independent means, he had no need to embroil himself in the technicalities of writs and pleadings on behalf of other people's money. After Phillips married Ann Terry Greene, the daughter of a rich merchant who was herself an ardent member of the Boston Female Anti-Slavery Society, his direction became clear. "My wife made me an out-and-out abolitionist," he recalled. "Wendell, don't shilly-shally!" Ann Phillips decreed.[6]

The masthead of the *Liberator* proclaimed the motto: "Our country is the world, our countrymen are Mankind." Garrison, recognizing Phillips's superb oratorical gifts, quickly pressed him into service as a key voice in the crusade beyond the boundaries of the Bay State. During the next twenty-five years Phillips would spend most of his time traveling throughout the northern states giving free lectures on abolition. Phillips also earned substantial fees (which he plowed back into the cause) by lecturing on history, philosophy, literature, and art on the lyceum circuit from Maine to Missouri. On these occasions he was warmly applauded, but when he mounted the platform to attack slavery, the greetings were more mixed. Phillips was heckled and mobbed again and again in the 1840s and 1850s—so often that he became a shrewd manipulator of crowds. Proud to fight the good fight, he could not be intimidated. His opponents lamented, partly in scorn and partly in despair, that "Wendell Phillips is an infernal machine set to music."[7]

Phillips did not shilly-shally, and he was radical. As early as 1842 he followed Garrison in publicly cursing the Constitution of the United States as a covenant with slavery and argued that political separatism was better than joining in evil. Both Garrison and Phillips recognized the impolitic character of their attack on the Constitution of 1787, but their realities were truth and virtue, and they *would be heard*. In 1840 they both were willing to see the American Anti-Slavery Society split over the ideological issues of women's rights and pacifism. Conservative abolitionists, who did not attack the Constitution, broke off from the American Anti-Slavery Society over the issue of women's voting rights. These "schismatics" opposed women's full participation and left the

American Anti-Slavery Society and organized the Massachusetts Abolition Society (not to be confused with Garrison's Massachusetts Anti-slavery Society). Garrison and Phillips supported full equality for women. For men who were in some sense disciples of Channing, the expedients of the moment and the survival of a particular organization were always subordinate to their perceptions of truth. And however impractical they may have been, however "counterproductive" their decision literally to burn the Constitution at a Fourth of July rally at Framingham in 1854, it was the intensity and sincerity of their commitment, rooted in individual judgment, that gave them their moral force. In a struggle that Garrison and Phillips believed concerned ideological absolutes, pragmatism had limited appeal.

As knowledge about the brutality of slavery became more widespread, due to abolitionist propaganda and the popularity of Harriet Beecher Stowe's 1850 classic, *Uncle Tom's Cabin*, many residents of Massachusetts changed their stance and became abolitionists or at least anti-expansionists. This was not a class issue. Elites that favored continued commercial intercourse with the South clashed with Brahmins who took a firm ideological position that slavery was evil, as did members of the middle and working classes. Many took no position at all. Nonetheless, opposition to slavery was so widespread that Boston and Massachusetts became national havens for fugitives from slavery. One of those who took a deep interest in this issue was Worcester's Unitarian minister, Thomas Wentworth Higginson.

Higginson was the son of a Boston merchant and descendant of a long line of Boston gentlemen prominently involved in the colony and the Revolution. Born in 1823 in Cambridge (where he died in 1911), he lived an active life as a minister, reformer, soldier, and author and editor. He entered Harvard at the age of thirteen, graduating at seventeen, and later training in its Unitarian-leaning divinity school to become a minister in 1847. He held few pastorates for long because of his impassioned opposition to slavery as well as his outspoken commitment to women's suffrage and temperance. He finally found a safe pastorate in the "Free Church" of Worcester, where he remained from 1852 until 1861. Higginson was one of those radical abolitionists, like Garrison, who saw the constitution as evil and called for its dissolution. His blunt rhetoric and his penchant to use violence for his cause branded him as a fanatic who was generally scorned by the Boston aristocracy. Nonetheless, when fugitives were arrested, Boston antislavery leaders invited the prominent abolitionist Higginson to come to Boston from his ministry in Worcester. In 1856 he journeyed to "bleeding" Kansas, where he met the fiery John Brown. In 1859 he was one of the "Secret Six" backers of Brown's raid on Harpers Ferry, along with other Boston abolition leaders, Reverend Theodore Parker and Samuel Gridley Howe. Afterward, during the Civil War, Higginson's reputation as a fighter against slavery earned him a colonelcy as the first to command an all black regiment, the First South Carolina Volunteers. Wounded in battle, he was forced to retire in 1864. He spent the rest of his long and fruitful life fighting for reform causes including women's rights, by writing books, articles, and giving speeches. As editor of the *Atlantic Monthly* he served as the first mentor of the Amherst poetic genius, Emily Dickinson. He was, truly, one the literary lights of late-nineteenth-century Massachusetts. However, it was the cause of fugitive slaves that brought Higginson to the reform fold when he was a young man.

The first public event centering on fugitive slaves occurred in 1836, when a slave agent had two black women, Eliza Small and Polly Ann Bates, arrested as runaways. In court, Judge Lemuel Shaw, chief justice of the Supreme Judicial Court, ordered them freed on a technicality, because the agent had not obtained a warrant before his action. Immediately responding to the judge's order, the agent requested the warrant on the spot, which Shaw granted. The courtroom, made up largely of blacks and white women who supported the two escapees, erupted in anger. Men from the crowd overcame the bailiff and removed the black women. Judge Shaw tried to block their escape, but he was knocked to the floor. Bostonians had embarked upon a new enterprise.

By 1850, fugitive slave rescues in Boston and elsewhere in the North became a major irritant to the South. The passage of a national proslavery fugitive slave law in September of 1850 led to more serious confrontations between those wishing to uphold the law and those abolitionists, such as the clergymen Theodore Parker and Thomas Wentworth Higginson and Wendell Phillips, who believed in a "higher law." The new law put the return of fugitives solely in the hands of federal agents, who were compensated ten dollars for finding the person a slave, five dollars for finding otherwise. Slave owners or their agents merely had to swear ownership. It was up to the accused African Americans to prove they were freemen. In a city with a free black population of more than two thousand, such a law put every African American, fugitive or not, at risk.

Two fugitive slaves, a married couple, William and Ellen Craft, had lived in Boston since 1848. In October of 1850, their owner appeared and had them arrested. Local blacks and white abolitionists were determined to protect them. Theodore Parker and others organized a rescue based on intimidation. A crowd of over two thousand blacks and whites harassed the owner and the slave catchers. Fearing for his life, the owner fled from Boston. With no one to press the case, the court reluctantly freed the Crafts. In February 1851, a crowd of blacks stormed a courtroom and took away by force a fugitive slave named Shadrach Minkins. The open violation of the law incensed President Millard Fillmore who issued a proclamation urging Bostonians to obey the law. The Whig municipal authorities expressed their regrets over the incident and made plans to prevent any future recurrence.

The next time Boston authorities arrested a fugitive—Thomas Sims, in April 1851—they took extreme precautions to prevent his rescue. The mayor ordered the entire police force to use barricades to guard the area around the courthouse. The antislavery forces divided on how to proceed. The majority led by Wendell Phillips thought of using legal remedies. Only Thomas Wentworth Higginson and black leaders Leonard Grimes and Lewis Hayden recommended force to free Sims. Higginson and Grimes and a few of their followers planned a forcible rescue. Higginson recalled the event:

> The colored clergyman of Boston, Mr. Grimes, who alone had the opportunity to visit Sims, agreed to arrange with him that at a specified hour that evening he should go to a certain window, as if for air—for he had the freedom of the room—and should spring out on mattresses which we were to bring from a lawyer's office across the way; we also providing a carriage in which to place him. All was arranged—the message sent, the mattresses ready, the carriage engaged as if for an ordinary purpose; and behold! in the dusk of that evening, two of us, strolling through Court Square, saw men busily at work fitting iron bars across this

safe third-story window. Whether we had been betrayed, or whether it was simply a bit of extraordinary precaution, we never knew.[8]

Soon after, a very strong police contingent of three hundred armed constables, reinforced by volunteers, escorted Sims to the docks, where they placed him on a ship to return to the South.

The last major attempt to rescue a captured fugitive slave occurred in 1854, when Higginson and a group of antislavery mechanics and freed blacks led a violent but unsuccessful attempt to free the fugitive Anthony Burns. After Burns had been arrested, abolitionists hired the famous lawyer Richard Henry Dana Jr. to defend him. But many believed that a legal response was fruitless in the face of the new law. The abolitionist Ann Phillips, Wendell Phillips's wife, wrote: "If this man is allowed to go back *there is* no anti slavery in Mass[achuset]ts—We may as well disband at once if our meetings & papers are all talk & we never are to do any [thing] but talk."[9] Higginson agreed, and once again the fiery minister planned violent action.

On Friday, May 26, Higginson and his band of zealots stormed the jail holding Burns. Federal marshals and local armed volunteers repulsed the attack with force. During the fray one of the special deputies was killed, and several men were wounded, including Higginson, who suffered a cut on his face and was later arrested.

After a week of court hearings, the Boston officials ordered Burns's return to slavery. Local businesses and offices draped black streamers and crepe from their windows to express their opposition when hearing the news. Large crowds began filling the streets. The authorities now had to transport Burns through an agitated populace to a ship at the docks. To ensure order, 1,500 militia, plus the entire police force, and 145 regular federal troops with cannon, with 100 special deputies began clearing the streets as they marched Burns to the waiting ship. Crowd members began hurling objects at the troops and they responded with brute force. Cavalry units struck bystanders with sabers, and troops beat spectators with their rifle butts. The blatant use of force scattered the crowds and Burns was returned to a life of slavery in the South. Events such as these increased antislavery sentiment in Massachusetts and beyond, and fostered widespread support for a new political party.

of the expansion of slavery gave rise to the Republican
n Massachusetts was able to forge a coalition between
, Free-Soilers, antislavery Democrats, and the powerful
things. The national Know-Nothing party was undecided on
very question, largely because of its prominent southern compo-
nt. In Massachusetts, however, Know-Nothings supported a modified version of the antislavery position. A goodly portion of its rank
and file members in Massachusetts were opposed to extending slavery
into the territories. Some abolitionists, such as Boston Unitarian minister Theodore Parker, made the connection between Catholicism and
slavery: "The Catholic clergy are on the side of slavery. . . . They like
slavery itself; it is an institution thoroughly congenial to them, consistent to the first principles of their church." [10]

Sentiment now prevailed in the Bay State that the territories must be
kept free of slavery in order to preserve the Republic. The victory of the
Republican party was not the work of charismatic political giants, such
as Charles Sumner, but was due to the coming together of men from
all walks of life who were opposed to the promulgation of slavery. Most
new Republicans were not abolitionists, but they thought slavery evil
and that it would eventually die if prohibited from being extended into
new lands. These men were moderates whose major concern was that
growth of the slave states would imperil democracy as they knew it.
One such man, Samuel Bowles Jr. of Springfield, was to use his position
as a journalist and editor, to help construct this new party.

In the 1850s, Bowles had become a national figure, both for his editorial prowess and the success of his newspaper, the *Springfield Republican*. Born in Springfield in 1826, Bowles was the son of a printer who
owned a weekly newspaper. The *Republican* had been founded in 1824
as an alternative to the weekly Federalist paper. By the 1830s, when
young Bowles was an apprentice, it—like Daniel Webster—had changed
its political orientation and was solidly Whig. Leaving school at the
age of seventeen, Bowles worked at various jobs on the paper, finally
convincing his father to change it from a weekly to a daily and weekly
in 1844. After his father's death in 1851, the young reporter took over
the ownership and the editorship of the paper. By 1860, Bowles had
build it up to such a degree that it dominated the Springfield region's
press, with a circulation of twelve thousand for the weekly and six
thousand for the daily.

As the Whig party deteriorated in the late 1850s, Bow[...]
tablishing an editorial position that was to be common fo[...]
in Massachusetts. He was opposed to the extension of [...]
felt the abolitionists were extremists. He supported the aim of the Free
Soil party in 1848, but could not vote for its candidate, the former
Democrat Martin Van Buren, whom he considered a puppet of the
slave masters. After the Burns debacle in 1854 and the controversy over
slavery in the Kansas and Nebraska territories, he took on a more ada-
mant antislavery position. He came to believe that it was time to put
together a new party, made up of old Whigs, disenchanted local Know-
Nothings, antislave Democrats, and temperance people. Acting alone,
and depending on his prestige among the powerful of Boston, he
chaired a gathering of sympathetic state leaders in Boston at which it
was agreed to form a new party. A convention of delegates from various
political factions met at Worcester on September 20, 1855, and formed
the Massachusetts Republican party. The major issue discussed was
preventing the expansion of slavery into the territories. The first political act of these new Republicans was to nominate Henry J. Gardner
for governor. Gardner was at that time the sitting governor and the
Know-Nothing candidate for that position in 1855. In 1856 Bowles
went to the first national convention of the Republicans, where they
nominated John C. Fremont. By 1860 Bowles was an ardent advocate
of preserving the Union, becoming a staunch supporter of the Republican presidential nominee, Abraham Lincoln.

The presidential election of 1860 gave Bay Staters a platform to express their opposition to slavery. Abraham Lincoln won a major victory
in Massachusetts, although he lost in Boston's heavily Irish wards. With
the onset of the Civil War, the Republicans controlled the Massachusetts governorship, the legislature, and the mayoralty of Boston. After
the shelling of Fort Sumter, Boston militia units began gathering in Boston for a joyous reception by large crowds of well wishers:

> It is impossible to overstate the excitement which pervaded the
> entire community through this eventful week [April 16, 1861].
> The railroad depots were surrounded with crowds of people; and
> the companies, as they arrived, were received with cheers of grate-
> ful welcome. Banners were suspended, as if by preconcerted ar-
> rangement. The American flag spread its folds to the breeze across
> streets, from the masts of vessels in the harbor, from the cupola

of the State House, the City Hall, in front of private dwellings; and men and boys, carried miniature flags in their hands or on their hats. The horsecars and express wagons were decked with similar devices; and young misses adorned their persons with rosettes and ribbons; in which were blended the national red, white, and blue.[11]

Throughout the war's duration, Massachusetts volunteers and draftees, white and black, Yankee and Irish, fought for the preservation of the union.

A young soldier from Granby, Joseph Taylor, wrote home to his father, describing the charge of Massachusetts troops during the battle of Fredericksburg in 1863:

> It was one of those sights which must be seen to be appreciated. . . . It was exciting I tell you to see them go up in an unbroken line, closing up their thinned ranks as they pressed on. Nothing could resist them. . . . We could see a long cloud of dust arise in the rear as the rebs skedadalled.[12]

Perhaps the most remarkable story of Massachusetts's contribution to the Civil War revolves around Robert Gould Shaw and the Fifty-fourth Regiment of Massachusetts Volunteers of African descent.

Shaw, a Boston native born in 1837, was the son of a rich and influential Brahmin family. His parents were enthusiastic abolitionists and members of Boston's fervent antislavery circle. Young Shaw was sent to preparatory schools in Europe and the United States. Although he was impressed with his parents' devotion to the abolitionist cause, he himself was not a reformer. He was in a quandary as to what to do for a career. In the 1850s, Shaw roamed Europe, more a dilettante than the student he was supposed to be. He entered Harvard in 1856 and performed there with little distinction or enthusiasm. Shaw left college in 1859 and entered business in New York. When Lincoln was elected he joined the Seventh New York National Guard as a private. After a few months he transferred to the Second Massachusetts Infantry as a lieutenant. He was a good soldier, was wounded at the battle of Antietam, was promoted to captain, and served a year and eight months with this Massachusetts regiment. His letters home to his parents show a devoted soldier committed to the Union cause, but one who was not particularly interested in the issue of slavery. It seemed he had found his calling—

gentleman soldier. A turn of events in the war and pressure from his parents were to lead him into the cause of abolitionism.

The Emancipation Proclamation of 1863 prompted little response from Shaw, but it was to change his life dramatically. Emancipation raised the possibility of forming black regiments, something that Massachusetts abolitionists had long demanded. Massachusetts governor and ardent Free-Soiler and Republican, John A. Andrew, determined that his state would lead the way. Gaining federal permission to raise a black regiment, Andrew went to his close friends, the Shaws, to persuade their son to become its colonel. For Andrew and the Shaws, an all black regiment would prove the righteousness of their past efforts; their honor was at stake. Shaw's father carried the governor's letter directly to Virginia, where his son was now camped after the battle of Fredericksburg. In spite of parental pleading and the governor's entreaties, Shaw at first refused the commission. However, due to pressure from his mother and the wide circle of the family's friends who were thrilled by the idea, Shaw relented.

The Fifty-fourth Regiment of Massachusetts Volunteers of African descent, Col. Robert G. Shaw in command, was formed amid hoopla and generous financial support from Boston's best families. Shaw threw himself into his work, writing to his fiancée "what I have to do is prove that a negro [sic] can be made a good soldier." [13] After a triumphant parade through Boston on May 28, 1863, the Fifty-fourth took ship and sailed to South Carolina. Once there, on July 18, Shaw led his troops in battle against the impregnable Fort Wagner. Shaw and many of his men were killed, and the young white officer was buried in a mass grave with his men. Shaw's troops demonstrated the fighting capacity of black men, elevating their regiment and their leader as an enduring symbol of men sacrificing themselves for liberty. A monument sculpted by Augustus Saint-Gaudens and erected in 1897 on Boston Common is a testament both to the courageous black soldiers and their leader and to the idealistic ardor of Massachusetts abolitionists who, along with black abolitionists such as Frederick Douglass (one of whose sons fought in Shaw's regiment), made a major contribution to ending slavery in the United States.

Another Massachusetts native who served the nation with distinction during the Civil War was Clara Barton, founder of the American Red Cross. Dedicated to the Union, like Shaw and many others Barton was at a loss as to how to contribute to the cause. She found her path amid the horrors of the battlefield, where she constructed a career based on service. Born in North Oxford, Massachusetts, in 1821, her life was generally uneventful, until her fortieth year, when she was working as a clerk in the United States Patent Office in Washington.

Barton was there when a Massachusetts regiment, the Sixth, was attacked by riotous secessionists in Baltimore. The troops were marching to board a train for Washington when rioters set upon them. They returned fire and a pitched battle ensued. Barton and several other women rushed to the station to meet the troops and to help with the wounded. With no real hospital facilities available, Barton took it upon herself to organize the care and provisioning of the wounded troops. After this event, recognizing the inadequate performance of the Quartermaster Corps, she began organizing with Massachusetts communities to send parcels with food and medical supplies for front-line troops. At her own expense, she stored these provisions in three warehouses. After convincing a colonel in the Quartermaster Corps, she received wagons and passes so that she could go to the front lines and help care for the wounded.

Working entirely on her own, she organized a volunteer system that would nurture and provide sustenance for those caught up in the maelstrom of the war. She was present at several battles, including Antietam, Fredericksburg, the siege of Charleston, the Battle of the Wilderness, Spotsylvania, and Petersburg. It was on the front lines that she began her career in nursing. Later, a Massachusetts general, Benjamin Butler, named her superintendent for nurses of his army.

After the war she went worldwide, caring for victims in dangerous places devastated by war, flood, and other disasters,. In 1881, she founded the American Red Cross and spent twenty-three years as the leader of an organization known for its main goal of helping casualties of warfare and natural disaster. She died in 1912, after fifty years of devotion to others. But it was in the Civil War that she received her baptism of fire, just like other "soldiers" from Massachusetts.

The story of Massachusetts in the Civil War is not without its darker side, specifically when it concerned the role of the Irish. As much as they disliked Lincoln, the Irish of Massachusetts grudgingly supported the war effort and the preservation of the Union. With the governor's support, the Irish recruited volunteers to create the Ninth Regiment, which served with distinction during the conflict. However, many Irish opposed the Emancipation Proclamation and the conscription law passed by Congress in 1863. The draft riot of 1863 disclosed the wide breach between the Yankees and the Irish.

The New York City draft riot of 1863 captured the nation's attention, because of its duration and the enormity of its violence, but Boston had one of its own. The new draft law passed by Congress in 1863 had a particularly devastating effect on the lower-class workers of America's cities. Besides calling for a general conscription, the law provided an exemption for anyone paying three hundred dollars for a substitute. The exemption meant the well-to-do did not have to go to war. This class-based legislation made poor men cannon fodder. Such an inequity resulted in a virtual rebellion among New York City's workers, both Yankee and immigrant. The New York riot was based on long-standing white hatred of the tiny black community and resentment against the rich. Thus, the targets of the rioters were innocent blacks and rich people and their possessions. The situation was somewhat different in Boston and was shaped by the peculiar animosity that existed between the Yankees and the Irish.

In New York blacks and whites intermingled in dense working-class settings where there were daily reminders of race conflict. Boston had relatively few black residents (3 percent of the population) but they lived largely segregated in an area surrounding Beacon Hill. Boston's Irish poor lived isolated under squalid conditions packed into the North End, near the wharves. The Boston rioters did not attack blacks; instead they vented their wrath upon the symbols of Yankee oppression visible in their own neighborhoods.

The riot started around noon on July 14, when a provost marshal entered a house on Prince Street in the North End to serve draft notices. A woman opposed him and struck him. He was whisked away to a nearby store by a policeman, while a crowd gathered. When the marshal and the policeman emerged, they were assailed by a large crowd of men, women, and children. Stones and brickbats were thrown, and the two officials were badly mauled. A journalist on the scene reported that women shouted: "Kill the damned Yankee son of a bitch." [14] The crowd then moved off to attack a local police station. After growing in numbers it stormed the armory at Cooper Street in the North End, with the obvious intention of looting its weapons. Cannon and musket fire turned the crowd back, leaving eight confirmed dead, although observers claimed that the crowd removed many of the dead and wounded when they dispersed, making accurate casualty figures impossible. Afterward, several crowds began attacking gun shops and hardware stores in order to arm themselves. By late in the evening, the rioters were dispersed by armed militia and federal troops. By the next day, peace had been restored by the troops, who now patrolled the city.

This event is evidence that many of the Irish felt oppressed by the Yankees and that they believed they had no political influence and that the war did not pertain to them. A historian of the Boston Irish, Thomas O'Connor, concluded that the war had actually worsened the political status of the Irish. They were "stubborn" Democrats who had supported Stephen A. Douglas against Lincoln. Besides opposing the Emancipation Proclamation, the Irish publicly backed the Democratic candidate, George McClellan, over Lincoln in 1864. The result was that the "Irish emerged from the war in political defeat."[15] The chasm between these newcomers and the Yankees was still unbridgeable.

The victory of the Union forces resulted in the almost total political eclipse of the state's Democratic party and its Irish followers. It would take years of patchwork among Yankee and Irish Democrats to construct a fragile alliance that would allow this party to make a partial comeback. The nativist-leaning Republicans were to monopolize political power for years to come. A revived Democratic party challenged Republican power from the 1880s on, but seldom achieved victory. Even in Boston, from 1865 to 1900, the Democrats were not the dominant political party. Five mayors were Democrats, seven were Republicans, and two were nonpartisan. Nathaniel Shurtleff, who held three one year terms (1868-70) was a Democrat who switched to the Republicans for his last election. With the exception of Irish-born Catholic Hugh O'Brien (1885–88), all Boston's mayors in this century were Yankees. The Irish first became powerful in Boston with the mayoral election of John Fitzgerald in 1910, but it was not until well into the twentieth century that the Irish, finally in control of the Democratic party, were to achieve full political assimilation in the Bay State. At the end of the Civil War, Yankees were still in ascendancy.

*Frederick Douglass (1817?–1895), famous fugitive slave and abolitionist leader.*

Courtesy National Park Service, Frederick Douglass National Historic Site.

*Clara Barton (1821–1912), founder of the American Red Cross.*

Copyright The Leslie Woman Suffrage Commission, New York. Sophia Smith Collection, Smith College.

*Bronze bas-relief by Augustus Saint-Gaudens honoring the Massachusetts 54th Regiment, one of the first African American military units to serve in the Civil War (detail).*
Photo Richard W. Wilkie.

*A typical industrial setting, the interior of a press works in midcentury Boston.* Drawn by J. H. Manning, woodcut by Frank Leslie. From *Gleason's Drawing Room Companion*, 1853.

*A view of industrial Lawrence in 1855.*
Museum of American Textile History, Lowell.

*Harvard College, founded 1636, as it appeared in the 1870s.*
From William Cullen Bryant, ed., *Picturesque America*, vol. 2, 1874.
Photo J. Douglas Woodward.

*View of downtown Holyoke, Massachusetts, c. 1907.*
Courtesy Ruth Owen Jones.

# CHAPTER 10

# Urbanization and the Emergence
# of Pluralism in the Gilded Age

F OR MASSACHUSETTS, AS WELL AS FOR THE UNITED STATES,
the Civil War marked a division between two eras. After the war the
old missionary zeal lingered, but its force was spent. Veterans of past
battles, such as Lucy Stone, Wendell Phillips, and Thomas Wentworth
Higginson, still found audiences for their reforming oratory; but although some people were willing to hear their arguments, the romantic,
idealistic faith of their day, in people and society, had become anachronistic. The dominant spirit throughout the United States between the
Civil War and the First World War was self-aggrandizement.

The setting was more competitive than ever; people who enjoyed
privileged social positions and inherited wealth found rivals among
"new" men of industry and commerce. Farmers and small businessmen, craftsmen and factory workers were also in competition. Although the rise of large corporations was beginning to introduce mo-
nopolistic elements into the nation's economy by the end of the century,
most people lived in a world where competitive self-seeking was necessary and legitimate. Old reformers and new ones challenged the Adam
Smith–Herbert Spencer philosophy that glorified individual pursuit of
self-interest. And although reformers denied the standard assertions
that competition enhanced the common good, the people who lived in
North Shore Italian villas and Back Bay brick mansions, as well as those
who lived in bleached clapboard farmhouses, in mill dormitories, and
in the alleyway shanties of East Boston, all knew that competition was
a fact of life, and they looked out for themselves first, and—often—

last. Ironically it was not just the poor or aspiring, but even the most highborn and wealthy who felt insecure in the dynamic social and economic environment of late nineteenth-century Massachusetts.

Some rhetorical commitment to the old ideal of disinterested service for the common good survived and exercised an influence on the language of public affairs and benevolence, but true believers were few in number, and they were generally located at the periphery of power. The old idea of an objective, disinterested definition of the public good—the ideal that magistrates had been righteously seeking from John Winthrop's day to John Adams's—was being transformed. Now the common good had come to be defined in relation to the interests of individuals banding together as groups. As a mass society developed, people became submerged politically into collective categories; social class, denomination, and ethnic background became primary identities, commanding substantial loyalty in public affairs. "Is it good for men of property [or working men; or Catholics]?" people asked themselves. "Class" loyalty, broadly construed, outweighed loyalties to particular towns and to the commonwealth. Patriotism, nourished by the Union cause and by the process of naturalization among immigrant citizens, became chiefly national. The importance of state and locality paled in comparison to class and nation.

The new industrial society created massive demographic change and the redistribution of the population into urban communities. Uprooted from farm and village, the migrant to the city was forced to reinvent the fabric of familial and social ties. High population densities accompanied by residential transience generated a sense of isolation and anonymity among newcomers. The total dependence of the working class on the unpredictable price system and business cycle, coupled with unsatisfying and routinized jobs, served to increase feelings of insecurity amid the strange urban environment. The transforming move to the city challenged the traditional moral order, but the attraction of plentiful jobs in the new factory towns was irresistible.

Manufacturing flourished in Massachusetts between 1850 and 1880, when three-quarters of the state's workforce could be considered members of the working class. The majority of Massachusetts residents were now involved either in industry or in areas supportive of industry—the definitive sign of an industrialized society. The decade beginning in 1860 was the period of the greatest growth of manufacturing; the numbers of manufacturing establishments jumped from 8,176 in 1860 to 13,212 in 1870, a rise of 61.8 percent. Capital investment expanded in this period by 61.6 percent. In the next decade, although the number of manufacturing units grew only by a modest 8.6 percent, capital investment rose by 31.1 percent. The number of textile workers had grown from 27,600 in 1837 to 93,000 in 1880. Similarly, the shoe industry, transformed by the introduction of the sewing machine in 1852, grew from 35,300 workers in 1837 to 61,500 in 1880. By 1880, 42 percent of the labor force was in manufacturing, 14 percent in trade and finance, 8 percent in construction, 19 percent in service areas (including public administration and household work), 7 percent in transportation, with only 10 percent in agriculture and 1 percent in fisheries. Measured by overall productivity, Massachusetts was third to New York and Pennsylvania, but on a per capita basis in 1880 it "was the most thoroughly industrialized state."[1]

An integral component of the movement to the factory system was the development of an effective transportation network. Though a distant second to New York in volume of shipping, by 1877 the port of Boston eclipsed Philadelphia and Baltimore combined. Easy access to overseas and coastal markets and to raw materials provided a natural incentive for capital investment in manufacturing. Even though the viability of the port began to decline when Philadelphia and Baltimore developed larger port facilities and had greater access to important railroad connections, in 1900, Boston was still the second most important port in the nation, controlling one-fifth of the aggregate foreign tonnage of the nation.

The railroad was vital to any industrial buildup. After a slow start in the 1840s, major railroad construction in Massachusetts, the most in the Union, took place in the 1850s. By the end of the decade every Massachusetts town of five thousand or more had a railroad connection. After the Civil War a new spurt of railroad building began. The creation of the consolidated Boston and Albany Railroad in 1867, the wealthiest corporation in the state, and the completion of the Hoosac Tunnel route in the 1870s finalized the statewide railroad network and opened up trade with the West. Railroad development increased the shipping capacity of the port of Boston. Reaching all corners of the state, the railroads brought in cotton, wool, iron, coal, livestock, wheat flour, and corn and on return carried westward and southward the finished manufactured goods. The railroads also provided the capability of moving large numbers of workers to the factory communities that urgently required their labor.

With the exception of Rhode Island, Massachusetts was the nation's most densely populated state and it continued to attract large numbers of newcomers. Increases of 22.4 percent, 25.6 percent, and 25.3 percent, respectively, in the three decades from 1870 to 1900, were almost identical to the overall growth rate of the entire United States. The proportion of foreign-born increased from 1 percent in 1830 to 25 percent in the 1870s. In 1895 the Massachusetts Census recorded that immigrants represented 30.6 percent of the population.

The major impetus in the migration to the city was the desire for economic betterment. In many instances, the call to the cities was encouraged by those who had already made the arduous journey. One French Canadian worker in Springfield wrote to a friend: "The pay is good Basile. We work from sunrise to sunset, but on Sunday the mills are closed and it is like a church holy day. The work is not hard. Some of the children are working and we make more money than we can spend. Let me know what you decide, and if you want to come I will speak to the foreman."[2] There seems little doubt that harsh as the conditions of urban life were, it was much better than the agrarian poverty these migrants left in Quebec. Bringing with them modest expectations, they saw material improvement in their new lives.

French Canadian immigrants followed in the wake of the Irish after the Civil War. The *Holyoke Transcript* of March 29, 1879, described the arrival of poverty-stricken French Canadians from the agrarian depression of Quebec: "They come with all their worldly goods packed in boxes and bundles, and the gents' room at the Connecticut River railroad depot is packed with their effects till it looks like a wholesale warehouse. . . . Some have friends or relatives here, expecting to find plenty of work on their arrival."[3] Throughout the 1870s, one-quarter to one-third of the farm land in Quebec was deserted. By 1880, twenty-five thousand French Canadians had arrived by train. But the close proximity to Canada also meant that many returned to Quebec, especially during the depression of 1893. It is estimated that half of the Canadians who immigrated to New England returned before 1900, but nonetheless, by the turn of the century they were a major presence in communities like Lowell, Fall River, New Bedford, Gardner, Leominster, North Adams, Chicopee, Granby, Ware, and a scattering of small towns throughout the state.

Arriving after the Irish, and like their predecessors willing to work at lower than prevailing wages, and hostile to labor unions, the French Canadian peasants were treated harshly by Yankee Protestant and Irish Catholic alike. On occasion Quebecers were used by employers as scabs to break up strikes, thus earning them the sobriquet of "Knobsticks." State labor commissioner Carroll D. Wright characterized them as "the Chinese of the Eastern states." He went on to say: "These people have one good trait. They are indefatigable workers and docile."[4] The French Canadians, for their part, hated the Irish, not only because of ill-treatment at their hands, but also because of the Fenian raids on Canada between 1866 and 1871. French immigrants were intensely clannish and ethnocentric, were ruled by their own priests, avoided unionization, and usually supported the Republican party. They added considerably to the volatile mix of ethnic groups that now made up the population of Massachusetts. Of a state population of 1,783,085 in 1880, 439,341 had at least one foreign-born parent. Successive generations of immigrants were to make up the varied populations of the Bay State's mushrooming factory towns.

The greatest surge in immigration occurred from 1890 to 1910, when over a million foreigners came to New England cities from eastern and southern Europe. These immigrants were to become the inhabitants of Massachusetts's new urban civilization; as early as 1870 the census revealed that well over a majority of the people (66.7%) lived in urban areas of the state. Only Rhode Island (74.6%), the exceptional District of Columbia (87.2%), and New York (50%), were more than half urban. By the end of the century fully 76 percent of the state's 2,805,346 residents lived in cities.

It was during the period known as the Gilded Age that the once-paternalistic factory towns made the rapid transition to industrial cities. The first factory town, Waltham, was a city of 18,707 by 1890. Forty-four percent of the population were Irish Catholics engaged in mainly blue-collar, low-paying work. With Yankee Protestants in higher-status jobs, the city was segregated into ethnic, class-oriented neighborhoods. By 1894, the presence of significant numbers of French Canadians led to formation of a separate Catholic church—a sign of ethnic divisiveness. Waltham's workers in the Gilded Age were not subject to the grinding poverty common to other factory towns. They did experience a measure of material success, but not enough to move them from blue-collar to white-collar ranks. The evidence suggests that these antagonistic and often warring ethnic and religious groups hammered out a reasonable accommodation within what the historian Howard Gitelman termed a "markedly stratified society."[5] However, no such accommodation developed in Lowell or Lawrence.

Lowell, the first planned factory town, was incorporated in 1826 with a population of 2,500. By 1895 the population of this city had expanded to 84,387, with 28,260 employed in industry. With the continuous expansion of the cotton industry, Lowell reigned supreme until 1890, when it was surpassed by Fall River, a still greater textile mill city. As in Waltham, the labor force of farmers' daughters first gave way to the flood of Irish immigrants in the late 1840s and 1850s. When the famines of 1845–55 brought Irish over in increasing numbers and, more important, when the Boston Associates dismantled the Waltham system and hired the Irish to work in the mills, Lowell was transformed. Rapid growth and dense settlement led to high land costs and the inevitable rise of slums and tenements. Inadequate sanitation created serious health problems. By the eve of the Civil War the Irish of Lowell lived in tenements and had twice the death rate of the Yankees. The poor health of the men and their migratory search for jobs meant that 31 percent of Irish households were headed by women. Low family income also required that many family members, including children, work in the mills.

After the Civil War large numbers of French Canadians came to the city to compete with the Irish for jobs. By 1890 the Irish and the French Canadians (twenty-three thousand by 1900) became the most numerous groups, easily surpassing the once dominant Yankees. Then Portuguese, Greeks, Poles, Lithuanians, and Italians began to arrive in ever-increasing numbers, adding to the city's variegated populace. The immigrants crowded into the central area of the city while natives moved to the outer districts. By the turn of the century, the French Canadians were the dominant ethnic group. Lowell had become a city beset with problems and dependent on the vagaries of a single industry that was now in decline.

Initially heralded as a model factory town, Lawrence too was to feel the brunt of change occasioned by immigration. While the Irish provided cheap labor—less than one dollar for a twelve-hour day in 1850, for example—they altered the community. They could only afford makeshift shanties where they were plagued by typhoid fever epidemics and tuberculosis. When Know-Nothingism reared its ugly head, Yankee mechanics attacked Irish neighborhoods in 1854. The squalor of Irish poverty, coupled with high rates of illiteracy and drinking, reinforced the rise of an intense nativism that divided the community for years. The revival of the cotton industry after 1865 marked the opening of new mills, and, as had happened in Lowell and Holyoke, there was a wave of migration from Canada. By 1900, the one-fifth of the immigrants were French Canadians, who were scorned by both natives and Irish.

In the last decade of the century Lawrence made some progress in efforts to improve housing, reduce mortality rates, and provide needed municipal services. Between 1900 and 1920 a large influx of southeastern European immigrants from Russia, Austria, and Italy increased the city's population from sixty-two to ninety-four thousand. The overall economic picture continued to be perilous for the city's ethnic working-class population.

Fall River and New Bedford, neighboring cities in the southernmost part of the state, joined a major urbanized belt bordering Rhode Island, and ranked among the nation's top twenty-five manufacturing cities in the nineteenth century. Located some fifty miles south of Boston, Fall River was referred to as the "Queen City of Cotton." Its natural advantages of water power and a humid climate good for cotton processing attracted investors from Providence and Boston. Ten mills were set up by 1837. With the changeover from water power to steam, Fall River's coastal location gave it the advantage of cheaper transportation costs for coal, so more mills were built. The mix of workers was somewhat different from that of Lowell and Lawrence. A mainly Yankee workforce was augmented by large numbers of English mill workers from Lancashire. The 1870s and 1880s saw an influx of Irish workers, but these were mill workers who had migrated previously to Lancashire and were already urbanized and familiar with the English trade union movement. By 1875, 13,000 of the population of 43,000 came from Lancashire, the next largest group being 5,000 French Canadians. Surpassing Lowell as textile leader in 1890, by 1900 Fall River had forty-two industrial corporations with a working force of 26,371, in a multi-ethnic population of 104,863.

Fall River's workers lived in densely packed clusters of slum "villages" surrounding the mill sites. The historian John Cumbler reported: "The mill-owned houses served as a means of control over employees and were frequently a source of profit."[6] As elsewhere, low wages forced entire families to work. Fall River had the highest proportion of child laborers (25 %), as opposed to other company towns (averaging 8 %). The workers themselves were divided into the skilled—with earnings of $524 a year in 1875—and the unskilled, largely French Canadians, earning $395 a year, just enough for subsistence. Dispersed slum villages kept the urbanized English and Irish apart from the rural French Canadians. A work style based on plentiful labor, excessive job pressure, a machine-tending technology, and many women and child laborers all prevented workers from organizing. Throughout the century, Fall River's workers suffered through periodic dislocations and the hardships of intermittent wage cutting, as well as periods of unemployment and labor conflict.

Circumstances in New Bedford paralleled those in neighboring Fall River. On the eve of the Civil War, the town was still a major whaling center but it was quickly transformed into a fine cotton goods center, with over forty-two mills by 1900. Again, the workforce was divided between skilled and semiskilled Lancashire men and the Irish. The French Canadians were the late arrivals who worked at the lowest-paying unskilled jobs. Early labor disputes concerned skilled workers— spinners and weavers who complained of long hours, wage cuts, and speedups. A strike in 1877 and later strikes were complicated by issues relating to ethnic differences and the level of skills among the workers. Refused admittance into the skilled workers unions, the French Canadians became the scabs of the community. Between 1883 and 1893 there were at least thirty-one strikes by crafts workers, most of which failed. Labor tensions increased with two major strikes in 1894 and 1898. Constant deskilling and introduction of new technology caused tensions among the varied crafts workers themselves. Backed by their priests, discriminated against by the Irish and Lancashire men, the French Canadians went back to work in 1898, thus destroying the strike. The arrival of new immigrant workers, Portuguese and Poles, at the turn of the century strengthened the hands of employers and heightened the ethnic divisions among the workers.

In New Bedford, the multiplicity of ethnic groups, burdened with feuds and dissensions, coupled with a jealously guarded occupational hierarchy, resulted in a divided working class unable to protect itself. The historian Thomas McMullin wrote: "The differing response of French-Canadian and English immigrants to American industrial conditions remained a source of tensions. . . . And ironically, the craft tradition of the English, the ethnic group most oriented to labor activism, would continue to be a divisive force among New Bedford textile operatives in the twentieth century."[7]

Although their industries were smaller in overall dollar volume, the state's boot and shoemaking cities employed many more workers. As early as 1860 the shoemaking industry employed more than sixty thousand workers in Essex, Middlesex, Worcester, Plymouth, and Norfolk counties. In the nineteenth century, Lynn became the country's leading shoe manufacturing center. In 1880 the city had more than 170 shoe factories that employed 10,700 workers out of an overall population of 28,274. Located close to Boston, and financed by Boston capital, the shoe industry was dramatically affected by the introduction of the sewing machine in 1852 and the automated stitcher in 1862. Casting aside individual shoe-sewing, labor had become so specialized by 1880 that it took thirty-three different jobs to complete one pair of shoes.

Unlike the textile industry, three-fourths of all shoe workers were native born and this monopoly remained until the end of the century. The historian Alan Dawley wrote that originally shoe production was done by outwork in rural hamlets. The move of shoe production to the factory system by 1870 resulted in the collapse of the outwork system. Impoverished Yankees moved in large numbers to places like Lynn in order to be employed. "In fact," Dawley continued, "Lynn had a larger proportion of native-born workers than nearly every other major manufacturing center in the state, a consequence of the development of large-scale shoe manufacturing before the existence of a factory system."[8]

Shoemaking was largely seasonal work. The *Boston Evening Transcript* of November 13, 1886, reported that "probably not more than one-half of the operatives would have more than eight months full work if they had that amount." Declining wage rates and life in densely packed tenements surrounding warehouse factories in the central area of the city contributed to generally harsh living conditions. Nevertheless, because there were many small manufacturers, and one-loft shops that required limited capital investment, some workers could rise in status. Moreover, centralization of work and residence led to integrated working-class neighborhoods that promoted interaction and cohesion among workers. This interrelatedness molded a class consciousness and solidarity that gave Lynn workers the distinction of being the first to join or form successful unions. Worker solidarity did much to alleviate some of the harsh conditions inevitable in an industry of uncertain production cycles.

The historian Mary Blewett pointed out that between 1870 and 1910, female workers, many of them Yankees, made up a significant portion of the workforce in shoes. In Essex and Middlesex counties "lady stitchers" of Yankee farm origins persisted as skilled workers because of gender segregation:

> In this industry, therefore, the sexual division of labor provided opportunities for female workers to develop a work-culture based on skill and gender pride. It enabled them to control part of the work process, which they defended successfully against any invasions by native-born male workers who might have been attracted by the relatively high wages for stitching.[9]

Invoking their rights as "freeborn American women," Yankee women shoe workers led several successful strikes because they were able to use gender issues to create a militant coalition with immigrant women shoe workers. In spite of internal dissension, the two groups succeeded because their independent female organizations specifically addressed the needs of women workers. In 1903 the Women's Trade Union League achieved the passage of a law intended to protect women workers by limiting the hours of weekly work. The self-sufficient women shoe-stitchers were dependent upon working long hours during the busy seasons, and the reform ironically resulted in their displacement by immigrant male newcomers who were unprotected. By 1920, 62 percent of the workforce was immigrant, mainly male Italians.

The financiers of Boston did not totally ignore the western portion of the state—Chicopee and Holyoke became grim replicas of the factory towns in the east. Boston Associates Harrison Gray Otis, Samuel

Eliot, George Bliss, and Edmund Dwight built the area's first cotton mill in 1825 on a Connecticut River tributary named Chicopee. As in other factory towns between 1840 and 1860, increased competition resulted in a search for cheaper supplies of labor. In the middle decades of the century the bulk of the Yankee laborers moved up the social ladder or migrated, and they were displaced by Irish and French Canadian immigrants. By 1875, 35 percent of Chicopee's population was foreign born (21 % Irish, 9.6 % French Canadian). Ten years later the French Canadians had increased to 11.8 percent of the population, and a new set of arrivals from Poland made up 8.8 percent of the immigrant population. The Yankees maintained control over the skilled jobs, and the usual separation of workers by religion, language, class, and customs stymied efforts at unified labor organization.

Long hours (seventy-two hours till 1869 and sixty-six per week thereafter) and repeated wage cuts throughout the 1860s and 1870s resulted in many small walkouts. But manufacturers easily dealt with labor discontent by importing new workers. The depression of the early seventies increased levels of unemployment and the owners, caught in a competition for low prices, cut wages further in 1874, 1875, 1876, and 1879. The next decade saw some improvement, but by 1885 there were more wage cuts. All efforts at unionizing were poorly organized and ineffective, largely because workers were unable to accumulate savings that would tide them over in hard times or enable them to better their circumstances.

Finding textiles overly competitive, Chicopee's outside investors began diversifying. Between 1890 and 1910, they turned to other products, including bicycles and automobiles, to expand the factory system in the community. When the legislature finally incorporated Chicopee as a city in 1891, the population was 43 percent foreign born. Like other industrial cities, Chicopee had a large working class earning low wages, but a much smaller middle class than usually was the case. Relying on commercial Springfield for retail businesses, lacking its own newspaper, and bereft of cultural amenities, Chicopee became a typical, one-dimensional, satellite industrial city.[10]

Its neighbor Holyoke struggled to make it as a textile town, but achieved economic success only when its leaders turned to papermaking. The antebellum period witnessed numerous unsuccessful local attempts to establish industry: a tannery, a wagon shop, a clock factory, a cement factory. In 1832 merchants in Enfield, Connecticut, established the Hadley Falls Company to produce cotton, but it went bankrupt. Boston Associates bought out the company in 1847 and built a new mill, only to close it because of the panic of 1857. Cotton was a volatile industry that had its ups and downs for several decades. Not until the Civil War and after, particularly with the trend to establishing paper mills instead of cotton factories, did investors achieve some measure of financial success. Small-scale machine factories opened as offshoots of the paper and cotton industries.

After the Civil War paper became the most prosperous industry, even though the majority of the labor force worked in textiles. The depression of 1873 had little impact on the growing prosperity of the newly incorporated city. Holyoke's population zoomed from 14,000 in 1873 to 21,961 in 1880. With capital from local industry, the 1880s witnessed further expansion of the paper mills. Constant growth of the paper industry was followed by a construction boom in housing and the establishment of subsidiary paper factories—making blank books, pads, boxes, envelopes, and paper mill machinery. In 1884, a papermakers' lodge was set up that in 1893 became the International Brotherhood of Papermakers. By 1895 Holyoke ranked eighth in factory production in Massachusetts, with the Irish and French Canadians as the primary labor source. The constant infusion of new workers through migration kept the labor supply abundant and jobs scarce.

Throughout the nineteenth century the workers of Holyoke, like workers everywhere, did not fare well. Wages were lower in Holyoke than in other factory towns, and workers faced wage cuts, accidents, fire risks, long hours, and housing shortages that led to crowding. The 1875 Report of the State Bureau of Labor Statistics recorded: "Holyoke has more and worse tenement houses than any manufacturing town of textile fabrics in the state. . . . It is no wonder that the death rate in 1872 was greater in Holyoke than in any large town in Massachusetts, excepting Fall River." Because of its dismal working and living conditions, the historian Constance Green called it a "hell hole."[11]

The depression of 1893 hit Holyoke more gradually than other factory towns, but when it did, it was more severe. With the prices of paper dropping by 50 percent, some factories closed and the work week was cut to three days by 1894. The building boom was checked and retail businesses suffered major losses. Since papermaking required infusions of large amounts of capital, the depression resulted in the elimination of many smaller concerns and the eventual establishment of four major consolidations initiated by outside investors.

By 1900, Holyoke's sixteen independent paper concerns were combined into one large monopoly, the American Writing Paper Company. The move to cartelization was typical of the combination movement affecting a wide range of American industries at this time. This paper-industry colossus thwarted further economic growth of the city and made its population totally dependent upon the decisions wrought in boardrooms elsewhere. After the depression of 1893, paper workers and textile workers began to organize in earnest, demanding the restoration of wages. A large number of strikes occurred between 1899 and 1903, climaxing in a major strike of 1903 that ended in defeat for the workers. The result was a largely disorganized working class that was impotent in the face of large-scale capital.

Nearby Springfield, once largely dismissed by the Boston Associates as lacking industrial potential, was to grow and flower as a commercial-financial metropolitan center. The variety of its commercial and industrial enterprises, coupled with moderate economic growth and small immigrant populations, accounted for relatively benign demographic conditions. An early development had been the construction in 1794 of the United States Armory, which attracted a wide range of artisans, skilled workers, and merchants. The creation of a railroad link with Boston by way of Worcester in 1839 and the building of the Hartford and Springfield Railroad in 1844 opened a direct route to New York City. Springfield became the transportation terminus of the western part of the state. Incorporated in 1852, the town slowly built up a balance between trade, manufacturing, and professional activity. The Civil War gave further impetus to weapons production, and firms of less than twenty workers produced a variety of goods and services: railroad cars, paper products, books, toys, subsidiary textile corporations, and, finally, in the 1890's, automobiles and motorcycles. A center for the wholesale trade of paper, wool, flour, cotton, and provisions, Springfield became the region's retailing and financial capital. Its major newspaper, the *Springfield Republican,* owned and edited by Samuel Bowles, had a national prominence that promoted the region's investment opportunities. Springfield's economic diversity engendered a stability uncommon for the period. Solomon Griffin, editor of the paper in the early twentieth century remarked, "Fortunately, not to this day has the city developed any one manufacturing interest so dominant . . . thereby to become a crushing liability in periods of financial distress." Griffin described the community as he remembered it in 1872 as a "homogeneous municipality of the best New England sort." [12] Only 25 percent of the population were foreign born in 1875, and 10 percent of this total were the easily assimilated English and Scottish; there were fifteen thousand Irish and some fifteen hundred Germans in 1885. Irish men were manual laborers, and the women were usually domestics. The Germans were skilled workers for the most part, tradesmen, teamsters, gunmakers, brewers, and cigar makers. The Irish did not achieve political influence until 1900, and by then they also owned twenty-two of the city's thirty-five saloons. The period of major immigration of Italians, Russian Jews, and Poles was not to come until the turn of the century. Springfield came to attain regional urban prominence.

The second largest city in the state, and by 1880 the twenty-eighth in the nation, Worcester had its own path of industrial development. An industrial city, it was unusual in that it was always diversified, unlike the one-product cities of Fall River or Lynn. Worcester became a center for manufacturing because of the opening of the Blackstone Canal in 1828 and because of its railroad connections made in 1835 and 1847. While boots and shoes was an early industry, by the 1880s, the metal trades and machines (producing wires, tools, lathes, paper machines, looms, plows, and woodworking machinery) became more important, accounting for more than 40 percent of manufacturing. There were also factories producing textiles, corsets, envelopes, and abrasives.

Different also were Worcester's factory owners and labor force. Instead of using Boston money, most of the industries were started by local Yankee mechanics who, by accumulating capital, worked their way up to owner. This Protestant gentry intermarried, controlled major economic decisions, and set up trade associations that helped foster monopolization of decision making in the community. The labor force itself was only partially native.

Laborers were largely first- and second-generation immigrants. After 1850 the Irish were the first arrivals, but by the 1880s, there were large numbers of Protestant Swedes. They were followed by many diverse groups of eastern and southern Europeans, including Lithuanians, Poles, Finns, Armenians, and Italians. Another difference in the workforce was that it was dominated by males, as the metal trades were not open to women. The variety of immigrants, in addition to the diversity of industries, meant that workers tended to be isolated from one another. Moreover, the division between Protestant and Catholic was quite severe. Workers usually lived in ethnic ghettos that further separated them. Consequently they were unable to organize and were easily manipulated by the more unified business classes. The result was that Worcester never developed a radical labor consciousness and had very few strikes.

Unlike other factory towns where workers were participating in politics, Worcester politics were controlled by the owners and managers of the factories and by the bankers, lawyers, and merchants of the community. Between 1885 and 1910, Republican business elites held a near monopoly of political offices. The minority Irish Democrats worked with the Republicans, who gave them just enough patronage to keep the Democrats in line. Thus, Worcester built a reputation as an anti-union city with a highly skilled, placid workforce, ruled by a small coterie of Yankee elites. Such was not the case for the metropolitan giant of the east, Boston.

Post–Civil War Boston's elite was suffused with the smug confidence embodied in Emerson's praise of the city "as the town which was appointed in the destiny of nations to lead the civilization of North America." Describing William Dean Howells's arrival from Ohio in 1866, twentieth-century author Van Wyck Brooks commented that Boston was "ripe for invasion," signifying the "commanding influence" of New England ideals in a city that was "a hallowed ground for thousands of the rising generations."[13] Actually, the invasion was to occur on a much different plane than that of the intellect. The Gilded Age was the period when Boston shed its small-scale, walking-city character to become a sprawling, volatile metropolis of the twentieth century.

By 1865 the "Athens of America," with its fabled commercial and literary reputation, had become the nation's fourth largest manufacturing city. The sewing machine revolutionized the clothing industry. The division of labor made Boston, between 1870 and 1890, the center for the manufacture of low-cost, ready-made clothing (until it was overtaken by New York City, which had a growing surplus of immigrant workers). New industries meant more jobs, and jobs meant more people flocking to the city in even greater numbers. The rate of population increase was well over 20 percent each decade from 1880 to 1900. The steady and continuous flow of Irish immigrants, 14.3 percent of the population in 1880, converged with that of migrant Yankee farmers; also twenty-five thousand French Canadians had arrived by that time. After 1890, record numbers of Jews, Italians, and others from southern and eastern Europe contributed to the rising material prosperity of the city as well as to its social problems.

Boston went from a tightly packed merchant city of two hundred thousand in 1850, to an industrial metropolis in 1900, with over a million people in thirty-one cities and towns within a ten-mile radius of Boston Common. Industrial and commercial expansion heightened demands on land use, and Bostonians responded by filling in the waters of the harbor and adjacent rivers to manufacture more land. From its original 780 acres, Boston by 1870 extended to over 24,000 acres, thirty times its previous size. Tons of gravel dumped into the waters between Boston and Roxbury created the South End; the landfill of the area south of Beacon Hill became the Back Bay. The quest for land continued unabated, with the city annexing nearby towns and villages: Roxbury (1867–68), Dorchester (1869–70), Charlestown, Brighton, and West Roxbury (1873–74).

No zoning regulations hindered the "privatistic" urges of streetcar magnates and land speculators. Developments in sanitary engineering and the extension of municipal services motivated large financial institutions, small investors, and thousands of prospective home buyers to build new residences outside the city limits. Between 1870 and 1900, 22,500 homes went up for 167,000 suburbanites. By 1900, the Boston region became the typical metropolis of the twentieth century: a central business district of retail stores, financial concerns, and leisure-time activities, an inner city of work and low-income residences abutting more affluent residential neighborhoods; and suburbs for a middle- and upper-income population. The consequences of a metropolis built by accidental traffic patterns and unregulated capitalism were class segregation of the suburbs and confinement of the poor to the inner city slums. For the most part, the vast majority of Boston's poor in the Gilded Age were the city's newcomers.

Prosperity was difficult to achieve for many Boston immigrants. Whereas 40 to 50 percent of Boston's families were middle class by

1900, at least one-third were poor. It was to take two or three generations before many immigrant families could advance to the middle
class. The newcomers encountered job shortages due to layoffs, depressions, and intense job discrimination. Years later, a successful Irish politician, James Michael Curley, recalled his first factory job in 1889 at
the age of fifteen:

> We slaved away in overalls and undershirts in the blistering tem-
> peratures required in those days in the manufacture of pianos. . . .
> During the nine months I worked there my weight dropped from
> 134 pounds to eighty. I was paid $7.50 a week until put on piece-
> work, and when my pay increased to as much as $16 a week the
> boss put me back on the former schedule.[14]

Curley complained and was fired. Immigrants lived in congested neighborhoods rife with disease. Furthermore, ethnic groups tended to co-
alesce into clannish enclaves, a situation that bred nativism, resentment,
and intergroup hostility.

The rapid industrialization and urbanization of late nineteenth-
century Massachusetts had dramatic results. Everywhere there were
changes that affected workers: the farmers' daughters gave way to
floods of immigrants; by the turn of the century three-quarters of the
industrial workforce was either foreign born or second generation;
workers suffered through periodic economic dislocations and the hardship of constant wage cuts, as well as periods of unemployment and
labor conflict. The immigrants crowded into the central areas of the
cities, while the native born moved to the outer districts and suburbs.
All attempts at corporate housing ceased. Competition for land use in
the central business district and its borders resulted in higher land costs
that led to the inevitable rise of slums and tenements. Health and sanitation became serious issues, and ethnic tensions were heightened.
Clearly, the industrial revolution had created great wealth, but at the
same time it had generated a wide gulf between the working and
middle classes.

With society divided among competing groups, Massachusetts politics became pre-eminently the art of coalition building. The Democratic
and Republican parties fulfilled this role by acting as brokers among
contending groups and by arduously locating common denominators.
More than ever before, the political parties functioned to bring a mea-

sure of harmony and coherence to a society that was more deeply and variously divided than at any time in the past. This was a world of public affairs that could no longer be guided by seeking rigid adherence to absolute principles. If an alliance, however unlikely, worked, it was a good one. Pragmatism, the doctrine that practical consequences must be the test of ideal principles, became the operating standard in public life. Harvard philosophers, chiefly Charles S. Peirce and William James, and the Harvard jurist Oliver Wendell Holmes provided the theoretical foundations that gave legitimacy to such mundane realities of decision making in Massachusetts.

The Civil War left the Massachusetts Democratic party in ruins. A full decade after 1865 would pass before the Democrats succeeded in winning a congressional district. In the 1850s the issue of slavery expansion had begun to deplete Democratic ranks seriously, as Know-Nothing and then Free-Soil candidates attracted Yankee farmers, tradesmen, and industrial workers. The battle to preserve the Union converted most of them, and even many Irish immigrants, into Republicans. The majority enthusiastically supported the war and contributed substantially to the Union triumph. Consequently, the Democrats' long uphill struggle began from deep in the valley of odium. Merchant advocates of free trade, people who lived by southern commerce, and Irish immigrants provided their nucleus of support. Ultimately the resurgence of the Democrats as competitors in a two-party system would be founded on the last constituency, for as the Irish became Irish Americans, they made their home in the Democratic party. They became the most loyal and powerful bloc within it; and although they could not dictate policy and select candidates themselves, by 1880 they possessed a decisive veto in party councils. The rebirth of the Democrats was linked to the emergence of the Massachusetts Irish.

Irish success in Massachusetts was met with Yankee bigotry. Time, service to the Union cause during the war, and their own ambitions and talents changed the circumstances of the Irish in the generation after 1865. The massive migration of famine victims slowed as conditions in Ireland moderated. People who had begun by taking any job thriftily accumulated savings, founded their own modest businesses, and bought homes. Deprived for centuries of any political voice, they quickly grasped the opportunities that local and state politics presented. For although they had spread throughout the commonwealth, patterns of employment, income, prejudice, and perhaps also preferences had segregated the Irish in particular neighborhoods in Boston and the mill cities, especially Fall River, Haverhill, Holyoke, Lawrence, Lowell, and Worcester. There they quickly entered the party that had been welcoming immigrant voters since the days of Thomas Jefferson and James Sullivan—the Democrats. Winning seats as aldermen first, later as delegates to the General Court, the former outcasts secured themselves from official harassment and gained a share of public patronage. For people who had trouble paying grocers and landlords and who were frequently subject to seasonal layoffs, political participation was not only an inspiring exercise of liberty, it was also practical. Since the Democrats had been so weakened by the conflicts over slavery in the 1850s and by the war that followed, Irish support of the party proved a blessing. The resurgence of two-party politics became a reality in the 1870s when the Democrats cracked the Republican monopoly in the congressional delegation, largely through Irish American participation. In the 1880s the Irish began to occupy positions of considerable importance, both symbolic and actual.

In 1881, Lawrence was the first major city to select an Irish Catholic mayor. Lawrence in 1880 was roughly the same size, forty thousand people, as Boston had been in the 1820s. Its population was 20 percent Irish-born and, next to Yankees, the Irish were the largest of several ethnic groups among the electorate. John Breen's victory combined support from working men from England, Scotland, Germany, and French Canada, as well as some Yankees; but the bulk of his strength came from the Irish. Breen, a native of Tipperary who had built up an undertaker's business among his fellow countrymen, was both a volunteer fireman and a city councilman before his election. When he took office in 1882 he used the patronage at his disposal to bring Irish Americans into the police, health, and public works departments. Though Breen left office three years later, Irish access to city jobs remained. Irish exclusion from public life was over.

At Boston, the metropolis of Yankee New England, the same pattern appeared in the 1880s, when Patrick Andrew Collins won a congressional seat and Hugh O'Brien won the mayoralty. Collins, a child of the famine migration, was born in 1844 at Ballinafauna in County Cork. His father was a politically active, respectable tenant farmer; but when he died in 1847, his wife and child were cast adrift in the world. Mrs. Collins chose to migrate to Massachusetts, and it was in Chelsea, just outside Boston, that young Patrick Collins attended public school. When the boy was thirteen, the family moved to southern Ohio and Patrick had a taste of coal mining; but two years later they came back to Boston, and Collins became apprentice to an upholsterer.

Collins mastered his trade, but it was politics that excited his imagination. At the age of twenty he joined the Fenian movement for Irish independence, and in 1867, at twenty-three, he won election to the Massachusetts House of Representatives. In the same year, Collins began to study law with a Democratic attorney, while also attending Harvard Law School on a part-time basis. He rose quickly. After three terms in the House he was elected to the state Senate, where he successfully sponsored a bill to open state hospitals and prisons to Catholic (as well as Protestant) chaplains. By 1874, when the thirty-year-old Collins was graduated from the law school, he had come remarkably far for the poor son of an Irish tenant.

Now he retired from public office and began to build up a practice. He had married Mary Carey of Boston in 1873, and he soon had family responsibilities. Gradually, as his social and economic position improved, Collins's political orientation shifted. In 1876 he decided to support John Adams's grandson, Charles Francis Adams, who was running for governor as the reform Democrat candidate. At the same time Collins broke with the Fenians, arguing the classic assimilationist position that whatever one's sympathies, Irish politics were foreign, and one must concentrate one's loyalty on America and its affairs. Collins was joining forces with Yankee Democrats in order to bridge the antagonisms that weakened the Democratic party.

In 1882 he was elected to Congress as a reform (Grover Cleveland) Democrat, and he served there for three terms. But he was frozen out of the Massachusetts patronage by the new president. Irish Democrats were divided and competing for Yankee alliances, and Cleveland had closer ties with the Brahmin leaders. Ultimately Collins became alienated. Cleveland sought to mollify him in 1893 when he appointed Collins the United States consul general in London, a prestigious and profitable post. But Collins's involvement in national affairs soon came to an end. He returned to Boston where he ran unsuccessfully for mayor in 1899, before winning successive terms in 1901 and 1903. By this time Collins was a respected elder statesman among Massachusetts Democrats, far from the cutting edge of ethnic politics.

Hugh O'Brien, who never attended college or law school, was almost twenty years older than Collins. O'Brien challenged native stereotypes—as Collins did—by demonstrating that an Irishman could be a prudent, sagacious public official of the highest integrity. His family brought him to Boston in 1832 when he was five years old, and he was educated in the common schools before being apprenticed to the printers of the *Boston Courier*. At the *Courier* O'Brien obtained some elements of a liberal training, since its editor, Joseph T. Buckingham, had broad literary interests, and his paper included book reviews and theatrical commentaries, as well as essays on literature and reform. The young printer also became conversant with "sound principles," since the *Courier* was a Whig organ. Later O'Brien would found his own commercial paper; he did not turn to politics until he was in his late forties and well established.

Because of his early arrival in Boston and his training at the *Courier*, Hugh O'Brien was a much more assimilated, "respectable" gentleman than most of his Irish constituents when he was elected an alderman in 1875. In city politics O'Brien distinguished himself for conscientious hard work, and after several years as an alderman he scored a concrete victory for laboring men by winning enactment of a two-dollar daily minimum wage for city employees. On the strength of this achievement and the support of Patrick Maguire's precinct organization, O'Brien won the mayoralty in 1884. Maguire, who dealt in real estate and published a weekly paper, the *Republic,* had become the leading Irish "boss" in Boston—but his success, like that of Collins and O'Brien, was based on his ability to retain Irish support while accommodating the native Democrats.

The emergence of the pluralism that this Yankee–Irish alliance within the Democratic party represented was symbolized by the selection of the Boston University–trained lawyer Thomas Gargan to deliver the city's Independence Day oration in 1885. Thereafter, for the next generation, the honor was divided equally between Yankees and Irish, who alternated from year to year. As hostile and suspicious as the two groups remained, divided by ethnicity, religion, and class, they had accepted the idea that Boston belonged to both. Ballot-box pragmatism ruled.

Outside the political marketplace, such pluralistic tolerance was far less common. But one early testimony to the possibilities was the meteoric career of the editor, poet, and novelist John Boyle O'Reilly. O'Reilly was a romantic man of action, a reformer, and a literary lion, who arrived in Boston in 1870 at the age of twenty-six. He had spent his youth in Ireland and England as a newspaper apprentice, soldier, and Fenian nationalist. After narrowly escaping the death penalty for subversive activity while in the army, he had been shipped as a convict to Australia. In 1869 he escaped aboard a Nantucket whaler, and in the following year he landed a job as reporter on the *Boston Pilot*. Founded in 1838, and named after the patriotic Dublin journal, the *Pilot* was the oldest and most popular Catholic paper in Boston, supported by laymen as well as churchmen. O'Reilly, whose intellect, magnetic charm, and energy transcended common prejudice, rapidly moved up. In 1876 the recently elevated archbishop of Boston, John J. Williams, made him his editor-in-chief and copartner in operating the *Pilot*. With this forum O'Reilly emerged as a vigorous Irish patriot and the spokesman of a humane, cosmopolitan Catholicism. His poetry moved from romantic, natural themes in the 1870s to reform ideals in the following decade when imperialism, race prejudice, and other forms of oppression—including capitalism—moved him to protest. O'Reilly found friends in literary Boston and Cambridge, and so while Collins, O'Brien, and Gargan were breaking down old political barriers, O'Reilly was enjoying comparable symbolic triumphs. His poetry was selected for the monuments to Wendell Phillips and to the black martyr of the Boston Massacre, Crispus Attucks. In 1889 his verse was part of the rededication ceremony for Plymouth Rock. With O'Reilly, a member of several established literary and social clubs, it would seem that cultural acceptance of Irish Catholics was not merely a token, but real and substantial.

Yet appearances are misleading. For one thing O'Reilly was an exceptional personality who combined literary gifts and reform social vision with orthodox Catholicism in a unique way. Moreover, O'Reilly's "sponsors" in Brahmin Massachusetts were chiefly drawn from the older generation of prewar idealists: Ralph Waldo Emerson, Julia Ward

Howe, Thomas Wentworth Higginson, Wendell Phillips, and John Greenleaf Whittier. If O'Reilly had lived longer (he died in 1890), perhaps he would have opened the way for other immigrants into the sanctums of literary and aesthetic culture in the commonwealth. But the record of literary, musical, and artistic organizations suggests otherwise. Wealthy Yankees made sure that high culture was their preserve.

Consequently, cultural pluralism emerged in a largely segregated context. "Second-class" associations emerged to satisfy the literary, musical, and artistic interests of aspiring, middle-class Irish Americans and other newcomers. The simultaneous rise of ethnic philanthropic and social organizations completed the pattern. The late nineteenth century marked the high tide of fraternal clubs and lodges throughout the nation. In Massachusetts such associations flourished within a setting where ethnic self-consciousness and class stratification provided members with a kind of social insulation. Booker T. Washington's classic 1895 Atlanta formula for race relations applied almost equally well to the heterogeneous peoples of Massachusetts: "In all things that are purely social we can be as separate as the fingers, yet one as the hand in all things essential to mutual progress."[15] In their commitment to economic growth and prosperity, the people of Massachusetts were united in a harmony that was only faintly disturbed by socialists and radicals.

In public life the Democratic party was the most prominent agent of inter-group and interclass coalition in Massachusetts, but the Democrats were a minority party. Between 1860 and 1919 Republicans monopolized Massachusetts's two places in the U.S. Senate and the vast majority of congressional seats. No Democrat served in Congress from the Bay State until 1876, and a comparable pattern of Republican dominance characterized state politics. The Civil War coalition of farmers and industrialists and of evangelical, deistic, and intermediate Protestants made Massachusetts a Republican stronghold. Advocating enterprise and industry, protective tariffs and sound currency, in addition to subsidies for transportation and education, Republicans controlled scores of Yankee townships year in and year out. Although some party politicians openly exploited anti-Catholic sentiment, Republicans were not so much hostile as they were indifferent to the wishes of immigrant voters. In cities and towns where the French Catholic and later the Italian Catholic voters held a balance of power, Republicans were courting them by the end of the century with rhetoric and petty patronage. More gradually than the Democrats, the Republicans too would function pragmatically, as vehicles for integrating diverse class interests and ethnic groups in a pluralistic society.

Yet the great leaders of the Republican party were two old-line, Harvard-educated Yankees: George Frisbie Hoar and Henry Cabot Lodge. Between them, Hoar and Lodge illustrated the accommodations that respectable Yankee Massachusetts was willing to accept in an era of dramatic social change. Their differences over civil rights, immigration restriction, and American imperialism suggested the conflicting elements that divided Yankees. Unity among Republicans was a matter of repeated compromise, and defections on questions of principle were a recurrent threat.

Republicans elected George Frisbie Hoar to the Senate in 1877, but Hoar's formative period had occurred before the war. He had been born into a Concord family of Unitarians in 1826. His grandfather Hoar had fought in the battle at Concord bridge in 1775, and his mother was a daughter of Roger Sherman, the Connecticut delegate who had helped draft both the Declaration of Independence and the Constitution. George was nurtured on Revolutionary idealism before he was sent to Harvard College and the law school in the 1840s. When he left Cambridge, Hoar settled at Worcester, where he soon became active in the Free-Soil party. Like his father, Samuel, and his elder brother Congressman Ebenezer Rockwood Hoar, George opposed slavery and slave expansion. If the Whigs were so bound up with cotton that they were deaf to conscience, then the Hoars were ready to assert their independence. Decades later, Senator Hoar would proudly recall how he had been one of the original founders of the Republican party in Massachusetts at Worcester in 1855. To George Frisbie Hoar, the Republican party would ever after be emblematic of the principles of the Declaration of Independence—liberty under a free, representative government.

When the war began, George was in his mid-thirties, married, a family man who chose to support the Union war effort at home rather than on the battlefield. Later, in 1868, he was elected to Congress as a radical, and he supported a thorough reconstruction of government and society in the South, including black civil rights. Hoar, who idolized

---

Massachusetts's abolitionist senator, Charles Sumner, whose seat he proudly filled, had firmly established his identity as an old-line Republican of principle by the 1870s.

One of Hoar's principles was to stand by his own party to fight for justice, so he did not bolt when the financial scandals of the Grant administration were revealed and when James G. Blaine, soiled with the corruption of the Crédit Mobilier, won the party's presidential nomination in 1884. Hoar felt a proprietary interest in the party he had helped create and, when he considered the long-term record of the Democrats, he never doubted that the Republican party alone offered the best hope for liberty and progress. Even though Hoar's prewar idealism was already becoming outmoded within the Republicans when he entered the Senate, Hoar clung to his party, preached to it, and, when he lost his battles, stayed to fight again. The year that Hoar came to the Senate as an advocate for the cause of black civil rights, the "compromise of 1877," which traded Republican control of the White House for unchallenged southern white rule in the South, marked the end of the party's egalitarian, reformist era. Hoar generally voted with his fellow Republicans on economic policy, but otherwise he was a maverick sustained by old-fashioned Massachusetts Yankees.

From the standpoint of legislation, Hoar's chief accomplishment was the Sherman Anti-Trust Act of 1890, which he redrafted and guided through shoals of conservative opposition. Though the statute actually did little to impede the progress of monopolies and trusts, Hoar pressed for its adoption because of his commitment, and that of small-town Republicans everywhere, to free, competitive enterprise with opportunities for petty capitalists. In Massachusetts such principles enjoyed overwhelming support across party lines. On other issues, however, Hoar was willing to advocate views that divided his own party.

Hoar's friendly position on black voting rights and his support for woman suffrage were less and less welcome among party contributors and regulars in the 1880s and 1890s. But since these issues were at the periphery of Massachusetts (and national) politics, they did not excite strong antagonisms. Immigration restriction and the development of an overseas American empire, however, were central policy questions, especially in the nineties, and Hoar's views marked a profound division in Massachusetts. Hoar, who had rejected the Know-Nothings in the 1850s, was not about to embrace the American Protective Association, in spite of its growing popularity among Protestant voters. Hoar was equally opposed to the more refined and respectable Immigration Restriction League which, through the device of a literacy test, aimed at keeping out masses of poor immigrants. The mission of America in 1776 had been to serve as the asylum for the oppressed. Hoar, true to family tradition, wanted to keep it that way; but in Massachusetts he spoke for a declining body of opinion, especially among Republicans.

The Spanish-American War and its sequel in the Philippines would further alienate Hoar from party regulars. Unlike some distinguished Boston Brahmins, Hoar supported the American effort in Cuba and stood by President McKinley. But when it came to the conquest of the Philippines and the military suppression of the native independence movement there, Hoar denounced United States policy. In the Senate Hoar worked tirelessly to defeat the peace treaty with Spain that made the nation a colonial power in Asia and the Caribbean. Indeed, had one more Republican or Democrat joined Hoar, the treaty would not have mustered the necessary two-thirds approval. But jingo pressures were intense, and even William Jennings Bryan, the leading Democratic anti-imperialist, yielded. Among Republicans, only Senator Eugene P. Hale of Maine stood by Hoar when the vote was cast. Gloating over the victory, Theodore Roosevelt contemptuously told his friend Henry Cabot Lodge that Hoar's actions could be "pardoned only because he is senile."[16] Roosevelt, Lodge, and indeed most people could not fathom the old man's adherence to the Revolutionary tradition of political independence for all peoples. The right to "life, liberty, and the pursuit of happiness" belonged to the Filipinos, Hoar asserted, and by seizing their liberty, Americans were repealing their own Declaration of Independence. Hoar's views commanded some respect in Massachusetts, especially with the politically heterogeneous members of the Anti-Imperialist League including, among others, the president of the Massachusetts Historical Society, Charles Francis Adams Jr., and Harvard professor Charles Eliot Norton. But Hoar's outspoken stand represented a strain of individualistic idealism that had become so odd by 1900 that it could be confused with senility. Hoar was an up-to-date, pragmatic, party man, loyal to the collective Republican cause, but he was also loyal to the beliefs of his family and of his own Massachusetts youth. To have embraced imperialism would have been to shed the identity that he had found in Concord, Cambridge, and Worcester.

Hoar's junior Massachusetts colleague in the Senate, Henry Cabot Lodge, was much more comfortable in the political environment of the era. Born in 1850, Lodge was a generation younger than Hoar, and his understanding of the old idealism was essentially rhetorical. Lodge spoke the language of principle, but he was worldly and ambitious; and as he matured, he learned that if he clung rigidly to principle he would be an outsider in a world where power brokers repeatedly laid principle on the shelf. A scrupulous regard for ideals or consistency would have consigned him to the fretful world of drawing-room politics, in which many of his peers dwelled.

In some ways Lodge entered life with every advantage—wealth, social prestige, health, talent, and doting parents. But his very advantages created handicaps in the competitive setting of mass democratic politics. He was definitely not born in a log cabin. The Lodges were relative newcomers, since his grandfather was an Englishman who had immigrated to Massachusetts in the 1790s, after escaping from the slave uprising in Santo Domingo. But although relatively recent arrivals, the Lodges were successful ones. Lodge's father, like his grandfather, prospered in trade; he married Anna Cabot, granddaughter of George Cabot, a North Shore merchant who made a fortune during the Revolution and moved to Boston, where he became the patriarch of Massachusetts Federalism. Cabot wealth and Cabot traditions heavily influenced the boy's youth, particularly after his father died, when Henry was twelve years old. His mother believed he resembled the Cabots "in mind & character as well as in looks & manner," and instead of being called Henry, he was called "Cabot." [17] Continually shielded from contact with people outside the family's social circle, Cabot Lodge attended Mr. Dixwell's private preparatory school and toured Europe for a year with his mother and tutor before entering Harvard in 1867. Raised in the Federalist tradition of elitism, and consistently reminded of his own social and cultural superiority both before he entered Harvard and while he was there, Lodge was splendidly suited by his background for a life of snobbish complacency. He never wished to escape from his breeding—he was proud of it. But though he became a shrewd and articulate defender of the status quo, he was not personally complacent. Born to hereditary prominence, he felt a compelling drive to make his own mark in the world. After he was graduated from Harvard in 1871, he spent a decade testing possible careers suitable for himself, a man who, already possessing wealth, sought additional recognition and prestige.

Lodge's initial choice was to become a scholar in the field of history. After graduation he had married a distant cousin and spent an extended honeymoon in Europe, where he avidly admired art and architecture. When the couple returned to Boston, Lodge reentered Harvard, enrolling in the law school and as a graduate student in Henry Adams's course on medieval institutions. Moreover, as one of Adams's favorites, Lodge also accepted a position as assistant editor of the *North American Review.* After earning his law degree in 1874, Lodge devoted himself chiefly to historical research and writing, in addition to his editorial duties. His training, which concentrated on the Teutonic origins of Anglo-Saxon political institutions, placed him in the mainstream of the new interest in linking the political and racial heritages of northern Europeans.

Like his mentor, Henry Adams, Lodge was only partly interested in scholarship. Both were deeply fascinated by power and eager to possess it. Adams, believing high office should seek him out because of his own brilliance and his distinguished lineage, sulked because it never did. Lodge, far more flexible and realistic, came to recognize that he would have to labor long, hard, and single-mindedly to grasp political power. He began among Henry Adams's refined, Harvard-bred coterie of high-principled, conservative reformers. Disgusted by the corruption of the Grant administration and the chicanery associated with Reconstruction in the South, they proposed civil-service examinations so that a meritocracy would control public administration; and they argued that southern Bourbons should be permitted to rule at home in accordance with the interests of their class and race. Ultimately much less fastidious than Adams and his other associates, Lodge started as a Republican reformer whose heroes were the elder Charles Francis Adams and Carl Schurz.

Through the 1870s Lodge dabbled with politics while also emerging as a prolific author of popular American history. Then in 1879 he ran for the Nahant seat in the General Court. Since childhood Lodge had spent summers in Nahant, and he was delighted when he won the election. Two years later he ran for the state Senate and lost, but in spite of this setback he persisted. Adams would never have deigned to run for such a humble office and, once defeated, would have scorned further battles. Lodge was more modest; he accepted his bruises and learned about the realities of Massachusetts politics as a participant. Throughout the early 1880s Lodge continued to run and to lose as he sought a seat in Congress. Ultimately the most profound lesson he drew from his experience was that he must close the gap between himself and the party rank and file and, after being narrowly beaten in 1884 by idealistic defectors who resented his support of James G. Blaine, he became devoted to party loyalty. When Lodge next ran for Congress in 1886, he won. Henceforth he would never be defeated.

The years 1883 and 1884 had been crucial for Lodge though he still remained out of office. He had finally broken with his social equals in the Adams circle and become a "professional" Republican. In 1883 he managed the gubernatorial campaign of respectable but lackluster Congressman George D. Robinson against the Democratic governor Benjamin F. Butler. This struggle assumed immense symbolic importance in Massachusetts, since many regarded Governor Butler as a wholly unprincipled "beast."

Butler, a shrewd and brazen opportunist, had begun his career in Lowell as a Democrat who championed Irish Catholic and labor issues in the General Court. During the Civil War he became a Unionist, a political brigadier general, and then a Republican. Serving as a radical alongside George Frisbie Hoar in the postwar congresses, Butler ended up close to General Grant and his cronies. After being defeated for reelection in 1875, Butler championed the inflationary "Greenback" cause before finally returning to the Democratic fold. Butler's willingness to move back and forth among the parties, his relish for patronage politics, and his own cultivation of lower-class and immigrant support convinced many middle- and upper-class people that he was vicious. Snubbed by Harvard and other elite establishments, Butler delighted in twitting his detractors. Indeed, the greatest scandal of Butler's administration was his Thanksgiving proclamation in 1882, a jeremiad pointing to the commonwealth's many sins and calling for repentance and reform. The upright were aghast when they read Butler's harsh criticisms. But Ben Butler had the last laugh, since his proclamation was copied verbatim from the arch-Federalist governor Christopher Gore's proclamation of 1810. Red faced and fuming, Republicans were not amused, and in 1883 ousting Butler became a holy cause.

But Butler was popular, and Lodge had an uphill struggle in which his organizing talents, his energy, and his shrewdness in assiduously presenting "honest" George Robinson to the voters were crucial. When Robinson won by a narrow margin, Lodge's stature in the party soared. He had gone into the political pits to labor not for his own glory but for the party and Massachusetts. He had succeeded in the grimy, tedious work of meeting people throughout the state, persuading them, speaking at scores of gatherings and arranging dozens more for Robinson. No other graduate of Mr. Dixwell's Latin school had ever achieved such a feat. When Lodge went to the Republican convention at Chicago the following year and came back supporting Blaine, some of his Brahmin friends cut him dead. Someone so devoid of principle, so opportunistic, they reasoned, should be beneath their notice. Lodge was hurt, but not so wounded that he altered his course. During the forty years of political activity that followed, Lodge remained a Republican regular, never doubting the wisdom of his judgment. When he subsequently won election to Congress, the wounds he had suffered earlier heightened his sense of satisfaction.

Urbane and wealthy, Cabot and Anna Lodge took naturally to high society in Washington and became part of a truly national elite. At the same time Lodge retained his Massachusetts roots, and his political views were always closely attuned to the Republican majority in the Bay State. By the time Lodge was elected to the Senate in 1893, he was closely identified with the orthodox positions on industrial tariffs, labor unions, and private capital of his senior colleague Hoar. Yet on other issues Lodge spoke for a different strain in Massachusetts opinion, and in the Senate he became the preeminent leader of the drive to curtail immigration into the United States.

In Massachusetts the movement to restrict immigration was not a distinctively Republican cause. Republicans liked protectionism in the form of tariffs, but they did not want the American labor market protected from low-paid immigrant workers. For different reasons, industrialists and their immigrant employees both favored the traditional policy of welcoming foreigners. But in the 1880s and 1890s especially, Massachusetts natives did become anxious. Now the Irish were being joined by Italians, Germans, eastern European Jews, French Canadians, Slavs, Syrians, Portuguese, and Scandinavians. Immigrant birthrates were higher than those of natives, and Roman Catholicism was on the way to becoming the largest denomination in the state. All the trends

---

suggested that in the not-too-distant future Yankees would become a minority in the land of their ancestors. Yankee pride and ethnocentrism grew more self-conscious as a result. Claiming free political institutions, social order, morality, and thrift as their special cultural achievements, Yankees became fearful of continuing, open-ended immigration.

The restriction movement began among a small group of well-educated reformers who viewed the immigrants as a key source of corruption. Because of the immigrants, they maintained, demagogy flourished, and unselfish, meritorious, well-bred people like themselves were displaced from the centers of power by politicians and industrialists who exploited foreigners' ignorance and poverty. Because of the immigrants a vice-ridden proletariat was emerging in the birthplace of liberty. Restrictionists believed that the clannishness of the foreigners exacerbated social divisions, and that their slow pace of assimilation destroyed all hope of restoring the homogeneous, harmonious society that they associated with the past and that they craved. For some elite Yankee Democrats and political independents the Immigration Restriction League, founded at Boston in 1894, offered hope. Public opinion might be awakened and legislation, similar to the recently enacted Chinese exclusion law, could result.

Lodge was the only prominent Republican in Massachusetts who embraced the league from the outset. His own views, however ethnocentric and snobbish, were also altruistic. Lodge, sharing the prevailing vogue for racial explanations of history and society, wanted Massachusetts and the United States preserved from further dilution by "inferior stocks." Ideally all immigration, except for Englishmen and Scots, would be stopped. But as a realist Lodge understood that such a program could never win public approval and that proposing it would mean political suicide. Already, by 1891, Lodge had stopped making derogatory allusions to the Irish in public—after all, they were voters. Restrictionism under Lodge's guidance would not seem to be directed at any particular national or religious group. It would appear disinterested, high minded, and couched in the language of the common good. The instrument of the league's indirect approach became the literacy test. Most people believed that literacy was an essential requirement for good citizenship, so by introducing this "nondiscriminatory" test the desired result, cutting off the massive new immigration from southern, central, and eastern Europe, could be achieved. Just as Lodge's

Bourbon allies in the South were using literacy tests to disfranchise black voters, the league could use the same technique to protect the racial stock of the North.

In advocating restrictionism in this form, Lodge was ahead of other Massachusetts politicians, although he was not alone for long. Workingmen, Yankee and Irish, liked the idea of a protected labor market. Progressives, concerned about political corruption, believed that literacy would help destroy bossism and demagogues. Bigots and xenophobes of every variety found the scheme palatable. By masking racial and ethnic elitism, restrictionism became good politics.

By proposing restrictions, Lodge made his mark nationally. In 1896 he reported the results of the "scientific" study his Senate Committee on Immigration had produced. Southern and eastern Europeans were disproportionately poor, diseased, and criminal. Culturally they were "aliens" whose presence in numbers threatened American civilization. American history proved, and here Lodge spoke as an authority, that Anglo-Saxons and northwestern Europeans were the ablest, most achieving peoples. From this platform Lodge launched his literacy-test statute, and it passed both houses of Congress handily. For an America gripped by high unemployment, immigrant restriction was widely attractive. Had it not been for President Grover Cleveland's veto, millions of lives would have been different, and the histories of Massachusetts and the United States altered significantly. Because of the veto, immigration continued, rising dramatically during the prosperous early years of the new century.

Characteristically, Lodge did not give up. He continued to lead on this issue both in Massachusetts and in the Senate. The literacy test suffered repeated congressional defeats for a decade after 1897, but finally passed again in 1913 only to be vetoed by the Republican president William Howard Taft. Two years later another version won approval, but this time Woodrow Wilson vetoed it. Not until after the First World War, when hypernationalism, the Red Scare, and economic recession sustained a renewed drive for restriction, would it become law. In the thirty-year interval from the time Lodge introduced his literacy bill, hundreds of thousands of Italian and eastern Europeans of various nationalities and faiths had made their way into the Bay State. The ethnic and cultural pluralism Lodge had hoped to stem was to dominate Massachusetts.

Actually, the social vision that had sustained elite restrictionism was already beleaguered by 1900. The neo-Federalist ideal of a homogeneous, hierarchical society united around a single orthodoxy of belief and behavior had always been a reactionary anachronism, even when grafted to "survival-of-the-fittest" social Darwinism. But except for the equally old-fashioned romantic Christian idealism, it had not faced a powerful rival during the post–Civil War era. By the beginning of the new century, however, a new outlook, one that grew out of contemporary experience, had taken shape in Massachusetts and across the country. Pragmatism, the view that the truth of abstract principles could not be established a priori, but must be tested by actual practice, was becoming prevalent.

Pragmatism gained adherents in many forms and at many levels. In a formal sense pragmatism was a Massachusetts creation. At the highest level the ideas were worked out by Harvard philosophers Charles Peirce, William James, and Josiah Royce. But at the most common, unselfconscious level, pragmatism was the everyday discovery of thousands of people throughout Massachusetts and elsewhere. In simplest terms, pragmatism meant that if an idea worked, it was a good one. To many self-righteous observers this was the very essence of unprincipled opportunism. All received, "absolute" truths, it appeared, could be laid aside if they did not suit the occasion. Like schoolchildren who discover that they have been speaking "prose" all their lives, politicians discovered that they were pragmatists. From here the step to relativism, where the truth varies according to one's perspective and the circumstances, was a short one. The groundwork was being laid among common people as well as the most highly educated for a society in which a variety of ideals, even conflicting ones, could peacefully coexist, and in which cooperation and compromise would achieve legitimacy because they were practical.

All these developments occurred in many states and in the nation at large. Yet because of Massachusetts's early experience with industrialization as well as with large-scale non-English immigration, it was on the leading edge of the new, pragmatic pluralism. Several generations of Massachusetts people had been actively seeking to reconcile diversity with the ideal of uniformity and to accommodate old truths with new realities. So it was not entirely coincidental that the jurist Oliver Wendell Holmes and his friend, the Boston attorney Louis Dembitz Brandeis, became central figures in national affairs, bringing legitimacy to pragmatism and relativism in public policy and jurisprudence.

Holmes was born in Boston in 1841. His father, a professor at Harvard Medical School, was a poet and essayist who was a leading figure in literary circles and his mother was the daughter of a justice of the Massachusetts Supreme Judicial Court. Young Holmes was raised in a most cultivated setting, and he prepared for Harvard at Mr. Dixwell's school. Holmes endured the pedantry of Harvard in the 1850s, but when the Civil War began, he left—weeks before graduation—to enlist. He was eager to escape from his sedate milieu and to plunge into the world of strenuous action. Earlier in his senior year he had already served as a bodyguard for Wendell Phillips in Boston, and Holmes was committed to abolition and the Union cause. He was romantically attracted to the prospect of valor on behalf of a noble cause, as Samuel Gridley Howe had been decades earlier when he joined the Greek effort for independence.

Holmes wanted the war to shape his life, and it did, decisively, though not as he might have predicted. The war for Holmes, an officer in the Twentieth Regiment of Massachusetts, began in tedium far more penetrating than Harvard's and was soon followed by horrors more gruesome than the young romantic had ever imagined. From his father, Holmes had some familiarity with anatomy; but now he saw the bloody fragments scattered on the ground, and he listened to cries of mutilation and death. Before the year was out, he himself was shot through the chest and narrowly escaped death. After several months of recuperation he returned to his regiment; in 1862, at Antietam, he was shot in the neck and briefly left for dead behind Confederate lines. Again Holmes recovered and resumed his duty, and once more he was wounded, taking a ball of grapeshot in the heel. For the third time in twenty months he was a casualty, and by now he had no more enthusiasm for war. He almost wished that his foot had been amputated so he would have been released from the duty of returning to the battlefield. "War, when you are at it," he later declared, "is horrible and dull." [18] When his three-year term was up in 1864, Holmes left to return to Cambridge and Harvard Law School. Though the war continued, neither a sense of idealism nor of duty obliged him to stay; he had had enough.

Although his appearance was not much different, Holmes was a changed man. He was still a tall, witty, and imaginative young gentleman with bright, piercing blue eyes. But now he was reserved, detached, and profoundly skeptical. The stresses of war had stripped away the hopeful shibboleths of liberal antebellum Massachusetts.

"I'm an out and outer of a democrat in theory," Holmes noted while in the army, "but for contact, except at the polls, I loathe the thick-fingered clowns we call the people—especially as the beasts are represented at political centers—vulgar, selfish and base." Repeated experience with the routines of killing fixed him with an aloof identity, and he knew it: "How indifferent one gets to the sight of death—perhaps because one gets aristocratic and don't value a common life—Then they are apt to be so dirty it seems natural—'Dust to Dust.'"[19] Holmes was a survivor who could no longer commit himself fully to abstractions. Truths were relative, to be tested as his own ideas had been, in the practical world.

When Holmes completed law school in 1866, he easily could have become a wealthy establishment lawyer had he so wished. He boasted a genealogy more distinguished, by Massachusetts standards, than Cabot Lodge, since he was descended from seventeenth-century governors Dudley and Bradstreet, the poet Ann Bradstreet, and an assortment of Olivers, Lees, Quincys, and Wendells. His family had, as he put it, for generations "been in the habit of receiving a college education,"[20] and he himself was recognized as both highly disciplined and brilliant. Moreover, he liked the lawyer's work, the research, the briefs, the pleadings, the precision, and the sophistication it demanded. Nevertheless, immersed as he was in the world of affairs, he also edited the *American Law Review* and became an intellectual in spite of his doubts about ideas and abstractions.

His companions in the early 1870s were the members of the Metaphysical Club that met in Cambridge. In the evenings Holmes would join William James, Charles S. Peirce, and Chauncy Wright, among others, and it was in their discussions that the principles of pragmatism were first articulated. Later, as Holmes developed his major treatise, *The Common Law* (1881), he interpreted legal history as a pragmatic, evolving phenomenon in which the law, instead of being a set of fixed, absolute principles, was continuously changing: "The life of the law has not been logic: it has been experience. The felt necessities of the time . . . have had a good deal more to do than the syllogism in determining the rules by which men should be governed."[21] The consequence of these views was a more flexible, open-minded approach to law than generally prevailed within the legal profession.

A year after *The Common Law* was published, an endowed professorship was created for Holmes at Harvard Law School, and he returned to what he regarded as "the sidelines" of mere theory. Academic law was not his preference, and when the opportunity came to take a seat on the Supreme Judicial Court of the commonwealth, his grandfather Jackson's old bench, Holmes seized it. For the next twenty years Holmes's impact on Massachusetts law and, through it, public policy in other states as well, would increase. Because of his sensitivity to "the felt necessities of the time," including the rights of labor, many of his peers on the bench and at the bar regarded him as a radical. Nonetheless, although he was not a doctrinaire supporter of capitalists, he won their sometimes grudging respect through his genius. One lawyer who often pleaded before Holmes reported:

> [H]is questions went so to the root of the case, that it was rather an ordeal to appear before him. In arguing a case you felt that when your sentence was half done he had seen the end of it, and before the argument was a third finished that he had seen the whole course of reasoning and was wondering whether it was sound.[22]

In time, Holmes became chief justice in Massachusetts.

Yet when Henry Cabot Lodge proposed to Theodore Roosevelt that Holmes be appointed to the U.S. Supreme Court in 1902, the suggestion was controversial. Many lawyers regarded Holmes as too unpredictable, and Senator Hoar, who did not really understand Holmes, believed his mind ran too much "to subtleties and refinements, and no decision of his makes a great landmark in jurisprudence."[23] But Lodge, who never forgot Holmes's kindnesses to him when other Brahmins were turning their backs after he supported Blaine in 1884, pressed Roosevelt, assuring him that on such key political issues as imperialism Holmes was sound. Once the president was convinced Holmes was not a political renegade, he appointed him to the Court, and Holmes's self-consciously pragmatic jurisprudence, born in Massachusetts, began to be asserted in national rulings.

But one swallow does not make a summer, and Holmes was a lonely, frequently dissenting figure in the Court for years. Only the passage of

---

time and the addition of new judges would change that. In many ways the turning point came in 1916 when the reforming Democratic president Woodrow Wilson appointed his adviser, Louis D. Brandeis, to the Court. Though Holmes and Brandeis had important differences in outlook and temperament, there were intellectual bonds between them.

Indeed, it had been the twenty-six-year-old Brandeis who had long before raised the money to create a professorship specifically for Holmes at Harvard. Brandeis, born in Louisville, Kentucky, in 1856, had come to Harvard Law School in 1875 by way of the Louisville public schools and the *Annen Realschule* in Dresden. Bringing an alien background—his parents were Jewish immigrants from Prague who had settled in Kentucky and founded a grain and produce business a few years before his birth—Louis Brandeis quickly displayed the intellectual and personal aptitude that would place him at the head of his class and at the top of his profession. Soon after he completed law school in 1877, he entered practice in Boston as a partner of his Brahmin classmate Samuel D. Warren Jr. while he simultaneously clerked for the chief justice of the Massachusetts Supreme Judicial Court. Through these connections Brandeis's legal practice flourished, and within a decade he became a prosperous and prominent member of the Massachusetts bar. Anti-Semitism, like the more generalized xenophobia that pervaded Yankee circles, was not a serious barrier for Brandeis, whose extraordinary abilities had led influential sponsors to befriend and to employ him. Somewhat in the manner of the exceptional John Boyle O'Reilly, Brandeis was insulated from much hostility by his own brilliance and ascetic charm. Even yachting and polo clubs opened their doors to Brandeis.

By the 1890s Brandeis was a wealthy man who had arrived. Now his social conscience awakened, and instead of serving privileged capitalists he turned to advocacy on behalf of common people. In the eyes of many lawyers he emerged as a radical in 1892 when he denounced steel company union-busting at Homestead, Pennsylvania. "Organized capital," he declared, had "hired a private army to shoot at organized labor for resisting an arbitrary cut in wages."[24] Hereafter, as Holmes sought to make law more flexible, Brandeis worked to make it more just and humane within the framework of capitalism and competition.

Ultimately, Brandeis rose to national prominence as a conservative defender of individual rights and a foe of monopoly. He fought railroad and utility monopolies on behalf of individual stockholders and consumers to purify the competitive system. Concerned about the rise of bureaucracy, he also took on the federal government when a lowly official was fired for revealing collusion between the Department of the Interior and special interests seeking access to Alaskan minerals. Like Holmes, Brandeis was a legal pragmatist. In his most notable case before the Supreme Court, Brandeis defended the Oregon law governing women's working conditions, which established the ten-hour day. He did not argue from abstractions; he argued from experience, confronting the Court with a fact-filled comparative analysis of the impact of excessive hours on health and productivity in the United States and overseas. Here, with regard to the hours of working women, the impact of that long-ago-and-faraway Metaphysical Club of Cambridge pragmatists was apparent in national social policy.

The practical, realistic approach to jurisprudence that Brandeis shared with Holmes gradually came to prevail during the first decades of the twentieth century. Recognition of social realities in courts of law meant that contemporary views of social justice could gain a hearing. Holmes made his greatest direct impact as an advocate of judicial restraint, repeatedly arguing that legislatures—which were responsive to the Progressives' ideals of social justice in the marketplace—had the right to act whether or not courts agreed with their policies. During this period the Supreme Court was zealously using the Fourteenth Amendment, which barred states from abridging "the privileges or immunities of citizens,"[25] to protect corporations (corporate "citizens") from the pressures of labor unions and regulatory legislation. The prevailing ideology on the Court favored a laissez-faire social Darwinism, in which corporations should be allowed to pursue the competitive struggle as they saw fit. Holmes, whose personal outlook was substantially influenced by Darwin's and Spencer's evolutionary views, believed that such beliefs were irrelevant to the issues of legislative power. "The Fourteenth Amendment," he declared in 1905, "does not enact Mr. Herbert Spencer's *Social Statics*."[26] Later Holmes commented that legislation was "like buying a ticket to the theatre. If you are sure you want to go to the show and have the money to pay for it, there is an end of the matter. I may think you foolish to want to go, but that has nothing to do with my duty."[27] Holmes did, in fact, think some of the legislation was foolish, and he was skeptical of altruism. By assuming an Olympian posture Holmes enhanced the credibility of his message.

In 1916 Brandeis was heavily criticized during his confirmation proceedings because he had been a partisan of reform. Again and again Brandeis had denounced "industrial absolutism," arguing that it was incompatible with democracy in the long run.[28] It must be transformed by the intervention of labor unions so that industrial democracy could become a reality. Brandeis was the altruistic, socially committed reformer Holmes so doubted, but on the bench they were allies against "judicial sanction" of what Brandeis called the "half-truths" of "survival of the fittest" doctrines.[29]

When they went to the Supreme Court, Holmes and Brandeis left Massachusetts, except for summers spent on the North Shore (Holmes) and on the Cape (Brandeis). But the issues that they were now confronting in the national arena were connected fundamentally to the historic dilemmas of individual and corporate rights in Massachusetts. How absolute were the rights of an individual? In what measure could groups prescribe limits on individuals? When people joined in concert to promote their aims, what was their status? In the 1630s the individual consciences of the migrants had been paramount, relative to the English Church and state. But in the same decade the corporate good of Massachusetts ruled over the consciences of dissenting individuals like Roger Williams and groups like the followers of Anne Hutchinson. In 1688 and again in 1775 and 1787 insurgent groups had gathered in the name of individual rights to challenge what they saw as usurping state power. Throughout the nineteenth century people had formed voluntary associations that were bent on asserting the rights of their members to free speech and assembly and on defining the common good even if it meant, as in the case of the temperance movement, limiting the rights of others. Holmes and Brandeis had been trained in Massachusetts, where conflicts between the individual and the group, between the private and the public good had been repeatedly articulated. Not even conflicts between organized labor and organized capital were new to Massachusetts. Holmes could recall the great Lynn shoemakers' strike of 1860, at the time the largest strike in American history. Brandeis could not forget the strike in Lawrence that closed up Massachusetts's largest mills in 1912. The actors and their interests in the conflicts changed, as did the settings, but whether the arguments were couched in religious or secular terms, whether voiced by Yankees or immigrants, the core political issues fundamental to a republican society remained.

What was new was the pragmatic willingness to accept social friction. Acknowledging the heterogeneity and competition among Massachusetts citizens and their interests, people learned that tolerance had become a necessity. But it did not come easily to everyone. Memories and traditions, as well as economic and electoral competition, sustained hostilities while they nurtured group consciousness. Haltingly, people adjusted to the multiethnic, urban, industrial character of Massachusetts.

Contributing to the process of social cohesion and peaceful coexistence in the new industrial commonwealth were the initial attempts of the state legislature to ameliorate the worst excesses of urban and factory life. Robert Woods, the pioneering settlement-house founder and social reformer, wrote that the immigrant "incursion" had precipitated "sanitary, industrial and moral problems so threatening that it became necessary to call upon the state for new and unprecedented forms of legislative action."[30]

Massachusetts was the first state to undertake some measure of regulation of competition and to enact early forms of factory legislation to protect helpless workers. One historian suggested that the state legislature's reform efforts in the area of industrial legislation predated the Progressive Era. Lord Bryce's comment that the General Court in 1888 was "substantially pure and does its work well" seems an overstatement, yet by the end of the century the legislature's actions were impressive. In 1869 the state established a railroad commission to mediate between railroads and the public interest. They created a Board of Gas and Electric Light Commissioners in 1885, with added powers in 1887, 1893, and 1894, allowing for rate fixing, the control of competition, and the governing of stock sales. Commissions on hospitals, asylums, libraries, charities, penal institutions, and a Bureau of Labor Statistics followed.

Massachusetts legislators passed a series of laws relating to labor regulation and governing political practices: the 1866 Factory Inspection Act; a ten-hour limit for women and children in 1874; an 1886 weekly payments measure; an employers' liability act; a law outlawing contract labor; an 1887 act making Labor Day a holiday; the Secret Ballot Act of 1888; the 1890 Lobby Regulation Act; the 1891 abolition of the poll tax for voting; and the 1892 Corrupt Practices Act. The salient fact here is that in Massachusetts, where the industrial era had first begun, the state legislature faced up to the realities of the industrial age well before the rest of the nation.

The end of the century brought more changes to Massachusetts. The economy seemed to be in an advantageous competitive position because of its early start. However, competition from other regions, such as the South with its lower labor and transportation costs for raw materials, and New York and Philadelphia with their major ports and financial power, now outpaced Massachusetts. Conspicuous in this economic decline was the diffusion of the capitalistic drives of Boston's elite and their increased commitment to an aristocratic tradition that looked askance at trade. Professor Barrett Wendell of Harvard lamented this loss of Brahmin power: "We are vanishing into provincial obscurity. . . . America has swept from our grasp. The future is behind us."[31] Not many shared this gloomy vision, and the continued immigrant flood of Italians, Jews, Poles, and hosts of others demonstrated that Massachusetts still offered attractive economic opportunities. The prosperity of Massachusetts in the twentieth century would lean heavily on the economic foundations built in the Gilded Age, farsighted progressive legislation, and the talents, vitality, imagination, and variety of its people.

*Matzo factory in Boston's North End, 1894.*
The American Jewish Historical Society, gift of Harriet Rosenberg.

*A woman textile worker at Pacific Mills, Lawrence, c. 1916.*
Museum of American Textile History, Lowell.

*W.E.B. Du Bois (1868–1963) at a meeting of the Niagara movement in Boston, 1907* (front, left). Courtesy Special Collections and Archives, W.E.B. Du Bois Library, University of Massachusetts Amherst.

*Striking workers marching through the streets of Lawrence, 1912.* From *New England Magazine*, March 1912.

*James Michael Curley
(1874–1958), mayor
of Boston, governor of
Massachusetts, and United
States congressman.*
Boston Public Library.

*John F. "Honey Fitz" Fitzgerald (1863–1950), Boston mayor
who began the Irish American takeover of city politics.*
Boston Public Library.

*Unemployed men shoveling snow in Boston as part of a public works project during the Great Depression.*

The Society for the Preservation of New England Antiquities, Boston.

*Mary Kenney O'Sullivan (1864–1943), feminist labor activist who helped organize the Women's Trade Union League in 1903.*

Schlesinger Library, Radcliffe Institute, Harvard University.

## CHAPTER 11

✤

# The Twentieth-Century Metropolitan Commonwealth

I N TWENTIETH-CENTURY MASSACHUSETTS, STRAINS BETWEEN groups and individuals were particularly keen. Every person, it seemed, had several identities, one that belonged exclusively to that individual, and others that were associated with an ethnic heritage, an occupation, and a social class. The rights of the majority, acting through the state and public opinion, could infringe on individuals and minorities. Such conflicts occurred repeatedly, from the first decades of the twentieth century onward. In Massachusetts many of the vital issues of contemporary America have been boldly articulated: civil liberties; minority and women's rights; the rights of labor.

Yet Massachusetts was not one continuously flaming battleground of discord. Parallel to the struggles over corporate and individual rights, Massachusetts was emerging as a substantially pluralistic commonwealth. Electoral politics channeled ethnic rivalry into routines that excited interest but not passionate commitment. In time, Massachusetts Yankees, Irish, Italians, and the other ethnic groups reached accommodations with one another so that in the Bay State, as throughout the United States, boundaries of color and class remain the most formidable sources of hostility and barriers to trust.

Here Massachusetts's electoral history furnishes revealing symbols of the nature of the emerging pluralism. People have fought vigorously over many questions, but when they have found a candidate who inspires confidence, they have yielded a portion of their ethnic and ideological commitment. Moreover, everyone can identify with some aspect of Massachusetts's past: the idealism of Puritans, Revolutionaries, and reformers, the aristocratic culture of the eighteenth and nineteenth centuries, or the upward struggle of more recent immigrants, the underdogs of the industrial era. People have moved into the future bringing their own past and that of the commonwealth. The past is always part of the present, and indeed old names and families have exhibited a rare staying power in politics because people remember, whether in the old industrial cities, the sprawling suburbs, or the countrysides of fields and forests, of rocks, of sand and salt air. If one wishes to escape the past, one must leave Massachusetts, because those who stay cannot forget, and its history comes to assimilate newcomers.

Massachusetts's remarkable and startling changeover from a rural to urban society became even more pronounced by the first half of the twentieth century. Following the late-nineteenth-century rapid growth of its central cities and factory towns, in the twentieth century Massachusetts witnessed even greater urbanization. Concomitant with the huge population rise in cities such as Boston, Worcester, and Springfield was the emergence of a more pervasive suburban way of life. Yet all the while the state was undergoing traumatic economic upheavals that were to affect all citizens. The motif that seemed to dominate this period was that of coping with changes brought on by economic dislocations and a new population mix and of adapting to the impact of the Great Depression and two world wars. Political accommodation was one important ingredient that allowed Massachusetts residents to overcome ethnic and class animosity exacerbated by declining industries. Another factor was the burgeoning of new industries (defense, service, and high tech) growing out of the technological skills of old industrial processes as well as advanced educational institutions. These new industries, coupled with the imperatives of wartime, set the stage for renewed economic vitality in Massachusetts.

Heralding the coming of the twentieth century, Massachusetts maintained its preeminence as one of the major industrial states of the nation. With the exception of a still-stagnant agriculture, the state's economy from 1900 to 1919 was vigorous. While agricultural products were valued at only $109 million, the value of industrial goods was well over $4 billion. Textiles and shoes, engaging over 250,000 workers, were the mainstay industries. Yet over 450,000 others worked in a wide range of manufacturing establishments all over the state. From west to east, factories produced paper, metals, machinery and machine tools, grinding tools, electrical apparatus, rubber products, watches, industrial machines, leather items, and a host of other goods. The state contained more than 11,000 factories averaging forty-two workers in each, compared to twenty-three workers for the U.S. factory average. By the turn of the century Massachusetts was third in manufacturing employment, just below New York and Pennsylvania—which each possessed populations several times larger than the Bay State.

In 1900, the port of Boston was the second most important in the country and the leading port in the value of its fish trade. The number of coastal arrivals (9,115) exceeded New York (5,470) and Philadelphia (4,280) in 1908. But the port began to decline, and by 1920 fell to sixth place nationally. Large increases in the labor force, brought about by internal rural-urban migration and rising European and Canadian immigration, kept wages low enough so that industry could prosper. Other factors, such as increasing productivity in factories, continued capital investments, a favorable climate for trade, and Boston's strength as a leader in national finance, all bespoke the commonwealth's attractive economic position. One historian wrote: "Certainly, not least important, however, was the simple fact that Massachusetts industry was established *early,* and therefore enjoyed the economic advantages of priority in important markets, and the political advantages of a vested interest."[1] Its dynamic prosperity continued to lure hosts of newcomers who sought to better their lives in the Bay State's industrial centers.

Continued population growth fueled by unabated immigration was to change the makeup of the state's population and to increase the urbanization process. Growing from 2.8 million inhabitants in 1900 to 3.5 million by 1915 and augmented by the arrival of more than a million immigrants between 1890 and 1914, the Bay State was no longer predominantly a Yankee state. Streams of more than 100,000 immigrants arrived each year.

Before 1880 the majority of citizens came from Great Britain and western Europe; but in 1907, 81 percent of newcomers came from the Austro-Hungarian Empire, Poland, Rumania, Russia, Greece, Italy, Turkey, and Spain. The 1920 Census showed that the Irish were still the largest immigrant group in the state with 183,171. Then came British Canadians with 153,330. For old-line Yankees the numbers of newcomers were startling and worrisome: Italians with 117,007; French

Canadians with 109,681; Russians with 92,034, 56 percent of whom were estimated to be Jews. By 1920, only 31.9 percent of the population could be classified as "native white," while 66.8 percent of the Bay State's people were immigrants or the children of immigrants. The African American population was relatively small, with 45,466 (1.2 percent of the state). The 1920 Census showed that 71.6 percent of Boston's total population was made up of first- and second-generation foreign stock. The major area of settlement for these ethnic groups were the fast-growing cities and towns of the state.

The immigrant tide inundated the urban areas of Massachusetts, taking up the space left by the middle classes who pursued the rural ideal in suburbia. Each new immigrant wave created a surging demographic flow that swiftly transformed neighborhoods, rearranging the nature of community life. Boston and its one thousand square mile metropolitan area, which included seventy-eight towns and cities, showed more than a 30 percent population increase over two decades. It was truly the hub of the Bay State and the New England region. Urbanization also affected other regions—with Worcester, Springfield, Lowell, Fall River, and New Bedford all having more than one hundred thousand residents. By 1920 Massachusetts was thoroughly urbanized; almost 95 percent of the population lived in urban areas, with over two-thirds residing in cities of twenty-five thousand or more. Because of the numerous factory communities of Massachusetts, however, urbanization and city growth were directly connected to a well functioning industrial base.

Crucial for the well-being of the urban-industrial mix was either the development of newer industries or the expansion of older ones. Too many cities, however, concentrated in producing only one or two products, textiles or shoes. In New Bedford 82 percent of the workers were in textiles; in Fall River 78 percent; in Lawrence 76 percent; in Lowell 62 percent. In Haverhill 84 percent of the total number of workers were employed in boots and shoes, as were 81 percent of the workers in Brockton. The prosperity of these communities was dependent on the growth of industries that were, owing to external low-wage competition, on the verge of a long-term slide into oblivion. The dramatic collapse of Massachusetts' two major industries between 1921 to 1949 created large-scale unemployment and suffering and wreaked havoc on the state's once thriving factory cities and towns.

The decline of the factory towns actually began late in the nineteenth century and was halted only temporarily by the short-lived surges in demand brought about by two world wars. To a degree, the geographic factors that turned Massachusetts from agriculture to trade, and then to industry, were significant in determining the downfall of the consumer-goods and durables industries. Massachusetts's early industrial boom had been due to investor daring, technological innovation, educated mechanics and middle-level managers, and a cheap and abundant supply of labor. But these factors came to be overshadowed by the South, which was closer to raw materials and thus had lower freight and shipping costs, and even cheaper nonunion labor.

While Massachusetts still possessed an oversupply of labor, employers grumbled about high wages and low productivity. For example, in the 1920s loom fixers received sixty-two cents an hour, while in North Carolina they earned forty-two cents an hour. Shoe workers in Haverhill made seventy cents an hour while workers in the Midwest received from fifty to fifty-eight cents an hour. Massachusetts workers had promoted their well-being by organizing unions, and they were protected by a well-intentioned and effective system of state social-service laws, both of which were costly to employers. In the South, however, political control by capitalists and an impoverished rural workforce blocked unionization and state-sponsored social-service laws. One textile manufacturer (Kendall Textiles) complained that the company paid 113 percent more for workman's compensation than the southern plant they operated, and unemployment taxes cost $108,000 in Massachusetts whereas they were $40,000 in North Carolina.

Another factor that gave the South a competitive edge was a Massachusetts law that prevented women and children from working after eleven at night. Southern textile factories, with no such strictures, could run an extra shift, produce more, and cut costs. But progressive labor laws were not the only cause of Massachusetts's economic decline. Backward management was also significant. Many Bay State textile communities used only Yankees in managerial positions, limiting their reservoir of talent and demonstrating that "the melting pot process had not advanced well" in Massachusetts.[2] More important was management's failure to utilize technological improvements in textile machinery, such as the Draper loom and automation, which was quickly appreciated by investors in the South. (Some of these investors were

Massachusetts businessmen who also owned stocks in less profitable Bay State mills.) Across the board, Massachusetts could no longer compete in the very industries with which it had launched the industrial revolution in the United States.

Even before the onslaught of the Great Depression, between 1919 and 1929 Massachusetts lost 154,000 jobs in manufacturing, of which over 94,000 were in textiles and shoes. The major decline for textiles began after 1924, with numerous mill closings and bankruptcies. Later the Massachusetts Textile Commission reported that between 1929 and 1948, ninety more plants were liquidated. A study of eighty-nine municipalities showed that seventy-three were producing less in 1939 than in 1919. In 1924, in Fall River the dominant Borden interests announced they were closing their mill to move to Tennessee; in 1929, eighteen mills closed, with nine more in 1930. Further liquidations increased unemployment and lowered production. When the town government went bankrupt it was clear that economic catastrophe had struck Fall River. In 1933, the Beacon Manufacturing Company of New Bedford moved most of its facilities to its southern plant, while the Appleton Company of Lowell moved to Alabama. Similar disastrous changes occurred in shoes. The period 1925–35 saw twenty-five thousand shoe workers lose their jobs, with total wages cut by half. Between 1930 and 1938, seventy-nine shoe firms relocated out of the state, leaving cities like Lynn with a surplus of skilled shoe workers. Other industries and areas were affected by the depression as well.

During these years that mill towns endured declining population, departure of industry, high unemployment rates, lower property values, and rising taxes, the middle class continued to move to the suburbs. It is ironic that the state's electric street railway systems, which had made possible the suburbanization process, careened into bankruptcy during the 1920s. Overbuilt, undercapitalized, facing high maintenance costs and competing with the new and cheaper motor coaches (busses), the street railway companies vanished. The region's three railroad monopolies—the Boston and Albany, the Boston and Maine, and the New York, New Haven and Hartford Company—were also unable to withstand competition from trucks and autos. Although each railroad controlled all traffic within specified areas, they were in a chronically weak financial condition, which was only temporarily interrupted when the federal government took over the railways during World War II. Although motor transit systems made it easier to move to the suburbs, the long, deep economic depression curtailed the social mobility that made suburbanization possible for many people. Between 1920 and 1950, the Boston metropolitan area was one of the slowest growing regions in the country.

The Great Depression, however, strongly influenced the rate of internal migration, particularly to Boston proper, with its population reaching a near peak of over 781,000 in 1930. In the desperate search for jobs, migrants came to Boston, only to discover that the city was reeling under the blows of bankruptcies, cutbacks, and unemployment. Over the 1929–39 decade the value of products produced in the city fell from $604 million to $413 million. Boston's industrial labor force earned 37 percent less in 1939 than in 1929, and the city lost 25 percent of its jobs as well. By 1939, Boston had an unemployment rate of 19.9 percent. The city's clothing industry alone had fired 30 percent of its employees. The Great Depression hit Boston hard; and it was especially brutal to those at the bottom levels of society, particularly the foreign born.

Citywide the Irish had the highest unemployment rate of all groups, 26 percent. But Irish South Boston had a rate of 33 percent, with sixty thousand out of work in that community. Some predominantly Italian communities were even worse off. By 1930, the North End had the highest density of population in the city, at 799 per square acre, also accounting for the city's highest juvenile delinquency rate. A few years later, in 1934, unemployment among the Hub's Italians reached 40 percent. Italian Americans expressed their frustration and alienation by holding pro-Mussolini rallies. A historian of depression-era Boston, Charles Trout, has suggested that widespread suffering among ethnic groups "manifested greater tendencies toward separatism" and "stimulated inter-group hostilities."[3]

Irish and Italian conflict spread into gang warfare, with the Irish resentful of Italian incursions into the North End and East Boston. By 1910, when Italians began moving into the North End in large numbers, the Irish shifted to Charlestown and South Boston. Irish gangs tried to hold sway over North and Commercial streets along the waterfront, attacking Italians after dark. This became especially galling for

Sicilian fishermen who had to walk home through these Irish neighborhoods after their day's work was over.

Once the Irish left for other neighborhoods gang wars began on a sectional basis. If an Italian was caught on the Charlestown bridge by Irish youths, he would signal for his own gang to appear and full-scale fighting would break out. One former gang member reported that after a fight began during a football game in Charlestown, the Italians sought retribution:

> Some of the boys got back to the North End, and pretty soon thirty, forty cars come across that bridge, all filled with North End fellows. By the time the cars got there, the field was deserted. But we drove around Charlestown in a procession. We rode up and down them streets, and wherever we went, we saw the women throw down the windows. They thought we was gangsters.[4]

There were rumbles (pitched battles between gangs with agreed-on rules) and widespread youth gang violence, which included attacks upon blacks moving into the South End. Thus, under pressure of intense job competition in a declining economy, ethnic awareness and solidarity was heightened.

Divisions among groups were part of the tumult produced by the nation's changeover from a rural to urban society. In a democracy, conflicts between minorities and majorities are inescapable. In the nineteenth century, Massachusetts was a staging ground for educational reformers, temperance advocates, feminists, and abolitionists who sought to persuade the majority of the justness of their cause. In the twentieth century several of the descendants of William Lloyd Garrison and his peers united with a handful of Massachusetts blacks to continue the drive for equal rights. Together they joined in founding the National Association for the Advancement of Colored People (NAACP), the principal agent of black rights in the new century and ultimately the architect of the national policy of desegregation.

The most remarkable of these founders was W. E. Burghardt Du Bois, who was born in the Housatonic Valley at Great Barrington in 1869. Raised among his mother's people, who had been in town for generations, Du Bois developed a strong, characteristically Massachusetts sense of place:

The social classes of the town were built partly on landholding farmers and more especially on manufacturers and merchants. . . . The rich people of the town were not very rich nor many in number. The middle class were farmers, merchants and artisans; and beneath these was a small proletariat of Irish and German mill workers. They lived in slums near the woolen mills and across the river clustering about the Catholic Church. The number of colored people in the town and Country was small. They were all, save directly after the [Civil] war, old families, well-known to the old settlers among the whites. The color line was manifest and yet not absolutely drawn. I remember a cousin of mine who brought home a white wife. The chief objection was that he was not able to support her and nobody knew about her family; and knowledge of family history was counted as highly important. Most of the colored people had some white blood from unions several generations past. That they congregated together in their own social life was natural because that was the rule in the town.[5]

Although his family was poor, it was respectable. Du Bois enjoyed Great Barrington, for its surroundings were "a boy's paradise: there were mountains to climb and rivers to wade and swim; lakes to freeze and hills for coasting. There were orchards and caves and wide green fields; and all of it was apparently property of the children." After school he did odd jobs "splitting kindling, mowing lawns, doing chores." Because his brilliance was recognized in the town school, the principal of the high school encouraged Du Bois to prepare for college, and a mill owner's wife purchased the necessary texts in algebra, geometry, Latin, and Greek for him. When Du Bois was graduated in 1884, he delivered a public oration on Wendell Phillips. Though neither he nor his audience knew it, his own career ultimately would carry on Phillips's devotion to human rights and social justice. "My heart was set on Harvard," Du Bois later recalled, since "it was the greatest and oldest college and I therefore quite naturally thought it was the one I must attend."[6] But the Great Barrington High School had not prepared him for the entrance exam, nor had he the necessary funds, so he went to work. Soon after, however, white sponsors came forward and offered to send him to the all-black Fisk University in Nashville, Tennessee. Fisk was not Harvard, but Du Bois was pleased to go. Going south was an adventure, and the move played a crucial role in establishing his sense of himself as a champion of black equality.

For the young black Yankee from the Berkshires, Fisk provided an awakening as to what it meant to be black in America. In the summers Du Bois taught school for the children of black sharecroppers in the Tennessee countryside, and as editor of the *Fisk Herald* he began to express "a belligerent attitude toward the color bar."[7] At graduation in 1888 he won a scholarship to enter Harvard, and when he joined the junior class he had already learned to accept the social segregation that prevailed there.

Eagerly, Du Bois took advantage of Harvard's faculty and library. Philosophy was his first love: "I was repeatedly a guest in the house of William James; he was my friend and guide to clear thinking; I was a member of the Philosophical Club and talked with Royce and Palmer; I sat in an upper room and read Kant's Critique with Santayana." But William James persuaded DuBois to turn toward history and social science because, he told his student, "it is hard to earn a living with philosophy."[8] Thus Du Bois became a protege of the historian Albert Bushnell Hart and went on, with his study of the suppression of the African slave trade, to become, in 1895, the first African American to earn a doctorate at Harvard. Du Bois proved that intellectually he had few peers.

For social life Du Bois turned to the small, cultivated black community in the vicinity. Some of his most rewarding evenings were spent at the home of Maria Louise Baldwin, the principal of the Agassiz grammar school. Baldwin who in 1889, at the age of thirty-three, had become the first black principal in Massachusetts, was a Cambridge native, a graduate of its high school and teacher training school, and a lecturer of note. She was also, in her modest way, a *salonière* for black intellectuals, and her home was the headquarters of the literary Banneker Club and the more wide-ranging Omar Circle. Du Bois, who was deeply appreciative and admiring, described her as "always serene, just slightly mocking, refusing to be thundered or domineered into silence and answering always in that low, rich voice—with questionings, with frank admission of uncertainty." Baldwin made a superb foil for Du Bois, who admitted he was then in his "hottest, narrowest, self-centered, confident period."[9] It was in Baldwin's parlor that Du Bois came to know the equally headstrong William Monroe Trotter, his ally years later when they worked on behalf of the NAACP to challenge white supremacy and the Booker T. Washington brand of accommodation. Maria Baldwin not only influenced the lives of several thousand students in her forty years at the Agassiz school, she also cultivated the aspirations of passing African American Harvard students to whom the college turned a cold shoulder socially.

Trotter, several years younger than Du Bois, came from a prominent black family and was a native of Boston who had come to Harvard from the suburban Hyde Park High School in 1891. His father, the son of a Mississippi slave owner and slave mother, had been raised as a free black in Cincinnati. During the Civil War James Monroe Trotter had enlisted in Holmes's friend Nathaniel Hallowell's black regiment, where he rose to the rank of second lieutenant and led the struggle for the principle of equal pay for black soldiers. After the war the senior Trotter settled in Boston, where he became the leading black Democrat. In 1884, one year before Thomas Gargan became the first Irishman to give the Fourth of July address in Boston, Trotter gave the oration in Hyde Park, and three years later President Cleveland named him to succeed Frederick Douglass in the lucrative position of recorder of deeds for the District of Columbia. Notwithstanding political differences, Senator Hoar endorsed Trotter, and he won the post for the two remaining years of Cleveland's administration.

It was no wonder that Monroe Trotter, who made Phi Beta Kappa in his junior year and graduated magna cum laude from Harvard in 1895, rejected Booker T. Washington's program of manual training for blacks and accommodation to segregation and disfranchisement. Like Du Bois, Trotter knew from firsthand experience that intellectual capacity was not a matter of race, and he had grown up competing successfully with whites. Several years after graduation Trotter came to realize that for him the advocacy of equal rights, becoming a "race champion," was more important than respectable prosperity. In 1901, together with George W. Forbes, a black Amherst College graduate, he founded the *Guardian,* a newspaper that quickly became the most militant defender of equal rights in the United States.

Soon Trotter became notorious as a renegade. In 1903 he was jailed for his part in disrupting a speech that Booker T. Washington was giving at the African Methodist Episcopal Zion Church on Columbus Avenue in Boston; and Washington, who did not brook opposition, ever after did his best to denigrate Trotter and destroy his influence. Since

Trotter sometimes had a sharp and abusive tongue, and the pages of the *Guardian* were often enlivened with personal invective, Washington had no difficulty in persuading whites of the danger Trotter represented. Even the descendants of William Lloyd Garrison, who had known the Trotter family for years, came to regard Monroe Trotter as unreasonable.

Yet he persisted. In 1907 he moved the *Guardian* to the old *Liberator* office, the very building where Garrison had been mobbed, and he adorned his desk with a bust of the abolitionist who would not equivocate or "retreat a single inch" and who had insisted that he would be heard. By now Trotter, who had joined Du Bois in organizing the Niagara Movement for equal rights, had made himself one of the key spokesmen for the growing minority of blacks who, rejecting "Bookerism," spoke in favor of complete equality of opportunity for blacks— in education, jobs, and politics. Although Trotter was a self-righteous individualist who was temperamentally unsuited to collaboration, he worked for a few years with Du Bois; and gradually several key whites, including Oswald Garrison Villard (grandson of Trotter's hero) and Moorfield Storey (former secretary of the abolitionist senator Charles Sumner), came to respect his principles. By 1910, when the NAACP was formed, Trotter was a militant gadfly rather than an insider. He was too irascible for the new organization that would ultimately supplant Booker T. Washington as the quasi-official voice of black Americans. Du Bois was by now an experienced educator and scholar who had taught for years in Atlanta and who had studied and traveled abroad. He had become more urbane and sophisticated than Trotter, and after his experiences at Fisk and Atlanta, Du Bois was ready to compromise lesser points for larger ones. Like his mentor, William James, his idealism merged with his pragmatism.

From here on, his path separated from Trotter's, as Du Bois became the chief spokesman of the NAACP and the editor of (and frequent author for) its publications. Trotter went his own way although he did collaborate with NAACP officials in working successfully in 1911 to defeat a bill in the General Court that would have banned interracial marriage in Massachusetts. In 1908 he had been key in forming the all-black Negro-American Political League which in a few years became a vehicle for his own leadership as the National Equal Rights League, a rival to the largely white NAACP. It was Trotter's independence from the more circumspect NAACP that led to his famous confrontation with President Wilson over the introduction of segregation in the federal bureaucracy.

In 1912 Trotter had played an unimportant role in the effort among northern blacks to support Wilson's candidacy, in the hope that Wilson would provide greater recognition of equal rights. But soon after Wilson took office the southern members of his cabinet persuaded the president that segregation should prevail. Trotter, who looked for more, not less, from Wilson, was alarmed. In late 1913 he led a delegation to meet with Wilson, and the president, as Trotter reported in the *Guardian,* "listened attentively to Colored citizens, . . . responded courteously and gave them thirty-five minutes of his time." Yet Wilson did not budge, and a year later Trotter and his colleagues returned. This time Wilson lectured them on the virtues of segregation. It was, he said, "a benefit, and ought to be so regarded by you gentlemen." Trotter, who with his father had been fighting patronizing white supremacists since Lincoln's day, was outraged. Speaking from personal experience he replied to the president: "For fifty years white and colored clerks have been working together in peace and harmony and friendliness, doing so even through two Democratic administrations. Soon after your inauguration began, segregation was drastically introduced." Interrupting, Wilson imperiously declared: "Your manner offends me." But Trotter was undaunted, and for nearly an hour the argument continued. When Trotter later revealed the contents of the interview to reporters, the White House was shocked by this breach of etiquette. But Wilson would not yield, and public opinion, especially in the South, supported his intransigence. There were few advocates of official segregation in Massachusetts and Republicans took pleasure from Wilson's difficulties, but an informal segragation was emerging. Trotter himself was denounced by the respected *Boston Evening Transcript* as an "impudent mischief-maker." [10] The white majority in Massachusetts recognized the political rights of the black minority, but the vision of a black man confronting a white official, the president, was offensive.

Besides confrontations with minorities, Massachusetts suffered through the agonies of nativist and class conflict, as indicated by spectacular disruptive events, such as the 1912 general strike of Lawrence, the Irish-Yankee conflict of the Boston police strike of 1919, and the decade long turmoil brought about by the Sacco and Vanzetti cause célèbre.

In 1912, Lawrence was truly an "immigrant city" with a population of eighty-six thousand, of whom seventy-four thousand had been born abroad, or were native born with foreign-born parents. The largest groups were French Canadians, Italians, Irish, Russians (including many Jews), and Syrians. Except for the Irish, many of these immigrants spoke little English. The "Bread and Roses" general strike of 1912, which laid bare the intolerable conditions of the workers, exposed the city's social crisis. Textile workers received poverty wages—the U.S. commissioner of labor, Charles P. Neill, found the "fulltime earnings of a large number of adult employees are entirely inadequate to maintain a family."[11] When the state legislature, in an effort to protect families, mandated that women and children under eighteen could work no more than fifty-four hours, the employers responded by cutting wages proportionately. On January 11, 1912, women weavers who could not read English and normally worked fifty-six hours per week found less pay in their envelopes, and they went on strike demanding higher wages. They were soon followed by the men who found their own wages intolerably low. In a few days the strike spread and most of the Lawrence mills closed. The early nineteenth-century model factory town had become a worker's nightmare in the twentieth century.

Workers organized strike committees along ethnic lines, while resisting the approaches of unions. They did welcome organizers from the International Workers of the World, who assisted them by suggesting tactics to deal with the employers. The IWW leaders Joe Etore and, later, William Haywood worked out picketing and parading procedures that were effective against the employers and their attempts to reopen the mills. Sometimes confrontations grew ugly, particularly when the police brutally attacked prominent women pickets. The resulting publicity created widespread support for the strikers, but the employers refused to meet with them, and daily picketing brought violence and increasing property damage. The nation's eyes were on Lawrence, and Governor Eugene Foss, hoping to keep the peace, called out the militia.

The plight of the workers and their children aroused sympathy, as they suffered through the winter months with little money or food and endured what appeared to be the cruel actions of the employers and local authorities. By early March, Governor Foss grew angry at the obdurate mill owners and their refusal to negotiate. He threatened to remove the militia. At the same time orders for textile goods increased and the mill owners decided to meet the demands of the workers. The workers received pay increases and promises that the strikers would not be punished. Ethnic solidarity among the working poor had won the day for the Lawrence strikers. However, owners would later retaliate by moving their plants to the South where unions could be suppressed.

Because the strike involved large numbers of women and children, many women reformers streamed to Lawrence to express their support. One such labor activist was Mary Kenney O'Sullivan, who collaborated with upper-class women to promote women's rights in Massachusetts. Born January 8, 1864, the daughter of Irish immigrants who worked together on the railroads, Mary Kenney knew from personal experience the plight of the working classes. The premature death of her father forced her to leave school in the fourth grade and go to work. In time she took on many industrial jobs, from dressmaker to printer and bookbinder. She began organizing women bookbinders, and at age twenty-eight in 1892, Samuel Gompers appointed her to continue this work for the American Federation of Labor (AF of L). She was sent to Boston where she met and married a labor reporter, John F. O'Sullivan. For a short time she served as deputy factory inspector of Illinois, but she returned to Boston where she and her family lived in the Denison Settlement House. This settlement house had been established by Vida Scudder and Emily Greene Balch, upper-class women who sought to create a female alliance that would bridge the gap between classes. Working with Boston society women who called themselves the "Allies," O'Sullivan organized the National Women's Trade Union League in 1903, in conjunction with New York social worker William English Walling.

This was the first national women's trade union. Its purpose was to create an alliance of women workers and their upper-class "friends" to promote legislation to protect women's rights in the trades and to work to get women to join existing men's labor unions. O'Sullivan went on to help garment and laundry workers to organize and was recognized for her efforts by her appointment in 1914 as inspector of industrial safety for the Commonwealth of Massachusetts. She served in that position until 1934 when she was seventy years old. She died in West

Medford early in 1943, having devoted herself to the working women of the state and the nation. But the Lawrence strike left an indelible imprint upon her. She wrote: "I had been in strikes in 1877 and had seen the poverty of underpaid workers in every form . . . but never in my labor experience had I seen or known so many men, women and children as badly housed and undernourished." [12]

Several years after the Lawrence strike of 1912, anxieties resulting from minority challenges to majority opinion generated a dramatic confrontation in Massachusetts when the Boston police, of largely Irish background, staged a strike. Coming within the context of ethnic suspicions, widespread labor discontent, and growing concern about political radicals during the "Red Scare," the strike revealed tensions inherent in the creation of a pluralistic democracy in industrial Massachusetts. Although the conflict was ostensibly Boston's alone, the whole state was involved, and Governor Calvin Coolidge, a modest Northampton lawyer, would parlay his role in the episode into the vice presidency.

The strike, which had been brewing for weeks, occurred in mid-September 1919. The central issue was whether the city would accept a police union affiliated with the American Federation of Labor. When the police went out on strike, an unprecedented step, they were rapidly maneuvered into becoming the scapegoats for the mob violence and the destruction of downtown property that resulted. Volunteer policemen, largely recruited from among middle- and upper-class suburban Protestants, together with National Guardsmen from around the state restored order in the weeks that followed, and the strikers were defeated. Calvin Coolidge, the prim symbol of Yankee Americanism, seized the opportunity to vindicate law and order; and indeed Yankee Republicans used the strike to put labor, new immigrants, and the Boston Irish "in their place." The issues that were publicly debated revolved around the rights of labor and the rights of the majority, Governor Coolidge declaring, "There is no right to strike against the public safety by anybody, anywhere, any time." [13] The common good was preeminent—an old fundamental principle in Massachusetts public life.

Beneath the surface, however, there was an undertow of ethnic division. Long ago the state legislature had reduced Boston's municipal autonomy because of the statewide Yankee Republican suspicion of the dangers of Irish rule. Now, in the aftermath of the First World War, when Irish patriots, preferring neutrality, were protesting the United

States's close alliance with Britain, some Yankees doubted Irish American loyalty. Indeed, the prescription of one police strikebreaker was simply to "select a few old-fashioned Yankees—full-blooded Americans to instill a little Americanism" in Boston.[14] Even though the Irish Americans of Massachusetts had participated heroically under arms in wartime, even though officials of the Catholic Church had firmly supported law and order, staying aloof from the strikers, the old doubts lingered.

Just a few months after the turmoil of the police strike subsided, two robberies occurred south of Boston in Bridgewater and Braintree. Although two men were killed in the Braintree holdup, these incidents were not in themselves remarkable. But the effort to solve these crimes, which led to the arrest, trial, and execution of Nicola Sacco and Bartolomeo Vanzetti, became one of the great dramas of Massachusetts history. Just as the trials of Anne Hutchinson and the Salem "witches" had aroused imaginations and readily lent themselves to symbolic interpretations, so did the Sacco and Vanzetti case. But in contrast to them, it developed in the glare of nationwide publicity and became, in the eyes of many, a test of the ability of American democracy to dispense even-handed justice.

Sacco and Vanzetti had come to Massachusetts from Italy in 1908 and had become marginal members of the industrial labor force. By the time of their arrest in 1920, Sacco was settled with a wife and child in South Stoughton, where he was an edger in Kelley's shoe factory. Vanzetti was living in Plymouth, where he peddled fish, door to door. Both men were in their early thirties, and both were active in a minor way among Italian immigrant anarchists. When they were arrested three weeks after the Braintree robbery, each was carrying a loaded pistol.

Within a few weeks Vanzetti was indicted for the Bridgewater robbery, and after a week-long trial he was convicted on July 1, 1920. A year later, in a trial that lasted six weeks, both Sacco and Vanzetti were convicted of the Braintree crimes. Then for six long years the case remained in litigation, with motions for new trials and finally an appeal to the Massachusetts Supreme Judicial Court. During this period left-wing and liberal activists succeeded in making the case a national, even an international cause célèbre. Left-wing and liberal groups believed that the defendants were innocent, and that as Italian anarchists they were victims of ethnic and political prejudice. Their case was used to arouse libertarian sentiments and as a means of challenging the legitimacy of the native white Protestant "establishment."

Finally, when the last appeal was denied, the fate of the two "martyrs" was left to Republican governor Alvan Fuller, a bicycle mechanic turned automobile entrepreneur and congressman, whose chief assets at the polls were his great wealth and his companionable nature. Fuller wanted to do right, but as a firm believer in the death penalty he did not mean to err on the side of leniency. Only recently he had denied the request of three Catholic mothers who, backed by a petition of 120,000 people including three ex-governors, had prayed on their knees in his office for their sons' lives. In that instance two of the three convicts were merely accessories to murder, but Fuller, seemingly immune to the pressure of humanitarian appeals, was content that their death sentences be carried out. When Fuller decided to review the Sacco and Vanzetti case and to appoint an advisory committee, headed by President Abbott Lawrence Lowell of Harvard, he wanted to do a thorough job that would appear so fair and meticulous that it would reinforce the legitimacy of Massachusetts government.

From Fuller's standpoint the choice of Lowell to advise him was perfect. By definition a Harvard president could not be corrupt; a man descended from several of the wealthiest, most distinguished Yankee families must be widely respected; and Lowell had long ago proved his civil-libertarian credentials. During the police strike when pressure at Harvard mounted to fire Harold Laski, a temporary lecturer in political science, Lowell, who disagreed with Laski's outspoken support of the strikers, defended him, declaring that if Laski was fired he would resign. What Fuller failed to appreciate was that to outsiders there was no better symbol of smug, self-righteous Yankee establishment than President Lowell. If Lowell's committee found in favor of Sacco and Vanzetti, he was a good choice; if not, the friends of the doomed men would see collusion by the Massachusetts elite.

As it turned out, Lowell's committee, like Governor Fuller, came to the conclusion that Sacco and Vanzetti had been fairly tried and sentenced, so on August 23, 1927, they were executed. That act symbolized Massachusetts's painful, seemingly irreconcilable divisions. W.E.B. Du Bois concluded ruefully that "the social community that mobbed Garrison, easily hanged Sacco and Vanzetti."[15] The trial records, as analyzed at the time by the Harvard law professor Felix Frankfurter, showed that a Yankee judge and jury had displayed prejudice and that the testimony of immigrant witnesses on behalf of the defendants had been ignored. Frankfurter concluded that if Sacco and Vanzetti had been Yankees, they would never have been indicted, much less convicted. The decision of Lowell, made in good faith, was also a reflection of his own ethnic prejudice. One of Lowell's old Harvard classmates explained to the confounded Frankfurter that he believed Lowell was simply "incapable of seeing that two wops could be right and the Yankee judiciary wrong." [16]

Though they became victims, these two anticlerical, immigrant anarchists generated profound concern in Massachusetts and the nation and this interest represents a measure of the emerging liberal pluralism. In the name of the common good, Americans had often ridden roughshod over minorities, sometimes employing the dignity of judicial procedures as in Anne Hutchinson's case, sometimes, as in the Ursuline Convent and Garrison mobs, with direct violence. The Sacco-Vanzetti case, like those of the Scottsboro boys in Alabama in the 1930s and the Rosenbergs in the early 1950s, was understood as being more than just another prosecution to determine innocence or guilt. In all these cases the balance between corporate, majority, and individual rights—procedural and political—was being tested.

One factor that would enable Bay Staters to withstand the ethnic-class pressures heightened by economic disaster was their willingness to use the system of participatory democracy to redress long-held grievances. For an urban and troubled Massachusetts, the primary avenue for societal accommodation among contending groups was the open political system. A democratic system imbued with the capitalist drive for individual achievement—"equality of opportunity"—prompted the possibility of expanding material prosperity. For those newly arrived urban groups initially outside the corridors of Yankee power in Massachusetts, majoritarian politics provided the vehicle for both individual social mobility and group social welfare.

Martin Lomasney, the Irish "Mahatma" of Boston's Ward Eight, conceived of politics as pure utilitarianism when he described the function of his political organization, the Hendricks Club, as "a machine for getting votes. And it gets them, by working 365 days a year, caring for people, being a big employment agency, being a generous benefactor, viewing with charitable and forgiving eyes lapses of human conduct." [17]

The path to power for Massachusetts ethnics was an arduous and complicated journey, which began with compliant compromise and then, when power came within reach, was marked by bitter infighting and almost suicidal bickering.

Clearly, the notion of absolute Irish supremacy in Boston and elsewhere in the state was largely mythical. The first and second generation of Irish never made up more than one-third of the city's population. By 1920, the Irish accounted for 31.9 percent, the Jews 15.7 percent (of various nationalities, but with substantial Russian and Polish immigrants), the Italians 14 percent, with a variety of other immigrant groups at 10 percent, for a total of 71.6 percent, making Boston second only to New York City in total percentage of first- and second-generation foreign stock. Between 1885 and his death in 1933, Martin Lomasney's Ward Eight in the West End dramatically changed its population mix from predominantly Irish to Jewish and then to Italian. All the while as "clan chief" he maintained absolute political control by bridging the polyglot ethnic gap and providing jobs and service to all. As the premier immigrant group, the Irish dominated ethnic politics, but only because they were adept conciliators and compromisers.

The two most famous of these Irish politicos were John Francis Fitzgerald and James Michael Curley. Both men were sons of Irish immigrants. Both gravitated to politics at least partly because other avenues of social mobility were closed to them, and both had the ebullient and vibrant personalities that made for political charisma. They symbolized ethnic success in a world of Yankee supremacy that controlled finances and a large portion of the professions. Politics attracted them as it did many of Boston's Irish. A Yankee social worker wrote in 1903 about the Irish "love of politics":

> The Irishman regards politics as a separate department of life. It is an end in itself. . . . To be sure he hopes by its means to be able to gain a living, but that is the stake of a game which has a fascination all its own. They are not merely the most easily organized of any nationality, but they are the most capable organizers.[18]

Curiously, more often than not Fitzgerald and Curley lost their political races, but nonetheless they were politicians who foreshadowed the eventual victory of the newcomers over the hosts.

John Francis Fitzgerald (1863–1950), maternal grandfather of John F., Robert F., and Edward M. Kennedy, grew up in the North End of Boston, the third sibling in a family of twelve children. His father, Thomas had come from Ireland as a simple laborer. He soon worked his way up the ladder of success, ending up as a merchant owning a grocery-liquor store. Young "Johnny Fitz," as he was called, grew up amid the wharfs and winding streets of the waterfront. He was one of the first Irish Catholics to attend the elite Boston Latin School, and he made another breakthrough when he began attending Harvard Medical College in 1884. But the death of his father meant the end to schooling, and he secured a political plum working in the U.S. Customs House, and then began selling insurance.

A short dapper man with a bouncing step and a readiness to sing "Sweet Adeline" on any occasion, he became a popular North End figure. He joined every social club he could and soon was keeping a list of all eligible voters in his district. He entered politics in 1892 when he was elected to the Boston Common Council at the age of twenty-nine. He became the undisputed "Boss" of his district, the "Napoleon of the North End." He organized a political club, scanned the death notices every morning and went to funerals, made it his business to help men find jobs, and attended dances and social functions to make himself indispensable to his neighbors. With the support of adjacent ward leader Martin Lomasney, Fitzgerald successfully ran for state senator in 1892, 1893, and 1894. He ran for U.S. Congress in 1895 and won, serving until 1901. With his eye on the mayoralty, he voluntarily left Congress to return to Boston and wait for his opportunity.

The unexpected death of Mayor Patrick Collins in 1905 gave Fitzgerald the chance he sought. Opposed by the other Democratic ward bosses, he ran a vigorous primary campaign, giving the city its first political motorcade, barnstorming with ten speeches a night, and spending over $120,000. He had made a fortune in the insurance business with his brother, and he owned a profitable weekly newspaper. To the surprise and anger of his fellow politicos, particularly Martin Lomasney, Fitzgerald won the primary. In the election the miffed Lomasney went as far as to direct his ward to vote for the Republican candidate, but the presence of an independent third candidate allowed Fitzgerald to eke out a narrow victory. He had succeeded in spite of the other Democratic bosses.

As mayor he became a bane to the bosses by creating jobs and thus limiting their patronage power; he also represented the first organized challenge to Yankee control over the city. His two years in office (1906–07) combined reform, patronage and ward politics, and corruption. He added new jobs to the city payroll to reward those who had supported him. Avoiding civil service limitations, he put people to work as "provisionals" or in emergency appointments, as watchmen to watch watchmen, inspectors to check on street watering crews, bridgeworkers on drawbridges that no longer worked, tree climbers, rubber boot repairers, and a host of invented positions. During his administration the city lost over $200,000 in bizarre dealings with a coal company, and several of his appointees were indicted for bribery. All the while he built new facilities for the harbor, constructed new schools, playgrounds, bathhouses, and municipal swimming pools for his working-class constituents. A historian of Boston, John Koren, wrote, "He gave much time to city planning, motor fire apparatus, garbage disposal, playground extension . . . laborers' retirement plan, the city hall annex and to new district municipal buildings . . . containing public halls, branch libraries, baths, etc." [19] He horrified the Yankees, disgusted the bosses, and delighted those who voted for him. But the scandals were too much, and despite the renewed support of Lomasney and the ward bosses, he lost to a strait-laced Republican, George Hibbard, in 1907.

Ever fearful of the return of Fitzgerald and his wild spending ways, the Yankee business establishment determined to make it difficult for a popular ward leader to become elected. With the full support of the Republican-dominated state legislature, Boston received in 1909 a new charter that strengthened the power of the mayor (who now held a four-year term and had control over the budget), reduced the Common Council and Board of Aldermen to a small city council elected at large, and eliminated the political parties in mayoral elections. Using the rhetoric of "Progressivism," the national reform movement that was sweeping the country, the Republicans were attempting to break the hold of the Democratic party in the wards. They envisioned a system with a strong nonpartisan mayor elected at large, who would need the support of the middle and business classes to win. To cap off their strategy, in the election of 1910 the determined Yankees put forward as their candidate the city's most respectable Brahmin, James Jackson Storrow, a wealthy banker, Harvard overseer, former president of the Boy Scouts of America, former president of the Boston School Committee, and Cleveland Democrat of the old school.

To meet this formidable challenge, John Fitzgerald created a political alliance with the new boss of Ward Seventeen, James Michael Curley. He convinced the former Republican mayor George Hibbard to run again so that the Storrow ticket would be split. His campaign was based clearly on class and ethnic hostility, calling it a contest between "an Irish boy from the slums and a wealthy encrusted Harvard blueblood." He went on to say: "My election will mean to every father and mother whose son is attending the public schools that their boy needn't become a millionaire in order to be mayor of Boston." Storrow countered with a charge of corruption: "I propose to put into operation as soon as possible a merit system, which will give our city employees a fair chance to earn promotion, instead of putting over their heads some political loafer or friend of the mayor." [20] Without scruples, Fitzgerald's cohorts started an underground rumor that Storrow was anti-Catholic. Spending freely, racing around the city speaking everywhere, "Fitz" made the staid Storrow look anemic. Yet even with his brilliant campaigning and divided opposition, he barely won by 1,402 votes, as the gulled Hibbard drained off enough votes to ruin Storrow's chances. Fitzgerald's narrow margin of victory demonstrates that the Irish never fully controlled Boston politics and that rivalries between the bosses and the allegiance of the minority Yankee contingent would make the difference in most election contests.

Fitzgerald's next four years in office (1910–14) provided more of the same, with brazen spending, generosity to his friends, and more public works projects to help the poor. He spurned his critics:

> Such things as playgrounds, parks, recreation piers, museums, and libraries, school lunches, municipal theaters, model tenements, social centers have been discussed as if they were frills. . . . As a matter of fact they come close to the real objects for which cities exist. [21]

He made good on his promises, and Boston benefited by getting a new tuberculosis hospital, the Franklin Park Zoo, a city aquarium, and public holidays for city workers. Aside from his picturesque peccadillos that outraged the Yankees, Mayor John Fitzgerald was demonstrating how one city was meeting the needs of twentieth-century urbanization. At the end of his administration in 1913, Fitzgerald surprised people when he announced he would not seek reelection. The opportunity for the mayoralty was now open for Boston's most aggressive new challenger, James Michael Curley.

The circumstances surrounding the election of 1914 illustrate the contentious and acrimonious relationships among the Irish bosses that blocked the creation of a well-coordinated political machine so representative of other cities in the nation. Fitzgerald suffered from health problems and was thinking of not running, but his mind was made up when Curley viciously attacked him on personal grounds. The foolish Fitzgerald was having an affair with a musical actress named "Toodles." Such a liaison was frowned on by the Irish who made much of family values. Curley announced that he would begin delivering a series of public addresses concerning graft: "Great Lovers from Cleopatra to Toodles," and on morals: "Libertines: From Henry the VIII to Present Day." He sent Mrs. Fitzgerald a black-bordered letter in which he threatened a public scandal over Fitzgerald's affair. Mrs. Fitzgerald confronted her husband, who suffered a nervous collapse and then pulled out of the mayoral race. Fitzgerald's withdrawal badly affected his career, as he was characterized as being afraid to stand up against his enemies and was prey to "petticoat power," a humiliating affront for an Irish politician. He ran unsuccessfully for office five more times (winning a 1918 election for Congress only to have the vote overturned by a federal court on charges of illegal registration and ballot stuffing).

The new dominant force in Boston politics from the 1920s to the 1940s was the irrepressible James Michael Curley (1874–1958), "mayor of troubled times." Son of impoverished Irish immigrants and without a formal education, he worked his way out of the slums of Roxbury to become one of the most memorable Massachusetts politicians of the twentieth century. Emulating Lomasney and Fitzgerald, the young newcomer organized a political club that became the centerpiece of his providing service to his constituents. His approach to politics was to avoid parties and organizations and to create a personality cult built on his talents as orator, generous benefactor, and gadfly against the Yankee establishment. There are many legends that surround the Curley era and one of the most notable is the "He did it for a friend" episode. In 1902, he was on the Common Council and one of Curley's constituents asked him to take the civil service test for the post office for him. Curley did, was recognized and indicted for fraud. Under indictment in 1903 he ran and won office as alderman. In 1904, after several appeals, he ended up in jail. While in jail he ran again for alderman and won easily. The voters of Ward Seventeen in Roxbury loved Curley's antics, especially when he manipulated the establishment in their favor.

Curley served as alderman from 1904 to 1909 (including sixty days in jail), and won election to the city council in the charter reform of 1909. In return for his support of Fitzgerald in the mayoral election of 1910, he took over Fitzgerald's old U.S. congressional seat. By 1913, he was ready to fight Fitzgerald and Lomasney, arguing "it was his turn" at the mayoralty. Curley was a beneficent ward boss, holding long office hours at his club to serve his voters. He wrote orders for butchers, grocers, and fuel suppliers, he called up doctors, wrote notes to creditors, went to police stations and court houses to plead for those in trouble, and in the afternoons he met groups of unemployed and walked with them around his district seeking jobs. When he held office he saw his major responsibility as providing services for the poor and needy of all ethnic backgrounds, and using the patronage system to get them jobs. The historian James J. Connolly put Curley in the progressive mold:

> The ability to project a benevolent persona throughout the city earned Curley the mayor's office, where he gained even more power to shape popular perceptions. Seizing on the rhetoric of Progressivism, he made himself the representative of Boston's ordinary citizens as they battled corrupt, hostile Brahmin interests. This image became reality for most Bostonians, a convincing explanation of the city's social order and their place within it.[22]

This vision of the humanitarian purpose of government ran counter to that of the Yankee business community and was to earn Curley popular support from the masses and the undying hatred of the rich.

When he announced for mayor in 1913 the Irish bosses and Yankee establishment coalesced against him. The Democratic city committee put up the city council president, Thomas Kenny, an Irish Democrat from South Boston, who was immediately supported by Storrow and the Boston Good Government Association. Curley defied both camps in typical rhetorical fashion:

> While the opposition indulged in invective, I made campaign promises that I kept after I was elected: Parks and Playgrounds and other recreational areas. These were social improvements that would increase the tax rate, but they were long overdue. Meanwhile, Mr. Kenny, echoing the pinch-penny economics of the "Goo Goos" [Good Government Association] was promising to reduce the tax rate, which was another way of saying that the rich would get richer, and the poor, poorer.[23]

Curley used showmanship and promises to the poor to win in 1914, beating Kenny by a vote of forty-two to thirty-seven thousand and carrying sixteen of Boston's twenty-six wards.

His first administration was to set the standard for all those following. He initiated the daily "spectacle of the corridors," in which people lined up in the corridors of city hall waiting to see Curley to ask for favors. He claimed to talk with two hundred people a day, or more than fifty thousand a year. (By dispensing patronage on a citywide basis, he soon made the ward bosses irrelevant.) Following in the footsteps of Fitzgerald, Curley focused on public works projects—hospitals, neighborhood health units, playgrounds, parks, subways, tunnels, and highways. He overspent and then, when out of money, went to the state legislature to borrow. In 1917, Curley found himself once again the center of controversy. Because of his opposition to World War I based upon Irish nationalist hatred of the British, Curley lost favor with many non-Irish voters. With the business interests, the ward bosses, and the newspapers against him, Curley was defeated. This time the local Democrats used a stratagem that had worked well for Fitzgerald—splitting the ticket. Three Democrats ran against Curley, siphoning off enough of his votes so that the choice of the reformers, the Yankee Democrat Andrew Peters, easily won.

Curley began to experience defeat more often than victory. He won again in 1921, largely because of the hard times associated with the postwar inflation and the chaos resulting from the Boston police strike. While he was in office the Republican state legislature took aim at him, amending the Boston city charter so that incumbent mayors could not succeed themselves. Seeking other opportunities, he ran for governor in

1924 but lost to Yankee Republican Frederick Gillett. Five years later, the fall of the stock market in October 1929 sent a clear signal to the people of Boston that economic distress and unemployment were imminent. Unease over the faltering economy led the poorer people of Boston to turn once again to Curley.

Facing another Irish American, the lawyer Frederick Mansfield, Curley waged an exuberant campaign pledging "work and wages." Mansfield was more ambiguous, calling for "necessary public works" that were "wise expenditures." Curley won the election (116,463 to 96,946). The poorer wards went strongly for Curley. Mansfield won eight wards that were among the highest in the city for median income and housing costs. The election of 1929 demonstrated that in times of trouble—which occurred again during the postwar unemployment of 1945—the poorer classes would turn to their savior, James Michael Curley.

Unable to run again for mayor, Curley won the governorship in 1934. Now he took advantage of New Deal deficit spending to build the gigantic Quabbin Reservoir, which required hiring three thousand Boston Irish tree cutters.[24] The governor's job was only a two-year term, so in 1936 he ran for the U.S. Senate only to lose again to a Yankee Republican, Henry Cabot Lodge Jr. By this time the sixty-three year-old Curley quarreled with President Franklin D. Roosevelt over an appointment as an ambassador and was at odds with state Democrats. He lost the mayoral race in 1937 to another Irish Catholic, Maurice Tobin. The Republican legislature so feared Curley that in 1941 they changed the charter again so that an incumbent mayor *could* run, and the popular Tobin defeated Curley that year. But Curley was indefatigable and won a seat in Congress in 1942 and 1944.

By 1945, Boston was in trouble again—the postwar recession had created significant unemployment and the people called for Curley to relieve their woes. At the age of seventy and under a federal indictment for mail fraud, Curley ran and won the mayor's office for a fourth time. His promise to solve economic discontent proved irresistible:

> During this campaign I jolted the complacent by warning that Boston would become a ghost town after the war unless I was elected. . . . Inflation was rampant and the housing shortage was serious. Meanwhile, such municipal facilities as parks, beaches

and roads were in a sad state of disrepair. Boston was in the throes of another depression.[25]

Two weeks after the election he went on trial, was found guilty, and sent to jail for five months. He returned to a tumultuous welcome and went about his business of frenetic public spending. But rising postwar prosperity, changes in residential voting patterns, and the development of high-tech defense and financial and educational service industries created a new electorate that rejected the old Curley patronage ways. He was defeated for reelection in 1949 (the "Last Hurrah"), and again at age seventy-six in 1951 and at age eighty in 1955. The old political warhorse, long accused by the Yankees of being a corrupt politician, died three years later at the age of eighty-four, leaving an estate valued at $3,768—proof that personal enrichment was never his goal.

Curley's historical image displays two exaggerated and conflicting viewpoints. The one held in middle- and upper-class circles is that Curley was a crook who was largely responsible for Boston's economic and physical decline in the first half of the century because of his hostility to the Yankee elites and his readiness to use class and ethnic hatred for political purposes. This derogatory theme permeates the journalistic 1992 biography by Jack Beatty which characterizes him as "the rascal king."[26] The other notion, still widely held among working-class and lower middle-class inner-city Irish and other ethnics, is that Curley was a Robin Hood figure who stood up for the poor against the oppressive Yankees.

But the most judicious interpretation comes from the city planning historian Lawrence W. Kennedy. Kennedy argued that Boston's woes were not Curley's fault but endemic to American cities during sluggish economic times. Curley, in fact, was a city builder who attempted to cooperate with the city's businessmen during his first two terms, and then later, during the depression and after, he took up the slack when the upper classes deserted the city. Kennedy maintained that "the enmity between the private sector and city hall predated Curley's mayoralty. In fact, the public-private cooperation which had traditionally shaped Boston failed to survive even the Fitzgerald years. The private sector offered no leadership and shunned cooperation with Curley. Equally important, old Boston money had long since exited the city." Kennedy concluded:

When the private sector abandoned planning leadership, the public sector assumed a more important role. The government was no longer handmaiden to the capitalists who shaped the city. Indeed, planning in Boston evolved during the Curley years into one of the most vital of all roles for city government. Curley changed the basic thrust of city planning by directing attention to the neighborhoods and by inviting government interest in new areas. Although the resulting physical changes to Boston were not of heroic proportions, they were nevertheless momentous. Streets, highways, parkways, tunnels, housing, schools, beaches, libraries, municipal buildings, and fire stations all required massive planning and construction, as did the national policy of accommodating the automobile and the dramatic regional population growth. Curley supported these projects partly to put people to work; in any case, planning was directed less by private-sector interests and more by public need and popular wishes. Although less dramatic, planning of this sort is more democratic and is Curley's legacy.[27]

Kennedy's interpretation puts Curley's contribution to Boston in a long-term national context.

The Curley saga also reveals the divisiveness among the Boston Irish and the long-standing political presence of the Yankees who successfully sustained their power by encouraging Celtic infighting. According to the Yankee Republican Henry Cabot Lodge Jr. : "Ah, the Irish. The minute one of them accomplishes anything, there's always another one behind him with a rock, waiting to bring him down."[28] After ousting the Yankee elites, the ward bosses and Irish leaders Lomasney, Fitzgerald, and Curley ferociously attacked each other, thus preventing any one group from emerging triumphant. This internal power struggle in Boston allowed a small Yankee contingent of independents to work closely with a Republican-dominated state legislature and state Democratic leaders such as another Irishman, David I. Walsh, to hamstring Boston's Irish politicians through "good government" crusades and continual charter reform. Feuding Irish chieftains and seesawing alliances with Yankee reformers were to typify Boston politics until Maurice Tobin's mayoral victory in 1937 and the supposed "decline of bossism." Although Curley kept reappearing on the political scene, the election of John Hynes as mayor in 1949 and the growing middle-classification of the electorate, Irish and non-Irish, heralded a new epoch for politics in Boston and the state. While immigrant groups, particularly the Irish, had made great headway in the political arena of Boston and other cities, the considerable power of the state legislature was in the hands of the WASP-dominated Republican party until after World War II.

Massachusetts had long been a Republican stronghold of businessmen, industrialists, white-collar workers, skilled and semiskilled Yankee workers, farmers, and small-town merchants and artisans who controlled the rural areas and townships of the state. The Republicans had been preeminent in state politics from the Civil War until 1930. They virtually monopolized the General Court until 1948; they dominated the delegation to the U.S. Senate and House; they elected the majority of governors between 1884 and 1930. They were indifferent, sometimes even hostile, to the needs of immigrant voters. On occasion, to counter the growing strength of the Democrats, they wooed newer immigrant groups. Italians and French Canadians initially sought Republican support and were reluctant to join the Democrats because of the enmity of their Catholic rivals, the Irish.

For years, the Irish had little access to political power except through the Democratic party, controlled by Yankees and disaffected ex-Republican Mugwumps. By the turn of the century urban second-generation Irishmen, like John F. Fitzgerald, Martin Lomasney, and James Michael Curley, broke their ties with the Yankee element in their party, at least at the level of city politics. That was not the case on the state level where the Republicans were too formidable an enemy. What emerged was a long-standing, uneasy alliance between Irish and Yankee Democrats that lasted well up to 1934. As the commonwealth urbanized, statewide slates of Yankee Democrats gave way to more and more urban-based ethnic Democrats. One landmark politician was David Ignatius Walsh of Fitchburg, who in 1913 became the first Irish American since James Sullivan served in 1807, to be elected governor (he was reelected in 1914), and, in 1918, the first elected as U.S. Senator (he was subsequently elected to an unexpired term in 1926, and then to full terms in 1928, 1934, and 1940).

Walsh was born in 1872 in Leominster, the son of Irish immigrants. His father, James, died in 1885, leaving a widow with ten children.

Overcoming the adversity of poverty, Walsh worked his way through Holy Cross College and Boston University Law School. In 1897 he passed the bar and set up a practice in Fitchburg. The following year he entered politics, and in 1899 won election as state representative. His chance for major office came in 1912 when Theodore Roosevelt's Bull Moose Progressive campaign split the Republican party, allowing Walsh to win the job of lieutenant governor. Symbolizing progressive reform and appealing to Irish Catholic voters, Walsh went on to gain the governorship. As governor he was able to achieve improvements in the state's labor codes, and he established a state-supported system of university extension courses for workers. He lost his bid for reelection in 1915, because the Republicans healed their party breach and once again became the state's dominant party.

But Walsh's growing popularity with ethnic voters resulted in his election to the U.S. Senate in 1918 against Republican William Weeks. In office he continued to promote a progressive agenda that included old-age pensions, aid to mothers with dependent children, and federal pensions for blind children. He lost in 1924 to Republican Frederick Gillett largely because he had rejected Wilson's League of Nations for its failure to provide independence for Ireland, and thus he faced retribution from fellow Democrats who did not have an Irish constituency.

Walsh ran again in 1926 for a two-year term left after the death of Republican Senator Henry Cabot Lodge. He stood out as the one Democrat who could attract working-class Yankees, upper-class reformers as well as the newer immigrants. Walsh's success was to signal the beginning of the realignment of political power from the Republicans to the Democrats in Massachusetts. From 1928, Walsh was unbeatable for years to come. During the 1930s he was the leading advocate of workers' causes, pushing for an end to child labor, speaking out in favor of slum clearance and housing subsidies for the poor, and becoming a champion of the environment. But the approach of World War II led to his undoing. He took an Irish, anti-British, and isolationist position, in opposition to that of President Franklin D. Roosevelt. Walsh's attacks upon the destroyer-base-deal and lend-lease became hollow after Pearl Harbor. This foreign policy stance geared to Irish nationalism led to his ignominious defeat by Henry Cabot Lodge Jr. in 1946. He died soon after he left office in 1947.

In most cases, however, in order for a Democratic to win a higher office, he had to be a Yankee, as were governors Eugene Foss (1911, 1912, and 1913) and Joseph Ely (1931–32, 1933–34).[29] The Republicans, led by Yankees such as Henry Cabot Lodge Sr., Winthrop M. Crane, Channing H. Cox, and Calvin Coolidge, could only be dislodged when national issues merged with state problems.

According to one historian, the presidential election year of 1928 "witnessed a striking transformation in the political status of Massachusetts, from a rock-bound Republican stronghold to a Democratic state."[30] David Walsh's senatorial victory in the special election of 1926 heralded a new Democratic coalition in the making. Because of large-scale unemployment in textiles and shoes, the Massachusetts Republican party was in the difficult position of explaining why the Bay State was excluded from the apparent prosperity of the Coolidge era. Another important factor was the party's support of Prohibition which galled the French Canadians and Italians who usually voted Republican. That the national Republicans, supporting "pure Americanism," were nativistic and anti-Catholic was enough to create a new coalition of Democrats in 1928.

For the first time, the majority of the Massachusetts electorate voted for the Democratic presidential nominee, Al Smith of New York City, a Catholic and a "wet" candidate. Not only did Smith do well with Irish Americans and Yankee Democrats, he broke records in gaining the support of Italians, French Canadians, Poles, Lithuanians, Portuguese, and Jews in districts that heretofore had gone Republican. Massive desertions from the Republican fold by ethnics in New Bedford, Fall River, Lowell, Chicopee, Gardner, and Fitchburg, and in solid working-class Republican strongholds such as Adams, Easthampton, Southbridge, Webster, Montague, Ludlow, Hadley, and Hatfield suggest that both economics and ethnicity were on the minds of the voters. Although the Republicans still controlled the state government, the Democrats began to make inroads there as well.

But bitter infighting and factionalism, such as that between James Michael Curley, and Joseph Ely and David I. Walsh, delayed the Democratic takeover of the state legislature until 1948. In 1932, Curley was pledged to support the presidential nomination of Democrat Franklin Delano Roosevelt, while party chieftains like Walsh and Ely again supported Al Smith. These state leaders punished Curley by denying him a delegate's seat to the national Democratic convention. The brash Curley came anyway, taking the seat of a delegate from Puerto Rico who was ill. Walsh and Ely steered the state delegation to vote for Smith. They were horrified to hear the chief delegate from Puerto Rico, Alcalde Jaime Miguel Curleo, announce in a Spanish accent six votes for Roosevelt. Ely castigated Curley, calling his actions "insulting to the Commonwealth" and "an undemocratic subversion of the will of the voters." Curley had great fun with the press discussing his new constituents and sniping at the Massachusetts Democratic leadership. Curley gave the seconding speech for the vice presidential nominee, John Nance Garner, by beginning with an allusion to "the beautiful island of Porto Rico."[31] With Roosevelt's victory, and the cornucopia of New Deal patronage jobs, Curley's prominence rose, and the Democratic leaders were forced to nominate him for the governorship in 1934. Nonetheless, his rift with Walsh and Ely never healed, and they successfully worked against his reelection bids for mayor of Boston in 1937 and 1941.

The Republicans attempted to stave off eventual defeat by adding more talented young aristocrats like Henry Cabot Lodge Jr. and Leverett Saltonstall to the leadership, but to little avail. The important point is that from 1928 on the Democratic party strongly competed to attract the support of the heterogeneous population of the state by advocating legislation that would address the state's economic crisis. For statewide offices, the Irish monopolized the Democratic party. But locally and as representatives and senators to the General Court, other ethnic groups were able to gain office, depending on their prominence in the community and their skill in compromising with Irish Democratic party leaders. For example, the first Italian American elected to the Massachusetts House was North Ender Edward A. Bacigalupo in 1934. Thus politics functioned to promote coherence and stability among diverse social groups during a time of severe economic distress and discontent.

Nevertheless, the economy of Massachusetts was changing profoundly by the time of demobilization in 1945. In 1900 the textile, woolen, and shoe industries, with their legions of immigrant factory workers living in congested urban areas, personified the Bay State. Yet these older industries, although buoyed up by two world wars, had already begun a long-term, sometimes precipitous decline. At the war's end, many wondered whether the state could adapt to the changes in society and technology emerging in the new postwar era. Would prosperous older industries, such as paper, machine tools, abrasives, chemicals, and financial services be able to combine or survive alongside the leading-edge defense businesses of the war years—aircraft engines, radar, ordinance, communications equipment, and computers? Would Massachusetts workers refashion their skills and education to flourish in a diverse and changing job environment? How would the new workplace affect unions and their relationships with employers? Would government need to reconstruct its pro–social welfare leanings to make entrepreneurs and businessmen more inclined to invest in Massachusetts?

The postwar years ushered in an era that opened new possibilities and questions for Bay Staters. To dramatically reverse the commonwealth's economic downturn, the people of Massachusetts would need to face these imperative challenges with the same vigor and cooperative effort they demonstrated when they launched the industrial revolution in the nineteenth century. Capital and labor, manager and technician, inventor and professional, all would need to reconstitute themselves to survive and prosper. It was the development of new industries, opportunely stimulated by the onslaught of the Second World War and lasting through its aftermath, the Cold War, that actually changed the Bay State from a place of stagnation and depression to one of growth and prosperity.

*The Kennedy family at their summer home in Hyannis Port, 1931.*
Left to right: *Robert, John, Eunice, Jean, Joseph Sr., Rose, Patricia,*
*Kathleen, Joseph Jr., and Rosemary.*
Courtesy The John F. Kennedy Library, Boston.

*Democratic congressman*
*John F. Kennedy* (left) *and*
*incumbent senator Henry*
*Cabot Lodge Jr.* (right)
*during 1952 senate*
*campaign.*

Courtesy The John F. Kennedy
Library, Boston.

*The Product Integraph, an early computer, developed
by Vannevar Bush* (left) *at MIT, 1927.*

Courtesy MIT Museum, Cambridge.

*Aerial shot of MIT's Lincoln Laboratory, along
Route 128, Boston's "high-tech corridor."*

Reprinted with permission of MIT, Lincoln Laboratory, Lexington.

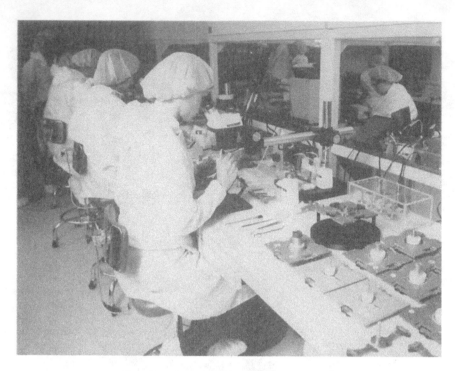

*At Honeywell, Inc., in the Electro-Optics Division, women work
at precise high-technology tasks, c. 1980.*
Courtesy Lockheed-Martin.

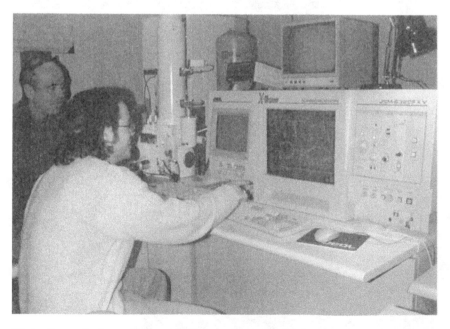

*Silvio Conte Polymer Research Center, University of Massachusetts Amherst.*

# CHAPTER 12

# Reinventing Massachusetts

T HE SECOND WORLD WAR AND ITS AFTERMATH GENERATED A
new worldwide economic order dominated by United States business and military interests. The domestic economy was dramatically
altered because of the large-scale governmental procurement policies
based upon defense needs. The postwar years transformed the economy
of New England from a factory system largely relying on textiles and
shoes to a service and high tech economy predicated on both highly
skilled and semiskilled white-collar workers. In Massachusetts during
the war the federal government built new facilities that were leased to
defense contractors—for example, General Electric (G.E.) leased new
plants in Lynn, Everett, and Pittsfield. After the war the federal government sold the plants cheaply, and G.E. bought fourteen electrical machinery facilities. The Cold War, the Korean War, and the Vietnam conflict all contributed to the prosperity of a state geared to developing
and producing highly specialized defense goods.

Innovations in weapons technology led to spin-offs in the high-
technology and consumer-durable industries that found easy access to
foreign markets. The combination of government contracts, private
venture capital, and the research facilities of the area's universities resulted in the development of an up-to-date industrial base in Massachusetts, which increased per capita income and generated widespread
employment. These pronounced economic changes transformed Massachusetts workers from primarily blue-collar factory laborers to white-
collar professionals, up-scale service employees, and numerous low-
wage service workers. These years saw a massive suburbanization

process and a decline of the Bay State's once politically powerful cities. Increased prosperity stimulated the rise of a fourth generation of a fully assimilated, well-educated middle class, while attracting new immigration from Asia, the Caribbean, Latin America, Africa, as well as from Portugal, Italy, Ireland, Greece, the former Soviet Union, and the American South.

The key to continued economic well-being for Massachusetts was the expansion of employment opportunities, particularly with jobs that were labor intensive, requiring a large human effort and a small volume of raw materials. The region had always been at a disadvantage because of higher fuel and power costs, a scarcity of raw materials, and steep transportation costs. New England's commercial prosperity depended on its ability to either produce specialty items or deliver specific services. For example, between 1947 and 1948, total manufacturing employment in labor-intensive industries rose from 74.7 to 77.3 percent, while the rate for the nation declined from 69.2 to 63.6 percent. Thus, New England manufacturers lessened production costs by avoiding high capital expenditures and by using the region's most valuable and plentiful resource—labor.

Central to the blossoming of new manufacturing and service industries was the cost of labor, which in the 1950s was lower in Massachusetts than elsewhere in the nation. From 1947 to 1964, overall wage rates in New England declined and were below the national average. For example, skilled male manufacturing workers received lower wages than in many other regions in the nation. Semiskilled and unskilled male workers earned lower wages than all but their southern counterparts. Wage rates for New England women office workers in manufacturing plants were well below the national average and below those in the South. The state's twentieth-century history of rising unemployment in textiles and shoes meant that there was a reservoir of labor available, which kept wages down. Jobs in textiles dropped from 264,000 in 1950 to 63,000 by 1979. The Massachusetts unemployment rate in 1950 was higher than in the rest of the nation, and cities such as New Bedford and Fall River had rates that hovered between 18 and 26 percent. Surveys taken among New England manufacturers in 1949 and 1954 found a high degree of satisfaction with both the availability of labor and the character of the workforce. Character meant productivity, dependability, and a low worker turnover rate.

Employers in electronics, metals, and service industries all benefited from the state's cheap and plentiful supply of labor, using profits to expand and thereby increase jobs. By 1972 the electrical/electronic equipment, metals, and machinery industries had the most employees, the largest payrolls, and the greatest value added by manufacturers of all Massachusetts's industries. For the first time, in 1977 there were more workers employed in electronics (103,100) than in the textile, apparel, and leather industries (90,800).

Intraregional migration was an important source of labor, with large numbers moving from rural to metropolitan areas, especially from the depressed areas of northern New England. Despite the relatively low wages, in-migration exceeded out-migration. Moreover, the state population increased by a modest 9.8 percent between 1950 and 1960, compared to 18.5 percent for the nation. Small population growth rates meant there was little pressure to create new jobs annually, whereas other regions with expanding populations that exceeded available jobs had increasing unemployment.

Other factors encouraged lower labor costs. The experience of plant relocation and closing contributed to rising anti-union sentiment among hostile businessmen and fearful workers. The Massachusetts American Federation of Labor claimed 525,000 dues-paying members in 1962, but by 1979 its membership was down to 250,000. The *Boston Globe* of September 7, 1990, reported a dramatic three-year drop of overall percentages of the workforce in unions from 23 percent in 1984 to 17 percent in 1987. In addition, the increased job participation of women and younger workers and the emergence of a new tide of unskilled immigrants from the Third World resulted in the creation of a "tractable supply of labor" creating "the most important condition" for a "new wave of economic growth in the region." [1]

Massachusetts was able to overcome locational disadvantages in the area of high technology because the products required small volumes of raw materials. Built-in obsolescence and continued product innovation through research and development insured the availability of markets that could continually absorb new items. The previous success story of textiles in New England was connected to its "close proximity to the source of technological change in the industry," wrote the economic analyst John Hekman. "Textile firms, machinery builders, and entrepreneurs formed an agglomeration of skills and other resources which made firms more productive than those located elsewhere during the period of rapid development in the production process."[2] It is important to note that the transition from the old textiles and shoe industries to state-of-the-art high-technology industries and the modern durables industries (electrical/electronic equipment, aerospace and aircraft engines, generators, metals and metal-working machinery) was possible only because of Massachusetts's industrial past. As far back as the nineteenth century machinists and metal workers were utilizing their accumulated skills to promote scores of technical breakthroughs.

Although much was new, these innovations were drawing on a long history of cooperation among the older industrial base, banking, and insurance. For example, in the 1880s a shoe manufacturer in Lynn, Charles Coffin, provided the capital, drew staff from nearby metalworking shops, and made use of the electronic inventions of Elihu Thompson to create the Thompson-Huston Electrical Equipment Company. New England's first electric street lights went on in Lynn in 1882, powered by a dynamo built by Elihu Thompson. Designer Frank Sprague founded Sprague Electric in Brockton in 1884, where he perfected the use of his industrial constant speed electrical motor, which opened markets for electrical machinery products, particularly for streetcars. The first large urban street railway company to adopt electricity based on the Thompson-Houston and Sprague innovations was Henry Whitney's Boston West End Street Railway Company, in 1889. In 1892, Thompson-Huston of Lynn merged with Edison General Electric of Schenectady, New York, to form the General Electric Corporation. Later, however, a critical factor in the flowering of new products was the role played by universities and research and development laboratories.

The Massachusetts Institute of Technology (MIT) started its first course in electrical engineering, taught by physicist Charles Cross, in 1882. In 1900, G.E.'s research laboratory was moved from Lynn to Schenectady, but the director was MIT professor Willis Whitney. MIT's course of study was enlarged to include a Department of Electrical Engineering (1902) and the Research Laboratory of Applied Chemical Engineering (1906). During World War I MIT scientists set up the nation's only naval aviation school and developed antisubmarine devices in conjunction with the Submarine Signal Company, a private laboratory pioneering in electronics. With these activities MIT scientists created new industries and stimulated the growth of new corporations, such as the radio tubes that gave Raytheon its start. After the war, MIT formed a Division of Industrial Cooperation and Research to promote faculty contracts with industries and to solve research problems.

In the decades after the 1920s new laboratories such as Instrumentation (later Draper Laboratories), Radiation Laboratory, and Lincoln Laboratory, all generated countless technologies. The Second World War spurred federally sponsored research at MIT to astronomic heights, from $18,923 in 1938–39 to $44,354,800 in 1944–45. (By 1987 the Department of Defense alone sponsored contracts at MIT worth $45,418,000). During World War II British scientists had developed radar, but Britain lacked skilled machinists to produce magnetrons. To promote the development of microwave radar, in 1940 the federal government funded the establishment at MIT of a civilian research facility, the Radiation Laboratory. The next important step was to manufacture the magnetron tubes. Raytheon did this, and in the process, using microwave technology, discovered microwave cooking.

Patterned after the old Radiation Laboratory, Lincoln Laboratory of Lexington was set up in 1951 to work with MIT to study air defense systems. With the onset of the Cold War in the 1950s, Raytheon, Avco-Lycoming, and Submarine Signal, working under government contracts with research laboratories at Harvard and MIT, produced instruments for navigation, aviation, and undersea measurement. In 1957 the MIT scientist Kenneth Olsen founded Digital Equipment Corporation. In 1968, Data General was started by employees of Digital. In 1982, MIT and the Charles Stark Draper Laboratories became one of Massachusetts's top ten defense contractors. Thus, government funding and university-related research activities provided indirect subsidies for the high-technology industries.

One of the men responsible for this high-tech take-off was MIT's Vannevar Bush (1890–1974). A professor of electrical engineering, Bush became a major force in both industry and government for high-tech development, rising to a peak of power in World War II and the Cold War, as the federal government's most influential science leader. Bush was born in Everett, Massachusetts, the son of a Universalist minister. After graduating from high school in Chelsea, he earned his way through Tufts University by tutoring in mathematics and physics. He worked briefly at G.E. in Schenectady, returned to Tufts to teach, and in 1916 wrote a Ph.D. thesis in electrical engineering in a joint Harvard-MIT program. Subsequently, he became consultant to a fledgling radio equipment company; working with his design for a thermostat, he formed his own company with partners, and eventually in 1925 he and others created Raytheon, a new company to produce power vacuum tubes for radio. In the same year, Bush and H. B. Stewart and Frank Gage, two colleagues at MIT, built the product integraph, the first of four analog computers. By 1929, one of Bush's students and coworkers, Harold Hazen, developed a more sophisticated computer, the network analyzer, constructed jointly by MIT and General Electric.

By 1932, Bush was both dean of the School of Engineering and vice president of MIT. As professor, consultant, and business entrepreneur in the dynamic new field of electronics, he gained national prominence. Bush was one of the leaders in bringing together university research laboratories with private venture capitalists, in tandem with funds supplied by the federal government. In 1939, as chair of the National Defense Research Committee, he set about reorganizing the procedures for new weapons development. His main contribution was the idea of funneling federal funds through grants to private research facilities both in business and at the universities, to conduct the necessary research and development for weapons promotion. This approach became the standard for all American scientific technology research and inspired the creation of new laboratory and science programs throughout the nation. Defense spending linked to higher education and high-tech laboratories became one of the keys to the post–World War II economic upsurge in Massachusetts.

Another example of the wedding of science and industry was Digital Equipment Corporation (DEC). The mastermind behind the enterprise was the Lincoln Laboratory researcher Kenneth Olsen. Born on February 20, 1926, in Bridgeport, Connecticut, he was the son of a machine tool designer. He and his three brothers grew up in a world devoted to mathematics and electricity. After a stint in the navy, he entered MIT as a student in electrical engineering in 1947. He received his bachelor's degree in 1950 and his master's in 1952. During this period he was working on a defense project at MIT, and from that he went on to do original research at MIT's Lincoln Laboratory, where he built a computer. In 1957, Olsen and Harlan Anderson founded DEC, a computer parts company, by borrowing $70,000 from American Research and

Development (ARD), the nation's first venture-capital corporation. ARD provided the money to the two unknown scientists with no business experience, and for their gamble, ARD insisted on owning 70 percent of the company, an arrangement that never troubled Olsen and Anderson. The fledgling company depended heavily on the investment company's business expertise, and they maintained a profitable relationship for many years.

With the money from ARD, the partners rented a loft in an old mill in Maynard, Massachusetts, a twenty-minute drive from Lincoln Lab. At start-up in 1957, the first employee was Olsen's brother Stan, a technician at Lincoln. (For many years, Lincoln Lab personnel would move from there to DEC.) After one year, DEC was making a profit selling computer parts, and by 1959 the company turned its attention to building and selling computers. Olsen's contributions to high-tech development were many, but two areas of innovation were his in particular. One was his idea to personalize the computer.

The world of the late 1950s was dominated by large mainframe computers, built by IBM and other companies, which, because of their cost, were limited to only the largest of enterprises. Olsen created a new industry that provided a product that allowed an individual to work a computer using a keyboard and a monitor. "We had a vision," he said, "of computing that we knew the world needed."[3] Eventually, this shrewd vision would lead to the personal computer, a revolutionary development for this century. DEC's first computer, the PDP-1 of 1959, was as big as a refrigerator and cost $120,000, but it was cheap compared to the room-sized mainframes of IBM.

Another of Olsen's important ideas concerned the administration of his new complex corporation, which was research facility, factory for production, and marketing entity. In its early years chaos reigned at DEC. In time, however, Olsen devised a system he called production-line management. A senior executive would take responsibility for one product, develop it, nurture it, market it, and make a profit. These line managers would also work together when it came to sharing information on sales, parts, manufacturing, marketing, and the negotiating of services from the company. This system came to be known in the industry as the Matrix System, and it would help create and make accessible the modern personal computer. It was men like Bush and Olsen, who, by bridging the gap between science and technology, promoted a new industry crucial for the new economy of the Bay State. In 1986 *Fortune Magazine* called Olsen "America's Most Successful Entrepreneur." In 1988, DEC was one of the leading forces in the computer industry, worth $11 billion, thirty-eighth on the *Fortune* 500 list, and with over 120,000 employees.

The commonwealth's prosperity also relied on the development and growth of a multitude of industries, both public and private, that "served" the new industries. A 1954 economic report showed that the labor force in Massachusetts was already undergoing a metamorphosis: the number of industrial workers had declined to 42.9 percent, while the number of service workers reached the high of 54.89 percent. By the late 1970s, two-thirds of all workers in New England were employed in the service sectors of the economy: transportation, communication, utilities, wholesale/retail trades, business services (fiscal, legal), recreation, repair, the reproductive services (health and education), and government. The Boston metropolitan area became the nexus of the new service economy for the region. The percentage change in the decade of the 1960s for service employment was phenomenal: growth rates, for example, of 233.3 percent in professional services, 68 percent in education, 54.8 percent in health, 53.6 percent in business services, 36 percent in financial and real estate services, 25.4 percent in communications, represented an overall 29.5 percent change in total service employment for greater Boston. Most of the newly created jobs were labor intensive and many were low paying, which gave Massachusetts business people a wage rate advantage over other regions.

Low-paying clerical or service jobs increased everywhere—hospitals became one of the biggest employers in the state. Women entered the workforce in larger numbers than ever before, generally for low-paying jobs, as in the nineteenth century. In 1979, women made up 41 percent of Boston's workforce, but they received only 25 percent of the total wages paid; they represented 74 percent of the clerical workforce whereas men occupied 72 percent of managerial and professional positions. By 1976, the labor force of those under twenty-five was 10 percent higher in Massachusetts than the national average. Inflation, the higher cost of living in Massachusetts, and the proliferation of low-wage, unskilled service jobs forced more family members to join the workforce, which meant that overall per capita earnings increased. Low unemployment rates mean that more teenagers work, increasing family earnings. Massachusetts in 1987, ranked in the top eighth of states with the highest participation of teenagers, sixteen to nineteen years old, in the workforce. Other factors that contributed to higher per capita income for the state were greater employment in nonagricultural jobs than other regions (which meant that patterns of employment were less affected by seasonal variaions), higher per capita transfer payments (Social Security, welfare), and higher employer contributions in the form of pensions, and workers' compensation. The commonwealth's total gross state product (the market value of all goods and services produced) increased almost threefold between 1969 and 1983, and the state held the nation's record for the lowest unemployment rates of the 1980s. High-tech and service industries accounted for 97.6 percent of all the jobs created in the state between 1979 and 1983. From the perspective of 1950, the turnabout in the fortunes of Massachusetts residents was certainly "miraculous."

Coincidental to the transformed economic system was the burgeoning of a massive suburbanization process that was triggered, in part, by the needs of the high-tech industries to have ample space for both laboratories and production facilities. Even before the building of new highways, research and development (R & D) companies sought open space with easy access to the higher education systems of Cambridge and Boston. In 1948, before the federal government's commitment to a huge program of subsidizing highway building instead of mass public transit, the Massachusetts Department of Public Works unveiled its own master highway plan.

The master plan envisioned a series of three ring roads surrounding Boston, linked by radial connectors that pierced the city's center, to open the suburban fringe for development and to provide commuters with access to the central city. Foremost was Route 128, the "fertile crescent" or "golden ring," circling Boston at a distance of twelve miles. A twenty-mile ring, Interstate 495, was to be built later to take up overflow from suburban residential and industrial expansion. The opening of Boston was to be achieved by a central artery (the Southeast Expressway, completed in 1956) and a river drive that eliminated much parkland (Storrow Drive). All would be connected to a major east-west roadway that crossed the circles and moved westward to New York State (the Massachusetts Turnpike completed in 1963). Also planned (but never completed) was an inner belt one or two miles from downtown Boston, and another central artery in the southwest corridor of the city. By the late 1960s, new highways were coming up against popular resistance because of destructive effects on Boston's neighborhoods, small businesses, and the environment. In 1970, when Governor Sargent declared a moratorium on highway building within the Route 128 circumference, Massachusetts became the first state to halt such road construction. But most of the master plan was implemented, and the infrastructure was put in place to allow for widespread investment in suburban development.

With construction begun on Route 128, electronics firms sprang up in communities like Waltham, Lincoln, Bedford, Lexington, Burlington, and Wilmington. R & D labs worked cooperatively with university engineers, scientists, entrepreneurs, and technicians to innovate and update the products of high tech. Ray Stata, the president of Analog Devices of Norwood, said in 1980: "The foundation of this industry emanates from the universities."[4] More than 156 high-tech companies in greater Boston came out of MIT departments and laboratories. By 1979 there were 300 computer and computer-related companies within two miles of MIT.

Most of the developmental capital came from Boston investment firms who saw the tremendous potential of the new high-tech and electronics industries. Between March 1954 and June 1956, sixty-eight new plants were built along Route 128. By 1963 there were four hundred new plants. Employment grew by 22 percent, although Boston lost 7.7 percent of its jobs. One of the first developers was Gerald Blakely, connected to the prestigious firm of Cabot, Cabot and Forbes (CC&F). Using CC&F venture capital, Blakely began raising large sums to build industrial parks. His work was facilitated by favorable mortgage deals from Boston bankers and tractable local communities that provided zoning variances. By 1959 an industrial park was in place in Needham, consisting of thirty-eight firms, employing thirty-six hundred workers, and paying annual wages of $12.2 million. The Waltham Industrial Center and the Waltham Research and Development Park, both astride Route 128, were early investments of CC&F. Soon others followed, and warehousing and transportation facilities were built as well. Between 1969 and 1982, high technology was the fastest growing industry in the state, and could be considered the third wave of Massachusetts industrialization.

Because many of the high-growth industries are defense related, their economic health has been closely tied to world and national politics. The 1970 recession and the beginning of federal cutbacks in defense spending affected Massachusetts severely. By 1973, unemployment reached 7.3 percent, which compared unfavorably with 4.8 percent in the nation. A second downturn in 1974 and the winding down of the Vietnam War further influenced the state's economy. By 1975 unemployment stood at 10.2 percent, the highest statewide average in the United States, which then had an overall rate of 8.5 percent. This boom-or-bust cycle had been typical of the industrialization process in Massachusetts since the early nineteenth century. Responding to the recession of the mid-1970s, the first administration of Governor Michael Dukakis (1975-78) drastically cut state spending and raised taxes. These fiscally necessary policies infuriated almost everyone and deprived Dukakis of renomination by his Democratic party.

The Soviet military involvement in Afghanistan and the Reagan administration's reemphasis on Cold War hostility in the late 1970s and early 1980s once again fueled increased defense spending. The stabilization of energy prices and the downward trend of inflation renewed prosperity for the nation and for Massachusetts. Computer applications and instrumentation usage expanded vigorously as areas of industrial growth. These consumer industries were able to employ the many engineers and technicians who had been recently laid-off from the defense industries. Services such as finance, education, health, and trade emerged as the fastest growing segments of the state's economy from 1982 to 1986. Low population growth combined with rapidly increasing job participation rates, so that the Bay State's unemployment rate dipped to new lows in 1987. New industries and an able workforce became the keys to the restored economic strength of Massachusetts as it entered the nineties.

One economist wrote in 1985, "We know that New England is an economy in transition. Indeed, it is a leading economy, not a declining economy. It is leading the nation in the transition from manufacturing to services."[5] Those high-technology industries that are able to remain innovative and the service industries have thrived in the Bay State. Between 1979 and 1983, these industries accounted for 97.6 percent of new jobs. Problems of job security and inadequate wages arose because many of the high-technology jobs and, more particularly, the service jobs tended to be low paying, were part time, and did not provide adequate health and retirement benefits. Furthermore, the low-paying, unskilled jobs are usually geared to those who traditionally suffered from discrimination, that is, blacks, Latinos, women, teenagers, and the newer immigrant groups.

In an analysis of high tech in Massachusetts one economist warned:

> While professional and technical occupations account for a greater share of jobs in the newer industries than in the traditional industries, blue collar and clerical jobs continue to account for the majority of workers in these high technology industries. In fact, unskilled assembler . . . was the largest occupation in the office, accounting and computing machines, electrical and electronic equipment, and instruments industries in Massachusetts in 1980; assembler was the second largest occupation, following engineer, in the guided missiles and space vehicles industry.[6]

Moreover, economic growth seemed concentrated around the strong labor markets of Boston, Lowell, and Worcester. The greater Boston metropolitan area labor market (from Marblehead to Hull and bound by Interstate 495) netted 62.3 percent of new service industry jobs created between 1980 and 1984. At the same time, 87.6 percent of all new high-tech jobs were developed in the Boston-Lawrence-Haverhill-Lowell Metropolitan Statistical Area (MSA). Although Worcester actually lost jobs in this period, it gained 49.1 percent of new high-tech jobs (compared with a statewide average gain of 11.3 percent). Some areas, like Fall River, lacked high-tech and service industries and remained dependent on slow-growth durables or consumer-items industries. In 1984, only 3.2 percent worked in high tech and only 19.2 percent worked in service areas, while the largest segment of the workforce (38.6 percent) was either in slow-growth durables like wood, glass, concrete, and metals, or in nondurable consumer items, such as food, textiles, paper, chemicals, and leather goods. Nonmetropolitan areas like Berkshire County have not attracted new jobs and have been losing population since the 1960s. Pittsfield reached its peak in 1960 and has declined ever since, but industrial North Adams reached its highest population in 1900 and suffered substantial losses throughout the century. Meanwhile, those areas benefiting from economic growth seem to be narrowly focused either on high-tech or service industry job creation, duplicating a dependence that may prove as precarious as textiles and shoes were in an earlier era.

Nonetheless, experts on New England's economic prospects remained quite sanguine. Two forecasters wrote: "The 'reindustrialization' of New England has come about not through reinvestment by existing industries but by their replacement with new ones."[7] A modest population growth combined with rapidly increasing job participation rates and a changing age structure led to dramatic improvements in the unemployment figures, dropping to 5.4 percent in 1979 below the national average of 5.8 percent. By 1987, Massachusetts ranked with Connecticut and New Jersey as states that led the nation in the percentage decline of unemployment, the percentage gain in jobs, and the percentage rise in per capita personal income. The Bay State's unemployment rate at the end of 1987 was at the remarkable low of 3.2 percent.

The decade of the 1990s, however, was to bring new economic challenges to the Bay State. The state underwent an unusual short-term fiscal crisis in 1989–90, which was largely due to political intervention and not the business cycle. One must go back to 1980 to understand what occurred. In that year a popular anti-tax referendum limiting increases in property taxes (Proposition 2 1/2) passed over the objections of the legislature. This measure severely curtailed revenues of cities and towns. Because the state had a budget surplus and predicted continued high revenues, the legislature appeased voters by picking up the local shortfalls. But another referendum put a cap on state spending and required a balanced budget. State revenues fell considerably, and as a result in 1990 the electorate chose a cost-conscious Republican, William Weld, as governor. But the main reason for the bust cycle of the early nineties was the decline of defense spending by the federal government which hurt high-tech regions severely. Computer giants, such as Wang Laboratories, a symbol of the "Massachusetts miracle" of the 1980s, went bankrupt because defense orders plummeted and it had not joined the personal computer revolution. Major cutbacks from the Massachusetts executive branch and belt-tightening by the legislature were necessary measures, but they were short-term solutions that did not promote an upturn in the state's economy. In the late 1990s Massachusetts had to "reinvent" itself once again in order to prosper.

The state's economy began to rebound largely due to the initiative and daring of its businessmen who were quick to adjust to peacetime pursuits. An article in the *New York Times* saw diversity, competitiveness, and a focus on markets as the keys to a rebirth of prosperity:

> Time and again, this region has transformed itself through pluck and brains, . . . So the region has responded to its latest slump by reinventing its economy once more. No miracle of growth this time, the economy has weaned itself from an overdependence on Pentagon money, outmoded mainframe computers and real estate dollars. Instead, it is developing a mix of entrepreneurial high-technology start-ups and services.[8]

The new economy draws both on established firms, such as Raytheon and Gillette, and on companies focusing on financial services, health care, telecommunications, and—the newcomer in the high tech field—biotechnology. Growth in banking, particularly in mutual funds (which includes the giant Fidelity Investment Corporation), and Boston's concentration of top educational institutions that provide the intellectual reservoir for the region's expanding economy are significant factors in the recovery process. For example, by 1994 MIT alumni and faculty were responsible for creating 1,065 companies in Massachusetts. These companies collectively employ 120,000 workers, with $53 billion in worldwide sales, in industries that run the gamut from manufacturing, financial services, and software to a host of businesses involved with international markets. A 1997 survey of the business community shows a remarkable turnaround in the attitude of businessmen who in a 1991 survey had considered Massachusetts to have a "fair" or "poor" business climate to one of "good" and "outstanding." In 1996, venture capitalists invested more than $1 billion in developing technology companies in the Bay State. There are pockets in which the recovery has not occurred, especially in western and southeastern Massachusetts, but cities such as Boston, Cambridge, and Lowell have shown major gains. The Boston metropolitan region's prosperity has carried over to other areas tied to the regional economy, including New Hampshire and southern Maine.

To a great degree, as in the nineteenth century, Massachusetts's continued prosperity relies on its continued success in exports, with its high-tech equipment, minicomputers, and semiconductors rebounding in export sales because of the weak dollar and the state's competitive products. In addition, the state's strength in service areas, such as law, finance, accounting, health, education, and insurance, is relatively insulated from fluctuating consumer demands and these areas continue to attract new firms who see the benefit of relocating to Massachusetts and New England.

One determinant for companies that desire to keep and attract highly trained professionals is the recognition that these workers seem to prefer living in the cosmopolitan, pluralist society the people of Massachusetts have created. Massachusetts's "quality of life," enhanced by sophisticated cultural, recreational, and leisure-time activities, the availability of an educated workforce, the high degree of health care choices, and the close proximity to universities that rank first in the nation in graduate science and technology, is one of the factors that replenish the pool of new industries setting up shop in the Bay State.

The availability of labor, both skilled and unskilled, is crucial to economic expansion. Historically, besides the indigenous Yankee rural poor of New England, labor for the burgeoning industrial revolution in Massachusetts was provided by the Irish and the French Canadians from the 1840s to the 1860s. Maturation of the industrial economy and disruptions in their own countries attracted eastern Europeans from the 1880s to the 1920s. Beginning in the 1960s a new wave of immigration began to replenish the labor supply just when the state was moving in the direction of high tech and services and away from textiles and shoes. While some European emigration continues, specifically from Portugal, Italy, Ireland, Greece, and the former Soviet Union, the majority of newcomers are Asian, West Indian, Latin and Central American, and African. The newest immigrants are from Southeast Asia. In 1988 the state's Office for Refugees and Immigrants estimated that there were eighteen thousand Cambodians, eleven thousand Vietnamese, and five thousand Laotians. Most of the state's Cambodians live in Lowell, making it the largest such community in the nation. There is also evidence that a sizable number of illegal immigrants are entering the state. One such large group is the Irish, who are once again looking to Boston as a place offering more opportunity than their homeland. The overall marked changes of the state's historic immigration patterns—from Europe and Canada to Asia, Africa, and Latin America—have added new dimensions to the polyglot population that makes up the quiltlike diversity of the peoples of the commonwealth. Room for these newcomers was found in the urban areas of the state, since growing numbers of assimilated second- and third-generation immigrants had moved to the middle-class suburbs.

The new prosperity of the postwar years helped stimulate a suburbanization process that took the nation and Massachusetts by storm. The federal government aided in the suburban process by providing access to funds for residential construction through the Federal Housing Authority and the Veterans Administration. In addition, the federal government became an important financial provider in the development of high tech with R & D defense funding as well as highway subsidies. So, high-tech and research firms, having no need for downtown services, settled outside the cities. They generated many skilled jobs and took advantage of the educated workers who were eager to move there and to fulfill the American dream of owning a one-family home. By 1980, the Boston metropolitan ring was twenty-five miles beyond the center of Boston, a fourfold increase in urbanized space. Once-small towns, such as Burlington and Framingham, witnessed phenomenal growth. Overall population change was the result of the central cities losing population to the suburbs, rather than pure population growth. The story of the postwar economic rejuvenation of Massachusetts had its parallel in the transformation of its capital city, Boston.

In the early 1950s, when its population had reached its all-time high, over eight hundred thousand, Boston, like many of the nation's older urban areas, was a decaying city. The median income for families in 1949 was the lowest of the nation's dozen largest cities. By 1950, the downtown vacancy rate stood at 25 percent, and the residential neighborhoods had one of the highest property tax rates in the nation. Over the decade of the fifties, Boston had lost many of its prime manufacturing and transportation jobs and had seen an expansion of nontaxable property such as hospitals, government agencies, universities, and churches. As happened elsewhere in the nation, retail stores were moving to suburban malls and public services were deteriorating. No new building construction took place downtown between 1929 and 1950. The *Boston Globe* lamented: "Boston is a dead city, living in the past. If you want to be successful in any business, get out of Boston."[9] Boston's economic prospects were bleak, and one of the main reasons for this condition was the political past of the city.

For years, the city's poorer ethnics, led by bedazzling politicos like James Michael Curley, secured power by constructing a fragile alliance against the Yankee elite. Irish American political bosses had kept the city government oriented to providing jobs and public service for the working and lower classes. And as that occurred, Brahmin financial brokers were reluctant to invest in a city they thought was a "sinkhole of corruption." In recalling those years, the *Boston Globe* wrote that "the negative attitudes of the Yankee-dominated insurance industry was so fervent that no mortgages on buildings in Irish-dominated Boston were granted." [10]

The old political style of patronage and machine politics, however, was not popular with the rising third- and fourth-generation of ethnics who had climbed into the middle class. They demanded a new brand of politics. Symbolic of the "new Boston" was the emergence of a different breed of Democratic politician—those wedded to the realistic understanding that the city's future lay with a close working relationship with business. The coalition of Brahmin capital and new-line Democrats was to be the force that would successfully lure huge federal urban renewal funds to the city. These federal funds helped to revamp Boston into New England's governmental, financial, commercial, legal, health, and educational center.

The alliance of mayors John Hynes (1950–60) and John Collins (1960–67) with influential business public service groups—the New Boston Committee, the Citizen Seminar, and the powerful and prestigious Boston Coordinating Committee (nicknamed the "Vault" because they first met in a boardroom near the vault of the Boston Safe Deposit and Trust Company)—focused attention on publicly funded construction of major downtown commercial projects to revitalize the Hub's economy. Mayor Hynes, who coined the term "the new Boston," began the process by working with the Eisenhower administration, with Boston bankers, and with a former Hynes aide turned developer, Jerome Rappaport. Hynes set in motion the transfiguration of the city with the massive demolition of an entire neighborhood, the West End, the conversion of the seedy downtown Scollay Square area into a new government center, and the plans for a major convention center, later named in his honor the Hynes Auditorium.

In 1947, Hynes had been Boston's city clerk. That year Mayor Curley went to prison for mail fraud and the Republican state legislature appointed Hynes as interim mayor. President Harry Truman pardoned Curley, and he returned to office and treated Hynes in ignominious fashion. The angered Hynes took Curley on in the special mayoral election of 1949, and won an upset victory. Hynes was admired for his rejection of Curley and the ward bosses. His public announcements related to curbing corruption and promoting a business revival for the city. He worked with the local business community to revitalize the city. With a more middle-class electorate and support of the business elite, he won reelection in 1951 against Curley and 1955 against state senator John Powers.

Progress was slow, however. Members of the city's business elite voiced their impatience with the lack of urban revitalization. Robert Ryan of Cabot, Cabot and Forbes, told a meeting of concerned citizens in 1957, "Gentlemen, we are marked men, Bostonians at midcentury! . . . Boston is crying for leadership."[11] The president of Raytheon, Charles Francis Adams Jr., complained that Boston was living beyond its means, and he demanded new leadership that would open the coffers of the federal government to promote the revival of the Hub.

A catalyst in the creation of the "new Boston" was the exclusive group of about a dozen prominent businessmen who formed the Coordinating Committee in 1959 with the purpose of stimulating downtown revival through urban renewal. This group of predominantly Yankee bankers, lawyers, and businessmen included the chief executive officers of the region's four largest banks, two largest retailers, two major industrial firms, a leading law firm, the city's public utility firm, and the area's third largest insurance company. Besides lending expertise to city officials, sponsoring studies and reports, Vault members were major backers of the little-known Suffolk County registrar of probate, John Collins, who in 1959 was seeking the mayoralty of Boston over the prominent president of the Massachusetts Senate, John E. Powers.

John Collins was a third-generation Irish American Catholic who was born in Roxbury in 1919. A lawyer and World War II veteran, he won a seat in the Massachusetts House of Representatives in 1948. In 1949, he upset the political establishment by supporting John Hynes against Roxbury's favorite, James Michael Curley. Elected to the state Senate in 1950, with a reputation as a "maverick," Collins served two terms. In 1955, while running for the Boston City Council, Collins became seriously ill with polio. He survived and won office, but he had to use crutches or a wheelchair for the remainder of his life. His illness was to serve his political interest, because it demonstrated his courage and reminded voters of polio-stricken Franklin Delano Roosevelt. Collins's 1957 appointmen as Suffolk County registrar of probate had been considered a political plum and a life-time sinecure, so it was a shock to the establishment when Collins threw his hat into the race for the mayoralty, against Powers.

In a race in which Powers appeared the heavy favorite, the financial support of the Vault and fortuitous circumstances surrounding an election eve "bookie raid" by federal agents of a saloon with Powers banners draped everywhere gave Collins a narrow victory. Once elected, Collins delivered on his promises to the business community by cutting the city budget and reducing municipal employees, and he went to the legislature to get a reduction in the Boston tax rate and a special tax abatement for the developers of the Prudential Center.

Collins was a frequent visitor at Vault meetings, and he worked hard to maintain cooperation with business leaders. For example, Ralph Lowell, the Brahmin president of the Boston Safe Deposit and Trust Company, known as "Boston's first citizen," usually presided over Vault meetings. After one such occasion, he wrote in his diary that the mayor gave a talk "on the prospects of keeping the tax rate down. He will make a list of things he thinks the State should pay for and will submit it to us in the near future."[12] A primary goal for the Vault was the redevelopment of downtown Boston, a half-vacant, highly taxed area in which Vault members had a huge financial stake. This approach became the linchpin of the John Collins administration.

The new mayor decided that a massive infusion of federal urban renewal funds was the way to curb Boston's economic decline: "There is only one program now available or even on the horizon by which Boston can begin to cope with all its major areas of slum and blight. This program is federally aided urban renewal."[13] Collins was the driving force behind the idea of redevelopment. Eminently successful in winning public and federal and state legislative support for urban renewal, Collins nonetheless recognized the need for an expert administrator to realize his ambitious goals for rebuilding the city. Collins accelerated Boston's urban renewal process by bringing in New Haven's city planner, Edward J. Logue, to head the Boston Redevelopment Authority (BRA).

Collins was able to convince the state legislature to expand the powers of the BRA by combining it with the Office of Development. This BRA agency could then provide certain corporations with major tax concessions, as well as variances from zoning and building codes. With the power of eminent domain and the constitutional authority to pro-vided tax concessions to private businesses, Logue received "the most massively centralized planning and renewal powers that any large city had ever voted to one man (other than New York's Robert Moses)," wrote one city planner.[14]

As Logue put it, the "BRA was a uniquely powerful instrument." The BRA under Logue went from a staff of seventeen and a budget of $250,000 in the early sixties to an organization of seven hundred with a budget of $25 million by the time Logue left in 1968. Logue wrote: "Our Boston Development Program proposed simultaneous large-scale planning, development, and renewal efforts for the entire downtown area and for most of the city's older neighborhoods. Rehabilitation was to be emphasized rather than reliance exclusively on the bulldozer. It was the largest urban renewal program seriously put forward anywhere up to that time."[15] In the process, Logue had secured over $200 million in investments in the city, raising Boston from seventeenth to fourth place per capita in renewal grants. Helpful in bringing monies to Boston was that Boston's John F. Kennedy was president from 1961 to 1963, while Boston native John W. McCormack was Speaker of the House of Representatives (1962–71). The BRA further generated over half a bil-lion dollars in private office building investments, such as the Prudential Center. Logue, working with a coalition of Boston bankers, university experts, and federal officials, and with the total support of the Vault, created a new skyscraper-dominated central business district that re-sembled the Manhattan skyline of New York City.

By the early 1970s, Boston had the fourth largest central business district office space in the country, with the highest construction rates. Over 3,223 acres were affected, as were over 50 percent of Boston's population. With the passage of further remedial state legislation in the form of tax abatements and tax exemptions, the building boom fe-ver infected more private investors. Even after urban renewal monies slowed, the skyscrapers continued to be built at a breakneck pace. Although the business community was delighted by the turnaround that made Boston a profitable investment center, others were not so impressed.

Urban renewal in Boston, as elsewhere, had staggering negative effccts upon the poor and the working classes who lived and worked nearby. As sociologist Herbert Gans noted, the West End, Boston's first major renewal area of the Collins administration, "was not a slum"[16] but a viable, working-class community with decent and affordable housing. This "urban village" was wiped out so developers could put up profitable high-rise, luxury apartments. The program destroyed thirty-eight blocks, forty-one acres, and homes for nine thousand residents between 1958 and 1960. Several studies demonstrated that most West End residents suffered either financially or psychologically because of relocation. Urban renewal tore some neighborhoods apart. In 1966, a *Boston Globe* survey showed immense dissatisfaction with urban renewal, dislike of Collins's too-close relationship with the business community, and complaints of the decline of public services in ethnic neighborhoods. Although he was reelected in 1963, Collins sought the Democratic nomination for U.S. Senate in 1966, only to lose to Endicott Peabody. An indication of the mayor's falling popularity was that Peabody, the Yankee, carried Boston in the primary, before losing to Edward W. Brooke, an African American Republican in the general election.

Popular discontent with the results of urban renewal ended the political careers of Collins and Logue. In 1967, Logue ran a dismal fourth in a preliminary election for the mayor's office. Urban renewal was viewed, accurately, as a program that benefited business and the suburbs and hurt particular neighborhoods. During the 1960s, the city actually lost more dwelling units than it gained. When Logue was finished with the city, 9,718 low-rent housing units had been erased from the Boston housing market, and of 3,504 new units constructed, only 982 could be considered low rent. Finally, urban renewal intensified the concentration of blacks in specific areas, thus increasing racial segregation and poverty. Aside from urban renewal's major contribution of the revival of downtown Boston and the rehabilitation of what became upper- and middle-class neighborhoods, the large numbers of poor, who were forced to relocate in spite of a tight housing market, found that their situations grew worse. In response to urban renewal horrors in Boston, neighborhood activists established political alliances that succeeded in halting many new projects, such as the expansion of Logan Airport and extending of the interstate highway system through

Boston neighborhoods. As the mayoral election of 1967 approached, the anger of the people in the neighborhoods became evident by the appearance of populist champion Louise Day Hicks.

The chair of the Boston School Committee (whose own children attended parochial schools) and staunch opponent of racial integration of the public schools, Hicks launched a direct attack against Collins and his policies: "What the people wanted was to be heard by City Hall, but they found that the mayor belonged to big business and special interests." [17] The first and only woman ever to run for mayor of Boston, Louise Day Hicks was a remarkable product of Irish American social mobility in the large cities of the nation.

Born in 1916 to a middle-class family in South Boston, she was the daughter of a part-time judge, lawyer, banker, and real estate man, John Day. In those days credit was hard to come by for the lower-middle class, and John Day became a popular figure in the community because his bank lent money to the credit-starved South Boston Irish. In 1932, her mother, Julia, died and the teenage Louise became the woman of the house to her father and three brothers. She married John Hicks, who promptly moved into the family home. She was her father's pride, and she dominated the male Day-Hicks family and sought to emulate John Day's career. After graduating from Wheelock College with a teaching certificate, she taught and then spent ten years as a law clerk in her father's office. It was there that she learned about the law and became convinced that she would one day carry on the mantle of her father. Three years after his death, this mother of two entered Boston University Law School, a rare occurrence in 1952 America. She passed the bar examination in 1956, and with her younger brother John opened the law practice of Hicks and Day. She did well, making good use of her father's reputation to amass several real estate holdings. In 1961, to the dismay of her family, she announced that she would run for school committee.

The Boston School Committee had changed from a Yankee bastion of Protestant values in the nineteenth century to an Irish dominated pork barrel. By the time Hicks sought a place on the committee, it was recognized as a place to launch a political career. Committee members controlled large numbers of jobs for custodians and administrators in the school department and issued lucrative city contracts; they used their position to raise money for political campaigns by selling tickets to so-called testimonial dinners. Campaigning as "the only mother on the ballot," she won easily. By 1963, she was elected chair, which put her directly into the public eye when the black community began efforts to desegregate the Boston public schools.

Led by the local NAACP, the black community wanted the school committee to recognize the de facto segregation of the schools. Hicks and her colleagues refused to acknowledge this reality. Her strong denial of this claim, her steadfast support for the neighborhood school, and her leadership in stubbornly refusing state efforts to balance school attendance, all increased her growing reputation as the protector of the white neighborhoods. While this stance led to attacks by the press and the liberal community, her popularity blossomed to such a degree that she was reelected and went on to a variety of public offices. Her only biographer stated: "She had found her issue or, more accurately, it had found her."[18] For Hicks and other would-be white politicians in Boston, a stalwart resistance to desegregation was a ticket to political stardom. Besides her run for the mayoralty in 1967, she ran and was elected to Congress in 1970, and voters gave her strong majorities for city council victories in 1969, 1973, and 1975, although she again lost the mayoralty in 1971, and a congressional race in 1972. Whatever the outcome, Hicks was Boston's most famous woman politician and a force to be reckoned with.

Noted for her elaborate hats with floral arrangements, Hicks had announced in 1967 that "my chapeau is in the ring."[19] She ran a campaign based on innuendo and scare tactics, avowing to the white neighborhoods, "You know where I stand," on desegregation. Her popularity frightened moderates and liberals, and leaders of the Vault and Senator Ted Kennedy readily coalesced behind the banner of the up-and-coming young secretary of state, Kevin Hagen White, also a scion of a Boston Irish political leader. Accused of running an amateurish campaign, ridiculed by the press for her rotund appearance, her brightly colored dresses, and her speaking style, Hicks could not overcome White's sophisticated, Kennedy-style campaign and his citywide coalition.

The 1967 mayoral victory of White, a man seen as a conciliator between the troubled neighborhoods and the downtown business interests, over the more insular South Boston favorite Hicks signaled a time of compromise and harmony for all groups. White was to be mayor of Boston for a record sixteen years, agilely adapting himself to several crisis situations, including the school busing controversy and a momentary fiscal decline of the city. His political acumen and survivability, his reputation for remarkable energy and intelligence, and his sincere desire to make a contribution enabled him repeatedly to win election in face of major attacks of corruption in his administration. His victory in 1967, however, was due largely to the coming together of many diverse forces who could not stomach Hicks, and for them White was the only choice.

That White would go into politics was almost a foregone conclusion based upon his background. Born in Boston in 1929, he was an assimilated fourth-generation Irish American. His grandfather, Henry Hagan, had been a Boston City Council president. His father, Joseph White, was another former city council president, state legislator, and school committee member. Young Kevin married Kathryn H. Galvin, daughter of another city council president, William Galvin. White's life was suffused with the politics of Irish Boston, and early on he harbored political ambitions. After graduating from Williams College in 1952 and Boston College Law School in 1955, he became an aide to the Middlesex County district attorney, and in 1958 was appointed as an assistant district attorney for Suffolk County.

The law school–district attorney route became a common path for young politicos starting their careers. White's problem was that his job was coveted by another up-and-coming young man, Edward Kennedy. When John F. Kennedy was elected president in 1960, he made clear that he wanted his youngest brother to inherit his senate seat. But Ted was too young, and the obedient state legislature appointed a temporary party stalwart to hold down the seat until he came of age. Meanwhile, he needed political experience, and the big guns of Massachusetts politics informed Kevin White that he was out of a job.

The action by the powerful Kennedy family forced Kevin White into electoral politics sooner than he might have wished, at the age of thirty-one. In 1960, he won the nomination of the Democratic party for secretary of state, and the election by beating another newcomer, Edward Brooke. The main job of the secretary of state was record keeping, which enabled White to familiarize himself with local politicians all over the state. He ran four times, winning two-year terms each time. By 1967, he was ready for bigger things.

Jumping into the mayoral race in 1967, White began a masterful campaign. He advertised for supporters, and when they arrived he sent them out to get other supporters. He held coffee hours throughout the city, beginning to get his name better known in the neighborhoods. As a Williams College graduate he was acceptable to upper-middle-class groups, and as the scion of an old Boston political family, he was welcomed by the city's ethnics. Although he came in second to Hicks in the preliminary election, he was the one candidate the Hicks opposition could accept. He noted his new recognition: "First I was a nice young kid! Then, when I started moving on reforms, I was a new breed Democrat."[20]

His goal as mayor was to bring together the discontented neighborhoods and the more affluent downtown business interests by providing something for everyone. White's new BRA head, Hale Champion, worked to conciliate activist neighborhood groups by halting housing demolition and attempting to increase subsidized housing units. Mayor White gave local communities a voice and a means to air grievances through his neighborhood "little city halls" initiative; and he worked to deflect racial tensions with his "summerthing" neighborhood programs. Between 1968 and 1975, the White administration spent over $500 million on neighborhood capital improvements, a sum vastly greater than that spent by the Collins administration. At the same time, he championed the progrowth desires of the business community, being careful that housing units would not be lost in the process of building skyscrapers.

The erstwhile collaboration of contending groups managed by White fell apart because of the economic recession and the racial conflicts of the early 1970s, and because in 1976 he sponsored a foolhardy charter change that would increase his power.

> To understand my own desire to centralize power in the mayor's office you must understand how much the city needs to be held together. This city has been saved by a strong executive. When I was re-elected in 1975, I tried to galvanize the city against the

forces that were hitting it from outside—[from] the suburbs and the federal government . . . but what I didn't realize was how little psychological pressure there was for the  city to hold together as a constituency against the forces that were killing it.[21]

White's admission that with this charter he wished to create an old-time "machine" that boosted the mayor's powers fell on unsympathetic ears. The business community, particularly the Vault and the *Boston Globe* reacted with dismay. They severed their relationship with White and from then on were his enemies. The *Globe* began a campaign against White that hinted at corruption and scandals that haunted his administration. Without the support of the power elite and facing increasing criticism from all sides, he refused to seek reelection in 1983. But the most calamitous event of his four terms had happened nearly ten years earlier, with the public school antibusing crisis that began in 1974.

The postindustrial transformation of Massachusetts, with decaying central cities and mushrooming suburban metropolitan areas, exacerbated tension among social classes and was a catalyst for the revival of virulent racial hatred. These racial divisions were particularly strong in Boston, but they were evident in other cities as well. Cities such as Lynn, Lawrence, Lowell, Brockton, and New Bedford shared the predicaments of Boston—declining populations, departing of industry, and middle-class flight. These problems combined with slipping property values, rising taxes, high unemployment, and competition among older ethnic groups and new nonwhite arrivals. Ethnic and racial conflicts were commonplace in the nation, but in Boston they reached levels that brought the city national attention.

From 1910 to 1970, the four prominent ethnic groups in Boston were the Irish, Italians, British Canadians, and eastern European Jews. While portions of these groups experienced sufficient social mobility to move to the suburbs, others remained behind in Boston's older immigrant neighborhoods. Ethnic segregation and restricted economic opportunities built up a "fortress" mentality among the Irish, the Italians, and the few remaining Jews. Boston's black population had been restricted to small portions of Beacon Hill and the South End for decades, but by the 1950s and 1960s, as earlier occupants joined the suburban exodus, they had moved steadily into decaying Jewish neighborhoods in Roxbury. As Boston's blacks began to seek housing in the affordable and stable Irish and Italian neighborhoods characterized by strong identities, they seemed to threaten the social fabric of these "tribal domains."

Unlike Detroit or Atlanta, cities that experienced long-term and continuous heavy black migrations, Boston's blacks were never able to marshal significant political power because of their fewer numbers. From 1870 to 1940, blacks averaged only between 1.4 and 3.1 percent of Boston's population. Throughout the period from 1870 to 1950, persistent discrimination against them had resulted in menial jobs, residential segregation, and unequal schooling. Denied equal opportunity at all levels, most working-class blacks experienced dismal conditions. One scholar wrote that "black economic progress did not fit the model of even the most limited example of nineteenth-century immigrant advance, that of Irish Bostonians." Another scholar bluntly stated: "There was virtually no improvement in the occupational position of black men in Boston between the late nineteenth century and the beginning of World War II." [22]

The northern migration of large numbers of blacks began in earnest in the 1950s. Like elsewhere this journey was predicated upon finding jobs and leaving the inhospitable South. But in Boston it was also based upon a kinship migration of blacks following family members and friends who had come earlier. Between 1950 and 1970, Boston's black population increased from 5 percent to 16 percent. Throughout this period, blacks appeared to make occupational gains into semiskilled, skilled, and clerical jobs. But these job improvements are misleading. Blacks were getting better jobs, but in comparison to whites their income levels actually fell:

> Despite these undeniable gains, however, the occupational distribution of Negro males in Boston remained quite distinctive in 1970. Seven of ten black men, but slightly less than half of the white males of the city, were manual workmen of some kind. As compared with the entire Boston labor force, there was a black excess of 59 percent among unskilled laborers, 81 percent among service workers, and 77 percent among semiskilled operatives. And there was a corresponding black deficit of 44 percent among professionals, and 60 percent among managerial and sales personnel. . . . In 1970 as in 1950 Negro males in Boston earned less than three-quarters of what their white counterparts earned. [23]

Because of their economic subordination, blacks lived under highly segregated living conditions. In a 1970s report on racial discrimination in
Boston, two geographers wrote: "Blacks are more segregated in Boston
than in most other large U.S. metropolitan areas, in the South as well
as in the North."[24] Lacking a substantial middle class, competing for
jobs with other ethnic groups in a city with a weak and narrow economic base for unskilled labor opportunities, and facing a white power
structure that resorted to racism to win elections, Boston's blacks were
ghettoized in a fashion almost comparable to Jim Crow days in the
South. Competing for unskilled jobs with other ethnic groups who were
favored by the ruling political machine, lacking sufficient numbers to
wield political power through voting, ignored and discriminated against
by the business and educational community, Boston's blacks found
themselves powerless. Inspired by national events, a small group of
black elites launched a campaign to promote civil rights through demonstrations and affirmative action initiatives. Finally, meeting little success in these endeavors, they focused on school integration and took
the issue of racial discrimination to the courts.

Boston working-class whites reacted in panic to growing numbers
of black migrants. Whites feared that these newcomers would take
their jobs, force down property values, bring crime to the streets, increase the welfare rolls, and lower the standards of their neighborhood
schools. The arguments put forth by the Irish in South Boston and
Charlestown, the Italians in East Boston and the North End, and the
Jews in Mattapan and Roxbury were the very ones that had been leveled against them generations earlier by the Yankees. Seeking a scape-
goat to explain their economic decline and the incessant challenge to
their neighborhood turf, Boston's white ethnics turned their discontent
into hatred of the city's most recent immigrant group.

The black community, led by the NAACP and by leaders such as
Thomas Atkins, Royal Bolling, and Mel King, fought the racial injustice
perpetrated by the city's public officials and by the negligent state government. The 1974 school desegregation order of federal judge W. Arthur Garrity of Wellesley ruled that the evidence was overwhelming
that the Boston School Committee had "knowingly carried out a systematic program of segregation."

Focusing on the demonstrated racism of the Boston School Committee, Garrity ordered that it come up with a desegregation plan by Sep-

tember 1974. The recalcitrant school committee members, elected because of their promise to protect the white "neighborhood school," dug in its heels and refused compliance, even under a contempt citation. Garrity responded by putting the Boston schools into federal receivership. Searching for a solution, he made a serious error when he selected an old and repudiated desegregation plan of the state board of education. This faulty Phase One plan used busing to integrate the schools, particularly the two poorest high schools in the city: all-white South Boston High, and all-black Roxbury High. He thus enraged the people of white neighborhoods (who invoked the sanctity of the neighborhood school which was entwined with racism). They were further outraged that Boston's two poorest neighborhoods had been chosen for busing, while suburbs like Garrity's Wellesley remained lily white and unintegrated.

It is true that Boston's white ethnics had fostered segregation, but the plan imposed on them exempted the white suburbs from any role in desegregation, making no attempt to promote educational progress. The issue of school integration recalled the old class warfare between the Yankees and the Irish. It unleashed a bitter and violent response by white ethnics that created an overt atmosphere of racial conflict in the city. Now, however, people of Irish descent were on both sides of the controversy. J. Anthony Lukas, a journalist, theorized that fourth-generation, assimilated, suburban Irish Americans supported busing for Boston as part of their new allegiance "to political and social ideals which transcend ethnicity or neighborhood."[25] Many middle-class Irish in the suburbs repudiated the tarnished spoils system of city hall politics for a new sense of regional politics based upon social responsibility, including a responsibility to black victims of poverty and racism.

The working-class inner-city Irish, led by Louise Day Hicks and an organization known as ROAR (Restore Our Alienated Rights) reacted to Garrity's decision with demonstrations and then with violence. The members of the group vowed: "I will not pledge allegiance to the Court Order of the United States, or to the dictatorship for which it stands, one law, under Garrity . . . with liberty and justice for none."

Kevin White's administration vacillated, and White himself, who never actively supported the law, sought to distance himself from the conflict, in part owing to his gubernatorial aspirations. In 1975, the second year of desegregation, Garrity rejected a moderate plan in favor of a more stringent one that increased busing and therefore opposition. In that second year of busing, because of worsening violence and resistance, federal marshals were called in to carry out Garrity's Phase Two order. For years, until 1984, a federal judge solely administered the school system of one of America's major cities.

One way or another the entire metropolitan community was somehow involved in the Boston school-busing controversy. In assessing the reasons for community defiance to court-ordered busing, a U.S. Commission on Civil Rights report extended the blame beyond the city limits. Cited for failing to act effectively were the metropolitan business community (personified by the Vault), the area's religious leaders of all denominations, the region's institutions of higher learning, the media (local and national), and even the federal executive branch. Boston's school desegregation issue could not be confined to the artificial and fixed boundaries of one city. Imposing a racial fix on inner city neighborhoods while asking nothing of the suburbs proved no solution. Indeed, whites either fled Boston to the suburbs or they sent their children to private and parochial schools. The result was that by the 1990s Boston had desegregated schools, but they were located in neighborhoods that remained, for the most part, as segregated as they had been in the 1970s.

But these retrograde outcomes have as much to do with Boston's peculiar history as they have to do with similar events across the nation. From a Yankee-dominated, nineteenth-century city which exploited the newly arrived Irish and other immigrant groups, Boston had become an ethnic stronghold with Irish political supremacy. Unfortunately, the success of the Irish and their eventual coalition with other ethnics were based on their continuing hostility to the Yankees, and that had much to do with the lack of compromise during Boston's busing crisis. Proof of the importance of that city's history can be found in the fact that Springfield, the other city in the state that faced court-ordered busing, had no such problems.

Springfield, the third largest city in the state, faced the typical problems of the nation's cities beginning in the 1960s, with its population declining from over 174,000 to 152,000 in 1980. Springfield's history, however, played an important role in the peaceful acceptance of court-ordered desegregation. A diversified commercial, transportation, and industrial city, Springfield never experienced the brutal ethnic and class conflict of Boston. While Yankees generally governed, no one ethnic group emerged to challenge their hegemony. There was no past hostility and no feelings that the ruling elites had oppressed anyone. All of the city's high schools were magnet schools for commerce, vocational education, or the liberal arts. Thus, students were already bused and the high schools did not play a major role in neighborhood conflict as they did in Boston. Most important, a state-ordered busing plan came to a community whose leaders agreed that segregation existed and were willing to abide by the court's decision. Although the Springfield School Committee had only one black elected member, it was clear that, unlike Boston, the school committee had not imposed practices that fostered segregation, but that the accident of residential choice had been the major culprit.

Initially, Springfield's leaders opposed change and did engage in delaying tactics. Eventually, however, after realizing that they had no legal recourse, virtually all opposition ended. The school committee and the school department worked with parents to promote full acceptance of the busing plan. The plan itself covered the entire city, so that everyone felt involved and no separate schools were singled out, as had happened with Boston's "Southie" and Roxbury High. Accepting the inevitable, Mayor William Sullivan abandoned his opposition to busing and even rode a school bus on the first day of the school year. The teachers, the media, the religious community, all came out in favor of the peaceful implementation of the plan. While some white flight to the suburbs occurred, it was not on the same scale as Boston's, and city residents did not move their children to parochial or private schools in significant numbers.

Crucial to the Springfield success, according to an unpublished study of this event, were the almost heroic activities of the superintendent of schools, Dr. John Deady. Unlike Boston superintendent William J. Leary, who refused to plan for the opening of school and who neglected to seek curriculum information from other school departments or to plan with teachers and parents, Deady threw himself wholeheartedly into carrying out the court order. His goal, he announced, was "to give all children an education at least equal to that which they had already received."[26] In fact, Deady wrote the desegregation plan that was to be implemented and put the full resources of the school department behind it. It was Deady who convinced the school committee to support the plan, and he arranged carefully in the preceding summer so that it would work. Moreover, he acted as a general liaison with the community in promoting the peaceful acceptance of the desegregation scheme. The media ran spots on TV and radio supporting the desegregation plan, and school teachers and staff participated in seminars designed to prepare them for classroom diversity. Thus Springfield experienced a tranquil desegregation of its schools because of its long political tradition of compromise and fairness. Unlike the situation in Boston, the city's political leaders chose not to make political capital out of opposition to busing. Springfield's politicians acknowledged the need to accept diversity and change, in part because of the transformation taking place in the state's political milieu. A new political understanding, spawned in the 1950s, came about largely because political power in the state was to dramatically change hands. To describe this phenomenon means looking back to the early post–World War II years and the coming to power of the Democratic party.

As a result of post–World War II economic expansion, suburbanization, and a growing generalized prosperity, a new middle class was emerging that was more cosmopolitan and heterogeneous than the predominantly small-town Protestant middle class of preceding generations. Economic and social changes that were national in scope were shaping a context for pluralism to flourish in a state that had been struggling with it for decades. By the beginning of the 1950s a new kind of ethnic politics was emerging that would encourage coalitions across traditional dividing lines in state and congressional elections. This new coalitional ethnic politics was dramatized by the ongoing struggle for control over state government between Republicans and Democrats.

From 1928 on, when Massachusetts voted for Democrat Al Smith for the presidency, the Democratic party strongly competed to attract the support of the heterogeneous population of the state by opening its ranks and by advocating legislation that would answer the state's economic needs. As second and third generations of ethnics moved into the middle class they maintained their political loyalties to the party that embraced their parents and grandparents. Unlike the nation at large, Massachusetts has a suburban middle class peculiarly loyal to the Democrats.

It was not until 1948 that feuding Democrats finally came together with a more unified ticket under the national banner of Harry S. Truman. Both Truman and Paul Dever, the Democratic candidate for governor, won major victories. Truman received 55 percent of the state's vote, and the Democrats carried all six of the state's constitutional offices. For the first time, the Democrats won the state House of Representatives, and the members chose Thomas P. ("Tip") O'Neill to be the commonwealth's first Democratic Speaker of the House. Also, for the first time, they tied with Republicans for senate seats, with each party winning twenty.

The election of 1952 brought the Republicans steam-rolling back to power under the aegis of General Dwight David Eisenhower. This instance of state officers riding on the general's coattails reversed the course of political history for a short time, as the Republicans won back the governorship with Christian Herter and regained control of the House and the Senate. But the momentum of the Democratic party could not be stopped. That election was the last time the Republicans would control both houses of the legislature and the governorship.

In 1954, the Democrats regained a majority in the lower house and held it for the rest of the twentieth century. The Republicans lost their hold on the upper house in 1958. By the late 1960s, Democratic margins in both houses were overwhelming. In the thirty years from 1950 to 1980, Republicans fell to having barely 20 percent of the membership in either branch. From a rough parity in voter registration in 1952 the GOP dropped to having fewer than one in four party registrants. They held no constitutional officers, and the state's congressional delegation was usually totally Democratic. The expanded middle classes of both cities and suburbs were Democrats, and after years of Yankee small-town rule, assimilated ethnics now governed. The symbolic moment of the coming Republican defeat, and the transformation of Massachusetts into a one-party Democratic stronghold, was the 1952 victory of Irish American Democrat John F. Kennedy over Yankee Republican Henry Cabot Lodge Jr. for the U.S. Senate.

The history of the Kennedy family in Massachusetts public life reveals much of this complex metamorphosis. The first Kennedy, Patrick, came to East Boston in 1848 at the age of twenty-five as part of the great famine exodus. In County Wexford he had been a tenant farmer, but in Boston he found work making barrels, so he became a cooper. After a few years he married a fellow migrant, Bridget Murphy, and they had three daughters and one son, Patrick Joseph Kennedy, born in

1858, just a few months before his father died. Bridget Kennedy worked heroically to keep her family together, and she succeeded by working in a shop and by taking a job dressing the hair of stylish women at the great downtown Jordan Marsh emporium. The baby Patrick was raised by his sisters and, for seven or eight years, attended parochial school before leaving to become a stevedore on the East Boston waterfront. It was there, in the year that Henry Cabot Lodge graduated from Harvard, that "P. J." Kennedy's real-life Horatio Alger rise to respectability and power began.

Longshoremen rarely became prosperous, but the brawny, hard-working P. J. Kennedy saved pennies, dimes, and dollars. After a few years he had saved enough to purchase a run-down saloon in the shadow of Faneuil Hall on Haymarket Square. From there he never looked back, gradually expanding his business until he became not only a saloon keeper in Boston and East Boston but a retail and wholesale liquor dealer as well. Before he was thirty, Kennedy became a power in East Boston politics, winning election to the state House of Representatives in 1886 during Hugh O'Brien's mayoralty, and later, in 1892, going to the state Senate.

Representative P. J. Kennedy married Mary Hickey in 1887, and the following year Joseph Patrick Kennedy was born. Young Joseph was raised in a privileged, middle-class setting. His prudent and calculating father continued his upward ascent, becoming a prominent fixture in municipal government and a prosperous capitalist with investments in Boston real estate and two small local banks. He carved out his career within the confines of the Boston Irish, but for his compatriots he wished all doors to open. Consequently he cultivated his son's competitive drives and sent him to the elite Boston Latin School where he could prepare for Harvard.

Young Joseph Kennedy was very bright, but not in an academic way, and he barely made it through the Latin school and into Harvard. But like his father, he did not look back. Harvard presented opportunities for a man with ambitions to acquire a social patina and to make useful acquaintances. Given the goals of P. J. Kennedy and his son, scholarship was a necessary evil, and many of Joe's highborn Protestant classmates agreed. Judging from his actions after he graduated in 1912, Joe Kennedy aimed to crack the remaining barriers to power and prestige in Massachusetts.

His chosen route was banking, and he quickly landed a job as a state banking examiner—a marvelous opportunity for on-the-job training. From there he moved to acquire the Columbia Trust Company in East Boston, in which his father had long had an interest. At twenty-five he became the youngest bank president in the state and perhaps the nation. But Kennedy was no specialist; as time went on, he sought out opportunities for profit in a wide range of investments including real estate, movie theaters, wartime shipbuilding, and common stocks. Yankee Boston saw him as a pushy, upstart speculator—but no one could deny his shrewd judgment and his talent for getting what he wanted.

In 1914 what he wanted was Rose Fitzgerald, the daughter of John F. ("Honey Fitz") Fitzgerald, Boston's mayor (1906–7 and 1910–14) and a perennial power in city politics. Rose, who had graduated from Dorchester High School and later studied at the Convent of the Sacred Heart, had been voted Boston's prettiest graduate, a distinction Kennedy appreciated. Rose Fitzgerald was already an accomplished hostess, and Kennedy was confident she would make a splendid wife. Their wedding, which was performed by Cardinal William O'Connell, was the highlight of the social season for Irish Boston.

But Kennedy was not content to live in an Irish ghetto, even at its apex. He and Rose settled in Brookline, then mostly Protestant, and as their children came along, they enrolled them in private schools where there were few if any Catholics. For a while the family summered at Nantasket, an Irish resort, but they soon tried Cohasset, where old Boston predominated. Here, in a humiliating episode, the Kennedys were barred when they sought admission to the country club. Kennedy's response was to create his own resort for his family at Hyannis on the Cape.

Joseph Kennedy wanted a pluralistic Massachusetts where he could be as good as the "best people" and be an Irish American Catholic too, but during the teens and twenties that was impossible. Finally he left, moving his family to New York in 1927. By then he was a multimillionaire, having greatly enlarged his fortune in the movie business. Except for spending summers on Cape Cod, the Kennedys became expatriates from Massachusetts. But when they returned, their reentry into Massachusetts public life after the Second World War revealed how Massachusetts was changing. The agent of their return was John Fitzgerald Kennedy, their eldest surviving son. John had been born in Brookline in 1919, he passed summers at Hyannis, and he had spent four years at Harvard from 1936 to 1940, but when he came home from the Pacific war in 1945, he might as reasonably have sought a congressional seat in New York or Palm Beach as from the Eleventh District of Massachusetts. But John Kennedy, under his father's tutelage and with his cousin Joe Kane, an old Boston "pol," for campaign manager, set out to capture the district that James Michael Curley had just vacated in order to resume Boston's mayoralty. In addition to Cambridge, the district included the North End and East Boston, birthplaces of his grandfathers Fitzgerald and Kennedy. It was an Irish and Italian working-class district with Harvard thrown in. John won, and from 1947 until 1953 he served in the House. Yet his own and his family's ambitions aimed higher.

Opportunity appeared in 1952. Senator Henry Cabot Lodge, grandson of the former senator, was so popular and well entrenched that major Democrats were reluctant to challenge him. Lodge had been in the Senate since 1936 and had regularly defeated Irish Democrats, including James Michael Curley, Joseph Casey, and David I. Walsh, the first Irish Catholic governor and senator in Massachusetts history. To compete with the widely respected Lodge seemed fruitless, but the Kennedys tried. For John it was a contest rich in significance, for Lodge's grandfather had narrowly defeated his own grandfather, Honey Fitz, in the election of 1916. Now the grandsons did battle in a new context.

From the standpoint of issues, little divided the two candidates other than the rhetorical nostrums of their respective parties. Lodge was experienced, honest, personable, and had always been able to attract Irish, Italian, and other ethnic voters to supplement his regular Republican support. He was a Brahmin Yankee candidate who had learned to campaign in a plural setting. But in John Kennedy he was facing something new in Massachusetts, a fourth-generation Irish immigrant who was so thoroughly "Americanized" that he could surmount ethnic stereotypes. Kennedy's well-financed, well-organized campaign won because he created a favorable impression among all sorts of voters. His ethnicity and family background were assets that he built on, outdoing Lodge at his own game. Running against the Eisenhower landslide that swept the state and defeated the Democratic governor, Kennedy won by seventy thousand votes. "At last," Rose Kennedy exulted, "the Fitzgeralds have evened the score with the Lodges!"[27]

When Kennedy ran again in 1958, the margin of his victory, 875,000 votes, demonstrated the breadth of his appeal. He had transcended ethnic politics in Massachusetts, and he was on his way to surmounting them nationwide. Ethnic politics were not dead, but in a pluralistic setting, they had become far more complicated and more entwined with other issues than ever before.

Joseph Kennedy's ambitions were not confined to his eldest son. In 1961, with John in the White House and Robert in the cabinet, he made sure that John's seat remained accessible to his youngest child, Edward ("Ted"), who was not yet old enough to enter the Senate. When the new election was held in 1962, it was in many ways a rerun of 1952. After defeating Edward McCormack (nephew of John W. McCormack, Speaker of the House of Representatives) in the primary, Ted Kennedy faced Henry Cabot Lodge's son George. Neither of the two was particularly well qualified for the Senate, and neither had previously held elective office. That scions of these two families should be again competing for high office testified to the hold that the past still possessed. Kennedy won.

The repetition of the Kennedy-Lodge contest was in some ways misleading, since it suggested that a bipolar Irish Catholic–Yankee Protestant division still dominated the state. In fact, electoral competition was coming to reflect the diversity of Massachusetts inhabitants. In 1957 the Democrat Foster Furcolo became the first Italian American governor in Massachusetts and the United States; he was then followed by another Italian American, the Republican John A. Volpe, in a state where Italian Americans were a distinct minority. Later, in the 1960s, there were Yankee governors from both parties, the Democrat Endicott Peabody and the Republican Francis Sargent. In the following decade the son of Greek immigrants, Democrat Michael Dukakis, won the governorship. Indeed even though people of Irish background are the most numerous single ethnic group, there has been only one Irish governor, Edward J. King (1979–83), since Paul Dever left office in 1953. This overall diversity became evident at the federal level as well: the Kennedys have held the Senate seat John won in 1952 for more than a generation, and the same Massachusetts voters made the Republican Leverett Saltonstall an institution, electing him to the Senate from 1944 until 1967. After Saltonstall's retirement in 1966 the Republican Edward W. Brooke became the first black member of the Senate since Reconstruction. Brooke served until 1978 and was succeeded by the former Democratic congressman from Lowell, Paul Tsongas, a Greek American who chose to retire in 1984; he was followed by John F. Kerry. Thus since 1978 until the end of the century both U.S. Senate seats were held by Democrats, and—since 1984—by elite, Ivy League Irish Americans. Ethnicity remains vitally important, especially within smaller constituencies, but coalition building across ethnic lines dominates state political organization. As elsewhere in the United States, appeals to the voters focus on personal qualities and even, from time to time, on questions of policy.

Unlike the close national election of 1960, John F. Kennedy beat Richard Nixon in Massachusetts that year by a half-million votes. Though Republicans were able to win the governorship with John Volpe, who served three two-year terms (1961–62, 1965–69), and Francis Sargent (1969–74), the party continued to decline. Republican gubernatorial victories were due in part to fielding attractive candidates, but also because continuing factional fights—urban versus suburban—regularly split the Democrats. This Democratic confusion was illustrated by the chaotic presidential primary of 1976.

Washington State's Henry Jackson, an old New Dealer and a conservative on defense, won the primary among seven candidates with 22.3 percent of the vote, the lowest in the history of Massachusetts presidential primaries. The anti–Vietnam War dove and liberal Morris Udall finished second, while ultraconservative George Wallace of Alabama, courted the antibusing constituency, followed closely. The moderate and eventual party standard bearer, Jimmy Carter, finished fourth, trailed by three other Democratic candidates. The total Democratic vote split almost evenly between liberals and conservatives. As a portent of what was coming in the Reagan years of the 1980s, the state's big cities went for the conservatives, while the suburbs went for liberals like Udall. Together, Jackson and Wallace captured two-thirds of the Boston vote, reflecting white discontent with the 1974 busing order promulgated to end school segregation.

Conservative Democrat Edward King capitalized on this division by upsetting Governor Michael Dukakis in the 1978 Democratic primary. But in 1982, Dukakis, as leader of the suburban reform faction, was able to put the party together once again and control the governor's office for two terms. Even though President Ronald Reagan won the state in 1984, it was by a very narrow margin. Like 1972, when the state stood alone and voted for the peace candidate, Democrat George McGovern, Massachusetts Democrats survived Reagan's national tide of victory. Although Governor Michael Dukakis lost his bid for the presidency in 1988 against George Bush, Dukakis won Massachusetts handily, demonstrating the strength of liberalism in the Bay State. While Republican patrician William Weld won the governorship in 1990, and again in 1994, Democrat Bill Clinton's victories in 1992 and 1996 illustrated the continuing saga of Democratic popularity in the state. At the end of the century, as in years past, Massachusetts remained a one-party state, except that the tables were turned and the more numerous Democrats controlled the commonwealth's political destinies.

Wholly apart from politics, the vitality of the old ethnic conscious-ness and the ethnic social hierarchy that it mantained have been pro-gressively undermined during recent decades. The Massachusetts econ-omy no longer sustained the old relationships, with Yankee owners and managers ruling immigrant labor, as in the old mill cities. In the last decades of the twentieth century many private employers were national corporations whose managers possessed only the faintest ethnic identi-ties, and labor unions stood between the employer and the employed. Moreover, many people worked for nonprofit enterprises like govern-ment and education, so relation between "bosses" and "workers" were transformed. In addition, large numbers of self-employed professionals, quasi-professionals, and small businesspeople emerged, serving all kinds of people. Domestic service, which once reinforced class and eth-nic identities all but vanished, and insofar as it survived, it relied as in the past on a congeries of impoverished newcomers.

Time also brought a general assimilation toward the national com-mon denominator purveyed in the mass culture. Just as Irish brogues were seldom heard, so the Yankee twang all but disappeared, and Har-vard men or women could no longer be identified by accent. Regional and class differences survived, but black dialect was the only really vig-orous, distinct ethnic mode of speech, and it was nourished by the single major postwar immigration—in this case from the South. In the generation following the Korean War, Massachusetts became a pre-dominantly heterogeneous, middle-class, suburban state. Under these conditions strong ethnic identities, including hostility to "outsiders," seldom had meaning, and marriages across old ethnic lines became common. Ethnic pluralism survived, but only within the melting pot of mass culture. Social values were changing. Gaining access to the inner sanctum of Yankee society had been a vital aspiration for Joseph and Rose Kennedy, but by the 1970s these old longings had become anachronistic. To outsiders, the exclusive Brahmin waltz evenings at the Ritz Carlton Hotel in Boston became equivalent to the polka nights at the Polish clubs. Such ethnic festivities helped groups preserve the vestiges of their identity across generations and played a minor role in encouraging marriage within the group. But the boundaries of power and prestige had become so inclusive that the old ethnic hierarchy that lingered in the mind was no longer grounded in reality. Wealth, education, personality, and, most of all, performance counted more than ethnicity.

In their acceptance of diverse ethnic identities, the people of Massachusetts found a partial resolution for the chronic tensions between the majority and the minority, between the community and the individual. For at some level of consciousness all citizens now thought of themselves as part of the majority in some circumstances, and as member of a minority in others. Perhaps it was these realizations that brought Massachusetts people to the forefront in testing new boundaries between individual liberty and community control over issues like school busing, abortion, and gay rights in the last quarter of the twentieth century. The particular conflicts had changed, and so had Massachusetts; it was no longer substantially a world of its own. Yet integrated as it was into the nation, the old questions that had divided its people remained. Did the majority possess the right to overrule the fundamental beliefs of minorities? Where should the boundary lie between individual liberty and community values? Bradford and Winthrop, Adams and Hutchinson, Garrison, Hoar, Du Bois, and Holmes had all confronted these issues. By the last decades of the twentieth century, Massachusetts people continued to take a leading role in American debates about the limits of liberty and equality.

Besides this noteworthy political heritage, one must keep in mind the long-term factors that have shaped the Bay State's economic fabric. Federal largess in the form of defense spending sowed the seeds for the post–World War II Massachusetts economic miracle. Its long history as an industrialized state, coupled with an efficient and educated labor force in a region with a stable population, led to the emergence of new service and high-technology industries, often linked to local university research and Boston-based venture capital. With an educated labor force, the economy can be reinvented if necessary, as it has been twice since the 1940s.

A 1967 forecast by economist Robert Eisenmenger holds true for Massachusetts at the start of the twenty-first century: "It appears therefore, that the future of New England's economy rests with the new technologically oriented manufacturing and service industries. . . . So far as public policy is concerned, this suggests that the New England states should place increasing emphasis on providing high-quality secondary-school and college training so as to provide the necessary high-skilled labor force for the region's growing industries."[28] The tradition of a skilled and educated workforce and the innovations and investment daring of the research and business communities have been the paramount ingredients in the uncertain mixture that brought forth Massachusetts's twentieth-century economic prosperity. Tolerance for diversity by a people is linked to their acceptance of innovation and there is a connection between being open to innovation in business and being open to social diversity. Both are aspects of what might be termed "coastal cosmopolitanism." The political tolerance and the high standard of material prosperity of Massachusetts' citizens augurs well for the Bay State in the twenty-first century.

# NOTES

## *1. The Country That the English Found*

1. Thomas Morton, *New English Canaan* (Amsterdam, 1637), Publications of the Prince Society, 14 (1883; reprint, New York: Burt Franklin, 1967), 180.
2. William Wood, *New England's Prospect* (n.p., 1634). Publications of the Prince Society, 3 (1865; printed from the 1764 edition; reprint ed., New York, 1967), 4, 5, 16.
3. Morton, *New English Canaan,* 180.
4. Wood, *New England's Prospect,* 37–38, 39.
5. Morton, *New English Canaan,* 89–90.
6. Wood, *New England's Prospect,* 15, 31.
7. Ibid., 29.
8. Ibid.
9. Morton, *New English Canaan,* 190.

## *2. The Worlds of Bradford and Winthrop*

1. Thomas Fuller, *Worthies of England* (1662), quoted in "Editor's Introduction," *Agriculture and Economic Growth in England, 1650–1815,* ed. Eric L. Jones (London: Methuen, 1967), 5.
2. Quoted in George Macaulay Trevelyan, *England under the Stuarts* (1904; Harmondsworth: Penguin, 1960), 74.
3. William Bradford, *Of Plymouth Plantation, 1620–1647,* ed. Samuel Eliot Morison (New York: Knopf, 1963), 17.
4. Ibid., 25.
5. Ibid.
6. William Shakespeare, *Troilus and Cressida,* act 1, scene 3, line 86.
7. Matthew Cradock, quoted in Charles McLean Andrews, *The Colonial Period of American History,* 4 vols. (New Haven: Yale University Press, 1934), 1:388.
8. "The Agreement at Cambridge" (August 26, 1629), quoted in *The Found-*

ing of Massachusetts: Historians and the Sources, ed. Edmund S. Morgan (Indianapolis: Bobbs-Merrill, 1964), 183.

9. Ibid., 184, 186.
10. Ibid., 202, 203.
11. Ibid., 203.
12. Ibid., 203–4.
13. Bradford, *Plymouth Plantation,* 59.
14. Ibid., 76.
15. Ibid., 72, xxiv.
16. Ibid., 77.
17. [Thomas] *Mourt's Relation,* quoted in ibid., 80n.
18. Bradford, *Plymouth Plantation,* 85.
19. Ibid., 90.
20. Edward Winslow, letter of December 11, 1621, printed in *Mourt's* Relation (60–61), and quoted in ibid., 90n.
21. Winthrop, quoted in Andrews, *Colonial Period,* 1:435.
22. Hutchinson, quoted in Darrett B. Rutman, *Winthrop's Boston* (Chapel Hill: University of North Carolina Press, 1965), 120.
23. Hutchinson, quoted in Edmund S. Morgan, *The Puritan Dilemma: The Story of John Winthrop* (Boston: Little, Brown, 1958), 152.
24. Hutchinson, quoted in Rutman, *Winthrop's Boston,* 121
25. Edward Johnson, quoted in ibid., 245.
26. Bradford, *Plymouth Plantation,* 333–34.
27. Winthrop, quoted in Rutman, *Winthrop's Boston,* 245.

## 3. *Piety and Plenty in the American Canaan*

1. Petition quoted in Kenneth A. Lockridge, *A New England Town. The First Hundred Years: Dedham, Massachusetts, 1636–1736* (New York: Norton, 1970), 4. In this book, *township* refers to a tract of land with political boundaries. *Town* and *township* are used synonymously; *town* does not mean an urban center, and the term *townspeople* refers to farmers and village dwellers within the town.
2. Ibid., *A New England Town,* 4, 5.
3. Quoted in Morgan, *The Founding of Massachusetts,* 203.
4. Bradstreet quotations are from *The American Puritans: Their Prose and Poetry,* ed. Perry Miller (Garden City, N.Y.: Doubleday, 1956), 270, 271, 279.
5. Thomas Hutchinson, *The History of the Colony and Province of Massachusetts Bay,* ed. Lawrence Shaw Mayo, 3 vols. (Cambridge: Harvard University Press, 1936), 2:160.
6. Corey, quoted in Marion L. Starkey, *The Devil in Massachusetts* (Garden City, N.Y.: Doubleday, 1961), 205.

7. Jonathan Edwards, *A Faithful Narrative of the Surprising Voice of God* (1737), in *American Colonial Documents to 1776*, ed. Merrill Jensen, vol. 9 of *English Historical Documents* (New York: Oxford University Press, 1962), 538.

## 4. Revolutionary Vanguard

1. The term *Yankee* was applied to the English colonists of New England by Massachusett Indians in the seventeenth century. By the early years of the eighteenth century the term was being applied to New Englanders of British origin by the Dutch of New York and by settlers of New England themselves. As used here, *Yankee* refers to the social and cultural characteristics of eighteenth-century settlers, who were more individualistic, competitive, secular, and provincial than their pious immigrant ancestors.
2. Thomas Hutchinson, *Diary and Letters,* 1:46. Quoted in Bernard Bailyn, *The Ordeal of Thomas Hutchinson* (Cambridge: Harvard University Press, 1974), 21.
3. Hutchinson to Francis Bernard, March 25, 1770, Massachusetts Archives, 26:471. Quoted in Bailyn, *Ordeal,* 12.
4. Hutchinson, *History of the Colony,* 3:64.
5. John Adams to William Tudor, Quincy, March 29, 1817, *Works of John Adams,* ed. Charles Francis Adams, 10 vols. (Boston: Little, Brown, 1856), 10:245, 247.
6. Peter Oliver, *Origin and Progress of the American Rebellion,* ed. Douglas Adair and John A. Schutz (Stanford: Stanford University Press, 1961), 39.
7. Samuel A. Bates, ed., *Records of the Town of Braintree, 1740 to 1793* (Randolph, Mass., 1886), 404–6.
8. John Adams, *Diary and Autobiography of John Adams,* ed. L. H. Butterfield, Leonard C. Faber, and Wendell D. Garrett, 4 vols. (Cambridge: Harvard University Press, 1962), 1:263.
9. J. Mayhew, *The Snare Broken* (Boston, 1766), 1–2.
10. Jensen, *American Colonial Documents,* 696.
11. Mayhew, *Snare Broken,* 20, title page.
12. Quoted in Bailyn, *Ordeal of Thomas Hutchinson,* 158.
13. *The Votes and Proceedings of the Freeholders and Other Inhabitants of the Town of Boston. . . .* (Boston, 1773), 1.
14. Town of Gorham (Maine), Proceedings, January 7, 1773. Massachusetts Historical Society, Boston Committee of Correspondence letters received, photostat 274.
15. Quoted in Richard D. Brown, *Revolutionary Politics in Massachusetts: The Boston Committee of Correspondence and the Towns* (Cambridge: Harvard University Press, 1970), 88.
16. *The Speeches of His Excellency Governor Hutchinson, to the General As-*

*sembly . . . with the Answers of His Majesty's Council and the House of Representatives Respectively* (Boston, 1773), 57, 58.

17. Adams, *Diary and Autobiography,* 2:77.

18. Quoted in Bailyn, *Ordeal of Thomas Hutchinson,* 227.

19. Adams to James Warren, December 17, 1773, *Warren-Adams Letters,* 2 vols. (Boston: Massachusetts Historical Society, 1917–25), 2:403–4. (*The Warren-Adams Letters,* vols. 1 and 2, were published as vols. 72 (1917) and 73 (1925) of *Collections of the Massachusetts Historical Society.*)

20. Samuel Adams to James Warren, December 28, 1773, *Warren-Adams Letters,* 1:20.

21. Thomas Young to Samuel Adams, Boston, September 4, 1774, Samuel Adams Papers, New York Public Library.

22. Adams, *Diary and Autobiography,* 2:134–35.

23. John Andrews to William Barrell, Boston, January 29, 1775, *Proceedings of the Massachusetts Historical Society,* 1st ser., 8 (1864–65): 398–99.

24. James Warren to John Adams, Boston, July 17, 1776, *Warren-Adams Letters,* 1:261.

25. Words inscribed in the copy Hutchinson sent to King George. Quoted in Bailyn, *Ordeal of Thomas Hutchinson,* 357n.

26. Malcolm Freiberg, ed:, *Thomas Hutchinson's Strictures upon the Declaration of Independence . . .* (London, 1776; reprint. Boston, 1958), 10.

27. John Adams to Abigail Adams, Philadelphia, July 3, 1776, *Adams Family Correspondence,* ed. L. H. Butterfield et al., 6 vols. (Cambridge: Harvard University Press, 1963), 2:28.

## 5. A Republic of Virtue or Liberty?

1. Paine to Elbridge Gerry, Boston, April 12. 1777, in James T. Austin, *The Life of Elbridge Gerry,* 2 vols. (1828; 1829; New York: DaCapo, 1970), 1:220–21.

2. "The Constitution of 1780" in *The Popular Sources of Political Authority: Documents on the Massachusetts Constitution of 1780,* ed. Oscar Handlin and Mary F. Handlin, (Cambridge: Harvard University Press, 1966), 441.

3. Ibid, 446.

4. Ibid., 442–43.

5. Ibid., 446.

6. Ibid., 456.

7. Ibid., 465.

8. Ibid., 467.

9. Ibid., 435, 434.

10. George R. Minot, *History of the Insurrection in Massachusetts . . .* (Worcester, 1788), 34.

11. Ibid., 35.
12. Ibid., 37.
13. Ibid., 64.
14. *An Address from the General Court to the People of the Commonwealth of Massachusetts* (Boston, 1786), 4, 34.
15. Ibid., 33–35.
16. Minot, *Insurrection,* 127.

## 6. Hive of Industry and Elite Paternalism

1. "Newburyport, 1808," quoted in Samuel Eliot Morrison, *The Maritime History of Massachusetts, 1783–1860* (1921; Boston: Houghton, Mifflin, 1961), 187.
2. Jonathan Prude, *The Coming of Industrial Order: Town and Factory Life in Rural Massachusetts* (New York: Cambridge University Press, 1983), 35.
3. Lowell, quoted in Robert F. Dalzell Jr., *Enterprising Elite: The Boston Associates and the World They Made* (Cambridge: Harvard University Press, 1987), 9.
4. Reported by Kirk Boott and quoted in George Sweet Gibb, *The Saco-Lowell Shops: Textile Machinery Building in New England, 1813–1949* (Cambridge: Harvard University Press, 1950), 67.
5. Lawrence, quoted in Dalzell, *Enterprising Elite,* 64.
6. Dalzell, *Enterprising Elite,* 65, 67.
7. Harriet H. Robinson, *Loom and Spindle or Life among the Early Mill Girls* (Kailua, Hawaii: Press Pacifica, 1976), 42.
8. Martineau, quoted in Norman Ware, *The Industrial Worker, 1840–1860: The Reaction of American Industrial Society to the Advance of the Industrial Revolution* (1924; Chicago: Quadrangle Books, 1964), 72–73.
9. Robinson, *Loom and Spindle,* 51–52.

## 7. Missions to the Nation

1. *Publications of the American Tract Society* (n.p., 1824), 6, 9.
2. Ernest Renan, quoted in Daniel Walker Howe, *The Unitarian Conscience* (Cambridge: Harvard University Press, 1970), 20.
3. Howe's report, quoted in Oscar Handlin, *The Americans* (Boston: Little, Brown, 1963), 225.
4. Howe, quoted in Gerald N. Grob, *The State and the Mentally Ill* (Chapel Hill: University of North Carolina Press, 1966), 190–91.
5. Stone, quoted in Louis Filler, "Lucy Stone," *Notable American Women, 1607–1950,* ed. Edward T. James et al., 3 vols. (Cambridge: Harvard University Press, 1971), 3:388.

6. Abigail Adams to John Adams, Braintree, March 31, 1776, *Adams Family Correspondence*, 1:370.
7. Francis Bowen, *The Principles of Political Economy* (Boston, 1856).
8. Ibid., 545.
9. Ibid., 545, 546.
10. Ibid., 27.

## 8. *Irish Immigration and the Challenges to Industrial Paternalism*

1. Robert A. Gross, "Culture and Cultivation: Agriculture and Society in Thoreau's Concord," *Journal of American History* 69 (June 1982): 42–61.
2. Arthur B. Darling, *Political Changes in Massachusetts, 1824–1848* (New Haven: Yale University Press, 1925), 2–3.
3. Alexander Keyssar, *Out of Work: The First Century of Unemployment in Massachusetts* (New York: Cambridge University Press, 1986), 26.
4. Gloria Main, "Inequality in Early America: The Evidence from the Probate Records in Massachusetts and Maryland," *Journal of Interdisciplinary History* 7 (1977): 559–81.
5. Peter Knights, *The Plain People of Boston, 1830–1860: A Study in City Growth* (New York: Oxford University Press, 1971), 123–24; Steven Herscovici, "The Distribution of Wealth in Nineteenth-Century Boston: Inequality among Natives and Immigrants, 1860," *Explorations in Economic History* 30 (July 1993): 321–35.
6. Van Wyck Brooks, *The Flowering of New England, 1815–1865* (Cleveland: World Publishing, 1946), 96.
7. The antebellum period was one in which parties proliferated, and issues or personalities dominated the political scene. While first Republicans and Federalists, then Whigs and Democrats seemed to represent a two-party system, such was not the case. These parties themselves were highly factionalized, and many splinter parties emerged to momentary national importance. Besides the above-mentioned parties there were a variety of subgroups within parties and several other parties. There were Adams Republicans, the National Republican party, Jeffersonian Democrats, Jackson Democrats, the Anti-Mason party, the Liberty party, the American or Know-Nothing party, the Temperance party, the Free-Soil party, the Workingmen's party, the Loco-Foco party, to name the most prominent. This party diversity was characterized by deep divisions, as in the presidential election of 1824, when four Republicans ran against each other, or in 1832 when the candidates were a Democrat, two National Republicans, and an Anti-Mason, or in 1836, an election that had three Whigs, a Democrat, and an Independent all competing.
8. Maurice G. Baxter, *One and Inseparable: Daniel Webster and the Union* (Cambridge: Harvard University Press, 1984), 186–87, 503.

9. Quoted in Ware, *The Industrial Worker, 1840–1860,* 76–77.

10. Ibid., 14–15, 1.

11. Wells, quoted in Roger Lane, *Policing the City: Boston, 1822–1885* (Cambridge: Harvard University Press, 1967), 28.

12. Quoted in Robert Lord et al., *History of the Archdiocese of Boston* (Boston: Pilot Publishing, 1945), 2:205.

13. *Mass Yeoman,* quoted in Ray Allen Billington, "The Burning of the Charleston Convent," *New England Quarterly* 10 (March 1937): 4–25; Judge [William C.] Fay, quoted in "Mob Law" *American Quarterly Review* 17 (March 1835): 209–31; "Destruction of the Charlestown Convent: Statement by the Leader of the Know Nothing Mob," United States Catholic Historical Society, *Historical Record and Studies* 12 (1918): 66–74.

14. Thomas M. Hammett, "Two Mobs of Jacksonian Boston: Ideology and Interest," *Journal of American History* 62 (1976): 846.

15. Robert C. Winthrop, "Reminiscences of a Night Passed in the Library of Harvard College," *Proceedings of the Massachusetts Historical Society* 23 (1886–87): 216–19.

16. Billington, "The Burning of the Charlestown Convent," 22.

17. *Hampshire Gazette,* December 17, 1834.

18. Thomas O'Connor, *The Boston Irish: A Political History* (Boston: Northeastern University Press, 1995), xvi.

19. Oscar Handlin, *Boston's Immigrants, 1790–1880,* rev. ed. (New York: Athenaeum, 1972), 54.

20. Sir Charles Lyell, quoted in *The Many Voices of Boston: A Historical Anthology, 1630–1975,* ed. Howard Mumford Jones and Bessie Zaban Jones (Boston: Atlantic, Little Brown, 1975), 222–23.

21. Brian C. Mitchell, *The Paddy Camps: The Irish of Lowell, 1821–61* (Urbana: University of Illinois Press, 1988), 135.

22. Ibid.

## 9. *Abolition and the Civil War*

1. *The Liberator,* January 1, 1831, 1.

2. Leonard Richards, *"Gentlemen of Property and Standing": Anti-Abolition Mobs in Jacksonian America* (New York: Oxford University Press, 1970), 5 n 4, 83.

3. "Garrison's Account of the Broadcloth Mob," in *William Lloyd Garrison,* ed. George M. Fredrickson (Englewood Cliffs, N.J.: Prentice-Hall, 1968), 45.

4. Austin, quoted in "In Defense of Lovejoy," in *Wendell Phillips on Civil Rights and Freedom,* ed. Louis Filler (New York: Hill and Wang, 1965), 6.

5. Phillips, quoted in ibid., 3, 8, 9.

6. Phillips, quoted in Richard Hofstadter, *American Political Tradition* (New York: Random House, 1954), 141, 143.

7. A Virginia newspaper, ca. 1860, quoted in Hofstadter *American Political Tradition,* 143.

8. Higginson, quoted in "The Fugitive Slave Epoch," in Jones and Jones, *The Many Voices of Boston,* 41.

9. Ann Phillips, quoted in Jane H. Pease and William H. Pease, *The Fugitive Slave Law and Anthony Burns: A Problem in Law Enforcement* (Philadelphia: Lippincott, 1975), 29–30.

10. Parker, quoted in William Bean, "Puritan versus Celt, 1850–1860," *New England Quarterly* 7 (March 1934): 70–89. The public position of Boston's Catholic Church gave credence to Parker's accusation. They remained loyal to the Democratic party in 1856, openly admired Stephen Douglas and his Kansas Nebraska Act, and agreed with the Dred Scott decision. They condemned Brown's raid in 1859, with the *Pilot,* the newspaper that spoke for the church, calling Brown a fanatic controlled by the Republicans. (Thomas H. O'Connor, *The Boston Irish: A Political History* [Boston: Northeastern University Press, 1995], 84.)

11. William Schouler, quoted in Jones and Jones, *Many Voices of Boston,* 273.

12. Taylor, quoted in Kevin Murphy, "Two Years in Blue: The Civil War Letters of Joseph K. Taylor," *Historical Journal of Massachusetts* 24 (Summer 1996): 145–63.

13. Quoted in Russell Duncan, ed., *Blue-eyed Child of Fortune: The Civil War Letters of Colonel Robert Gould Shaw* (Athens: University of Georgia Press, 1992), 32.

14. These events were reported in several Boston newspapers, e.g., see *Boston Evening Transcript,* July 15, 1863.

15. O'Connor, *The Boston Irish,* 90–94.

10. *Urbanization and the Emergence of Pluralism*

1. Carl Siracusa, *A Mechanical People: Perceptions of the Industrial Order in Massachusetts, 1810–1880* (Middletown, Conn.: Wesleyan University Press, 1979), 36.

2. Quoted in *Springfield's Ethnic Heritage: The French and French-Canadian Community* (Springfield, Mass.: USA Bicentennial Committee of Springfield, 1976), 9.

3. Ibid., 5.

4. Wright, quoted in ibid.

5. Howard M. Gitelman, *Workingmen of Waltham: Mobility in American Urban Industrial Development, 1850–1890* (Baltimore: Johns Hopkins University Press, 1974), 180.

6. John T. Cumbler, *Working-Class Community in Industrial America: Work, Leisure, and Struggle in Two Industrial Cities, 1880–1930* (Westport, Conn: Greenwood, 1979), 108.

7. Thomas A. McMullin, "The Immigrant Response to Industrialism in New Bedford, 1865–1900," in *Massachusetts in the Gilded Age: Selected Essays,* ed. Jack Tager and John Ifkovic (Amherst: University of Massachusetts Press, 1985): 117.

8. Alan Dawley, *Class and Community: The Industrial Revolution in Lynn* (Cambridge: Harvard University Press, 1976), 138.

9. Mary H. Blewett, "'We Are Freeborn American Women': The Persistent Politics of Native-Born, New England Women as Nineteenth-Century Industrial Workers," in *Labor in Massachusetts: Selected Essays,* ed. Kenneth Fones-Wolf and Martin Kaufman (Westfield: Institute for Massachusetts Studies, 1990), 127.

10. Vera Shlakman, *Economic History of a Factory Town: A Study of Chicopee, Massachusetts* (Northampton, Mass.: Smith College, 1935), 14–15, 24, 31, 35–37.

11. Constance M. Green, *Holyoke, Massachusetts: A Case History of the Industrial Revolution in America* (New Haven: Yale University Press, 1939), 12–16, 64, 116–17, 148–50, 163, 175–87, 195.

12. Solomon B. Griffin, *People and Politics Observed, by a Massachusetts Editor* (Boston: Little, Brown, 1923), 14, 3.

13. Van Wyck Brooks, *The Flowering of New England, 1815–1865* (1936; Cleveland: World Publishing, 1946), 5.

14. James Michael Curley, *I'd Do it Again: A Record of All My Uproarious Years* (Englewood Cliffs, N. J.: Prentice-Hall, 1957), 43.

15. Booker T. Washington, "The Atlantic Exposition Address" (1895) in *Up from Slavery* (1901; New York: Bantam Books, 1963), 156.

16. Roosevelt, quoted in Richard E. Welch, Jr., *George Frisbie Hoar and the Half-Breed Republicans* (Cambridge: Harvard University Press, 1971), 249n.

17. Anna Cabot, quoted in John A. Garraty, *Henry Cabot Lodge* (New York: Knopf, 1953), 5.

18. Oliver Wendell Holmes, Memorial Day address, 1895, "A Soldier's Faith," quoted in George M. Fredrickson, *The Inner Civil War: Northern Intellectuals and the Crisis of the Union* (New York: Harper and Row, 1968), 219.

19. *Touched with Fire: Civil War Letters and Diary of Oliver Wendell Holmes, Jr., 1861–1864,* ed. Mark DeWolfe Howe (Cambridge: Harvard University Press, 1946), 71, 78.

20. Holmes statement, in Harvard Class of 1861 yearbook; quoted in Mark DeWolfe Howe, *Justice Oliver Wendell Holmes: The Shaping Years, 1841–1870* (Cambridge: Harvard University Press, 1957), 76.

21. Holmes, quoted in Mark DeWolfe Howe, *Justice Oliver Wendell Holmes: The Proving Years, 1870–1882* (Cambridge: Harvard University Press, 1963), 155.

22. James M. Morton, October 9, 1937. Quoted in Felix Frankfurter, "Oliver Wendell Holmes," *Dictionary of American Biography,* Supplement One (New York: Scribner's, 1944), 21:422.

23. Hoar, quoted in Garraty, *Lodge,* 224.

24. Brandeis, quoted in Paul A. Freund, "Louis Dembitz Brandeis," *Dictionary of American Biography,* Supplement Two (New York: Scribner's, 1958), 22:94.

25. U.S. Constitution, amend. 14, sec.1.

26. Holmes, quoted in Richard Hofstadter, *Social Darwinism in American Thought,* rev. ed. (Boston: Beacon Press, 1955), 47.

27. Holmes to Franklin Ford, April 6, 1911, Holmes Letters, Harvard Law School Library, Cambridge, Mass.

28. Brandeis, May 4, 1905, address, "The Opportunity in the Law," in *Free Government in the Making: Readings in American Political Thought,* ed. Alpheus Thomas Mason, 2nd ed. (New York: Oxford University Press, 1956), 692.

29. Brandeis, January 3, 1915, address, "The Living Law," in ibid., 693.

30. Robert A. Woods, *Americans in Process* (Boston: Houghton-Mifflin, 1903), 7.

31. Wendell, quoted in Brooks, *The Flowering of New England,* 419.

## 11. *The Twentieth-Century Metropolitan Commonwealth*

1. Richard M. Abrams, *Conservatism in a Progressive Era: Massachusetts Politics, 1900–1912* (Cambridge: Harvard University Press, 1966), 20.

2. Seymour E. Harris *Economics of New England: Case Study of an Older Area* (Cambridge: Harvard University Press, 1952), 51.

3. Charles H. Trout, *Boston: The Great Depression and the New Deal* (New York: Oxford University Press, 1977), 258.

4. William Whyte, "Race Conflicts in the North End of Boston," *New England Quarterly* 12 (1939): 623–42.

5. W.E.B. Du Bois, *Dusk of Dawn: The Autobiography of a Race Concept* (New York: Schocken, 1968), 9–10.

6. Ibid., 13, 20.

7. Ibid., 31–32.

8. Ibid., 38, 39.

9. Du Bois, quoted in Dorothy B. Porter, "Maria Louise Baldwin," in *Notable American Women, 1607–1950,* ed. Edward T. James et al., 3 vols. (Cambridge: Harvard University Press, 1971), 1:87.

10. Trotter, quoted in Stephen R. Fox, *The Guardian of Boston: William Monroe Trotter* (New York: Atheneum, 1970), 175, 180, 183.

11. Henry Bedford, *Trouble Downtown: The Local Context of Twentieth-Century America* (New York: Harcourt, Brace, Jovanovich, 1978), 15.

12. O'Sullivan, quoted in John Galvin, "A Heroine for Labor Day," *Boston Globe,* September 4, 1984.

13. Calvin Coolidge, telegram to Samuel Gompers, September 14, 1919, quoted in Francis Russell, *A City in Terror: The 1919 Boston Police Strike* (New York: Viking, 1975), 191.

14. Quoted in Russell, *A City in Terror,* 195.

15. Du Bois, *Dusk of Dawn,* 40.

16. Quoted in Francis Russell, *Tragedy in Dedham: The Story of the Sacco-Vanzetti Case* (New York: McGraw-Hill, 1971), 374.

17. Lomasney, quoted in Leslie G. Ainley, *Boston Mahatma* (Boston: Bruce Humphries, 1949), 13.

18. Frederick A. Bushee, *Ethnic Factors in the Population of Boston* (New York: Macmillan, 1903), 63.

19. John Koren, *Boston, 1822–1922: The Story of Its Government and Principal Activities during One Hundred Years* (Boston: City of Boston, 1923), 62.

20. *Boston Globe,* January 9 and 10, 1910.

21. Fitzgerald quoted in Doris Kearns Goodwin, *The Fitzgeralds and the Kennedys: An American Saga* (New York: Simon and Schuster, 1987), 243.

22. James J. Connolly, *The Triumph of Ethnic Progressivism: Urban Political Culture in Boston, 1900–1925* (Cambridge, Mass.: Harvard University Press, 1998), 139. Connolly's argument is that both Fitzgerald and Curley were progressives.

23. Curley, *I'd Do It Again,* 117.

24. In response to the burgeoning need for water by the city of Boston and its suburbs, the legislature in 1922 began planning a large reservoir in the western part of the state. The choice of site was dictated in part by the position of the Swift and Ware rivers and in part by the physical setting of hills and bedrock, ideal for the necessary dams. Land acquisition required the flooding of four towns—Greenwich, Dana, Enfield, and Prescott—and several small villages. Twenty-five hundred inhabitants had to be resettled. Construction began in 1928, with the six dams completed in 1939. Considered filled by 1946, the Quabbin Reservoir began to deliver its pure water in time to meet the heightened demands of the wide-spread urbanization of eastern Massachusetts.

25. Curley, *I'd Do It Again,* 313.

26. Jack Beatty, *The Rascal King: The Life and Times of James Michael Curley, 1874–1958* (Reading, Mass.: Addison-Wesley, 1992).

27. Lawrence W. Kennedy, *Planning the City upon a Hill: Boston since 1630* (Amherst: University of Massachusetts Press, 1992), 154–55.
28. John Strahinich, "Only Irish Need Apply," *Boston Magazine* 85 (March 1993): 133.
29. In 1920 the governor's term increased from one to two years.
30. J. Joseph Huthmacher, *Massachusetts People and Politics: 1919–1930* (Cambridge: Harvard University Press, 1959), 260.
31. Curley, quoted in Charles Trout, *Boston: The Great Depression and the New Deal,* 107–8.

## 12. *Reinventing Massachusetts*

1. Bennett Harrison, "Regional Restructuring and 'Good Business Climates,'" in *Sunbelt/Snowbelt,* ed. Larry Sawers and William Tabb (New York: Oxford University Press, 1984), 68.
2. John Hekman, "The Product Cycle and New England Textiles," *Quarterly Journal of Economics* 94 (June 1980): 697–717.
3. Olsen, quoted in Glenn Rifkin and George Harrar, *The Ultimate Entrepreneur: The Story of Ken Olsen and Digital Equipment Corporation* (Chicago: Contemporary Books, 1988), 38.
4. Stata, quoted in Sarah Kuhn, *Computer Manufacturing in New England* (Cambridge, Mass.: Joint Center for Urban Studies, 1982), 36, 61.
5. Roger Bolton, "New England," in *Economic Prospects for the Northeast,* ed. Harry W. Richardson and Joseph H. Turek (Philadelphia: Temple University Press, 1985): 164–74.
6. Patricia M. Flynn, "Lowell: A High Technology Success Story," *New England Economic Review* (Sept./Oct. 1984): 39–49.
7. Lynn E. Browne and John S. Hekman, "New England's Economy in the 1980s," *New England Economic Review* (Jan./Feb. 1981): 5–28.
8. *New York Times,* March 17, 1997.
9. *Boston Globe,* May 7, 1950.
10. Ibid., March 19, 1973.
11. Ryan, quoted in ibid., January 16, 1957.
12. Ralph Lowell diaries, December 17, 1963, in the Charlotte Loring Lowell Papers, 1961–64 folder, Massachusetts Historical Society.
13. John F. Collins, "Rebuilding an Old City," *Journal of the Boston Society of Civil Engineers* 97 (January, 1961): 4.
14. Quoted in "Boston," *Architectural Forum* 120 (June 1964): 82.
15. Edward J. Logue, "Boston, 1960–1967—Seven Years of Plenty," *Proceedings of the Massachusetts Historical Society* 84 (1972): 82–96.
16. Herbert Gans, *The Urban Villagers: Group and Class in the Life of Italian Americans* (New York: Free Press, 1962, 1982), x.
17. *Boston Globe,* September 15, 1967.

18. J. Anthony Lukas, *Common Ground* (New York: Random House, 1985), 129.
19. Hicks, quoted in *Boston Globe,* May 2, 1969.
20. White, quoted in Alan Lupo, *Liberty's Chosen Home: The Politics of Violence in Boston* (1977; Boston: Beacon Press, 1988), 109.
21. White, quoted in Philip Heymann and Martha W. Weinberg, "The Paradox of Power: Mayoral Leadership on Charter Reform in Boston," in *American Politics and Public Policy,* ed. Walter Dean Burnham and Martha W. Weinberg (Cambridge: MIT Press, 1978): 297.
22. Elizabeth H. Pleck, *Black Migration and Poverty: Boston, 1865–1900* (New York: Academic Press, 1979), 7–8; Stephan Thernstrom, *The Other Bostonians: Poverty and Progress in the American Metropolis, 1880–1970* (Cambridge: Harvard University Press, 1973), 194.
23. Thernstrom, *The Other Bostonians,* 201.
24. Michael P. Conzen and George K. Lewis, *Boston: A Geographical Portrait* (Cambridge, Mass.: Ballinger Publishing, 1976), 90.
25. J. Anthony Lukas, "All in the Family: The Dilemmas of Busing and the Conflict of Values," in *Boston, 1700–1980: The Evolution of Urban Politics,* ed. Ronald P. Formisano and Constance K. Burns (Westport, Conn.: Greenwood, 1984), 248.
26. Deady, quoted in Joshua Rice, "Two Sides of Desegregation: Springfield and Boston" (master's thesis, University of Massachusetts at Amherst, December 10, 1996), 21.
27. Rose Kennedy, quoted in Richard J. Whelan, *The Founding Father: The Story of Joseph P. Kennedy and the Family He Raised to Power* (New York: New American Library, 1966), 423.
28. Robert W. Eisenmenger, *The Dynamics of Growth in the New England Economy* (Middletown, Conn.: Wesleyan University Press, 1967), 113.

# SUGGESTIONS FOR
# FURTHER READING

One of the joys of pursuing Massachusetts's history is discovering the wealth of original scholarship it has stimulated. The list that follows includes only a fraction of the excellent books that exist, and none of the articles. Readers are encouraged to pursue their interests from the leads they will find in the end-notes as well as in the citations and bibliographies published in the works cited below. These titles, spanning only the last two generations of scholarship, are a sampling of the riches that are available.

Several historical reference works supply a starting point for almost any topic: John D. Haskell Jr., ed., *Massachusetts: A Bibliography of Its History* (Boston: G. K. Hall, 1976); Martin Kaufman, John W. Ifkovic, and Joseph Carvalho III, eds., *A Guide to the History of Massachusetts* (Westport, Conn.: Greenwood, 1988); and Richard W. Wilkie and Jack Tager, eds., *Historical Atlas of Massachusetts* (Amherst: University of Massachusetts Press, 1991). In addition, Albert Bushnell Hart, ed., *Commonwealth History of Massachusetts, Colony, Province, and State* (New York: States History Company, 1927–30), a five-volume work, remains valuable for the centuries before 1920.

The colonial and revolutionary periods supply the most abundant scholarship. The first volume of Charles McLean Andrews's magisterial four-volume *The Colonial Period of American History* (New Haven: Yale University Press, 1934) won a Pulitzer Prize and remains a lucid account of the institutional origins and early years of the Plymouth and Massachusetts Bay settlements. Even more influential among scholars have been Perry Miller's dense analyses of Puritan thought: *The New England Mind: The Seventeenth Century* (1939; Cambridge: Harvard University Press, 1954) and *The New England Mind: From Colony to Province* (Cambridge: Harvard University Press, 1953). See also Darren Staloff, *The Making of an American Thinking Class: Intellectuals and Intelligentsia in Puritan Massachusetts* (New York: Oxford University Press, 1998). One of the most distinguished American historians of the twentieth century, Samuel Eliot Morison, presented a dozen readable portraits of the Puritan elite in *Builders of the Bay Colony* (1930; Boston: Houghton Mifflin, 1958).

For precolonial inhabitants there are two powerful studies: Howard S. Russell, *Indian New England before the Mayflower* (Hanover, N.H.: University Press of New England, 1980); and Neal Salisbury, *Manitou and Providence: Indians, Europeans, and the Making of New England, 1500–1643* (New York: Oxford University Press, 1982). These works are complemented by an important study that treats the Indian-European transition, William Cronon's *Changes in the Land: Indians, Colonists, and the Ecology of New England* (New York: Hill and Wang, 1983).

Early English settlement is treated in many works and from a variety of perspectives. Among migration studies readers will want to consult David Grayson Allen, *In English Ways: The Movement of Societies and the Transferal of English Local Law and Custom to Massachusetts Bay in the Seventeenth Century* (Chapel Hill: University of North Carolina Press, 1981); Virginia DeJohn Anderson, *New England's Generation: The Great Migration and the Formation of Society and Culture in the Seventeenth Century* (Cambridge: Cambridge University Press, 1991); and David Cressy, *Coming Over: Migration and Communication between England and New England in the Seventeenth Century* (New York: Cambridge University Press, 1987). A migration study that is also the first of the modern community studies is the history of Sudbury presented in Sumner Chilton Powell's *Puritan Village: The Formation of a New England Town* (Middletown, Conn.: Wesleyan University Press, 1963). The key study of early Boston is Darrett B. Rutman's *Winthrop's Boston* (Chapel Hill: University of North Carolina Press, 1965). For early Plymouth, see George D. Langdon Jr., *Pilgrim Colony: A History of New Plymouth, 1620–1691* (New Haven: Yale University Press, 1966). For the history of family and community, Philip J. Greven Jr.'s *Four Generations: Population, Land, and Family in Colonial Andover, Massachusetts* (Ithaca: Cornell University Press, 1970) has been influential. A communitarian interpretation distinguishes Kenneth A. Lockridge, *A New England Town, The First Hundred Years: Dedham, Massachusetts, 1636–1736* (New York: Norton, 1970). The hierarchical and profit-oriented elements of early settlement are evident in Stephen Innes, *Labor in a New Land: Economy and Society in Seventeenth-Century Springfield* (Princeton: Princeton University Press, 1983), and in John Frederick Martin, *Profits in the Wilderness: Entrepreneurship and the Founding of New England Towns in the Seventeenth Century* (Chapel Hill: University of North Carolina Press, 1991). Some perspectives on legal culture are provided in David Thomas Konig, *Law and Society in Puritan Massachusetts: Essex County, 1629–1692* (Chapel Hill: University of North Carolina Press, 1979). Richard S. Dunn supplies a commentary on elite leadership in *Puritans and Yankees: The Winthrop Dynasty of New England, 1630–1717* (Princeton: Princeton University Press, 1962). See also, James G. Moseley, *John Winthrop's World: History as a Story, the Story as History* (Madison: University of Wisconsin Press, 1992); Kenneth Silverman, *The Life and Times of Cotton Mather* (New York: Harper and Row, 1984); and Selma R. Williams, *Divine Rebel: The Life of Anne Marbury Hutchinson* (New York: Holt, Rinehart and Winston, 1981). For popular culture, see Roger Thompson, *Sex in Middlesex: Popular Mores in a Massachusetts County, 1649–1699* (Amherst: University of Massachusetts Press, 1986). A religious perspective is sketched in Francis J. Bremer, *The Puritan Experiment: New England Society from Bradford to Edwards* (New York: St. Martin's, 1976), and on religious politics in James F. Cooper, *Tenacious of Their Liberties: The Congregationalists in Colonial Massachusetts* (New York: Oxford University Press, 1999).

Warfare with the Native Americans was a crucial part of Massachusetts's seventeenth-century history. Two military accounts are Douglas Edward Leach's, *Flintlock and Tomahawk: New England in King Philip's War* (New York: Macmillan, 1958) and Alden T. Vaughan's, *The New England Frontier: Puritans and Indians, 1620–1675* (Boston: Little, Brown, 1965). For a cultural interpretation see Jill Lepore, *The Name of War: King Philip's War and the Origins of American Identity* (New York: Knopf, 1998). See also, Jean M. O'Brien, *Dispossession by Degrees: Indian Land and Identity in Natick, Massachusetts, 1650–1790* (Cambridge: Cambridge University Press, 1997); Richard W. Cogley, *John Eliot's Mission to the Indians before King Philip's War* (Cambridge: Harvard University Press, 1999).

Witchcraft beliefs were an important part of the culture of the settlers, and there are several revealing studies of their impact: John Putnam Demos, *Entertaining Satan: Witchcraft and the Culture of Early New England* (New York: Oxford University Press, 1982); Carol F. Karlsen, *The Devil in the Shape of a Woman: Witchcraft in Colonial New England* (New York: Norton, 1987); Paul Boyer and Stephen Nissenbaum, *Salem Possessed: The Social Origins of Witchcraft* (Cambridge: Harvard University Press, 1974); and Richard Weisman, *Witchcraft, Magic, and Religion in Seventeenth-Century Massachusetts* (Amherst: University of Massachusetts Press, 1984). In addition, Marion L. Starkey has written a popular account, *The Devil in Massachusetts: A Modern Inquiry into the Salem Witch Trials* (New York: Knopf, 1949).

There is a wide array of works treating eighteenth-century Massachusetts. Among the broad-ranging studies, Michael Zuckerman's *Peaceable Kingdoms: New England Towns in the Eighteenth Century* (New York: Knopf, 1970) concentrates on rural Massachusetts communities. Douglas Lamar Jones considers the same period in *Village and Seaport: Migration and Society in Eighteenth-*

*Century Massachusetts* (Hanover, N.H.: University Press of New England, 1981). Several topical studies of special interest are William E. Nelson, *Dispute and Conflict Resolution in Plymouth County, Massachusetts, 1725–1825* (Chapel Hill: University of North Carolina Press, 1981); Fred Anderson, *A People's Army: Massachusetts Soldiers and Society in the Seven Years' War* (Chapel Hill: University of North Carolina Press, 1984); Richard L. Bushman, *King and People in Provincial Massachusetts* (Chapel Hill: University of North Carolina Press, 1985); David W. Conroy, *In Public Houses: Drink and the Revolution of Authority in Colonial Massachusetts* (Chapel Hill: University of North Carolina Press, 1995); and Daniel Vickers, *Farmers and Fishermen: Two Centuries of Work in Essex County, Massachusetts, 1630–1830* (Chapel Hill: University of North Carolina Press, 1994). For treatment of particular individuals, towns, and regions see G. B. Warden, *Boston, 1689–1776* (Boston: Little, Brown, 1970); Christopher M. Jedry, *The World of John Cleaveland: Family and Community in Eighteenth-Century New England* (New York: Norton, 1979), which is set in Chebacco parish in the town of Ipswich; Patricia J. Tracy, *Jonathan Edwards, Pastor: Religion and Society in Eighteenth-Century Northampton* (New York: Hill and Wang, 1980); Christine Leigh Heyrman, *Commerce and Culture: The Maritime Communities of Colonial Massachusetts, 1690–1750* (New York: Norton, 1984); Benjamin W. Labaree, *Patriots and Partisans: The Merchants of Newburyport, 1764–1815* (New York: Norton, 1975); Gregory H. Nobles, *Division throughout the Whole: Politics and Society in Hampshire County, Massachusetts, 1740–1775* (New York: Cambridge University Press, 1983); and Robert J. Taylor, *Western Massachusetts in the Revolution* (Providence: Brown University Press, 1954).

The minority, non-European inhabitants of Massachusetts are treated in : Lorenzo J. Greene, *The Negro in Colonial New England, 1620–1776* (New York: Columbia University Press, 1942); William D. Piersen, *Black Yankees: The Development of an Afro-American Subculture in Eighteenth-Century New England* (Amherst: University of Massachusetts Press, 1988); Yasuhide Kawashima, *Puritan Justice and the Indian: White Man's Law in Massachusetts, 1630–1763* (Middletown, Conn.: Wesleyan University Press, 1986); and Daniel Mandell, *Behind the Frontier: Indians in Eighteenth-Century Eastern Massachusetts* (Lincoln: University of Nebraska Press, 1996).

Just as Massachusetts figures prominently in the history of English settlement of North America, so does it command attention in the era of the American Revolution and, to a lesser extent, the early republic. For Massachusetts people, the Revolution was in many respects an intensely personal and local affair. The following studies convey how closely intertwined micro- and macro-historical events were during the independence movement and the formation of the United States: John J. Waters Jr., *The Otis Family in Provincial and*

*Revolutionary Massachusetts* (Chapel Hill: University of North Carolina Press, 1968); Hiller B. Zobel, *The Boston Massacre* (New York: Norton, 1970); Richard D. Brown, *Revolutionary Politics in Massachusetts: The Boston Committee of Correspondence and the Towns, 1772–1774* (Cambridge: Harvard University Press, 1970); Benjamin Woods Labaree, *The Boston Tea Party* (New York: Oxford University Press, 1964); John W. Tyler, *Smugglers and Patriots: Boston Merchants and the Advent of the American Revolution* (Boston: Northeastern University Press, 1986); William Pencak, *War, Politics, and Revolution in Provincial Massachusetts* (Boston: Northeastern University Press, 1981); and *America's Burke: The Mind of Thomas Hutchinson* (Washington, D.C.: University Press of America, 1982); and Bernard Bailyn, *The Ordeal of Thomas Hutchinson* (Cambridge.: Harvard University Press, 1974); Andrew S. Walmsley, *Thomas Hutchinson and the Origins of the American Revolution* (New York: New York University Press, 1999); Esther Forbes, *Paul Revere and the World He Lived In* (Boston: Houghton Mifflin, 1942); Jane Triber, *A True Republican: The Life of Paul Revere* (Amherst: University of Massachusetts Press, 1998); Robert A. Gross, *The Minutemen and Their World* (New York: Hill and Wang, 1976); and David Hackett Fischer, *Paul Revere's Ride* (New York: Oxford University Press, 1994). William Fowler wrote two studies of important Revolutionary leaders: *The Baron of Beacon Hill: A Biography of John Hancock* (Boston: Houghton Mifflin, 1980) and *Samuel Adams: Radical Puritan* (New York: Longman, 1997).

For the years after independence, the period leading up to the formation of the national government under the Constitution, and the era of early national politics, some of the important studies are: Stephen E. Patterson, *Political Parties in Revolutionary Massachusetts* (Madison: University of Wisconsin Press, 1973); Van Beck Hall, *Politics without Parties: Massachusetts, 1780–1791* (Pittsburgh: University of Pittsburgh Press, 1972); David P. Szatmary, *Shays' Rebellion: The Making of an Agrarian Insurrection* (Amherst: University of Massachusetts Press, 1980); Robert A. Gross, ed., *In Debt to Shays: The Bicentennial of an Agrarian Rebellion* (Charlottesville: University Press of Virginia, 1993); Martin Kaufman, ed., *Shays' Rebellion: Selected Essays* (Westfield: Institute for Massachusetts Studies, 1987); Marion L. Starkey, *A Little Rebellion* (New York: Knopf, 1955); William E. Nelson, *Americanization of Common Law: The Impact of Legal Change on Massachusetts Society, 1760–1830* (Cambridge: Harvard University Press, 1975); Paul Goodman, *The Democratic-Republicans of Massachusetts* (Cambridge: Harvard University Press, 1964); James M. Banner Jr., *To the Hartford Convention: The Federalists and the Origins of Politics in Massachusetts* (New York: Knopf, 1970). The economic history of the first half of the nineteenth century is illuminated in Samuel Eliot Morison's *The Maritime History of Massachusetts, 1783–1860* (Boston:

Houghton Mifflin, 1961) and in George Sweet Gibb's *The Saco-Lowell Shops: Textile Machinery Building in New England, 1813–1949* (Cambridge: Harvard University Press, 1950). On commerce and fishing, see Edward Byers, *The Nation of Nantucket: Society and Politics in an Early American Commercial Center, 1680–1820* (Cambridge: Harvard University Press, 1986); J. R. Dolan, *The Yankee Peddlers of Early America* (New York: Potter, 1964); Edward C. Kirkland, *Men, Cities, and Transportation: A Study in New England History, 1820–1900* (Cambridge: Harvard University Press, 1948). On agriculture, see Howard S. Russell, *A Long Deep Furrow: Three Centuries of Farming in New England* (Hanover, N.H.: University Press of New England, 1976), and Clarence H. Danhof, *Change in Agriculture: The Northern United States, 1820–1870* (Cambridge: Harvard University Press, 1969). For regional studies, see John L. Brooke, *The Heart of the Commonwealth: Society and Political Culture in Worcester County, Massachusetts, 1713–1861* (1989; Amherst: University of Massachusetts Press, 1992); Christopher Clark, *The Roots of Rural Capitalism: Western Massachusetts, 1780–1860* (Ithaca: Cornell University Press, 1990); Robert Doherty, *Society and Power: Five New England Towns, 1800–1860* (Amherst: University of Massachusetts Press, 1977), a comparative statistical study of five communities analyzing social and economic mobility; and Alan Taylor, *Liberty Men and Great Proprietors: The Revolutionary Settlement on the Maine Frontier, 1760–1820* (Chapel Hill: University of North Carolina Press for the Institute of Early American History and Culture, 1990).

There are a host of thoughtful works on the industrial revolution and its impact. Oscar Handlin and Mary Flug Handlin's *Commonwealth, a Study of the Role of Government in the American Economy: Massachusetts, 1774–1861* (New York: New York University Press, 1947) explores a central theme in Massachusetts development. Specific studies include Robert F. Dalzell, *Enterprising Elite: The Boston Associates and the World They Made* (Cambridge: Harvard University Press, 1987), which should be read in conjunction with the earlier work by Ronald Story, *The Forging of an Aristocracy: Harvard and the Boston Upper Class, 1800–1870* (Middletown, Conn.: Wesleyan University Press, 1980). Other works include Alan Dawley, *Class and Community: The Industrial Revolution in Lynn* (Cambridge: Harvard University Press, 1976); Paul Faler, *Mechanics and Manufacturers in the Early Industrial Revolution: Lynn, Massachusetts, 1780–1860* (Albany: State University Press of New York, 1981); Conrad Edick Wright and Katheryn Viens, eds., *Entrepreneurs: The Boston Business Community, 1700–1850* (Boston: Massachusetts Historical Society, 1997); John S. Garner, *The Model Company Town: Urban Design through Private Enterprise in Nineteenth-Century New England* (Amherst: University of Massachusetts Press, 1984); Gary Kulik, Roger Parks, and Theodore Z. Penn, eds., *The New England Mill Village, 1790–1860* (Cambridge: MIT Press, 1982); Judith McGaw, *Most Wonderful Machine: Mechanization and Social Change in Berkshire Paper Making, 1801–1885* (Princeton: Princeton University Press, 1987); Jonathan Prude, *The Coming of the Industrial Order: Town and Factory Life in Rural Massachusetts, 1810–1860* (New York: Cambridge University Press, 1983); Winifred Rothenberg, *From Market-Places to a Market Economy: The Transformation of Rural Massachusetts, 1750–1850* (Chicago: University of Chicago Press, 1992), and Carl Siracusa, *A Mechanical People: Perceptions of the Industrial Order in Massachusetts, 1815–1880* (Middletown, Conn.: Wesleyan University Press, 1979).

For the early nineteenth-century growth of Boston beginning with the "great mayor," Josiah Quincy, and the decline of the Federalists, see Matthew Crocker, *The Magic of the Many: Josiah Quincy and the Rise of Mass Politics in Boston, 1800–1830* (Amherst: University of Massachusetts Press, 1999), and Roger Lane, *Policing the City: Boston, 1822–1885* (New York: Atheneum, 1971). Other works about Boston's elite, besides Dalzell's and Story's are—to name a few: Tamara P. Thornton, *Cultivating Gentlemen: The Meaning of Country Life among the Boston Elite, 1785–1860* (New Haven: Yale University Press, 1989); Betty Farrell, *Elite Families: Class and Power in Nineteenth-Century Boston* (Albany: State University of New York Press, 1993); and Frederic Cople Jaher, *The Urban Establishment: Upper Strata in Boston, New York, Charleston, Chicago, and Los Angeles* (Urbana: University of Illinois Press, 1982). A good introduction to Boston politics are the essays in Ronald Formisano and Constance Burns, eds., *Boston, 1700–1980: The Evolution of Urban Politics* (Westport, Conn.: Greenwood, 1984). For Boston during the Civil War see *Thomas H. O'Connor, Civil War Boston: Home Front and Battlefield* (Boston: Northeastern University Press, 1997). For Boston's demography, see Peter Knights's population study, *The Plain People of Boston, 1830–1860* (New York: Oxford University Press, 1971), and his sequel *Yankee Destinies: The Lives of Nineteenth-Century Ordinary Bostonians* (Chapel Hill: University of North Carolina Press, 1991). On the remarkable story of Boston's fill-ins to create more land and the steady expansion of the city, one must begin with the classic work of Walter Muir Whitehill, *Boston: A Topographical History* (1959; Cambridge: Harvard University Press, 1968). Other fine studies on this subject are Lawrence Kennedy's *Planning the City upon a Hill: Boston since 1630* (Amherst: University of Massachusetts Press. 1992), and, Douglass Shand-Tucci's *Built in Boston: City and Suburb, 1800–2000*, rev. ed. (Amherst: University of Massachusetts Press, 2000).

For consideration of women in society and culture there are Nancy Cott, *The Bonds of Womanhood: Woman's Sphere in New England, 1780–1835* (New Haven: Yale University Press, 1970); Susan Juster, *Disorderly Women:*

*Sexual Politics and Evangelicalism in Revolutionary New England* (Ithaca: Cornell University Press, 1994); Laurel Thatcher Ulrich, *A Midwife's Tale: The Life of Martha Ballard, Based on Her Diary, 1785–1812* (New York: Knopf, 1990); Martha H. Verbrugge, *Able-bodied Womanhood: Personal Health and Social Change in Nineteenth-Century Boston* (New York: Oxford University Press, 1988); Thomas Dublin *Women at Work: The Transformation of Work and Community in Lowell, Massachusetts, 1826–1860* (New York: Columbia University Press, 1979), and Dublin's collection of women's letters, *Farm to Factory: Women's Letters, 1830–1860* (New York: Columbia University Press, 1981); Susan L. Porter, ed., *Women of the Commonwealth: Work, Family, and Social Change in Nineteenth-Century Massachusetts* (Amherst: University of Massachusetts Press, 1996). A fascinating study of the Bay State's women shoe workers is Mary Blewett's *Men, Women, and Work: Class, Gender, and Protest in the New England Shoe Industry* (Urbana: University of Illinois Press, 1988). Blewett also edited an oral history of workers in the textile industry, *The Last Generation: Work and Life in the Textile Mills of Lowell, Massachusetts, 1910–1960* (Amherst: University of Massachusetts Press, 1990). A recent work is Ardis Cameron's *Radicals of the Worst Sort: Laboring Women in Lawrence, Massachusetts, 1860–1912* (Urbana: University of Illinois Press, 1993). Among the many fine histories of workingmen, see Henry Bedford's *Socialism and the Workers in Massachusetts, 1886–1912* (Amherst: University of Massachusetts Press, 1966); Mark Erlich's *With These Hands* (Philadelphia: Temple University Press, 1988), a history of the state's carpenters; James Green and Hugh Donahue's *Boston's Workers* (Boston: Boston Public Library, 1980); and a major study of unemployment in the Bay State, Alexander Keyssar's *Out of Work: The First Century of Unemployment in Massachusetts* (New York: Cambridge University Press, 1986). A study of working-class life in Worcester is Roy Rosenzweig, *Eight Hours for What We Will: Workers and Leisure in an Industrial City, 1870–1920* (New York: Cambridge University Press, 1983). Studies of mobility include Howard M. Gitelman, *Workingmen of Waltham: Mobility in American Urban Industrial Development, 1850–1890* (Baltimore: Johns Hopkins University Press, 1974); Michael Frisch, *Town into City: Springfield and the Meaning of Community, 1840–1880* (Cambridge: Harvard University Press, 1972); William Hartford, *Working People of Holyoke: Class and Ethnicity in a Massachusetts Mill Town, 1850–1960* (New Brunswick, N J.: Rutgers University Press, 1990); and two works by Stephan Thernstrom, *Poverty and Progress: Social Mobility in a Nineteenth-Century City* (Cambridge: Harvard University Press, 1964) and *The Other Bostonians: Poverty and Progress in the American Metropolis, 1880–1970* (Cambridge: Harvard University Press, 1973).

Massachusetts reformers have been studied chiefly through the medium of individual biography; however, there are some outstanding general works. *The*

*Unitarian Conscience: Harvard Moral Philosophy, 1805–1861* (Cambridge: Harvard University Press, 1970), by Daniel Walker Howe, reveals the patterns of thought and belief that conditioned many of the reformers and their constituents. Christopher Clark explores the views of radical critics of industrializing America in his study of the rise and fall of a Northampton utopian commune in *The Communitarian Moment: The Radical Challenge of the Northampton Association* (Ithaca: Cornell University Press, 1995). Gerald N. Grob's *The State and the Mentally Ill: A History of Worcester State Hospital in Massachusetts, 1830–1920* (Chapel Hill: University of North Carolina Press, 1966) is a penetrating analysis of reformers in action within the framework of current medical thought as well as state politics. A new look at abolitionist William Lloyd Garrison is Henry Mayer, *All on Fire: William Lloyd Garrison and the Abolition of Slavery* (New York: St. Martin's, 1998). A study combining history and literature is Albert J. Von Frank, *The Trials of Anthony Burns: Freedom and Slavery in Emerson's Boston* (Cambridge: Harvard University Press, 1998), and Gary Collison, *Shadrach Minkins: From Fugitive Slave to Citizen* (Cambridge: Harvard University Press, 1997). See also, Richard H. Abbott, *Cotton and Capital: Boston Businessmen and Antislavery Reform, 1854–1868* (Amherst: University of Massachusetts Press, 1991), and Donald M. Jacobs, ed., *Courage and Conscience: Black and White Abolitionists in Boston* (Bloomington: Indiana University Press, 1993). Two books on social services for children are Peter Holloran, *Boston's Wayward Children: Social Services for Homeless Children, 1830–1930* (Rutherford, N.J.: Fairleigh Dickinson University Press, 1989), and Eric C. Schneider, *In the Web of Class: Delinquents and Reformers in Boston, 1810s-1930s* (New York: New York University Press, 1992). For a study of the elderly, see Brian Gratton, *Urban Elders: Family, Work, and Welfare among Boston's Aged, 1890–1950* (Philadelphia: Temple University Press, 1986); on abused women, see Linda Gordon, *Heroes of Their Own Lives: The Politics and History of Family Violence, Boston, 1860–1960* (New York: Viking, 1988).

Oscar Handlin's searching examination of the arrival of the Irish and their place in Massachusetts, *Boston's Immigrants,* rev. ed. (Cambridge: Harvard University Press, 1959), is a classic not only of Massachusetts but of United States history. A more recent and indispensable work is Thomas O'Connor's *The Boston Irish: A Political History* (Boston: Northeastern University Press, 1995). Among other valuable works on the Irish are Brian C. Mitchell, *The Paddy Camps: The Irish of Lowell, 1821–61* (Urbana: University of Illinois Press, 1987), and John F. Stack Jr., *International Conflict in an American City: Boston's Irish, Italians, and Jews, 1935–1944* (Westport, Conn.: Greenwood, 1979); Gerald H. Gamm, *Urban Exodus: Why the Jews Left Boston and the Catholics Stayed* (Cambridge: Harvard University Press, 1999). To discover how Catholicism fared in Boston, see Thomas O'Connor, *Fitzpatrick's Boston, 1846–1866: John Bernard Fitzpatrick, Third Bishop of Boston* (Boston: Northeastern University Press, 1984); Paula M. Kane, *Separatism and Subculture: Boston Catholicism, 1900–1920* (Chapel Hill: University of North Carolina Press, 1994), and James M. O'Toole, *Militant and Triumphant: William Henry O'Connell and the Catholic Church in Boston, 1859–1944* (Notre Dame: University of Notre Dame Press, 1992). A few representative samples of ethnic studies are Paula J. Todisco, *Boston's First Neighborhood: The North End* (Boston: Boston Public Library, 1976); Gerard J. Brault, *The French-Canadian Heritage in New England* (Hanover, N.H.: University Press of New England, 1986); Lawrence Harmon and Hillel Levine, *The Death of an American Jewish Community: A Tragedy of Good Intentions* (New York: Free Press, 1992); Marilyn Halter, *Between Race and Ethnicity: Cape Verdean American Immigrants, 1860–1965* (Urbana: University of Illinios Press, 1993), and Jerry R. Williams, *And Yet They Come: Portuguese Immigration from the Azores to the United States* (New York: Center for Migration Studies, 1982).

For works on the post–Civil War and the early-twentieth-century development of Lynn, Fall River, Lawrence, Worcester, and Lowell respectively, see John T. Cumbler, *Working-Class Community in Industrial America: Work, Leisure and Struggle in Two Industrial Cities, 1880–1930* (Westport, Conn.: Greenwood, 1979); Donald B. Cole, *Immigrant City: Lawrence, Massachusetts, 1845–1921* (Chapel Hill: University of North Carolina Press, 1963); and Marc Miller, *Irony of Victory: World War II and Lowell, Massachusetts* (Urbana: University of Illinois Press, 1988). The classic study of the metropolitan growth of Boston is Sam Bass Warner Jr., *Streetcar Suburbs: The Process of Growth in Boston, 1870–1900* (Cambridge: Harvard University Press, 1962).

For changes in state politics, see Ronald P. Formisano, *The Transformation of Political Culture: Massachusetts Parties, 1790s–1840s* (New York: Oxford University Press, 1983); Harlow W. Sheidley, *Sectional Nationalism: Massachusetts Conservative Leaders and the Transformation of America, 1815–1836* (Boston: Northeastern University Press, 1998); John R. Mulkern, *The Know-Nothing Party in Massachusetts* (Boston: Northeastern University Press, 1990); and Dale Baum, *The Civil War Party System: The Case of Massachusetts, 1848–1876* (Chapel Hill: University of North Carolina Press, 1984). Geoffrey Blodgett's study of post–Civil War political reformers illuminates politics and society broadly, considering the monographic focus of *The Gentle Reformers: Massachusetts Democrats in the Cleveland Era* (Cambridge: Harvard University Press, 1966). Valuable essays on a wide variety of issues can be found in Jack Tager and John W. Ifkovic, eds., *Massachusetts in the Gilded Age: Selected Essays* (Amherst: University of Massachusetts Press, 1985). The politics of the late nineteenth and early twentieth centuries are treated in Richard M.

Abrams, *Conservatism in a Progressive Era: Massachusetts Politics, 1900–1912* (Cambridge: Harvard University Press, 1964) and J. Joseph Huthmacher, *Massachusetts People and Politics, 1919–1933* (Cambridge: Harvard University Press, 1959). On Boston's politics see Charles H. Trout, *Boston: The Great Depression and the New Deal* (New York: Oxford University Press, 1977); James J. Connolly, *The Triumph of Ethnic Progressivism: Urban Political Culture in Boston, 1900–1925* (Cambridge: Harvard University Press, 1998); and Gerald H. Gamm, *The Making of New Deal Democrats: Voting Behavior and Realignment in Boston, 1920–1940* (Chicago: University of Chicago Press, 1989). Two popular studies of dramatic episodes by Francis Russell are both informative and insightful: *A City in Terror: The 1919 Boston Police Strike* (New York: Viking, 1975) and *Tragedy in Dedham: The Story of the Sacco-Vanzetti Case* (New York: McGraw Hill, 1971). A major study of the origins of the Kennedy dynasty is Doris Kearns Goodwin's impressive *The Fitzgeralds and the Kennedys: An American Saga* (New York: Simon and Schuster, 1987).

For the economic situation in the post–World War II period, see Robert W. Eisenmenger, *The Dynamics of Growth in the New England Economy* (Middletown, Conn.: Wesleyan University Press, 1967), and Bennett Harrison, *Rationalization, Restructuring and Industrial Reorganization in Older Regions: The Economic Transformation of New England since World War II* (Cambridge: MIT Press, 1982). For a study of labor unions and their attempt to forestall deindustrialization, see William Hartford's look at Fall River, New Bedford, and Lawrence, *Where Is Our Responsibility? Unions and Economic Change in the New England Textile Industry, 1870–1960* (Amherst: University of Massachusetts Press, 1996). Another study of industrial decline is Laurence F. Gross's *The Course of Industrial Decline: The Boott Cotton Mills of Lowell, Massachusetts, 1835–1955* (Baltimore: Johns Hopkins University Press, 1993). For high-tech development, see Karl L. Wildes, *A Century of Electrical Engineering and Computer Science at MIT, 1882–1982* (Cambridge: MIT Press, 1985), and Dorothy Nelkin, *The University and Military Research: Moral Politics at M.I.T.* (Ithaca: Cornell University Press, 1972). For the development of service industries, see A. A. Bright, ed., *The Economic State of New England: Report of the Committee of New England of the National Planning Association*, 2 vols. (New Haven: Yale University Press, 1954). On higher education, see Richard M. Freeland, *Academia's Golden Age: Universities in Massachusetts, 1945–1970* (New York: Oxford University Press, 1992). For suburbanization and metropolitan growth, see Matthew Edel, Elliot D. Sclar, and Daniel Luria, *Shaky Palaces: Homeownership and Social Mobility in Boston's Suburbanization,*(New York: Columbia University Press, 1984); Henry Binford, *The First Suburbs: Residential Communities on the Boston Periphery, 1815–1860* (Chicago: University of Chicago Press, 1984), and Sam Bass Warner Jr., *The*

*Way We Really Live: Social Change in Metropolitan Boston since 1920* (Boston: Boston Public Library, 1977). For problems such as urban renewal and its effects upon the neighborhoods and ethnic and racial tensions in Boston, see Herbert Gans, *The Urban Villagers: Group and Class in the Life of Italian Americans* (1962; New York: Free Press, 1982); John Mollenkopf, *The Contested City* (Princeton: Princeton University Press, 1983); J. Anthony Lukas, *Common Ground* (New York: Knopf, 1985); Alan Lupo, *Liberty's Chosen Home: The Politics of Violence in Boston* (1977; Boston: Beacon Press, 1988), and the definitive study by Thomas H. O'Connor, *Building a New Boston: Politics and Urban Renewal, 1950–1960* (Boston: Northeastern University Press, 1993). A history of Boston's early black migration is found in Elizabeth H. Pleck, *Black Migration and Poverty: Boston, 1865–1900* (New York: Academic Press, 1979). On Boston's black elite, see Adelaide M. Cromwell, *The Other Brahmins: Boston's Black Upper Class, 1750–1950* (Fayetteville: University of Arkansas Press, 1994). The major historical analysis of the turmoil surrounding busing is Ronald P. Formisano, *Boston against Busing: Race, Class, Ethnicity in the 1960s and 1970s* (Chapel Hill: University of North Carolina Press, 1991).

# INDEX

Anderson, Harlan, 280–81
Andover (Massachusetts), 146–47
Andrew, John A., 196
Andros, Sir Edmund, 48–50, 59
Anglicans, 17, 21, 30, 48, 49, 52
Anthony, Susan B., 156
Anti-Imperialist League, 225
Appleton, Nathan, 123, 126, 128, 133, 176
Appleton Company, 246
Appleton family, 158
*Arbella* (ship), 20–21
ARD (American Research and Development), 280–81
Armenian immigrants, 214
Asian immigrants, 276, 289
Atkins, Thomas, 302
*Atlantic Monthly,* 190
Attucks, Crispus, 221
Austin, James T., 187
Austrian immigrants, 206, 243
Avco-Lycoming, 279

Bacigalupo, Edward A., 273
Back Bay (Boston), 215
Bacon, Francis, 11
Bagley, Sarah, 136
Balch, Emily Greene, 255
Baldwin, Maria Louise, 250–51
Baltimore (Maryland), 202
Banks, 128, 170, 278
Banneker Club, 250
Baptists, 49, 52, 95, 110, 111
Barnstable (Massachusetts), 34, 80
Bartlett, Ezekiel, 183
Barton, Charles, 132
Barton, Clara, 196–97
Bates, Polly Ann, 190
Beacon Hill (Boston), 198, 300
Beacon Manufacturing Company, 246
Beatty, Jack, 268
Beecher, Lyman, 174
"Benefit of Clergy," 69
Benton, Thomas Hart, 169
Berkshire County (Massachusetts), 100, 102, 114, 117, 286
Berkshire Hills, 2, 4

Bernard, Francis, 59, 67, 96
Bill of Rights, 108, 109
Blackstone Canal, 125–26, 213
Blackstone River, 120, 121
Blackwell, Alice Stone, 156
Blackwell, Henry, 156
Blaine, James G., 224, 228, 229, 235
Blakely, Gerald, 284
Blewett, Mary, 209
Bliss, George, 210
"Bodies of the People," 64
Bolling, Royal, 302
Bootmaking. *See* Shoemaking
Boott, Kirk, 128
Boott and Sons, 123
Borden Manufacturing Interests, 246
Boston (Massachusetts): and abolitionism, 185, 186; African Americans in, 181–82, 191, 198, 296–97, 300–304; blockade of, 79, 81, 82, 90; British troops stationed in, 67–70; as capital of Massachusetts, 58; Catholic church in, 173, 324n.10; charters for, 137, 138, 262, 266, 267, 269, 299–300; commerce and investors in, 36, 75, 114, 120–21, 126–28, 243, 288, 315; constitutional convention in, 94; Great Awakening in, 54; growth of, 215, 244; as hub of Dominion of New England, 47; Irish immigrants in, 173, 178–79, 215, 218–21, 260, 300; Loyalists in, 85–86; manufacturing in, 114, 137, 214–16; mayors of, 199, 260–70, 290–95, 297–300, 303–4; police strike in, 253, 256–58, 266; population growth in, 137, 173, 178, 215, 242, 244, 247; as port city, 52, 243; pre–Revolutionary War activities in, vii, 64–69, 71–72, 75–80; reform movements in, 149; riots in, 177, 198–99; school system in, 181–82, 300–304, 312; settlement of, 27; twentieth-century transformation of, 286, 290–304; urban renewal in, 291–95; wealth in, 51, 167. *See also* Suburbs; *Particular parts of Boston*
Boston and Albany Railroad, 202, 246

Cotton manufacture. *See* Textiles

Council for the Safety of the People, 49

Council of New England, 26

County conventions: pre-revolutionary, 80–82, 86; on Shays's Rebellion, 101–2

Covenants: in Dedham, 37–38, 40; "halfway," 40, 44–45, 51, 53; of Puritanism, 21–22, 94–95

Cox, Channing H., 272

Cradock, Matthew, 18, 19

Craft, Ellen, 191

Craft, William, 191

Crane, Winthrop M., 272

Crawford, William, 141

Crédit Mobilier, 224

Cromwell, Oliver, 47

Cross, Charles, 278

Cuba, 225

Cumbler, John, 207

Curley, James Michael, 216, 260, 263–70, 272–73, 290–92, 310

Cushing, John, 126

Dalzell, Robert, 127

Dana, Richard Henry, Jr., 191

Darling, Arthur B., 166

Dartmouth College case, 168

Darwin, Charles, 237

Data General, 279

Dawes, William, 84

Dawley, Alan, 208

Day, John, Jr., 296

Day, John, Sr., 296

Day, Julia, 296

Deady, John, 305–6

DEC. *See* Digital Equipment Corporation

Declaration of Independence, 86–87, 99, 223

Declaratory Act (of Parliament), 65

Dedham (Massachusetts), 37–41, 44

Defense industries, 275, 280–85, 287, 314

Deists, 110–11

Democratic Party, 141; and Boston mayors, 199, 260–70, 290–95, 297–300, 303–4; Irish support for, 173, 180, 194, 199, 214, 217–18, 220–22, 270,

273; rise of, in Massachusetts, 271–72; strength of, in Massachusetts, 311–13; support for, in Gilded Age, 216–21

Democratic-Republican Party, 89, 107–8, 111–12, 116, 140–41

Denison Settlement House (Boston), 255

Depressions (economic): in nineteenth century, 166, 172, 211–12; in twentieth century, 242, 246–47

Derby family, 91

Dever, Paul, 307, 311

Dexter, Franklin, 176

Dickinson, Emily, 190

Digital Equipment Corporation (DEC), 279, 280–82

Dix, Dorothea, 148–54, 157

Dominion of New England, 47–48, 51

Dorchester (Massachusetts), 27, 215

Dorchester Company, 18, 27

Douglas, Stephen A., 199, 324n.10

Douglass, Frederick, 196, 251

Draft riots, 198–99

Drake, Sir Francis, 11

Draper Laboratories, 279

Du Bois, W.E.B., 248–52, 258

Dudley (Massachusetts), 120

Dudley, Joseph, 47, 48

Dudley, Thomas, 19, 29, 42, 47, 234

Dukakis, Michael, 285, 311–13

Duxbury (Massachusetts), 34

Dwight, Edmund, 126, 128, 210

Dwight, Jonathan, Jr., 126

Dwight, Louis, 150

Earl of Lincoln, 19

East India Company, 75, 76, 78, 79

Economy (of Massachusetts): after American Revolution, 90–91, 100–101, 109, 110; effects of King Philip's War on, 46–47; industrialization of, 200–240, 273–74; and nineteenth-century depressions, 166, 172, 211–12; transformation of, from farming to manufacturing, 113–17, 242; transformation of, from goods production to services, vii, 275–315; and twentieth-century depression, 242, 246–47

Edison General Electric, 278
Education: and busing crisis, 300–304, 312; in Massachusetts constitution, 97
Edwards, Jonathan, 53, 54
Eisenhower, Dwight David, 307, 310
Eisenmenger, Robert, 315
Electronics industry. *See* High-tech industries
Eliot, John, 44
Eliot, Samuel, 209–10
Eliot family, 128
Elites. *See* Class and class differences
Elizabeth I (queen of England), 11
Ely, Joseph, 272, 273
Emancipation Proclamation, 196, 198, 199
Embargo Act, 115–16, 141, 168
Emerson, Ralph Waldo, 148, 214, 221
Endecott, John, 18, 27
England: in age of Elizabeth I, 11–13; in age of James I, 14–16; under Charles I, 17–20; colonial boycott of, 80, 90; Glorious Revolution in, 49, 56; immigrants from, 173, 206, 207–8, 243; imperial wars of, 55–56; influence of, on America, 51, 58, 109; manufacturing in, 121–22, 127; patriotism for, in Massachusetts, 56; reaction of, to Boston Tea Party, 77–78; as threat to Massachusetts Bay Colony, 45, 47–51. *See also* American Revolution; Parliament
Essex County *Free Press,* 183
Ethnicity: conflict over, in Massachusetts, vii, 128, 172–82, 198–99, 204, 206, 207–8, 247–48, 255–70, 290–91, 300–304; diversity of, in Massachusetts, 113, 205, 213–14, 229–31, 311–12; as primary identity, 201, 241, 248; undermining of consciousness of, 313–14. *See also* Pluralism; *Specific ethnic and racial groups*
Etore, Joe, 254
Europe, 115–16; Dix in, 150; embargo on trade with, 115–16; Massachusetts trade with, 114. *See also Specific European countries*
Everett (Massachusetts), 275

Extractive industries, 129, 163. *See also* Fish and fishing; Forests

Factory development. *See* Manufacturing
Factory Inspection Act, 239
Fall River (Massachusetts), 171; conditions in, 211; French Canadians in, 203; Irish in, 218; population growth in, 117, 164, 244; textile manufacture in, 205, 206–7, 213, 244, 246; unemployment in, 276, 286
Faneuil Market (Boston), 139, 187
Farming: changes from subsistence to market, 90–91, 115, 124, 162–64; decline of, 113, 118–19, 129, 165, 242; by Indians, 1, 6–7, 24–25; by Plymouth colonists, 26; workers in, transformed for industry, 133–36
Federal Housing Authority, 290
Federalists: decline of, 137–41, 167; vs. Jeffersonian Democratic-Republicans, 89, 107–8, 111–12, 116, 140–41
Fidelity Investment Corporation, 288
Fifty-fourth Regiment of Massachusetts Volunteers, 195–96
Fillmore, Millard, 170, 191
Finney, Charles G., 174
Finnish immigrants, 214
Firemen's riots, 177
First South Carolina Volunteers, 190
Fish and fishing (in Massachusetts): by English fishermen, 13; by Indians, 5, 8–9, 25; as occupation, 114, 163. *See also* Whaling
Fisk University, 249–50
Fitzgerald, John Francis (Honey Fitz), 199, 260–66, 268–70, 309, 310
Fitzgerald, Mrs. John Francis, 264
Fitzgerald, Rose. *See* Kennedy, Rose F.
Fitzgerald, Thomas, 261
Forbes, George W., 251
Forbes, John Bennett, 126
Forbes, John Murray, 126
Forests (in Massachusetts), 4–6, 163. *See also* Extractive industries
*Fortune Magazine,* 281
Foss, Eugene, 254–55, 272

Hartford (Connecticut), 29
Hartford and Springfield Railroad, 212
Harvard College (later, University): as college of capitalism, 158; Congregational clergy trained at, 32, 49, 95, 146; fears of Irish attacks on, 176; financial support for, 97, 143, 158; and pragmatism, 217, 232; research laboratories at, 279; Unitarianism at, 146
Hatfield (Massachusetts), 101–2
Haverhill (Massachusetts), 218, 244, 245
Hayden, Lewis, 191
Hayne, Robert Y., 169
Haynes, Ann, 133
Haynes, Cynthia, 133
Haynes, Gideon, 133
Haynes, Sabre, 133
Haynes, Sophia, 133
Haywood, William, 254
Hazen, Harold, 280
Hekman, John, 277
Hendricks Club, 259
Hepplewhite, George, 109
Herscovici, Steven, 167
Herter, Christian, 307
Hibbard, George, 262, 263
Hicks, John, 296
Hicks, Louise Day, 296–99, 303
Higginson, Stephen, 91
Higginson, Thomas Wentworth, 148, 156, 189–92, 200, 222
Higginson family, 126
High-tech industries, 275, 277–90, 314–15
Highways, 283–84, 290, 295–96
Hingham (Massachusetts), 109, 117
*History of the Rise, Progress, and Termination of the American Revolution* (Warren), 107
Hoar, Ebenezer Rockwood, 223
Hoar, George Frisbie, 223–26, 228, 229, 235, 251
Holmes, Oliver Wendell, 217, 232–38
Holyoke (Massachusetts), 206, 209, 210–12, 218
*Holyoke Transcript*, 203
Homestead Steel Strike (Pennsylvania), 236

Housatonic River, 2
Housing: company, 207; of Indians, 7; and industrialization, 128. *See also* Company towns
Howe, Elias, 171–72
Howe, Julia Ward, 221–22
Howe, Richard, 85, 86
Howe, Samuel Gridley, 150, 151–54, 157, 190, 233
Howells, William Dean, 214
Hudson River, 15, 23
Humphrey, John, 18, 19
Hunt, Harriot K., 157
Hunting and gathering, 1, 5–6, 9
Hutchinson, Anne, 31–32, 55, 59, 173, 238, 257, 259
Hutchinson, Sarah Foster, 59
Hutchinson, Thomas (father of royal governor), 59–60
Hutchinson, Thomas (royal governor of Massachusetts Bay Colony), 59–61, 63, 65–71, 73–80, 86, 87, 91, 96
Hyannis (Massachusetts), 309
Hynes, John, 270, 291–92
Hynes Auditorium (Boston), 291

IBM, 281
Ice Age, 2–4
Immigration (to Massachusetts), vii, 203–8, 213–14, 243–44, 276, 289; by French Canadians, 203–7, 210, 211, 215, 222, 229, 243–44, 254, 289; by Irish, 172–82; and poverty, 215–16; and reform, 239; restrictions on, 224–25, 229–32. *See also* Ethnicity: conflict over; Migration; Pluralism; *Specific nationalities*
Immigration Restriction League, 225, 230
Imperialism (American), 224, 225
Indians: arrival of, in Massachusetts, 6–7; Christian, 44, 46; warfare with, vii, 29–30, 45–47. *See also Specific tribes and peoples*
Industrialism. *See* Defense industries; High-tech industries; Manufacturing; Service industries
Industrial parks, 284
Instrumentation (lab), 279

Laud, William, 17, 21
Lawrence (Massachusetts), 171; creation of, 127; Irish immigrants in, 179, 205–6, 218; strike of 1912 in, 238, 253–56; textile manufacture in, 244; urban problems of, 300
Lawrence, Abbott, 128
Lawrence, Amos, 127, 128
Lawrence family, 158
League of Nations, 271
Leary, William J., 305
Leather goods, 129. *See also* Shoemaking
Lee, Henry, 121, 176
Lee, Joseph, 121
Lee family, 91, 126, 234
Leicester (Massachusetts), 54
Leominster (Massachusetts), 203
Lexington (Massachusetts), vii, 84
Leyden (Netherlands), 14–16, 36
*Liberator,* 184–86, 188, 252
Lincoln (Massachusetts), 284
Lincoln, Abraham, 194, 197, 199
Lincoln, Benjamin, 94, 104, 105
Lincoln Laboratory, 279–81
Literacy tests, 230–31
Lithuanian immigrants, 205, 213
Lobby Regulation Act, 240
Lodge, Anna Cabot, 226, 229
Lodge, Cabot, 234
Lodge, George, 311
Lodge, Henry Cabot, vii, 223, 225, 226–31, 235, 271, 272
Lodge, Henry Cabot, Jr., 267, 269, 271, 273, 307, 310, 311
Logan Airport (Boston), 295
Logue, Edward J., 293–95
Lomasney, Martin, 259–62, 264, 265, 269, 270
Loring, Charles, 176
Louisburg (Cape Breton Island), 55–56
Louisiana Purchase, 140–41
Lovejoy, Elijah P., 186–87
Lowell (Massachusetts), 288; conditions in, 171, 179, 205, 206; creation of, 124–25, 127; immigrants in, 203, 218, 288; Know-Nothingism in, 182; population growth in, 117, 244; strike in,

135; textile manufacture in, 130, 131, 134–35, 205, 244, 246; twentieth-century jobs in, 286; urban problems of, 300
Lowell, Abbott Lawrence, 258–59
Lowell, Francis Cabot, 121–27, 130, 171
Lowell, Ralph, 293
*Lowell Courier,* 171
Lowell family, 128, 158
Lowell Female Labor Reform Association, 136
*The Lowell Offering,* 134, 136
Loyalists, 79, 80, 85–86, 91, 94
Lukas, J. Anthony, 303
Lumber. *See* Forests
Lundy, Benjamin, 184
Lutherans, 52
Lyman, Theodore, 186
Lynn (Massachusetts): defense industry in, 275; electricity in, 278; opposition to abolitionism in, 186; shoemaking in, 129, 131, 208–9, 213, 246; strikes in, 172, 238; urban problems of, 300

Machine-building, 129, 130–31, 177. *See also* Mechanics
Machine politics, 259–69, 290–92, 299–300. *See also* Patronage; Politics
Madison, James, 168
*Magnalia Christi Americana* (Mather), 51
Maguire, Patrick, 220
Main, Gloria, 167
Maine: as part of Dominion of New England, 47; as part of Massachusetts Bay Colony, 47–48; Plymouth Colony's trade with, 26; as separate state, 113, 138
Mann, Horace, 148, 150, 152, 153
Mansfield, Frederick, 267
Manufacturing: as basis for high-tech industries, 276, 278; as chief Massachusetts occupation, vii, 113–37, 142–43, 164–65, 202, 244–46, 276; decline in, 244–46, 282; impact of rise of, 128, 165, 201–23, 239–40. *See also* Labor; Urbanization; Wages

Northbridge (Massachusetts), 131
North End (Boston), 247
Norton, Charles Eliot, 225
"Nullification," 169, 170

Oberlin College, 155–56
O'Brien, Hugh, 199, 218, 220, 221, 308
*Observations on the New Constitution* (Warren), 107–8
O'Connell, William, 309
O'Connor, Thomas, 199
Oliver, Andrew, 75
Oliver, Peter, 69
Oliver family, 63, 66, 234
Olsen, Kenneth, 279, 280–82
Olsen, Stan, 281
Omar Circle, 250
O'Neill, Thomas P. (Tip), 307
O'Reilly, John Boyle, 221–22, 236
O'Sullivan, Mary Kenney, 255–56
Otis, Harrison Gray, 109, 128, 137–41, 176, 209
Otis, James, 59, 61, 62, 68, 107, 187
Otis family, 63, 107–8
Oxford (Massachusetts), 120

Paine, Robert Treat, 91
Palfrey, John Gorham, 158
Palmer, George Herbert, 250
Papermaking industry, 210–12
Parker, John, 84
Parker, Theodore, 148, 190, 191, 193
Parliament, 11, 17, 51, 56; right of, to legislate over colonies, 65, 73–74, 78–79, 87
Parris, Samuel, 50
Parsons, Eli, 104
Paternalism, 133–37; decline of, 170–72, 205
Patronage: gubernatorial, in Massachusetts, 93; by Irish politicians, 259–60, 291–92; under John Hancock, 99–100; by political parties, 214, 223, 228; royal, 93
Patuxet Indians, 24–25
Peabody, Endicott, 295, 311
Peirce, Charles S., 217, 232, 234
Pemberton Mill, 179

Pennsylvania, 85, 135, 202, 243
Pequot Indians, 8; Puritan war against, 29–30, 46, 47
Perkins, Thomas H., 126, 128, 152–53
Perkins Institute for the Blind, 143, 153, 154
Peters, Andrew, 266
Philadelphia (Pennsylvania), 202
Philanthropy, 127, 143, 152, 158–60, 222
Philippines, 225
Phillips, Ann Terry Greene, 187, 192
Phillips, John, 139
Phillips, Wendell, 157, 158, 183, 187–91, 200, 222, 233; monuments to, 221; as subject of Du Bois speech, 249
Phips, Sir William, 49–50
Pierce, Franklin, 150
Pilgrims: experiences of, 22–27, 34; origins of, 14–16; as part of national legend, vii; reasons of, for coming to America, 36. *See also* Mayflower Compact; Plymouth Colony
Pittsfield (Massachusetts), 117, 275, 286
Pius IX (Pope), 150
Pluralism (in Massachusetts), 55, 200–241, 259, 289, 306, 315; in politics, 311–12. *See also* Class and class differences; Ethnicity
Plymouth (Massachusetts), 109, 115, 117, 118, 163
Plymouth Colony: consolidation of, into Massachusetts Bay Colony, 49; dispersal of members of, 40; in King Philip's War, 45–46; settlement of, 23–27. *See also* Pilgrims; Plymouth Rock
Plymouth Rock, 23, 221
Pocumtuc Indians, 7, 45
Polish immigrants, 205, 207, 210, 214, 240, 243
Political parties: diversity of, 322n.7; rise of, 111–12. *See also* Names of specific parties
Politics: and pluralism, 241, 259–73, 290–92. *See also* Political parties; Representation; *Names of specific political parties*
Port Act, 78

Portuguese immigrants, 205, 207, 229, 276, 289

Poverty: and industrialization, 170–72, 179, 204–12; in Massachusetts Bay Colony, 44; post-Revolutionary concerns about, 90–93, 97–98, 101–2; and urban renewal, 295. *See also* Class and class differences; Economy; Labor; Wages

Powder Alarm, 81–83

Powers, John E., 292, 293

Pragmatism, 217, 232–34, 237, 252

Presbyterians, 52

*The Principles of Political Economy* (Bowen), 158

Prison reform, 149–50

Privateering, 91

"Production-line management," 281

Progressive movement, 237, 239, 262. *See also* Reform movements

Prohibition, 272

Property: for Christian Indians, 44; in Dedham, 38, 39; ownership of, in Massachusetts Bay Colony, 27, 33; ownership of, in Plymouth Colony, 26; payment for, 48; and political rights, 96–98, 157; Puritan attempts to gain Indians', 29–30

Proposition 2–1/2, 287

Protestants: vs. Catholics in America, 172–79, 193, 204, 214; vs. Catholics in England, 11, 13; in England, 56; as reformers, 143; in state constitution, 95, 97, 98; in Worcester, 213–14. *See also* Pilgrims; Puritanism; *Specific denominations*

Provincial Congress, 80, 82–84, 92, 99

Prude, Jonathan, 120

Prudential Center (Boston), 293, 294

Puritanism: covenant of, 21–22; in Dedham, 37–41; in England, 33, 36, 44; Federalism's similarities to, 112; and Great Awakening, 54–55; and "half-way covenants," 40, 44–45, 51, 53; of John Winthrop, 13, 21; in Massachusetts Bay Colony, 27–32, 37–44, 113, 148; and religious dissenters, 30–32; as subversive movement in England,

17–18; waning of, 51–52; of William Bradford, 14–16

Putting-out system (of production), 164, 165

Quabbin Reservoir, 327n.24

Quakers, 95, 173

Quartering Act, 78–79, 95

Quebec (Canada), 203

Quincy, Josiah (patriot's son), 137–40, 143, 158, 176

Quincy, Josiah, Jr. (patriot), 69, 187

Quincy family, 63, 128, 234

Radiation Laboratory, 279

Railroads, 119, 128, 163, 202–3, 212, 213, 246–47; regulation of, 239

Raleigh, Sir Walter, 12, 26

Rappaport, Jerome, 291

Raytheon, 279, 280, 288, 292

Reagan, Ronald, 285, 312–13

Reconstruction, 223, 227, 231

"Red Scare," 231, 256

Reed, Henry, 132

Reed and Barton Company, 132

Reform movements: called for, after Shays's Rebellion, 103–5; and immigration, 239; Know-Nothing Party's contributions to, 181–82; in Massachusetts, vii, 144–61, 200–201

Relativism, 232–34

Religion: diversity of, in Massachusetts, 95, 113, 125; growing tolerance of, in Massachusetts Bay Colony, 49, 52, 55, 173; Puritan intolerance of differences in, 30–32. *See also* Great Awakening; Protestants: vs. Catholics; Second Great Awakening; *Specific religions and denominations*

*Remarks on Prison and Prison Discipline in the United States* (Dix), 150

Representation: as issue after American Revolution, 93, 96–98, 101; as issue before the American Revolution, 63–65, 70–71

Republicanism, 59, 89–112, 145, 176

Republican Party, 192–94, 199, 214; and Boston mayors, 262, 269–70; and Boston police strike, 256; decline of, in Massachusetts, 271–72, 312; nativism in, 272; splits in, 271; support for, in Gilded Age, 216–18, 222–24. *See also* National Republican Party; Yankees

Research and development laboratories, 278, 281–84, 290

Revenue Act, 63, 66–68

Revere, Joseph Warren, 131

Revere, Paul, vii, 83–84, 131–33

Rhode Island: banishment to, 32; manufacturing in, 120, 121; as part of Dominion of New England, 47; population density of, 117, 165, 203

Richards, Leonard, 185

Roanoke Colony, 12

ROAR (Restore Our Alienated Rights), 303

Robinson, George D., 228, 229

Robinson, Harriet Hanson, 133–36

Robinson, John, 16

Robinson, William S., 134

Roosevelt, Franklin D., 267, 271, 272–73, 293

Roosevelt, Theodore, 225, 235, 271

Rosenberg, Ethel and Julius, 259

Roxbury (Massachusetts), 300–301, 303, 305; Boston's annexation of, 215; settlement of, 27

Roxbury High School, 303, 305

Royce, Josiah, 232, 250

Rumanian immigrants, 243

Russell, Thomas, 91

Russian immigrants, 206, 243–44, 254, 276, 289

Ryan, Robert, 292

Sacco and Vanzetti case, 254, 257–59, 279–81

Saint-Gaudens, Augustus, 196

St. John, Sister Mary Edmond, 175, 176

Salem (Massachusetts), 81, 118; architecture in, 109; origins of, 18; as port city, 52, 114, 118; Roger Williams in, 30; witchcraft trials in, 50, 257

Saltonstall, Leverett, 273, 311

Saltonstall, Sir Richard, 18, 19

Samoset, 24

Sandwich (Massachusetts), 34

Santayana, George, 250

Sargent, Francis, 284, 311, 312

Saybrook (Massachusetts), 29

Scandinavian immigrants, 213, 214

Schurz, Carl, 227

Scollay Square (Boston), 291

Scott, Dred, 324n.10

Scottish immigrants, 173

Scottsboro Boys, 259

Scudder, Vida, 255

Second Great Awakening, 110, 145–49

Secret Ballot Act, 240

Segregation (in Massachusetts), 184; in neighborhoods, 198, 204, 214, 215, 218, 295, 296–97, 303–4; in schools, 181–82, 296–97, 300–304

Separatists. *See* Pilgrims

Service industries, vii, 275–77, 282–83, 285–89, 314–15

Sewall family, 63

Sewing machines, 171–72, 202, 208, 214

Shakespeare, William, 11

"Shanty Irish," 179

Shaw, Lemuel, 176, 190

Shaw, Robert Gould, 195–96

Shays, Daniel, 101, 102, 104–5

Shays's Rebellion, 89, 100–106, 111

Sheffield (Massachusetts), 106

Shepard, William, 104–5

Sherman, Roger, 223

Sherman Anti-Trust Act, 224

Shirley, William, 55, 60, 70

Shoemaking: collapse of industry of, 244–46, 273; in Massachusetts, 126, 129, 130, 171–72, 202, 208–9, 242; strikes in, 172

Shurtleff, Nathaniel, 199

Silversmiths, 131, 133–34

Sims, Thomas, 190, 191–92

Slater, Samuel, 120

Slavery: and Daniel Webster, 170; expansion of, 167, 193, 194, 217; opposition to, in Massachusetts, vii, 142, 154, 156, 183–96; and Whig Party, 180. *See also* Fugitive Slave Law

Slavic immigrants, 229

Small, Eliza, 190

jobs in, 286; women's rights convention in, 156

CPSIA information can be obtained
at www.ICGtesting.com
Printed in the USA
JSHW080731260123
36572JS00008B/167

9 781558 492493